Jacksonian Politics
and Community Conflict

Jacksonian Politics and Community Conflict

The Emergence of the Second
American Party System in
Cumberland County
North Carolina

HARRY L. WATSON

Louisiana State University Press
Baton Rouge and London

Designer: Joanna Hill
Typeface: Linotron 202 Times Roman
Typesetter: G & S Typesetters, Inc.
Printer: Thomson-Shore, Inc.
Binder: John Dekker and Sons

The author gratefully acknowledges permission granted by Claude N. Kent to quote from the James Evans Papers passages that appear in Chapters 1 and 7, herein.

Library of Congress Cataloging in Publication Data

Watson, Harry L
  Jacksonian politics and community conflict.

  Bibliography: p.
  Includes index.
  1. Cumberland County (N.C.)—Politics and government. 2. United States—Politics and government—1815–1861. 3. Jackson, Andrew, 1767–1845.
I. Title.
F262.C9W37   324'.09756'373   81–2414
ISBN 0–8071–0857–X   AACR2

FOR MARGOT

Contents

Acknowledgments   xi

Introduction   1

I. The Citizens of Town and Country   17

II. A Frequent Recurrence to Fundamental Principles: Some
Aspects of Prepartisan Political Culture   60

III. A Right to Vote for Who I Pleased: Political Alignments
After 1772   82

IV. Andrew Jackson and the Will of the People: The Election
of 1828   109

V. Banners of Political Faith: The Development of Party
Platforms, 1828–1834   151

VI. Aristocracy Against the Farmers: Party Growth and Social
Composition, 1834–1836   198

VII. Exclusively a Party Conflict: The Panic of 1837 and the
Election of 1840   246

VIII. A Calm Quiet State of Things: Party Routine in the 1840s   282

IX. Conclusion: Cumberland County and the Second Party System   314

Appendix I: North Carolina Antebellum Tax Lists as Historical
Sources   325

Appendix II: Statistical Methods   330

Bibliography   335

Index   349

Figures

1. North Carolina and Cumberland County, 1836   25

2. Cumberland County militia and tax districts before 1855   26

3. Voting turnout, congressional elections, 1791–1859   63

4. Voting turnout, presidential, gubernatorial, and legislative
elections, 1824–1860   64

5. The value of the Cape Fear valley cotton crop, 1831–1840   255

6. Anonymous political cartoon, 1840   273

7. Percent Democratic in Cumberland County presidential
elections, 1836–1860   305

8. Percent Democratic in Cumberland County gubernatorial
elections, 1836–1860   306

Tables

1 Social and Economic Characteristics of Cumberland County, 1827–1830   32

2 Per Capita Production of Selected Crops, 1840   33

3 Cumberland County Population, 1820–1840   45

4 Presidential Vote by Precincts, 1824   100

5 Committee Members and the Electorate, 1828–1829   128

6 Committee Rank by Age, 1828   130

7 Committee Rank by Residence, 1828   131

8 Committee Rank by Ethnicity, 1828   131

9 Property of Committee Members by Age, 1828   134

10 Property of Committee Members by Ethnicity, 1828   135

11 Property of Committee Members by Residence, 1828   136

12 Property of Committee Members by Rank, 1828   137

13 Candidate Preference by Age, 1828   138

14 Candidate Preference by Residence, 1828   139

15 Candidate Choice by Ethnicity, 1828   140

16 Property of Committee Members by Candidate Preference, 1828   142

17 Property of Rural Committee Members by Candidate Preference, 1828   143

18 Property of Fayetteville Committee Members by Candidate Preference, 1828   144

19 The House of Commons Election of 1831   171

20 Cumberland County Gubernatorial Election, 1836   209

21 Correlations Between Social, Economic, and Political
Variables, 1835–1837   210

22 Committee Members and the Electorate, 1836   215

23 Committee Members' Residence, 1828 and 1836   216

24 Property of Committee Members, 1828 and 1836   218

25 Property of Anti-Jacksonians, 1828 and 1836   219

26 Property of Jacksonians, 1828 and 1836   220

27 Party Rank by Age, 1836   221

28 Party Rank by Ethnicity, 1836   221

29 Party Rank by Residence, 1836   222

30 Party Rank by Residence, 1836, Controlling for Party   222

31 Property of Committee Members by Age, 1836   224

32 Property of Committee Members by Residence, 1836   225

33 Property of Committee Members by Party Rank, 1836   226

34 Party by Ethnicity, 1836   228

35 Party by Ethnicity, 1836, Controlling for Residence   229

36 Party by Age, 1836   229

37 Party by Residence, 1836   230

38 Property of Committee Members by Party, 1836   231

39 Property of Rural Committee Members by Party, 1836   232

40 Property of Fayetteville Committee Members by Party, 1836   233

41 Cumberland Merchants by Party and Business Size, 1835   234

42 Corporate Positions by Party   235

43 Timing of Railroad Support by Party   236

44 Changing Support for the Democratic Party, 1836–1840   278

45 Correlations of Social and Political Variables in Rural
Precincts, 1836–1840   279

46 Party Leaders by Residence, 1838–1848   301

47 Occupations of Party Leaders, 1838–1848   302

48 Intercorrelations of Percents Democratic Among Twelve
Cumberland County Precincts: Presidential Elections, 1840–1852   307

49 Intercorrelations of Percents Democratic in Gubernatorial
Elections, 1836–1848   308

50 Mean Percent Whig in North Carolina County Seats and Rural
Precincts, 1836–1842   312

Acknowledgments

I would not have been able to write this book without the generous assistance of many helpful individuals and institutions. The Office of Research and Sponsored Programs of Northwestern University made the indispensable computer time readily available. On a more personal level, the librarians and archivists of the North Carolina State Archives in Raleigh and the Southern Historical Collection and the North Carolina Collection in the library of the University of North Carolina at Chapel Hill gave me every consideration that a researcher could wish for. I would especially like to thank Dr. Thornton W. Mitchell and all of his staff in the Archives Search Room for extending me all the privileges of their magnificent collection. George Stevenson, Ellen Z. McGrew, and Joe Mobley of the Archives staff were particularly helpful in locating documents for my use. In Cumberland County itself, Mr. and Mrs. George Ake, Msgr. Frederick A. Koch, Mr. and Mrs. Wilson Marsh, and Mr. Thurmond Smith made special efforts to locate church records and to make them available to me. Mr. and Mrs. Claude N. Kent of Columbus, Georgia, gave me access to the James Evans Papers and every other expression of hospitality during my visit to their community. A grant from the College of Arts and Sciences of the University of North Carolina at Chapel Hill covered the cost of the illustrative material. For all these favors I am deeply grateful.

I would also like to thank Marc Kruman, Roger Ekrich, Thomas Jeffrey, and David Wilson for hours of stimulating conversation and for generous and friendly assistance to a fellow historian of North Carolina. Colleagues who have read this manuscript at several stages of its preparation, particularly William Barney, Robert Calhoon, Don Higginbotham, Marc Kruman, Donald Mathews, and Donald Scott, have given me invaluable suggestions and support on every occasion. I am especially grateful to Professor Edward Pessen and Professor Michael Holt for their thoughtful and stimulating criticisms.

Each one of these gracious and talented people has made my work more meaningful and more interesting.

The contribution of Professor Robert H. Wiebe of Northwestern University to the initiation and completion of this book has been invaluable at every stage. I have constantly drawn on what he has taught me in scholarship and in style. For the remaining deficiencies in either category, I remain solely responsible.

My final and greatest debt is to Margot B. Stein. She has contributed trenchant criticism and ready encouragement for as long as I have known her, and combined with grace the challenging roles of teacher, colleague, friend, and spouse.

Jacksonian Politics
and Community Conflict

Introduction

Social and political transformation swept the United States between 1824 and 1848. As President James Monroe faced retirement, an older vision of republican tranquility faded, and the stately tenor of public life gave way to impassioned competition for the presidency. In the same period, technological changes spurred by the search for cheaper ways to carry men and goods opened the continent for further exploitation. In the Transportation Revolution, commerce boomed, cities grew, immigration surged, and wilderness gave way to the plow, all of which brought sharper social pressures into thousands of American communities. Sensing their opportunity, constitutional and ideological revisionists reworked earlier precepts to meet new conditions. Participation in elections shot upward and high-toned gentlemen who wished to stay in office turned to the arts of the professional demagogue. Political structures which former statesmen had execrated became the basis for a new electoral system.

Americans viewed these changes with a mixture of dismay and exhilaration. For many citizens, decaying standards and fluid rules were tokens of national collapse. For others, the chance to build a finer, purer government stimulated support for active change. Not infrequently, these feelings were combined, and nostalgia for the old republic inspired an unwitting contribution to the birth of a new order. A small-town editor in North Carolina mirrored the ambivalence of these citizens exactly. "The present political *mellee*, which has been carried on for the last ten years has thrown everything into confusion," wrote John A. Cameron in 1831. "So much art has been used to make error look like truth, and so many opinions inculcated to serve the purposes of the time, which were not entertained by those who promulgated them, that the community has become a chaotic mass of mingled and warring factions." Despite his alarm in the face of political degeneracy, Cameron rejoiced to see a man who could mend the nation's ills. "In this state of things," the editor observed, "it is desirable that a banner be spread to the breeze, which may be seen by all, that the principles for which it is advanced may be distinctly understood, and that a large majority at least, of the country, should have a well founded confidence in him who holds it. This General Jackson now does."[1]

The editor's evocation of Old Hickory was emblematic of political transition. Andrew Jackson was president of the United States from 1829 to 1837. In spite of the general's association with simple and old-fashioned principles, his administration witnessed basic changes in American government. The Carolina editor very correctly observed that Jackson's conduct in office polarized the "mingled and warring factions" of the 1820s, dispelled demoralizing uncertainty, and reduced American politics to a simple dichotomy. In the new order, politically active citizens were for Andrew Jackson or against him, and these lines of cleavage became the basis for America's second political party system.

The nation's first political parties had pitted Jeffersonian Republicans against Hamiltonian Federalists. Competition between the two had fizzled out after 1815 amidst widespread distrust of partisanship itself. The second party system endured long after Jackson's death and persisted in some states until the outbreak of the Civil War. The party battles between Jacksonian Democrats and anti-Jacksonian Whigs carried the nation from a period in which organized political opposition still bore the odor of disloyalty and unpatriotic conspiracy to an age when political party conflict was normal, continuous, and even admired as beneficial to democracy. Thus when the second party system crumbled, its place was taken by a third system, and from then until perhaps quite recently, the United States has never lacked a vigorous two-party system.

The significance of the Jacksonian transformation extended far below the Congress, the White House, and the major metropolitan newspapers. It reached every county and crossroads hamlet and recruited village solons into multiple networks of committees, conventions, platforms, and caucuses. It stretched out further, beyond the circles of local notables, and enlisted individual citizens who never sought an office, never made a speech, and never chaired a meeting. By the thousands, Americans turned out to vote who had never done so before. Richard P. McCormick has found that the proportion of adult white males who cast ballots in the presidential election roughly tripled, rising from 26.5 percent in 1824 to 78.0 percent in 1840.[2] The new political

1. Fayetteville *North Carolina Journal*, July 27, 1831.
2. Richard P. McCormick, "New Perspectives on Jacksonian Politics," *American Historical Review*, LXV (1960), 292.

enthusiasts stood in the rain and the broiling sun for hours to hear and applaud partisan speeches. They pondered interminable editorials in the party press. They chose a party and stuck by it loyally, as they sang its songs, marched in its parades, fought its enemies, and cheered its friends. What Ronald P. Formisano has called "the birth of mass political parties" was not simply a political event.[3] It was arguably the largest social movement of its day, far more widely appealing than any romantic reform movement and even more pervasive than religious revivalism.

The end result of this transformation was a unique political system that diverged from the general patterns of other western democracies. Ever since Jackson's presidency, two broadly based parties have dominated access to political power in the United States. These parties have not represented the irreconcilable opinions of opposing monolithic interests in society. The major parties have been diverse coalitions which specialized in generating consensus, muffling or appeasing dissent, rewarding faithful service with tangible benefits, and winning public office for professional party workers. Intellectuals and reformers have charged to no avail that the major parties are and always have been ideologically erratic, programmatically indistinct, and socially miscellaneous. During most of United States history, good citizenship for the majority of American voters has meant steadfast loyalty to one of the major parties, in spite of the parties' basic similarity in several respects. The persistence of stable party structures and fierce party loyalties in the presence of widespread agreement on basic political principles may have been paradoxical, but the combination has long been the pride of American pragmatists and the near-despair of its radicals.

This enduring framework of American government was the creation of Jacksonian politics.[4] The birth and growth of the second American party system has therefore been as significant for American historians as it was for the Carolina editor in 1831. Traditionally, historians have sought to link the political developments of the period with the vast social changes occurring at the same time by invoking the concept of Jacksonian democracy. In this view, economic growth, equal opportunity, and democratic reform swept away old elites and enabled the common man to realize the promises of the Declaration of Independence. In the works of Progressive historians like Charles Beard and Frederick Jackson Turner, Andrew Jackson and the Democratic party were the vanguard of this revolution and the Whig party stood for the dying and reactionary forces of wealth, privilege, and the old order. Arthur M.

3. Ronald P. Formisano, *The Birth of Mass Political Parties: Michigan, 1827–1860* (Princeton, N.J., 1971).
4. Edward Pessen, *Jacksonian America: Society, Personality, and Politics* (2nd rev. ed.; Homewood, Ill., 1978), 170.

Schlesinger, Jr., codified this view after World War II with the publication of *The Age of Jackson.*[5]

The Progressive interpretation has lost persuasiveness in the last generation. A swarm of Schlesinger's critics attacked the notion that Jackson's party had special attractions for workingmen and asserted instead that the Democratic party was the favorite home of aspiring capitalists.[6] The innovative essays of Richard Hofstadter and Louis Hartz demonstrated that the national leaders of both parties held similar ideas on the basic questions of political economy. More recently, Edward Pessen has drawn on a large body of historical literature to conclude that Jacksonian politicians had similar origins in the economic and social elite, that they frequently acted contrary to their professed principles, and that they often seemed more interested in winning office for themselves than in serving the needs of any mass constituency. The pioneering research of Lee Benson demonstrated that the concept of Jacksonian Democracy as traditionally formulated had little or no empirical validity, while several scholars questioned whether social mobility improved at all. Robert Kelley has used the concept of long-standing division between significantly different cultural blocs as a basis for understanding the complete span of American political history, but no critique of "consensus history" has restored the Progressive account of politics in the Age of Jackson.[7]

The view of the major parties as fundamentally similar has led some scholars to label them electoral machines whose members and principles were more or less interchangeable. Richard P. McCormick has written an intricate description of party formation and development which rests on this basic premise. According to McCormick, parties were deliberate contrivances which were put together by leaders to accomplish the task of electing a presi-

---

5. Arthur M. Schlesinger, Jr., *The Age of Jackson* (Boston, 1946).
6. William A. Sullivan, "Did Labor Support Andrew Jackson?" *Political Science Quarterly,* LXII (1947), 569–80; Edward Pessen, "Did Labor Support Jackson? The Boston Story," *Political Science Quarterly,* LXIV (1949), 262–74; Edward Pessen, "The Workingmen's Movement of the Jacksonian Era," *Mississippi Valley Historical Review,* XLIII (1956), 428–43; Bray Hammond, "Jackson, Biddle, and the Bank of the United States," *Journal of Economic History,* VII (1947), 1–23; Joseph Dorfman, *The Economic Mind in American Civilization* (3 vols.; New York, 1946–49), II, 601–637.
7. Richard Hofstadter, *The American Political Tradition: And the Men Who Made It* (New York, 1948), 56–85; Louis Hartz, *The Liberal Tradition in America* (New York, 1955), 89–113; Pessen, *Jacksonian America,* 171–96; Lee Benson, *The Concept of Jacksonian Democracy: New York as a Test Case* (Princeton, N.J., 1961); Edward Pessen, *Riches, Class, and Power Before the Civil War* (Lexington, Mass., 1973); Sidney H. Aronson, *Status and Kinship in the Higher Civil Service: Standards of Selection in the Administrations of John Adams, Thomas Jefferson, and Andrew Jackson* (Cambridge, Mass., 1964); Robert Kelley, "Ideology and Political Culture from Jefferson to Nixon," *American Historical Review,* LXXXII (1977), 531–62, and *The Cultural Pattern of American Politics: The First Century* (New York, 1979).

dent when an older contrivance, the congressional caucus, broke down.[8] Mc-Cormick's careful account of organizers' actions did not explain why voters chose to follow them. One suspects that if ordinary Americans of the Age of Jackson had perceived the two parties as Tweedledum and Tweedledee, they never would have responded to partisan appeals as resoundingly as they did. Historians' desire to relate political metamorphosis to the social and economic changes of the period is likewise as strong as ever. It is therefore quite important to know how parties originated among the electorate, how they touched the lives and feelings of voters, and how their supporters distinguished between them.

Social and political historians of the nineteenth-century United States have offered imaginative answers to these questions. The most important conceptual contributions have come from Lee Benson and Samuel P. Hays. Drawing explicitly on the ideas of Hofstadter and Hartz, Benson suggested that in a diverse country whose voters shared many common convictions, party conflict would not be based exclusively on economic interests. Instead, "almost every social conflict, tension, and disagreement may function potentially as a significant determinant of voting behavior." Specifically, in his study of New York politics, Benson found that rivalry between hostile ethnic and religious groups was far more important than economic differences in shaping the course of party development. Subsequent studies have extended the ethnocultural interpretation to states and regions throughout the North and Midwest.[9] In many localities, it now seems clear, voters acquired their political preferences as part of their membership in particular religious or ethnic communities.

Historians who followed Benson have usually insisted that economic con-

8. Richard P. McCormick, *The Second American Party System: Party Formation in the Jacksonian Era* (Chapel Hill, 1966), 13–16.
9. Benson, *The Concept of Jacksonian Democracy*, 292. See also the following articles by Samuel P. Hays: "History as Human Behavior," *Iowa Journal of History*, LVIII (1960), 193–206; "The Politics of Reform in Municipal Government in the Progressive Era," *Pacific Northwest Quarterly*, LV (1964), 157–69; "The Social Analysis of American Political History, 1880–1920," *Political Science Quarterly*, LXXX (1965), 373–94; "Political Parties and the Community-Society Continuum," in William Nisbet Chambers and Walter Dean Burnham (eds.), *The American Party Systems: Stages of Political Development* (New York, 1967), 152–81. Three major applications of the ethnocultural interpretation of political conflict to antebellum history are Formisano, *The Birth of Mass Political Parties*; Michael F. Holt, *Forging a Majority: The Formation of the Republican Party in Pittsburgh* (New Haven, Conn., 1969); and Paul Kleppner, *The Cross of Culture: A Social Analysis of Midwestern Politics, 1850–1900* (New York, 1970). A judicious review of the literature using this approach to political history which also discusses its application in the postbellum period is Richard L. McCormick, "Ethno-Cultural Interpretations of Nineteenth-Century American Voting Behavior," *Political Science Quarterly*, LXXXIX (1974), 351–77.

flicts in society only rarely affected the course of political development. According to Joel H. Silbey and Samuel T. McSeveney, "American mass politics—the conflict between parties, candidates, and issues—has been primarily shaped by the clash of cultural values." On the specific subject of the second party system, Ronald P. Formisano, one of Benson's leading students, has written that "historians who believe that the Bank War, states rights, or similar issues gave rise to political parties among the masses are wrongly extending the issue-orientation of limited segments of the electorate to all of it." William G. Shade, who has investigated the issues of banking and currency in the Old Northwest, explains that voters responded to these questions in terms of their cultural predispositions, not simply by following their economic interests, narrowly defined.[10]

These historians acknowledge an important intellectual debt to the work of social scientists who study modern voting behavior. Using the data of survey research, sociologists and political scientists have concluded that the outcome of elections depends primarily on the party preference of voters, that party preference is adopted for reasons that long antedate the issues of any particular election, and that it may have very little to do with those issues. Summarizing these findings, Philip E. Converse has asserted that the mass electorate has very little comprehension of issues or ideologies in the conventional sense, and maintains that "large portions of the electorate do not have any meaningful beliefs at all."[11] Coherent and consistent opinions are common, Converse believes, only on questions related to reference groups, i.e., to identifiable subgroups in the population which may elicit strong feelings from others, either positive or negative. Examples of common American reference groups would be blacks, Catholics, bankers, union organizers, New Yorkers, white southerners, and so forth.

If Converse is correct, and the opinions of modern voters do not reflect ideological consistency or an understanding of complex political issues, it does not follow automatically that nineteenth-century voters were similarly confused. Nevertheless, it is plain that Converse's concept of political opinion facilitates an understanding of political parties in the electorate which is based on ethnic and religious conflict. If a voter viewed the Irish as a negative reference group, he could easily decide that he belonged in the opposite party

10. Joel H. Silbey and Samuel T. McSeveney (eds.), *Voters, Parties, and Elections: Quantitative Essays in American Popular Voting Behavior* (Lexington, Mass., 1972), 3; Formisano, *The Birth of Mass Political Parties*, 11; William G. Shade, *Banks or No Banks: The Money Issue in Western Politics, 1832–1865* (Detroit, 1972), 18.
11. Philip E. Converse, "The Nature of Belief Systems in Mass Publics," in David E. Apter (ed.), *Ideology and Discontent* (New York, 1964), 234–38, 245. See also Angus Campbell, Philip E. Converse, Warren E. Miller, and Donald E. Stokes, *The American Voter* (New York, 1960) and *Elections and the Political Order* (New York, 1966).

from most Irishmen, and he could make this choice without having to form an opinion on the tariff or the national bank, or on any of the other policy issues which divided Whigs and Democrats in Washington. Formisano therefore rejects economic or ideological interpretations of party formation because they rest on assumptions "warranted neither by recent studies of voter issue-awareness nor by what we know about the electorate of 1840." [12]

The discoveries of the ethnocultural historians have been valuable, but their findings should be placed in the broadest possible context to be properly appreciated. Critics of their works have observed that religious and cultural movements do not erupt in a social vacuum. [13] In different but related ways, David Montgomery's examination of Protestant-Catholic rioting in Philadelphia and Paul E. Johnson's investigation of revivalism in Rochester have both explored the means by which religious and cultural struggles of the Age of Jackson drew much of their power from the pressures of material change on the lives of their participants. [14] The experience of states and regions which did not experience ethnocultural conflict must also be taken into account. Eventually, we may come to understand a whole range of political and cultural struggles in this period as varieties of response to a connected set of social pressures stemming from the Transportation Revolution and its accompanying economic changes.

The search for social explanations of political change that may subsume both ethnocultural and other sources of conflict leads logically to the South. Almost all southern voters were white Protestants of British ancestry whose families had lived in America for several generations, yet southern politics showed the same party divisions as those of the northern states. Indeed, McCormick found that "the most crucial development in the extension of the second party system was the abrupt emergence of a two-party South between 1832 and 1834." [15] Most historians who have attempted to explain the development of political parties in the South have tied political developments more or less directly to basic cleavages in the economy, geography, or social structure of the region. [16] Burton W. Folsom II has urged southern historians to

12. Formisano, *The Birth of Mass Political Parties*, 11.
13. James E. Wright, "The Ethnocultural Model of Voting: A Behavioral and Historical Critique," in Allan G. Bogue (ed.) *Emerging Theoretical Models in Social and Political History*, Sage Contemporary Social Science Issues, IX (Beverly Hills, Calif., 1973), 35–56; James Green, "Behavioralism and Class Analysis: A Methodological and Ideological Critique," *Labor History*, XIII (1972), 89–106.
14. David Montgomery, "The Shuttle and the Cross: Weavers and Artisans in the Kensington Riots of 1844," *Journal of Social History*, V (1972), 411–46; Paul E. Johnson, *A Shopkeepers' Millennium: Society and Revivals in Rochester, New York, 1815–1837* (New York, 1978).
15. McCormick, *The Second American Party System*, 15.
16. Major studies of the second party system in the South include Ulrich Bonnell Phillips, "The Southern Whigs," in Guy Stanton Ford (ed.), *Essays in American History Dedicated to Frederick*

"examine the question of party formation in the Jacksonian South . . . without the conceptual blinders of economic or sectional determinism," but many have not seen fit to do so.[17]

Two very important recent studies of southern politics continue to emphasize the importance of economic and sectional issues. William J. Cooper, in *The South and the Politics of Slavery*, discounts the role of banking and currency controversies, but he holds that "slavery remained the central axis of political debate in the South" throughout the antebellum period.[18] J. Mills Thornton's massive study of Alabama emphasizes the importance of a wide variety of "hobbies" or perceived threats which politicians exploited rhetorically to stimulate the electorate. The hobbies or issues which produced party differences were "proposals which tended to pit the values of an organized and style conscious urbanism against the more traditional values of an individualistic and isolated rural world—proposals which often, though by no means exclusively, invited governmental activity to develop the economy." In most heterogeneous counties, Thornton found, urban centers leaned to the Whig party, and rural neighborhoods favored the Democrats.[19]

In the light of this literature, it may be that southern Jacksonian voters had greater receptivity to arguments based on political ideology or on economic and sectional differences than their northern or modern counterparts. The massive daily reality of slavery may have focused the attention of white citizens very closely on measures to preserve their sectional interests. In the absence of ethnic diversity, contrasting economic orientations of local communities may have assumed critical public significance and become the basis for hostile political subcultures. One of the major purposes of the present study has been to explore these possibilities.

This is a book about the social and cultural origins of the second party sys-

---

Jackson Turner (New York, 1910), 203–229; Arthur Charles Cole, *The Whig Party in the South* (Washington, 1913); Charles Grier Sellers, Jr., "Who Were the Southern Whigs?" *American Historical Review*, LIX (1954), 335–46; Lynn L. Marshall, "The Genesis of Grassroots Democracy in Kentucky," *Mid-America*, XLVII (1965), 269–87; Thomas B. Alexander, Peggy Duckworth Elmore, Frank M. Lowery, and Mary Jane Pickens Skinner, "The Basis of Alabama's Ante-Bellum Two-Party System," *Alabama Review*, XIX (1966), 243–76; and James R. Sharp, *The Jacksonians versus the Banks: Politics in the States after the Panic of 1837* (New York, 1970). These authors disagree among themselves as to whether the defense of slavery, the Bank War, or the overall orientation to the market economy was more significant to the drawing of party lines, but none have identified ethnocultural conflict as the linchpin of southern antebellum politics.

17. Burton W. Folsom II, "Party Formation and Development in Jacksonian America: The Old South," *Journal of American Studies*, VII (1973), 217.

18. William J. Cooper, *The South and the Politics of Slavery, 1828–1856* (Baton Rouge, 1978), xii.

19. J. Mills Thornton III, *Politics and Power in a Slave Society: Alabama, 1800–1860* (Baton Rouge, 1978), 41–45.

tem in the South. I have sought to discover what social groups composed the voting strength of the two parties, what themes and values appeared in the rhetoric of party politicians, how political discourse reflected social realities, and what were the characteristics of antebellum party leaders. More generally, this is an exploration of public life and civic culture in the transition from the early republic to the modernizing world of the midnineteenth century. I have tried to measure the tangible characteristics of Jacksonian voters and leaders; I have also tried to discover what they believed. Both approaches are necessary for a thorough investigation of political change.

I have examined the development of Jacksonian politics in the context of a single county. Cumberland County, North Carolina, attracted me because of its intrinsic interest as a center of economic and ethnic diversity in a southern setting. In addition, the second party system was especially vigorous there, each party published a county newspaper which contained rich lodes of political data, and the county's governmental records contained a very full collection of social information. Like every southern county, Cumberland was unique. Like the others, it also shared a culture and a social structure that extended, with variations, through the large and heterogeneous region. It has given me very rich answers to the questions I wished to investigate.

The values of a local study are manifold for an inquiry into social structure, political culture, and leadership. Nineteenth-century America was not a country where big government impinged directly on citizens' lives, nor did people learn about the state from nationally uniform and impersonal mass media. The activities of government in Jacksonian America, including tax collection, law enforcement, electioneering, and even community defense, reached the ordinary citizen in a framework of local institutions which varied considerably from place to place. The men who composed these institutions were almost never career bureaucrats. They were local residents who occasionally alternated in office with others like themselves and for whom office was not the principal means of making a living. They were known by the other citizens, related to many of them by blood or marriage, seen by them often in nongovernmental contexts, and subject in some fashion to continuous public oversight. This is not to say that the state was a noncoercive institution, that local communities were immune to oligarchy, that all officials were loved and trusted, or that all citizens enjoyed equal influence in government. The state was coercive as it must be by its nature, some officials were hated scoundrels, and certain citizens benefited from the government while others suffered. But state authority was mediated through so many local agencies of control that its influence appeared as a smooth extension of the patterns that held every other aspect of neighborhood life in its place.

As Samuel P. Hays has observed, political activity had a special local meaning in this setting.[20] Party competition did not appear only as distant warfare in Congress; it was also organization against foes in one's own neighborhood. If voters abandoned the antiparty values of the early republic and followed politicians in the second party system, they changed their minds in response to local conditions and as a result of face-to-face conversations, unamplified speeches delivered within earshot, and editorials in locally published newspapers. The reasons why some voters became Democrats and others became Whigs were likewise matters of local importance. If differences existed between Whig and Democratic candidates, they had to be visible to local voters. If successful candidates of both parties resembled one another at the state level, moreover, these similarities may have disappeared when officeholders stood beside their losing counterparts back home. For the electorate, the local context of parties was paramount in every case.

The objective of a local study of parties should be exploration of the process of social and political development. It need not be the inauguration of a county-by-county survey of the United States, to nail down the problem of party composition once and for all. It is important to abstract from the particular details of partisan maneuver in a local setting the overall patterns of action and perception which affected community politics. We do not fully understand how party activists reached the average voter, how they harnessed preexisting political alignments to new movements, and how they linked pressing local concerns to state or national platforms. Nor do we know what party identity meant to ordinary citizens, how or whether local demands affected state or regional party positions, or how the introduction of party politics affected standing patterns of social and political control in communities. For these purposes, an explanation of the process of local political change is more important than the simple knowledge of who was a Whig and who was a Democrat.

The discovery of a "typical" community is therefore not the principal desideratum in the study of national history through the local experience. No single county or town contained within it all the important social or political elements which influenced its state or its region. If such a place existed, it could not serve as a miniature version of a larger political arena, for the differences in scale between the two theaters were qualitatively significant. Nor should the historian necessarily search for an ideal-type community in which some important social formation like the plantation or the small farm reached its perfect expression. Such a place was no more typical than a heterogeneous community, and possibly less so, since there is strong evidence that political party competi-

20. Hays, "Community-Society Continuum," 157–58.

tion was and is unlikely to develop in such places.[21] I am reminded of the observation of Clifford Geertz that "anthropologists don't study villages . . . they study *in* villages." [22] By the same token, if political *process* is the object of the historian's attention, it is far more important to examine that process where it is clearly visible than to search out the magic community that can somehow take the place of all the others.

The methodology of a local study of political change should combine analysis of issues and rhetoric with an examination of political leaders and attention to the behavior of the electorate. Each approach has special advantages which make it indispensable, but each has special weaknesses which the others can remedy. The assumption that political language was "mere" rhetoric, for example, can hamper the understanding of local issues. Historians and certain political scientists have emphasized the importance of symbolism in political discourse and have pointed out that if we are to penetrate the meaning of parties in the minds of the voters, we must analyze the language that they used.[23] To do so requires an inferential assumption that the local politician or editor whose written opinions have survived somehow spoke *for* his audience as well as *to* it. This assumption rests on an intuition about the reciprocal relationship between leaders and followers, namely that county politicians with locally unpopular opinions would not have survived in office and that voters must have chosen their political opinions from the ideas that were locally available. When used with discretion, this intuition is indispensable to the historian of political culture, but it cannot be rigorously tested and ought to be buttressed by other information.[24] Records of voting behavior are especially useful in this regard. Within limits, we can test the popularity of a political position by counting the votes received by men who espoused it. We may also compare the pattern of votes cast in a group of districts with the distribution of various social and economic characteristics in those districts. These comparisons run the risk of

21. Thornton, *Politics and Power in a Slave Society*, 41; Douglas S. Gatlin, "Towards a Functionalist Theory of Political Parties: Inter-Party Competition in North Carolina," in William J. Crotty (ed.), *Approaches to the Study of Party Organization* (Boston, 1968), 217–45; Paul Goodman, "The First American Party System," in Chambers and Burnham (eds.), *The American Party Systems*, 68–69.

22. Clifford Geertz, *The Interpretation of Cultures: Selected Essays* (New York, 1973), 22. *Cf.* Hays, "Community-Society Continuum," 152–57.

23. Besides the ethnocultural historians already named, see John William Ward, *Andrew Jackson: Symbol for an Age* (New York, 1955); Marvin Meyers, *The Jacksonian Persuasion: Politics and Belief* (Stanford, Calif., 1957); Murray Edelman, *The Symbolic Uses of Politics* (Urbana, Ill., 1964).

24. Local studies which concentrate on rhetoric and issues almost exclusively include Kim T. Phillips, "The Pennsylvania Origins of the Jackson Movement," *Political Science Quarterly*, XCI (1976), 489–508, and Donald J. Ratliffe, "The Role of Voters and Issues in Party Formation: Ohio, 1824," *Journal of American History*, LIX (1973), 847–70.

the "ecological fallacy" or of magnifying the importance of spurious correlations. Perhaps more important, they may distort the context in which local party systems operated.[25] In spite of these potential pitfalls, the record of voting is still the most direct evidence we have of nineteenth-century public opinion.

The nature of party leadership is also a crucial component of inquiry into local politics. From a practical standpoint, it is essential to study individuals who in fact led their parties. This seems elementary, but some scholars have based major conclusions on the ethnic, economic, and occupational characteristics of men whose names appeared on lists compiled for journalistic or filiopietistic purposes, sometimes years after the fact.[26] Comparisons of leaders across party lines should be based on exhaustively inclusive lists of men who participated in politics at comparable levels of activity. The effect of occupation or religion on party choice, moreover, should not be based on lists of party leaders which may have originated from a process of ticket balancing. The pattern of party affiliation within exhaustive lists of members of particular professions or churches is a more appropriate test for that purpose.[27]

The hundreds of men who participated in politics at the very lowest level of leadership were especially useful to the present study. These were the men who composed the county committees of vigilance and who mobilized their neighbors at the precinct level. They were an elite of sorts, but their ranks were open to any moderately substantial householder and most of them had no reasonable hope of patronage as a reward for their party service. In the election of 1836, for example, the combined membership of Cumberland County's two committees of vigilance equaled one quarter of the electorate. Observing comparable men in Alabama, Thornton has found that state and county office seekers may have been look-alike opportunists, but that neighborhood leaders were disinterested participants whose primary motivation was moral or ideological.[28] If social differences existed between the parties, they ought to have manifested themselves among these men if anywhere.

The complex relationship between leaders and followers is important for

25. Leo A. Goodman, "Some Alternatives to Ecological Correlation," *American Journal of Sociology*, LXIV (1959), 610–25; Grady McWhiney, "Were the Whigs a Class Party in Alabama?" *Journal of Southern History*, XXIII (1957), 510–22; Thomas B. Alexander, Kit C. Carter, Jack R. Lister, Jerry L. Oldshue, and Winfred G. Sandlin, "Who Were the Alabama Whigs?" *Alabama Review*, XIV (1963), 5–19.
26. Benson, *The Concept of Jacksonian Democracy*, 156–64; Frank O. Gatell, "Money and Party in Jacksonian America: A Quantitative Look at New York City's Men of Quality," *Political Science Quarterly*, LXXXII (1967), 235–52; Burton J. Folsom II, "The Politics of Elites: Prominence and Party in Davidson County, Tennessee, 1835–1861," *Journal of Southern History*, XXXIX (1973), 359–78.
27. *E.g.*, Richard Jensen, "The Religious and Occupational Roots of Party Identification: Illinois and Indiana in the 1870s," *Civil War History*, XVI (1970), 325–43.
28. Thornton, *Politics and Power in a Slave Society*, 160.

evaluating comparisons between political elites. If it is true that "those who find striking contrasts in the beliefs and actions of the major parties tend to believe that the Whigs and Democrats appealed to different *constituencies*," it does not necessarily follow that "in this view, Democrats were *led* by plebeians, Whigs by aristocrats" (italics added).[29] Historians have found increasingly that American officeholders have owned more wealth than their average constituents and that they have often resembled each other more than they have typified the "common man." This is a valuable insight, but it should not distract us from the further social analysis of parties. Political transformation was a social process that calls for analysis below the level of senior leadership. The fact that the men who led the movement were similar in many respects may not prove anything about the nature of their followers.[30] In some cases, a reasonable measure of central tendency may be the practical way to find real variations between activists of different parties, while an analysis of parties as social coalitions may be necessary at other times. The analogy to a lawsuit may be useful, for the social similarity of rival attorneys is no guarantee of harmony between their clients. Whatever the approach, we ought not to finish the discussion of leadership with the elementary observation that senators and congressmen had more money than ordinary folk.

The evidence from rhetoric, leadership, and voting behavior indicates strongly that the Age of Jackson brought profound changes to North Carolina and Cumberland County. The political innovations of the period revolutionized the style and content of local civic culture. The older practices which had been geared to low participation, ideological consensus, and social stability gave way in the 1820s and 1830s to a system which mobilized larger numbers of voters and drew them into lively political controversy. To sum-

29. Pessen, *Jacksonian America*, 233.
30. Evidence on the property of elite members appears in Formisano, *The Birth of Mass Political Parties*, 42–47; Shade, *Banks or No Banks*, 135–41; Pessen, *Riches, Class, and Power*, 281–99; Folsom, "The Politics of Elites," 378; H. Wayne Smith, "Jacksonian Democracy on the Chesapeake: Class, Kinship, and Politics," *Maryland Historical Magazine*, LXIII (1968), 55–67; McWhiney, "Were the Whigs a Class Party in Alabama?"; Alexander, *et al.*, "Who Were the Alabama Whigs?"; Randolph Campbell and Richard Lowe, *Wealthholding and Power in Antebellum Texas* (College Station, Tex., 1977), 107–123; Ralph Wooster, *Politicians, Planters and Plain Folk: Courthouse and Statehouse in the Upper South, 1850–1860* (Knoxville, 1975), *passim*; Harold J. Counihan, "North Carolina, 1815–1836: State and Local Perspectives on the Age of Jackson" (Ph.D. dissertation, University of North Carolina, 1971), 19–24; Thomas Edward Jeffrey, "The Second Party System in North Carolina, 1836–1860" (Ph.D. dissertation, Catholic University of America, 1979), 154–84; Marc Wayne Kruman, "Parties and Politics in North Carolina, 1846–1865" (Ph.D. dissertation, Yale University, 1978), 10–18; Whitman H. Ridgway, *Community Leadership in Maryland, 1790–1840: A Comparative Analysis of Power in Society* (Chapel Hill, 1979), 215–339. Some of these authors go further and suggest that the similarity of leaders is an indication of the irrelevance of social factors to the question of party identity. I would argue that this conclusion is too hasty. Ridgway's discovery that diversity among leaders changed over various periods and settings is a major conceptual advance.

marize the argument briefly, I have concluded that in Cumberland County, the pivotal partisan controversy arose over questions of political economy. In effect, the voters had to decide how they wanted their community to fit into the rapidly developing world of international capitalism. Their alternatives were exceedingly complex, but by oversimplifying drastically, they can be stated in a couple of sentences. Would Cumberland County become an expanded regional market for staple crops exported to the factories of New England and Britain, with a few mills of its own as well? If so, powerful banks and expensive internal improvements would be necessary. Ultimately, overall community wealth would increase, there would be wider extremes between rich and poor, and the community would ride the dizzying swings of the business cycle through boom and bust. Or would Cumberland County remain an isolated backwater, experiencing almost certain poverty and a decline in the marginal return to slave property, possibly nursing the dream of a virtuous yeoman's utopia, but probably falling victim to the unwelcome aspects of capitalist market relations anyhow? These were the bare bones of the Jacksonian party debate. The choices were not usually put so starkly, and not everybody in the community understood them in the same way, but the questions had to be answered, if only by default.

To avoid misunderstanding, I should hasten to add that the citizens' answers to these questions emerged from a framework of commonly held assumptions which derived from their Anglo-American cultural inheritance and from their status as moderate property holders. And however self-conscious certain leaders may have been, the majority of voters and activists appeared most attuned to the symbolic aspects of the debate. Their responses, moreover, did not fit any simplistic dichotomy between the "people" and the "interests." Instead, the citizens formed political parties to uphold their respective images of good government and the good life. Subsequently, the parties provided them with useful stock answers to urgent problems and forestalled any further debate or redefinition of the issues. Cumberland County achieved a new version of stability.

The book which follows traces Cumberland County's political transformation through three roughly defined stages. In the first, the career of Andrew Jackson disrupted the informal politics of the Era of Good Feelings, and simultaneously, county leaders began to face the economic and political implications of the Transportation Revolution. This stage ended in 1829. In the second phase, political organizers drew on prior community values to build plausible linkages between political and economic issues at the local, state, and national levels. At the same time, they used long-standing regional, ethnic, and class alignments to assemble two rival voting blocs, each with a different perception of the issues. The pressing and connected questions of banking and government aid to internal improvements made these intellectual linkages both possible and necessary. The process of constructing coalitions and shaping ideologies continued throughout Jackson's first six years in office. It climaxed with the formation of recognizable Whig and Democratic party organizations in the town elections of 1834. The third and final stage began in the state and national elections of 1836, as country voters accepted the partisan perspectives hammered out by party leaders in the county seat and joined the townsmen in the routines of stable party operation. By 1840, the process was substantially complete.

How much can we learn from the study of Cumberland County? The community was no microcosm of North Carolina or the United States, but the same conditions which stimulated party politics there operated in many other places. Likewise, most American communities developed partisan politics at approximately the same time. To generalize dogmatically from a single case would be indefensible, but a case study without broader implications would have minimal significance. To strike a hopeful balance between these extremes, I would like to leave the reader with a series of educated guesses.

Putting aside those communities which were virtually unanimous for one party or the other and for which the party system was an expression of local agreement rather than controversy, I would suggest that the party systems generally emerged from the same approximate pattern that we see in Cumberland County. Undoubtedly, voters elsewhere faced somewhat different questions and even radically different social divisions; the attendant stages of party formation may also have varied from place to place, and the particular profiles of party membership were almost certainly nonuniform nationally. In the free states especially, many communities responded to the Age of Jackson by emphasizing ethnic and religious rivalries, and party composition there reflected these concerns. Nevertheless, I am inclined to believe that ethnic and religious conflicts broke into open hostility under the stresses of pervasive economic change. It was the power of cultural symbols for conveying what I have called rival images of good government and the good life that brought these values into politics. Regardless of these local variations, I suspect that the process of political development which we observe in Cumberland County repeated itself elsewhere. First, social and economic change ruptured traditional political patterns by generating demands for novel applications of government power. Second, leaders struggled to reassemble values and social blocs behind alternative stances or responses, groping simultaneously to answer constituents' complaints and to solve their own problems of winning electoral office. Third and finally, they settled on a set of party ideologies and constituencies that made practical and emotional sense to all citizens. Party leaders may not have believed or acted on their slogans, but for the mass of American voters, the credos of political faith were clear, convincing, and consistent with daily reality. When the process was complete, American political culture had experienced indelible change.

But if the culture of the old republic had been transformed, it is striking how the new political parties also captured and defused the potentially violent set of conflicts which created them. Obviously, the second party system could not resolve sectional tensions with the same facility that it deflected other conflicts. Civil war was the bloody monument to that failure. But American politics has been preeminently successful in containing the community conflicts which industrialization stimulated in other countries. In the United States, as in Cumberland County, the end result of party formation was a political system that expressed deep divisions within each community but which left the basic patterns of economic and social relations undisturbed. In other words, the development of liberal democracy first embodied a crisis and then neutralized it. To that extent, the experience of Cumberland County was indeed the history of American politics.

I. The Citizens of Town and Country

In 1824 and 1825, the United States received a distinguished visitor. The Marquis de Lafayette, French political leader and hero of the American Revolution, returned to America for a farewell tour. Throughout the republic, citizens thronged to see the grand old major-general who had left fortune and aristocratic splendor behind him as a youth to serve with Washington in the cause of American liberty. Everywhere Lafayette went, the nation's people turned out to see him and to thank him for his services to republicanism.[1]

One of the many places on the general's route was Fayetteville, North Carolina, the county seat of Cumberland County. Fayetteville was a small town, but its citizens had good reason to make their welcome of the general unrivaled for cordiality and enthusiasm. Back in 1783, when the American and French triumph at Yorktown was still fresh, Fayetteville had been the first town in the United States to be named for the gallant French officer.[2] Now, in 1825, Fayetteville was finally able to welcome its patronal hero. Preparations were intense, for the townspeople were determined to make a good impression. When the general's itinerary became known, a town meeting authorized the commissioners to entertain Lafayette at public expense, "in a manner as shall comport with the dignity of a distinguished personage and the respectability of the town of Fayetteville."[3] The citizens tried to make Lafayette comfortable, but they also made his visit an elaborate civic ritual which expressed some of their most important concerns about the meaning of the past and the future of their nation and their community.

As Lafayette's party finally arrived in town at five o'clock on the afternoon

1. Fred Somkin, *Unquiet Eagle: Memory and Desire in the Idea of American Freedom, 1815–1860* (Ithaca, N.Y., 1967), 131–74.
2. John A. Oates, *The Story of Fayetteville and the Upper Cape Fear* (2nd ed.; Fayetteville, N.C., 1972), 160.
3. Fayetteville *Observer*, February 24, 1825.

of March 4, 1825, pervasive excitement was not diminished by the downpour of rain that had been falling steadily for days. In his memoirs of the trip, Lafayette's private secretary remembered the occasion vividly. "The road for several miles before we reached the place was crowded with men and boys on horseback and militia on foot," wrote Alain Levasseur. "The streets of the town were filled with a throng of ladies, in full dress, hastening across the little streams of water, to approach the General's carriage, and so much occupied with the pleasure of seeing him that they appeared insensible of the deluge which threatened almost to swallow them up." [4]

Lafayette's carriage crossed the Clarendon Bridge over the Cape Fear River and passed through the waterfront neighborhood of Campbellton. Turning into Person Street, the party entered the commercial heart of Fayetteville through a double line of troops, and halted in front of the imposing Town House. Lafayette dismounted in the mud and ascended a newly erected scaffold, crowded with distinguished dignitaries. The hour was late, the general was tired, and the rain was still coming down; Judge John B. Toomer kept his welcoming speech mercifully short, but he managed to touch most of the rhetorical themes which made the visit so significant for local citizens.

Judge Toomer, an old Federalist who was Fayetteville's most distinguished orator, began by commending the simplicity of Fayetteville's welcome. "We receive you with joy and exultation at our family altars," he told the Nation's Guest, "and request your participation in our domestic comforts. We are plain republicans, and cannot greet you with the pomp common on such occasions. . . . We have no splendid arches, gilded spires, or gorgeous palaces to present you, but we tender the hospitality of our homes, and the grateful homage of devoted hearts." The reason for Fayetteville's gratitude, Toomer reminded Lafayette and his audience, was the immensity of Lafayette's sacrifice for the political principles of republicanism. "You disinterestedly lavished your treasure, and shed your blood in the hallowed contest; and by the influence of your high example, you consecrated the principles for which our ancestors contended. . . . Never, never can we forget the youthful stranger who, in the darkest hour of adversity, so generously flew to our succour, and so gallantly fought the battle of freedom." Concluding his address, the aging judge saluted the promise of the future. He foretold the coming greatness of Fayetteville and North Carolina generally, and then extended his prophecy to include the whole world. Because of the sacrifices of Lafayette and the other Founding Fathers, Toomer predicted that republican ideals would flourish everywhere and bring in an era of unequaled human happiness.

4. A. Levasseur, *Lafayette in America, in 1824 and 1825 or Journal of Travels in the United States* (2 vols.; New York, 1829), II, 44.

The darkness of error is vanishing before the light of truth. The doctrines of divine right and passive obedience are viewed as relics of ancient barbarism. Our political institutions are founded on the sovereignty of the people, from whom all power is derived; and here the
jargon of legitimacy is not understood. We recognize no Holy Alliance,
save that of religion and virtue, liberty and science. The sun of freedom
is extending the sphere of his genial influence; South America is "re-
generated and disenthralled;" the thrones of Europe are supported by
bayonets, and must totter to their fall; and the genius of our country is
ready to hail the spirit of "universal emancipation." [5]

The visitor made a short reply and the crowd of several hundred responded
with three cheers, after which the welcoming committee escorted Lafayette to
his quarters at the home of Duncan MacRae, Esq., president of the Fayetteville branch of the State Bank of North Carolina.

Writing almost seventy years later, another witness of the spectacle remembered Lafayette's visit as the momentous civic event of his childhood. "Great
preparations were made by the citizens of Fayetteville to receive their honored
guest," wrote William Kennedy Blake, onetime merchant and teacher in
Fayetteville. "Military companies, Artillery, Infantry, Calvary [sic]—Civic
Societies—schools and academies—and citizens of town and country all arrayed in their holiday attire, went forth at the sound of music and with flying
banners to welcome this generous friend of America from a foreign shore."
Lafayette's visit was marked by two banquets, a ball, a reception, cannon fire,
military parades, and numerous rounds of speechmaking and toasts. But to
young Blake, who was nine years old at the time, the climax of the celebration
came as he watched his grandfather, Isham Blake, who had been a member of
Lafayette's guard at Yorktown, lead a group of Revolutionary veterans in presenting a flag to his former commander. "Amid profound silence the eloquent
speeches of presentation and acceptance were spoken; and when the flag was
unfurled, and its silken folds floated on the breeze, a shout went up that made
the welkin ring. The roar of cannon, peals of musketry, ringing of bells, and
the martial notes of drum and fife, all swelled the universal joy of the multi-
tude." [6] Concluding its account of the visit, the Fayetteville *Carolina Observer* echoed William's enthusiasm. "It was a period in which none but the

5. Fayetteville *Observer*, March 10, 1825, reprinted in Edgar Ewing Brandon (ed.), *A Pilgrimage of Liberty: A Contemporary Account of the Triumphal Tour of General Lafayette
Through the Southern and Western States in 1825, As Reported by the Local Newspapers* (Athens,
Ohio, 1944), 31–34.
6. William Kennedy Blake, "Pen Sketches of My Life Written for the Gratification of My Children" (Typescript in Southern Historical Collection, University of North Carolina at Chapel
Hill), 8.

nobler feelings of the heart were exhibited. It was a period, the happiness of which may be imagined, not described." [7]

The day that Lafayette spent in Fayetteville was evidently a memorable event. Wherever Lafayette visited in the United States, his welcome was similar. Citizens gathered by the thousands to thank Lafayette, to support the republican principles he fought for, and to express their desire to keep alive the special meaning of the American Revolution. The response to the marquis' tour was so fervent that Fred Somkin has concluded that "the living Lafayette disappeared entirely behind the multiple facade of his social meanings" and that "in praising Lafayette a generation of Americans were explaining themselves to one another and the world." This certainly seemed to be the case in Fayetteville, where the citizens used the occasion to show that they were a unified community, that they were inspired by the ideals of the past, and that republican government would bring them future greatness. In Somkin's judgment, however, some of the celebrants betrayed a sense of insecurity. "The more Americans insisted on the 'spontaneous,' and hence pure, character of the national gratitude to the returned representative of the Fathers, the more shaky appeared their own self-confidence in the moral continuity of American history." [8] In other words, some Americans in 1825 seemed to doubt that their own age was as fine or as good as the age of the Founding Fathers. Judge Toomer admitted as much when he declared that the best part of America was in its past. "The freemen of America, when asked for their jewels," he acknowledged, "point not to their sons, but to the surviving heroes of the Revolution." [9] The testimonials of Judge Toomer and others before the marquis may have served to shore up Americans' own sense of assurance as much as they proved something directly to Lafayette.

Fears of moral discontinuity in 1825 were not limited to welcoming committees of provincial dignitaries. Fifty years after the battles of Lexington and Concord, the last survivors of the Revolutionary generation were dying. The future of the American experiment was passing into the hands of a new generation who might not be able to match the achievements of earlier patriots. Coincidentally, the day that Lafayette sloshed into Fayetteville was also the day that John Quincy Adams took office as fifth president of the United States. Delivering his Inaugural Address in the chamber of the House of Representatives, the new president spoke anxiously of the Constitution he swore to preserve, protect, and defend. "That revered instrument," he declared, "is the work of our forefathers. . . . We now receive it as a precious inheritance

7. Brandon (ed.), *A Pilgrimage of Liberty*, 36.
8. Somkin, *Unquiet Eagle*, 169.
9. Brandon (ed.), *A Pilgrimage of Liberty*, 32.

from those to whom we are indebted for its establishment, doubly bound by the examples which they have left us and by the blessings which we have enjoyed as the fruits of their labors to transmit the same unimpaired to the succeeding generation." [10] Adams' words implied a familiar admonition to a generation who feared the profligate tendency of heirs.

Unfortunately for the tranquility of his administration, some of his listeners thought John Quincy Adams was a perfect example of the declension he warned against. Himself the privileged son of a dying Founding Father, Adams won the presidency in a political horsetrade that reeked to many Americans of "bargain and corruption." [11] In Fayetteville, Judge Toomer affirmed that "our political institutions are founded on the sovereignty of the people" and in Washington, Adams maintained that "the will of the people is the source . . . of all legitimate government." But Adams' election over Andrew Jackson by the House of Representatives appeared to violate that principle, and when Adams addressed Congress ten months later and asked that the United States government not "proclaim to the world that we are palsied by the will of our constituents," many Americans feared that Adams could lead them to despotism. Adams asked his countrymen to abandon the "collisions of party spirit," but his term in office was marked by repeated political conflict and by the revival of party dissension. At the end of his term, Adams lost the presidency in an election that became infamous for bitterness, calumny, and personal vilification of the candidates. Eventually Adams' call for "discarding every remnant of rancor against each other" was rebuffed by continuous political partisanship. [12]

The same aversion to parties which Adams expressed appeared in the rhetoric of North Carolina's welcome to Lafayette. One of the general's hosts offered a toast to "the Unanimity of Parties—Their country's good the basis, may the National Column be inscribed *Peace*, *Good-will* and *Reconciliation*." [13] But in another coincidence, Fayetteville was the place where an im-

10. James D. Richardson (comp.), *A Compilation of the Messages and Papers of the Presidents* (20 vols.; New York, 1927), II, 860.
11. John Quincy Adams, Andrew Jackson, William H. Crawford, and Henry Clay were all candidates for president in 1824. No candidate received a majority of the electoral votes, but Jackson received the largest plurality, followed by Adams, Crawford, and Clay in descending order. In such cases, the Constitution provides for the election of one of the top three candidates by the House of Representatives. Clay was thus disqualified, but he threw his support to Adams in the House and Adams was elected over Jackson. Following his inauguration, Adams named Clay to be his secretary of state. Adams' political enemies widely alleged at the time that the chief magistracy had been bartered for a promise of high office. For a standard account of Adams' election, see Samuel Flagg Bemis, *John Quincy Adams and the Union* (New York, 1956), 11–70.
12. Richardson (comp.), *Messages and Papers of the Presidents*, II, 882, 862.
13. Brandon (ed.), *A Pilgrimage of Liberty*, 28.

portant piece of "evidence" appeared of a corrupt agreement between John Quincy Adams and Henry Clay to rig the election of 1825.[14] Cumberland County experienced the election of 1828 as a strident factional conflict, and the second American party system eventually replaced the local political harmony that had characterized the reception of Lafayette.

When General Lafayette died in the summer of 1834, the leading citizens of Fayetteville solemnized the occasion with respectful resolutions of mourning, but their real attention lay elsewhere.[15] Thomas L. Hybart had challenged James Seawell for Fayetteville's seat in the General Assembly, and the town rocked with tumult in its first party contest between Democrats and Whigs. The memoirs of another old-time resident of Fayetteville testify to the transformation which parties effected on the local scene. Writing as "Senex," Robert Cochran Belden published his recollections in the Fayetteville *Observer* in 1893. "Never had the borough witnessed such excitement as on the day of the election," Belden wrote. "The two parties marshalled their forces in Campbellton and marched up town to their respective rendezvous. The Whigs occupied an upper room in the Hooper building above the store then occupied by the late E. J. Lilly, and there liquor, from pure French to mean whiskey, flowed freely." The Democrats located their headquarters not far away, and the two parties were soon engaged in accusations of fraud. "To secure if possible a party triumph, subterfuge was resorted to," by the issuance of false deeds to qualify ineligible voters. "A tender of a vote which the Whigs charged was fraudulent gave rise to an angry discussion," remembered the old-timer, "and, except for a conciliatory speech by Edward Lee Winslow, would have brought on bloodshed." A duel between the Whig editor and a Democratic orator was narrowly averted. "Friends were alienated," Belden wrote, "and wounds were inflicted that time was long in healing." [16]

The drunkenness, violence, and resentment which Belden remembered

14. In the spring of 1827, Carter Beverley of Virginia visited Andrew Jackson at the Hermitage. While there, Beverley heard Jackson say that Clay's friends had offered to throw the election of 1825 to Jackson if only Jackson would signal his interest, but the general had indignantly refused. Beverley told the story in a letter to a friend in Fayetteville, and the letter was published in the *Carolina Observer*. Jackson's accusation was reprinted in other newspapers and led to a national scandal, with elaborate charges and countercharges hurled among the contending parties. Fayetteville itself was apparently unruffled by the furor, and Jackson's correspondence with Carter Beverley does not reveal the identity of Beverley's Fayetteville friend. Fayetteville *Carolina Observer*, April 5, 1827; Andrew Jackson to Carter Beverley, June 5, 1827, Carter Beverley to Andrew Jackson, June 9, 1827, both in John Spencer Bassett (ed.), *Correspondence of Andrew Jackson* (6 vols.; Washington, 1928), III, 355–57, 362–63; Marquis James, *The Life of Andrew Jackson* (Indianapolis, 1938), 458–61.
15. Fayetteville *North Carolina Journal*, July 9, 1834.
16. Robert Cochran Belden [Senex], "Traditions of Cross Creek and Reminiscences of Fayetteville," Fayetteville *Observer*, September 28, 1893.

were not really new in 1834, but they were a far cry from the ritual unity displayed for Lafayette nine years earlier. The return of party warfare, moreover, was not temporary. Six years later, in 1840, political conflict in Cumberland County was so severe that one political activist sighed for the good old days when everyone could "follow his business in peace and quietness—undisturbed by the bitter party combinations of the neighbourhood." [17] This leader's hope was not fulfilled in his lifetime. Political parties dominated Cumberland County elections for the rest of the nineteenth century. In the federal government, partisan conflict has been normal and continuous from the election of Andrew Jackson in 1828 to the present day.

The public life of community and nation evidently experienced a transformation in the years between 1825 and 1834. The emergence of professional politicians, the noisy proclamations of universal political equality among whites, and the creation of contentious mass political parties were all part of a rejection of the stately and genteel republicanism which dominated public affairs in the early national period. The new parties were heterogeneous assemblages which reflected an American talent for building consensus. Subsequent observers have been hard-pressed to define consistent differences between the Whig and Democratic ideology or social composition, and the two coalitions were indeed quite similar in many respects. From time to time, commentators have praised the American party systems as reflections of fundamental national unity or deplored their tendency to obscure significant differences by the use of "empty" rhetoric. Regardless of how they interpret it, virtually all observers would agree that the unique political culture of the American republic has been central to the national experience. For better or worse, that culture was born in the Age of Jackson.

Though historians have long recognized that the permanent creation of a two-party system was a crucial aspect of American history, most studies of the process have focused on state or national leaders. The concentration on leadership from above does not do justice to the intensely local character of antebellum life and politics. Americans boasted proudly that their country was no consolidated empire of homogeneous institutions, but a federated republic of semiautonomous local units. Legalistic politicians usually identified those units as states, but in fact, thousands of what Robert H. Wiebe has called "island communities" were the basic components of the larger national whole.[18] Each of these diverse localities reflected several aspects of Jacksonian social ferment. The adulation of national heroes, the vilification of

17. John W. Huske to Solomon Van Hook, November 14, 1840, in Solomon Van Hook Correspondence, Holeman Collection, microfilm copy in North Carolina State Archives, Raleigh.
18. Robert H. Wiebe, *The Search for Order, 1877–1920* (New York, 1967), 44.

partisan enemies, and the anxiety to get ahead were all local passions expressed in particular neighborhood ceremonies of praise, hostility, and hope. Many of the epic battles of the Age of Jackson took place on a national stage in Washington, D.C., but those larger-than-life encounters acquired their cultural significance as they reverberated through the consciousness of the neighborhoods. The calculations of officeholders closely followed changes in the mood of the folks at home, while opportunities for local actions depended on the turn of events in Washington and the state capitals. To overlook the local dimension of "Jacksonian Democracy" is to miss one of the essential qualities of the antebellum national experience.

Cumberland County, North Carolina, is an appropriate setting for the local study of Jacksonian politics. In the second quarter of the nineteenth century, the county contained a mixture of social elements that was characteristic of most rural counties in the antebellum South. Cumberland County also contained an important white ethnic minority, the Highland Scots. The people of the county faced challenges to the future of their community which involved them in some of the most absorbing controversies of their time. They responded by creating a vigorous two-party system and a flourishing local example of Jacksonian politics. Cumberland was exceptional in the way that most localities claim some distinction to set themselves apart from others, but on the whole, the county was an average southern community in a critical period of social and political change.

Located on the western edge of North Carolina's coastal plain, Cumberland had been set off from neighboring Bladen County in 1754. [19] The first white settlers had arrived about twenty years earlier. Some of the earliest inhabitants were Presbyterians who came to the area directly from the Highlands of Scotland. More of their countrymen followed in the 1750s and 1760s. Other pioneers were families with English surnames who probably immigrated from other colonies and from other parts of North Carolina. These settlers brought African slaves with them. A century after first settlement, immigration and natural increase had raised the number of the county's inhabitants to approximately fifteen thousand. Of these, about nine thousand were white, about five thousand were slaves, and the remainder were known as "free persons of colour." [20]

19. David Leroy Corbitt, *The Formation of North Carolina Counties, 1663–1943* (Raleigh, 1950), 79–83. Between 1784 and 1855, Cumberland County included all of modern Harnett County, most of Hoke County, and part of Moore County.
20. Oates, *The Story of Fayetteville*, 9–46; *Census for 1820* (Washington, 1821), 25; *Fifth Census; or, Enumeration of the Inhabitants of the United States: 1830* (Washington, 1832), 90–91; *Compendium of the Enumeration of the Inhabitants and Statistics of the United States, As Obtained at the Department of State from the Returns of the Sixth Census* (Washington, 1841), 42–43.

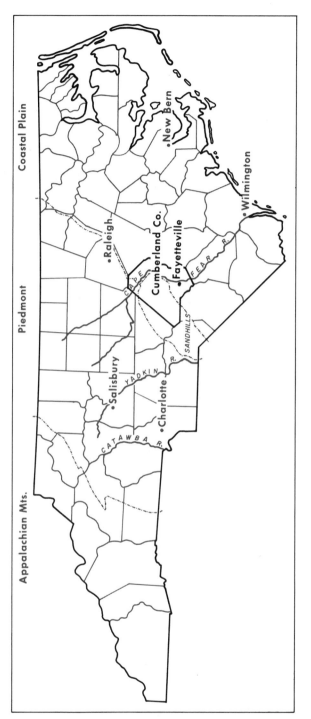

Figure 1. North Carolina and Cumberland County, 1836.
Map by Keith Adams

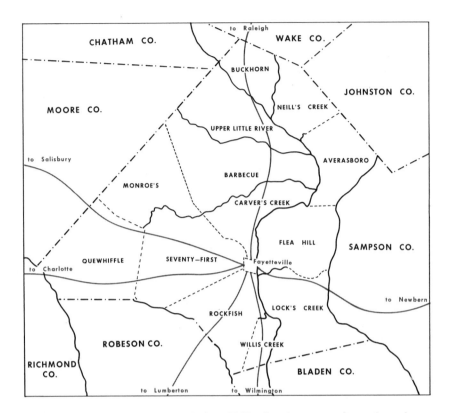

Figure 2. Cumberland County before 1855, showing approximate boundaries of militia and tax districts. A polling place was located in almost every district.

Map by Keith Adams

The Cape Fear River bisected Cumberland in a north-south direction and separated its two geographical sections. Fanning out west of the river and extending across several adjacent counties was a region of ancient dunes, covered with longleafed pines and known as the "sandhills." Though relieved by patches of better soil in the creek bottoms, the sandhills were generally infertile in the nineteenth century. By contrast to this poorer region, both banks of the river and most of the region to the east consisted of more valuable sandy loam soils.[21] It was here in eastern, northern, and southern Cumberland that most of the county's agriculture took place.

The farmers of Cumberland were a diverse group. In 1830, 38.9 percent of the rural heads of household were slaveholders and 3.0 percent owned more than 20 slaves, the number which designated them as members of the planter class. These proportions were roughly equivalent to conditions in North Carolina as a whole. Some planter families were wealthy by state standards. The largest single slaveholder in the county was William Lord, who owned 89 bondsmen in 1830 and 2,164 acres. Three other planters owned 50 slaves or more in that year.[22] The history of two planter families suggests that the large county fortunes began in the eighteenth century. George Elliott, for example, settled in Cumberland County before the American Revolution and acquired "Ellerslie," an estate of 30,000 to 40,000 acres. He represented Cumberland County in the Hillsborough convention of 1788 and voted there to ratify the United States Constitution. In 1830, his widow Mary and his three sons, Alexander, Henry, and John, owned 154 slaves and 34,000 acres, making the Elliots the wealthiest planter family in Cumberland.[23] The Evans family was also quite notable. Before 1736, the first Jonathan Evans came to the Cumberland County area from Pennsylvania, where his father, Thomas Evans, had been deputy governor. Two of his sons, David and Theophilus, were promi-

21. U.S. Bureau of Soils, *North Carolina Soil Map*, Cumberland County Map Sheet (Washington, 1922), Hoke County Map Sheet (Washington, 1918), Harnett County Map Sheet (Washington, 1916); S. H. Hobbs, Jr., *North Carolina: Economic and Social* (Chapel Hill, 1930), 5, 70.
22. The other three owners of 50 or more slaves were John B. Williams (55), Flora McKay (50), and Jonathan Evans, Sr., (69). United States Manuscript Census Returns, Population Schedule, Cumberland County, North Carolina, 1830, pp. 72, 44, 54, 77, microfilm copy in North Carolina Collection, University of North Carolina at Chapel Hill. In 1860, 2.7 percent of the households in North Carolina contained 20 slaves or more while 27.7 percent contained at least one slave. Cumberland County lay on the border between the planting districts of eastern North Carolina and the small farm country of the Piedmont. A total of 5.2 percent of eastern households contained 20 slaves or more but the comparable figure for the Piedmont was 2.0 percent. J. Carlyle Sitterson, "Economic Sectionalism in Ante-Bellum North Carolina," *North Carolina Historical Review*, XVI (1939), 136, 139–40; Guion Griffis Johnson, *Ante-Bellum North Carolina: A Social History* (Chapel Hill, 1937), 55–56.
23. Oates, *The Story of Fayetteville*, 828; MS Census Returns, Population Schedule, Cumberland County, North Carolina, 1830, pp. 44, 46; Will of George Elliott, typed copy in John Elliot Papers, Southern Historical Collection; Cumberland County List of Taxables, 1829, in Cumberland County Records, North Carolina State Archives.

nent in the local movement for independence in 1775. In 1830, his three grandsons, Josiah, Henry, and Jonathan, and two great-grandsons, Josiah, Jr., and Jonathan, Jr., were his principal male descendants still living in Cumberland County. They owned 124 slaves and 13,000 acres between them. The county historian records that "many of the most substantial citizens of the county and state are descended from the Evans line." [24]

The Evans' experience indicates that wide disparities of wealth and personal security could exist within families of the planter class. Jonathan Evans II was the wealthiest of the first Jonathan Evans' grandsons. He owned 64 slaves, which made him the second largest slaveholder in the county. Jonathan Evans II owned a large plantation and he was also a partner of Alexander and Henry Elliott in the ownership of 19,000 acres of "speculation land" on Jumping Run in the sandhills. For tax purposes, this modest tract was valued at $200 in 1830; Jonathan Evans himself was the magistrate who drew up the district tax list that year. [25] Jonathan's cousin Josiah was a moderate planter who owned 33 slaves, but cousin Henry owned only 11. Josiah Evans had 10 children; he was able to give each one a few hands and a farm, but great wealth was not his to bestow. The papers of Josiah's son James show that younger child struggling bitterly against bad luck and bad business conditions in the 1830s, and gradually clawing his way back to respectability as a planter by the 1850s. James's brother Dickson became a successful physician, but his brothers John and Jonathan died bankrupt. Several of their sisters made bad marriages which left them penniless and hostile, dependent on James to find their children apprenticeships as clerks or artisans. [26] The Evans' hold on planter status was precarious at best. Nevertheless, they and the 41 households in 1830 which contained more than 20 slaves defined the upper limits of rural county society.

Planters were not the typical farmers of Cumberland County. The majority of farmers were not slaveholders, but in 1830, a few less than 85 percent of the rural heads of households owned their own land. Their holdings averaged 419 acres in size, an unusually high figure for North Carolina, which probably stemmed from the cheapness and relative infertility of sandhills land. [27] The

---

24. Delancey Evans, "The Evans Family" (Typescript in Delancey Evans Papers, Southern Historical Collection); MS Census Returns, Population Schedule, Cumberland County, North Carolina, 1830, p. 77; Cumberland County List of Taxables, 1829, in Cumberland County Records; Oates, *The Story of Fayetteville*, 829.

25. List of Taxables for Lock's Creek District, 1830, in James Evans Papers, in possession of Mr. and Mrs. Claude N. Kent, Columbus, Georgia.

26. James Evans Papers, 1831–61, *passim*.

27. MS Census Returns, Population Schedule, Cumberland County, North Carolina, 1830, pp. 20–98; Cumberland County List of Taxables, 1829. Irregularities in land tenure patterns and record-keeping make it difficult to state precisely the proportion of farmers who owned their own land. Many of the owners listed in the tax records were women, minor children, or estates. In

nonslaveholding landowners were the largest group in Cumberland County's white population and comprised the majority of its electorate. As a group, they constituted the rural middle class. The political events of the Age of Jackson were decisively affected in Cumberland County by the way these men cast their ballots.

Not all farmers in Cumberland County were landowners. County records for 1810 mention the presence of transient tenant farmers who appear to have resembled postbellum sharecroppers. Other rural inhabitants divided their time between agricultural labor on the farms of others and "following the river" as boat hands. Perhaps the largest portion of the landless ignored formal rental agreements and squatted in the sandhills. When Frederick Law Olmsted visited the county in 1854 he was informed by a "gentleman of Fayetteville . . . that he had, several times, appraised, under oath, the whole household property of families of this class at less than $20." [28] These families were the rural poor. They appear in the electoral records occasionally as men who were accused of selling their votes for whiskey or of voting in violation of residency requirements. They were not central actors in the transformation of county politics, but they were a significant element of society that no politician could entirely ignore.

A special segment of the Cumberland County rural population belonged to a white ethnic minority. These were the descendants of the Scottish Highlanders who had settled in the county in the middle of the eighteenth century. Modern scholarship has rejected the tradition that these pioneers were expelled from Scotland as punishment for their participation in the Jacobite rebellion of 1745. But it is true that Flora MacDonald, the Jacobite heroine and benefactor of Charles Stuart, the Young Pretender, lived briefly in Cumberland County among the Highland community. In the American Revolution, these recent immigrants showed great opposition to the whiggish values of their patriot neighbors and formed a Loyalist regiment to defend North Carolina's royal governor. As late as 1780, large numbers of Scots in Cumber-

---

other cases, taxes were listed by agents, not by owners, and it is difficult to determine whether the owners in these cases were temporarily absent or incapacitated or actually absentee landlords. In all of these exceptional cases, it is difficult or impossible to determine whether the users of the land were in fact owners for all practical purposes (in the case of an adult son farming the land of his widowed mother, for example) or whether they were renters or squatters. Dividing the 1,142 rural landholders listed in the tax records for 1828 by the 1,350 rural households counted in the census of 1830 yields 84.6 percent as an outside estimate of the proportion of rural families who owned land. Record linkage of these two long lists was thought to be unnecessary, since a more precise knowledge of land tenure patterns would not have affected the major conclusions of this study.

28. Frederick Law Olmsted, *A Journey in the Seaboard Slave States in the Years 1853–1854, With Remarks on their Economy* (2 vols.; New York, 1904), I, 389; Deposition of William Cook, November 9, 1810, Deposition of Nathan Pearce, November 24, 1810, Deposition of Richard Cade, November 24, 1810, all in Legislative Papers, Box 245, North Carolina State Archives.

land County were still refusing to swear loyalty to the Revolutionary state government.[29]

Two generations after the Revolution, the Scottish community of Cumberland was still a distinct group. Tax lists show that Scottish-surnamed heads of households were relatively poor and concentrated in the sandhills districts of Barbeque, Quewhiffle, Rockfish, and Seventy-first. An especially conservative version of Presbyterianism helped to hold them together. Their continued use of the Gaelic language was another important source of cohesion. Community institutions like the "Old Scotch Fair" in neighboring Robeson County kept alive ethnic traditions of food, clothing, music, games, dances, folklore, and amusements. A trickle of continued immigration replenished the community with a small but regular number of newcomers from Scotland itself. The result was a large Scottish element in Cumberland County that maintained a separate cultural identity for most of the antebellum period. This community was sufficiently conspicuous to attract the attention of several antebellum travel writers, including Captain Basil Hall, Mrs. Anne Royall, and Frederick Law Olmsted. The ethnic identity of the group was decisive in the politics of the early national period, but less conspicuously influential in the Age of Jackson.[30]

The ethnic identity of the other white inhabitants of Cumberland was vague. They were simply the non-Scots. Their surnames were mostly English and like most North Carolinians of English descent, their ancestors probably arrived in Cumberland by way of other colonies. Although Cumberland was a center of Scottish immigration, the non-Scots had comprised a majority of the population since at least 1790. By the 1820s, almost two-thirds of Cumberland's free residents had non-Scottish surnames.[31]

29. R. D. W. Connor, *Race Elements in the White Population of North Carolina*, North Carolina State Normal & Industrial College Historical Publications (Raleigh, 1920), 44–68; Duane Meyer, *The Highland Scots of North Carolina, 1732–1776* (Chapel Hill, 1961), 69–162; Ian Charles Carghill Graham, *Colonists from Scotland: Emigration to North America, 1707–1783* (Ithaca, N.Y., 1956), 150–83; Carole Watterson Troxler, *The Loyalist Experience in North Carolina* (Raleigh, 1976), 21.

30. Johnson, *Ante-Bellum North Carolina*, 349–50; William K. Boyd, *The History of North Carolina: The Federal Period, 1783–1860* (Chicago, 1919), 191; Captain Basil Hall, *Travels in North America in the Years 1827 and 1828* (3 vols.; Edinburgh, 1829), III, 121–22; Una Pope-Hennessey (ed.), *The Aristocratic Journey: Being the Outspoken Letters of Mrs. Basil Hall Written During a Fourteen Month Sojourn in America, 1827–28* (New York, 1931), 205; Olmsted, *Seaboard Slave States*, I, 396; Fayetteville *Carolina Observer*, September 17, 1829, and September 24, 1829; Fayetteville *North Carolina Journal*, September 23, 1829; Fayetteville *North Carolinian*, May 22, 1858.

31. Harry Roy Merrens, *Colonial North Carolina in the Eighteenth Century* (Chapel Hill, 1964), 68; Connor, *Race Elements*, 19–39; Meyer, *Highland Scots*, 116–17; *Heads of Families at the First Census of the United States Taken in the Year 1790: North Carolina* (Washington, 1908), 38–42. For the proportions of Scots in the 1820s, see Table 1. Scottish names were verified in George F. Black, *The Surnames of Scotland* (New York, 1946).

Generally speaking, the Scots of Cumberland County were poorer than the non-Scots. A number of wealthy Scottish families lived on the riverbanks with other members of the rural elite, but most of their clansmen occupied poor land. Table 1 illustrates this concentration with data from the 1827 county tax list. The table shows that the sandhills tax districts were largely Scottish and sandhills land was worth less per acre than land in other districts. The coefficient of correlation between land values and percent Scottish is very high (r = .9218). A high degree of "per taxpayer" wealth was also associated with a low percentage of Scots (r = .5076).

Table 1 suggests that wealth, residence, and ethnicity divided the tax districts of Cumberland into four distinct groups. Fayetteville was in a class by itself. Because of the value of their homes and stores, its inhabitants controlled the lion's share of the county's wealth. Some affluent town dwellers also held large quantities of land and slaves in the countryside. A second group of districts, including Carver's Creek, Flea Hill, Averasborough, and Lock's Creek, bordered on the Cape Fear River and were heavily involved in plantation agriculture.[32] A third set of districts, Willis Creek, Neill's Creek, and Buckhorn, was dominated by small farmers who held few slaves and whose lands were relatively high in unit value. Both the plantation and the small-farm districts were characterized by a low proportion of Scottish residents. The fourth group comprised the sandhills, populated largely by poor Scots living on cheap land.

If their land was fertile enough to grow staples, the favorite crops of Cumberland County farmers were cotton and corn. The cotton was sold in Fayetteville, but much of the corn was eaten locally by people or animals.[33] Tobacco was not grown in the antebellum period because the soil was not considered appropriate. The best land in the county produced cotton that was superior to that of South Carolina, according to some local observers.[34] But on the whole, the county's land was not very fertile, so the farmers of Cumberland

32. In 1830, eleven households in Carver's Creek district contained twenty slaves or more. Flea Hill contained six planter families, Little River five, and Lock's Creek four. These four districts contained 63.4 percent of the plantations in the county. MS Census Returns, Population Schedule, Cumberland County, North Carolina, 1830, pp. 20–98.

33. The census of 1840 found substantial crops of cotton and corn in Cumberland. Surviving business records indicate that the cotton·was exported but that the corn was not. *Compendium of the Sixth Census*, 180; "Accounts for the Boat Clipper," 1816–23, in Orin Datus Davis Account Books, Southern Historical Collection; Unidentified Merchant's Ledger, 1815–17, Account Book 341, North Carolina State Archives; William MacLennon Letter Book, 1810–11, Thomas J. Curtis Letter Book, 1830–31, and Elijah Fuller Barter Book, 1833–38, all in Elijah Fuller Papers, Southern Historical Collection.

34. A. S. McNeill to Neill McNeill, February 18, 1830, in Harnett County Papers, Southern Historical Collection; John Huske, *et al.*, "The Undersigned, traders in the Town of Fayetteville," Fayetteville, N.C., October 24, 1833, (Broadside in the Rare Book Room, Duke University Library, Durham, N.C.).

Table 1. Social and Economic Characteristics of Cumberland County, North Carolina, 1827–30, by Tax Districts

District names[a]	Mean assessed wealth per taxpayer in dollars	Mean acres of land per taxpayer	Mean value of land per acre in dollars	1830 population	Percent slave, 1830	Percent taxpayers with Scottish names	Predominant soil type
Barbecue	218.87	365	.60	1,097	26.5	77.3	sandhills
Quewhiffle	225.75	389	.58	830	27.1	82.0	sandhills
Rockfish	298.64	352	.85	1,066[b]	33.7[b]	63.0	sandhills
Flea Hill	326.56	268	1.22	1,558	30.6	43.5	mixed
Buckhorn	398.38	313	1.27	965	28.1	10.7	sandy loam
Seventy-first	406.42	522	.65	1,781	31.4	68.4	sandhills
Upper Little River	433.20	405	1.07	978	42.4	46.8	mixed
Willis Creek	458.62	294	1.56	N.A.	N.A.	2.7	sandy loam
Neill's Creek	523.59	401	1.30	942	30.1	15.6	sandy loam
Lock's Creek	599.09	489	1.22	856	36.0	16.8	sandy loam
Averasborough	735.46	556	1.32	811	26.5	15.0	sandy loam
Carver's Creek	988.87	556	.90	1,082	53.9	39.8	mixed
Fayetteville	1,320.71[c]	273	1.09	2,868	39.8	16.2	mixed
TOTAL	625.68	419	1.01	14,834	34.5	36.3	

[a]The tax districts are arranged in ascending order by "mean assessed wealth per taxpayer."

[b]Includes Willis Creek.

[c]This figure includes $1,024.04 in town property per taxpayer, in addition to the value of rural land held by town dwellers.

SOURCES: Cumberland County List of Taxables, 1824–1829, in Cumberland County Records, North Carolina State Archives, Raleigh; George F. Black, *The Surnames of Scotland* (New York, 1946); U.S. Bureau of Soils, *North Carolina Soil Map*, Cumberland County Map Sheet (Washington, 1922), Hoke County Map Sheet (Washington, 1918), and Harnett County Map Sheet (Washington, 1916).

Table 2. Per Capita Production of Selected Crops in Cumberland County and the State of North Carolina, 1840

Crop	Cumberland County	North Carolina
Corn	26.5 bushels	32.4 bushels
Cotton	40.8 pounds	70.3 pounds
Tobacco	——	22.7 pounds
Potatoes	5.7 bushels	3.5 bushels
Wool	1.5 pounds	0.9 pounds
Cattle	1.3 head	0.8 head
Sheep	1.4 head	0.7 head
Swine	2.6 head	2.2 head

SOURCE: *Compendium of the Enumeration of the Inhabitants and Statistics of the United States, As Obtained at the Department of State from the Returns of the Sixth Census* (Washington, 1841), 170–81.

experienced lower yields of cotton and corn than farmers in other North Carolina counties. The other crops listed in table 2 were probably for local consumption. Potatoes, which thrived in poorer sandy soil, were abundant in Cumberland County. Wool and livestock production were also well suited to the county's soil conditions. Land that could not be cultivated profitably would still support grazing. In the colonial period, some Cumberland residents drove large herds of livestock to northern markets, but commercial animal husbandry was not an economic mainstay in the nineteenth century.[35]

Lumbering was one means for farmers to make up for low crop yields. Pine forests were almost everywhere, and the Cape Fear River provided easy transportation to the sea. Some of the logs were sawed into timbers in local sawmills; others were floated in rafts to the port of Wilmington for sale and processing there. Most of the timber was then exported to the West Indies by dealers in Wilmington. Lumbering was attractive to farmers of every level of wealth in Cumberland County. Advertisements for plantations with sawmills dotted Fayetteville's press. One advertiser reminded his readers that the forests and the river would guarantee that "there is no fear of their ever wanting timber, which can always be had to saw on halves." The business records of several planter-lumbermen show that they frequently bought timber or timbering rights from smaller farmers in the vicinity. For the poorest men, rafting and sawmill work provided an opportunity to earn ready cash. In 1840, Cumberland County led the state in the value of lumber produced.[36]

35. Oates, *The Story of Fayetteville*, 358; Merrens, *Colonial North Carolina*, 137.
36. Fayetteville *American*, December 5, 1816, and April 26, 1816; Fayetteville *North Carolina Centinel*, August 8, 1795; "Harnett County" (Typescript in Arthur T. Wyatt Papers, North Car-

It is not possible to calculate precisely how much the farmers of Cumberland County were involved in the market economy. The planters and lumbermen were heavily committed to selling raw materials to the expanding capitalist economy of the nineteenth-century world. The wage earners who were employed by these rural entrepreneurs were also dependent on conditions in the world market, while the unusual farmer who remained in a state of pure self-sufficiency was isolated from it. In between were the majority of Cumberland County farmers, who were more or less involved with exporting staples as their opportunities or inclinations directed.

The reports of the U.S. Census made no distinction between crops which were grown for sale and those which were used at home. Scattered evidence indicates, however, that Cumberland County farmers used the market economy much less than the residents of Fayetteville and even somewhat less than farmers in adjacent counties. One Fayetteville retailer, for example, recorded 228 credit transactions in his ledger for the years 1838 to 1841. Of the 140 customers from Cumberland County, all but 27 came from Fayetteville itself while 14 surrounding counties sent 88 additional purchasers.[37] Residents of rural Cumberland were also underrepresented among cotton broker Elijah Fuller's clientele. Fuller kept a "Barter Book" to record his business with petty producers who traded their staples—chiefly cotton, flour, and pork—for consumer goods and a cash balance. Aaron Thomas of Chatham County typified such customers. On December 4, 1834, Thomas brought in 1 bale of cotton worth $28.35 at the current price and left for home with 10 pounds of sugar, 5 pounds of coffee, 29 pounds of wide iron, 5 gallons of molasses, 1½ bushels of salt, 1 handkerchief, and 1 wool hat, while pocketing a cash balance of $21.60. Fuller had 502 customers like Aaron Thomas in the years between 1834 and 1837, but only 37 of them came from Cumberland County. The great majority came from the shell of counties bordering directly onto Cumberland or lying no more than a hundred miles away at the most. Chatham County sent 89 customers, 41 came from Guilford County, and there were 35 from Orange, 34 from Moore, 32 from Robeson, and 27 from Sampson. Fourteen other counties provided between 1 and 17 customers each.[38]

Further evidence on the local market comes from the state Board of Internal Improvements. In an effort to gauge the demand for a proposed railroad to

---

olina State Archives); *Compendium of the Sixth Census*, 182. For receipts of timber purchased from neighbors, records of wages paid to raftsmen, and correspondence with timber agents in Wilmington, see the business papers of Neill McNeill, Archibald S. McNeill, and Henry M. Turner, in the Harnett County Papers. The production of turpentine in the county did not become profitable until the 1840s. See Fayetteville *Observer*, March 10, 1846.

37. Unidentified Merchant's Ledger, Fayetteville, N.C., 1838–41, Account Book 345, North Carolina State Archives.

38. Elijah Fuller Barter Book, 1833–38, in Elijah Fuller Papers.

Fayetteville, the board asked several county courts to collect information on crop production for 1838. Compliance was spotty, but half the districts of nearby Chatham County responded. The magistrates there found 203 farmers who produced a total of 457 bales of cotton, 1,672 barrels of flour, and 38,408 pounds of bacon, pork, and lard, all of which they sold in Fayetteville. One magistrate remarked at the bottom of his return that "there was a considerable quantity of wheat and oats sent to Fayetteville which is not accounted for— a[nd] yet a great deal more that might have been sent provided it would of born carriage to market." [39]

No comparable statistics survive for Cumberland County, but one suspects that other factors besides transportation costs inhibited the county's farmers. Sandhills acreage could not match the fecundity of Chatham County's thick red clay, so Cumberland residents could not take full advantage of their relative proximity to market. Instead, they found themselves sandwiched between the commercial townsmen of Fayetteville and the ambitious tillers further west. When political parties blossomed, it was probably no coincidence that Fayetteville and Chatham County favored the Whigs, but rural Cumberland chose the Democrats.

When the farmers of Cumberland County turned from their homes to the county seat, they met a vivid contrast to the world of their daily lives. The marketplace was not an abstraction in Fayetteville. Standing exactly in the center of the town, in an elevated square formed by the intersection of four main streets, Fayetteville's imposing Market House or Town House dominated the visitor's field of vision from all approaches and stood as a forceful visual embodiment of the borough's principal concerns. The original building had been completed in 1789, just in time to house the convention which ratified the U.S. Constitution and brought North Carolina into the federal union. Thereafter, the graceful brick arches of the Market House sheltered vendor's stalls on the ground floor and supported civic chambers overhead. Slaves were sold from its steps and debating politicians made it their podium. Although fire gutted the structure in 1831, citizens quickly replaced its classic Georgian simplicity with a fashionable Victorian pastiche of round and pointed arches, Ionic capitals, and mansard roof. A bell and a new town clock took their places in the cupola and tolled out lessons in punctuality to slaves and freemen alike.[40] The rebuilt Market House stood stronger than ever, a powerful memorial to civic pride and the lure of progress, to the demands of commerce and

39. Returns for Pittsboro and Captains Stewart's, Perry's, Edwards', Mann's, Womack's, and Mare's districts, Reports to the Board of Internal Improvements on the Crops and Markets of Chatham County, 1839, in Governor's Office Papers, Box 139, North Carolina State Archives. The observation concerning wheat and oats was made by Robert Faucette, J. P., on the return for Captain Womack's district.
40. Oates, *The Story of Fayetteville*, 188–90, 257–59.

the pull of national integration. Viewing it, the visiting countryman was reminded that if self-sufficiency was possible at home, trade was the lifeblood of Fayetteville.

The town was located on the western bank of the Cape Fear River, where Cross Creek joined the larger stream. This spot was the head of navigation on the Cape Fear. Originally known as Campbellton, Fayetteville had been founded in 1762 to "encourage honest and able traders to reside therein." [41] Within a few years, a rival settlement named Cross Creek sprang up near a millsite further inland, and eventually the two villages combined. The so-called "upper town" became the center of merchandising, while Campbellton remained a rundown neighborhood of shanties, docks, and warehouses. In 1830, Fayetteville had 2,868 inhabitants, of whom 39.8 percent were slaves. [42]

Seventy years after its founding, Fayetteville's economy still depended on trade. Distant farmers were then in the habit of bringing their staples to Fayetteville for sale or barter. Their chief products were cotton, tobacco, corn, wheat, and flaxseed. Sometimes the farmers brought their grain already ground into flour or distilled into spirits. If not, Fayetteville millers and brewers were prepared to do the job for a fee. The town also featured sawmills and a tannery for the primary processing of other raw materials. As early as 1824, one Fayetteville businessman was experimenting with a cotton yarn factory. He failed at first, but by 1840, eight others had succeeded. [43]

In exchange for agricultural staples, Fayetteville merchants supplied farmers with salt, sugar, molasses, iron, imported textiles, imported spirits, and manufactured goods. The larger traders also had a wholesale business in which they supplied country merchants with the same articles. The Fayetteville merchants, in turn, obtained their supplies from wholesale houses in New York, Philadelphia, and Boston. Three banks existed in the town to finance this traffic. Two were branches of state banks, the Bank of Cape Fear and the State Bank of North Carolina. The other was an office of Nicholas Biddle's "monster," the Bank of the United States. Steamboats and smaller

41. Colin McIver (ed. and comp.), *Laws of the Town of Fayetteville: Consisting of all the Acts and Parts of Acts Now in Force Passed in Relation to Said Town . . . From A.D. 1762 to A.D. 1827* (Fayetteville, N.C., 1828), 2.

42. Oates, *The Story of Fayetteville*, 72–73; MS Census Returns, Population Schedule, Cumberland County, North Carolina, 1830, p. 98.

43. Reports to the Board of Internal Improvements on the Crops and Markets of Chatham and Randolph Counties, 1839, in Governor's Office Papers, Box 139; "Statement of Articles Transported on the River and the amounts of Tolls Thereon for the Year Ending May 1831 to 1840, Inclusive," Fayetteville *North Carolinian*, June 13, 1840; Oates, *The Story of Fayetteville*, 92; *Compendium of the Sixth Census*, 184; Fayetteville *North Carolina Minerva*, March 31, 1796. Records of the early textile mills are unfortunately lost. In 1840, there were 14,234 spindles in Cumberland. By comparison, Chesterfield County, Virginia (Richmond), contained 20,110 spindles and Middlesex County, Massachusetts (Lowell), contained 189,664. *Compendium of the Sixth Census*, 156, 108.

craft transported the freight between Fayetteville and Wilmington, while four daily and two triweekly stage lines provided mail and passenger connections with the interior.[44]

These business activities made Fayetteville a bustling and ambitious town eager to share the prosperity of Jacksonian America. In a certain measure, the townsmen succeeded. Within North Carolina, Fayetteville was second in population to the port of Wilmington and second in the value of its commercial investment to the port of New Bern. The value of urban property far outweighed the poverty of the rural areas, so that Cumberland was fifth in total tax payments to the state after the revaluation of 1837, though it was sixtieth in rural land values.[45] A catastrophic fire in 1831 almost obliterated the town, but the determined community rebuilt itself. The comforts of Fayetteville were impressive to visitors and conspicuous beside the rest of the state's rugged interior. When Captain Basil Hall visited Fayetteville in 1827, he found it to be "a very pretty and flourishing town" with "one of the best hotels in the country."[46]

Fayetteville offered amenities to its inhabitants as well. Two newspapers and a library company were the means of public information; two militia companies and a fire company were the means of public safety. Two academies existed for the education of youth; balls, races, and taverns were sources of their amusement; and five churches vied for their salvation. A temperance society and a chapter of the American Colonization Society enjoyed an off-and-on existence, while a Masonic lodge, a Mechanic Benevolent Society, and a short-lived county agricultural society practically completed the list of voluntary associations. By comparison to the quiet rural districts, Fayetteville was crowded with things to do.[47]

44. Belden, "Traditions of Cross Creek," 2; [Duncan MacRae], "Fayetteville!" Fayetteville *Observer*, June 27, 1889, 2, 4; McIver (ed.), *Laws of Fayetteville*, 20–30, 35; Elijah Fuller to Jones Fuller, December 1, 1838, N. J. King of the firm of King and Moring to Elijah Fuller of the firm of Hart and Fuller, February 21, 1837 and August 3, 1837, all in Elijah Fuller Papers.
45. "A Statement of the Revenue of the State of North Carolina," bound in back of *Laws of the State of North Carolina at the Session of 1838–'39* (Raleigh, 1839).
46. Hall, *Travels in North America*, III, 118. When she visited shortly after Captain Hall, Mrs. Anne Royall had a very different experience in Fayetteville. She collected only one dollar in subscriptions to her publications there, so she branded the town as "the poorest hole I was ever in." Anne Royall, *Mrs. Royall's Southern Tour, or Second Series of the Black Book* (3 vols.; Washington, 1830–31), I, 147.
47. McIver (ed.), *Laws of Fayetteville*, 24, 25, 31, 38; Fayetteville *Carolina Observer*, January 17, 1828; Fayetteville *Observer*, January 24, 1838, April 17, 1839; Fayetteville *North Carolina Journal*, June 30, 1830; Fayetteville *Gazette*, November 22, 1822; Fayetteville *North Carolina Minerva*, October 29, 1796; Ball Invitations, March 7, 1825, and December 15, 1829, Lafayette Hotel folder, Miscellaneous Papers, 1820–1917, in Cumberland County Records; "Tax Received from Retailers of Spirituous Liquors by the Small Measure Licensed in 1842," Cumberland County Court Minutes, 1842, in Cumberland County Records; Minutes of the Cumberland County Agricultural Society, in Cumberland County Records; Oates, *The Story of Fayetteville*, 264, 478–509.

Fayetteville's churches were voluntary associations with a special place in the life of the community. The three oldest churches in the county were rural Presbyterian congregations founded by the Scots at Barbecue, Bluff, and Longstreet. These congregations developed a reputation in the eighteenth century for insistence on precise Calvinist orthodoxy, leading one visiting minister to complain that "he would rather preach to the most polished and fashionable congregation in Edinburgh than to the critical little carls of Barbecue." [48] Unlike the Scotch-Irish of the Piedmont, the Highland Scots of the sandhills tended to reject the revivalism of the Second Great Awakening. In 1802, when the Great Revival was at its height in North Carolina, Rev. Angus McDiarmid, the Scottish-born pastor of Barbecue, Bluff, and McCoy's churches, was ejected from the Orange Presbytery for refusing to participate in the Presbytery "until the young puppies who are continually yelping about bow-wow-wow-wow would be turned out," and for saying that a certain revivalist "was a limb of the Devil, that the present revival of religion was a work of the devil, that the Devil had a synagogue at all the Presbytery's meetings, and that the ministers were Balaam's prophets." In spite of his expulsion, McDiarmid ministered to mostly-Scottish congregations in Cumberland County as late as 1825. [49]

Unlike the rural Presbyterian churches, which were filled with the descendants of Scottish Highlanders, the Fayetteville Presbyterian church was led by Scotch-Irish ministers from the 1790s onward. When they rebuilt the church after the fire of 1831, the congregation worshiped in one of the largest and handsomest structures in the county. Its members in the 1830s included a cross section of the town's population, including slaves, artisans, a federal judge, a future secretary of the navy, and a number of wealthy merchants and lawyers. [50]

The congregation of St. John's Episcopal Church was smaller than that of the Presbyterian Church but at least as prestigious. The first senior warden of the parish was Fayetteville's magistrate of police, or mayor, and one of its earliest rectors was the grandson and namesake of a signer of the Declaration of Independence. The church's records for the 1830s contained the names of a United States senator, two subsequent magistrates of police, the two principal

48. William Henry Foote, *Sketches of North Carolina, Historical and Biographical, Illustrative of the Principles of a Portion of Her Early Settlers* (New York, 1846), 133.

49. Robert Hamlin Stone, *A History of Orange Presbytery, 1770–1970* (Greensboro, N.C., 1970), 26, 261, 368; Lucile Johnson, "Galatia Records Date Back to 1825," Fayetteville *Observer*, March 15, 1964, p. 10B; Rev. Neill McKay, *A Centenary Sermon, Delivered Before the Presbytery of Fayetteville, at the Bluff Church, the 18th Day of October, 1858* (Fayetteville, N.C., 1858), microfilm copy in North Carolina State Archives.

50. Foote, *Sketches of North Carolina*, 490; Session Minutes, May 8, 1832, First Presbyterian Church, Fayetteville, N.C., microfilm copy in North Carolina State Archives. It was many years before there was any need to designate any church in Fayetteville as the "first" of its denomination.

newspaper editors, and numerous prominent merchants, lawyers, doctors, manufacturers, and other leading citizens. More than half of its white male communicants took an active role in county politics.[51]

In contrast to the Episcopalians and the Presbyterians, Fayetteville's Methodists, Baptists, and Roman Catholics were relatively isolated from the heights of wealth, power, and prestige. Hay Street Methodist Church contained a generous number of Fayetteville's leading white artisans, but few merchants and no prominent officeholders. The church had been founded by Henry Evans, a free black shoemaker whose first converts were also black. Whites later came to the fore, but blacks maintained an active role in the church, perhaps more than in any other local congregation.[52]

Unlike the Methodists, who started in Fayetteville and later spread to the country, Baptist churches originated in rural Cumberland County, especially in the small-farm, non-Scottish districts. Cape Fear Baptist Church, the oldest in the county, was at least forty years old before Baptists felt the need for a church in town. In 1837, twenty-nine men and women, all of them white, founded the Fayetteville Baptist Church. They grew to include more than three hundred members by 1850, of whom relatively few were Scottish. Virtually none of its white male members can be identified by occupation, which suggests that many of them were employees of other men.[53] The church was apparently a spiritual home for rural whites who had joined the humbler ranks of urban society.

Fayetteville's tiny Roman Catholic parish was also isolated from the social and political mainstream, but not particularly for economic reasons. One of the pillars of St. Patrick's Roman Catholic Church was John Kelly, a self-made Irish immigrant who became one of the largest planters in Cumberland County. Irish-born merchant Dillon Jordan, Sr., and planter Charles Montague were also active Catholics who achieved positions of wealth and respectability in the county. The Catholics' isolation was more cultural than economic. Their priest traveled all over North and South Carolina to reach his widely scattered flock. He rarely officiated at more than one marriage, one funeral, or ten baptisms a year. Mixed marriages were almost unknown, many

51. Collier Cobb, "William Hooper," in Samuel A. Ashe *et al.* (eds.), *Biographical History of North Carolina from Colonial Times to the Present* (8 vols.; Greensboro, N.C., 1905–1917), VII, 245–50; Parish Register, 1828–36, St. John's Episcopal Church, Fayetteville, N.C., microfilm copy in North Carolina State Archives; C. W. Broadfoot, *Address of Col. C. W. Broadfoot at the Centennial Celebration of St. John's Church, Fayetteville, N.C.* (Fayetteville, N.C., 1917), 6–24.
52. Elizabeth Lamb, *Historical Sketch of Hay St. Methodist Church, Methodist Episcopal Church, South, Fayetteville, North Carolina* (Fayetteville, N.C., 1934), 33; Quarterly Conference Record, 1825–39, Hay Street Methodist Church, Fayetteville, N.C., microfilm copy in North Carolina State Archives.
53. Oates, *The Story of Fayetteville*, 501–504; Church Minutes, 1837–50, First Baptist Church, Fayetteville, N.C., microfilm copy in North Carolina State Archives.

of the funeral records indicated that the deceased was born in Ireland, and most of the adults and at least half the children baptized were slaves of Catholic masters. All of these details testified to the uniqueness of Catholicism in Protestant North Carolina. The notation beside a crossed-off name in the Presbyterian session minutes conveyed the majority attitude eloquently: "Joined the Romish ch. & cut off from this ch. without a recommendation." [54]

Except for the Roman Catholics, the religious folk of Fayetteville shared an evangelical approach to Christianity in spite of their other differences. A historian of North Carolina Presbyterianism recorded that revivals were frequent in the Fayetteville church after 1809. Fayetteville's most popular Presbyterian minister in this period was renowned for his support of evangelical projects in foreign and domestic missions, Bible and tract distribution, primary and theological education, and the promotion of revivals. When the Presbyterians dedicated their new sanctuary in 1832, the preacher assured the assembly of worshipers that "revivals are yielding back to the church its primitive glory" and prayed that "this house may become more glorious by the outpouring of the Holy Spirit, and the conversion of sinners." Without embracing the more demonstrative aspects of evangelicalism, the rector of St. John's Episcopal Church stayed active in the North Carolina Bible Society and rejoiced in the strengthened position of religion which had accompanied the Second Great Awakening. The rector's commitment to evangelicalism was stronger than that of his parish, however, and eventually he left the Episcopal Church to become a Baptist. [55]

Revivals were particularly important to Baptists and Methodists. According to reports in the *Carolina Observer* in 1825, a Methodist camp meeting eight miles from town attracted an estimated crowd of six thousand persons, "particularly on Sunday, when this town was nearly depopulated." [56] Similarly, the Cape Fear Baptist Association complimented the Cape Fear Baptist Church in Cumberland for the quantity and quality of its evangelistic activities. In its minutes for 1833, the association reported that "this church appears to enjoy a regular work among them. Thirty have been added by Baptism the past year. They recommend in their Letter, the N.C. Baptist Convention in very strong terms. There is a Missionary Society in the Church, which sends delegates annually to the same Convention. There is also an interesting Bible class in this church, and a Temperance Society." Three years

54. Parish Register, 1831–50, St. Patrick's Roman Catholic Church, Fayetteville, N.C., manuscript copy in the church; Session Minutes, May 8, 1832, First Presbyterian Church.
55. Foote, *Sketches of North Carolina*, 499; Henry A. Rowland, Jr., *The Real Glory of a Church* (New York, 1832), reprinted in Harriet Sutton Rankin, *History of the First Presbyterian Church, Fayetteville, North Carolina* (Fayetteville, N.C., 1928), 96, 97; William Hooper, *An Address Delivered Before the North Carolina Bible Society* (Fayetteville, N.C., 1819), 1–6.
56. Fayetteville *Carolina Observer*, July 21, 1825.

later, when other congregations in the association were flagging, Cape Fear Church was still continuing its "regular work." [57] Throughout the rest of the 1830s and 1840s, revival activity spawned more Baptist churches, especially in the rural areas. When the census of 1850 made the first regular survey of county churches, Baptists appeared to be the most numerous denomination, followed by approximately equal numbers of Methodists and Presbyterians. [58]

The widespread commitment to evangelicalism may have been a source of cultural unity in Fayetteville and Cumberland County and may have underlain the fact that political parties, when they emerged, did not divide over clearly religious issues. Within this broad doctrinal unity, however, there were significant disparities in style and social composition of the churches. Revivals outdoors in the rural Methodist brush arbor, in a mixed crowd of six thousand penitents and curiosity seekers, cannot have felt the same as revivals in the elegant and spacious Presbyterian church of Fayetteville, which held eight hundred worshipers and was valued at $12,500. These contrasts in religious expression would not be irrelevant to conflicting versions of republicanism when Cumberland County citizens divided into political parties.

Like the farmers who surrounded them, the residents of Fayetteville were a diverse group. The most prominent citizens belonged to a circle of substantial merchants, bankers, and lawyers, many of whom were related by blood or marriage. Several of these families had roots or connections in New England. John Winslow, for example, was a merchant who was allegedly descended from a *Mayflower* pilgrim. Winslow had three sons in Fayetteville: Edward Lee, Warren, and John. The first two were associated in E. L. & W. Winslow & Co., the town's largest cotton brokerage. Their brother John was a promi-

---

57. Cape Fear Baptist Association, *Minutes*, 1833 (Fayetteville, N.C., 1833), Cape Fear Baptist Association, *Minutes*, 1836 (Fayetteville, N.C., 1836), 9, microfilm copies in North Carolina Collection.

58. The 1850 census counted the number of churches of each denomination, the value of church property, and the number of "accommodations" in each church building. These data are not entirely reliable evidence on the influence of churches on a county's population. As people of relatively slender means, however, Baptists and Methodists would be least likely to build churches which were unnecessarily numerous or large. The following table summarizes the information on Cumberland County churches found in the 1850 manuscript census returns.

	Baptist	Methodist	Presbyterian	Episcopal	Roman Catholic
Number of Churches	12	8	5	1	1
Total accommodations	4,850	3,900	3,300	600	400
Average value of church property	$300	$1,044	$3,180	$13,000	$3,000

SOURCE: United States Manuscript Census Returns, Schedule 6, Social Statistics, Cumberland County, North Carolina, 1850, pp. 90, 94, microfilm copy in North Carolina State Archives.

nent lawyer. John Winslow, Sr., had been a merchant in partnership with John Huske, who was at different times president of the Fayetteville branches of the Bank of the United States and the State Bank of North Carolina. John Huske was married twice, both times to one of the Tillinghast sisters. They were the daughters of a mercantile family transplanted from Providence, Rhode Island. John Huske named one of his sons John Winslow Huske. He became a lawyer too. John Winslow Huske's law partner was his brother-in-law, James C. Dobbin, the son of another merchant and later U.S. secretary of the navy. The mercantile firm of Winslow and Huske had been the executors of the estate of Peter Mallett, a large merchant who died in 1813. Mallett's descendants included Charles P. Mallett and his son Charles Beatty Mallett, both pioneers in Fayetteville's antebellum textile industry. Another member of the Mallett family married a daughter of a governor of Rhode Island and established a branch of the family in Providence. When John Huske died in 1848, Charles P. Mallett succeeded him as president of the Fayetteville branch of the Bank of the State of North Carolina. Similar family and business connections could be multiplied almost indefinitely to include most of the wealthiest families in town.[59]

The capital these families acquired from commerce was invested in a variety of ancillary activities. They owned stock in banks, transportation companies, and textile mills. They also owned sawmills, gristmills, tanneries, and warehouses. Most Fayetteville businessmen were slaveholders, and several owned plantations and woodlands in rural Cumberland. This network of a dozen or so families was Fayetteville's economic elite.[60]

Not all storekeepers were members of the elite. William Kennedy Blake's father was a merchant who struggled all his life to repay debts incurred in the disastrous fire of 1831. For security in his old age, he became the superintendent of a Methodist female seminary. The middle class also included the less

59. Oates, *The Story of Fayetteville*, 92, 867, 104, 176, 177, 414, 558, 846; Fayetteville *Observer*, November 28, 1848; Fayetteville *North Carolinian*, December 30, 1848; Collection Descriptions of Charles W. Broadfoot Papers and Bartholomew Fuller Papers, both in Southern Historical Collection; Collection Description of Edward J. Mallett Papers, in Manuscripts Division, Library of Congress; Collection Description, Tillinghast Family Papers, in Manuscripts Department, Duke University Library; R. D. W. Connor, "James Cochran Dobbin," in Ashe *et al.* (eds.), *Biographical History of North Carolina*, IV, 209–226. Other prominent townsmen with New England connections were Elisha Stedman, a Connecticut-born merchant and ruling elder of the Presbyterian church, and Dr. Benjamin Robinson of Middlebury, Vermont, who served for three decades as chairman of the county court. Fayetteville *Carolina Observer*, October 2, 1832; Fayetteville *North Carolina Argus*, March 14, 1857.

60. "A List of Stores' Pedlars' Rowlett, and Retailers Taxes Received for the Year 1835," Cumberland County Court Minutes, September Term, 1835, in Cumberland County Records; Fayetteville *North Carolina Journal*, June 6, 1827, June 4, 1828, May 30, 1832, June 6, 1832, June 3, 1835, November 4, 1835, July 21, 1836, February 2, 1837; Oates, *The Story of Fayetteville*, 92; Cumberland County Lists of Taxables, 1837–41, in Cumberland County Records.

wealthy and less well-connected lawyers, doctors, editors, and ministers. One of these was Thomas L. Hybart, a lawyer and editor who was probably the son of Mrs. Hybart the midwife, who arrived from London in 1807.[61] Members of the middle group in Fayetteville society were active members of the political community and often participated in political conventions and party committees.

The position of artisans in Fayetteville was ambiguous. The commerce of the town required a number of skilled services necessary for the export of agricultural products. Business opportunities were good for millers, tanners, blacksmiths, wagonmakers, saddle and harness makers, coopers, and wheelwrights. Fayetteville also needed the normal complement of workers to make clothing, furniture, and buildings. Successful practitioners of these trades could become leading citizens. Charles T. Gardner and Alfred A. McKethan were carriagemakers who eventually built a wagon factory which employed over seventy hands. James Gee was a hatter whose sons David and James R. Gee made their father's business a sizable and prosperous concern.[62] Other examples of remarkable upward mobility were infrequent. Constant turnover in the names of artisans who advertised in the columns of Fayetteville's press suggests that many skilled workers did not find enough encouragement to stay very long. Some artisans may never have owned their own shops, remaining journeymen all their lives. White workers of this description competed with black workers, both slave and free. Poor white families seeking to apprentice a son to a skilled trade sometimes met the humiliating notice that "coloured boys would be preferred." [63] The artisan in Fayetteville thus occupied a respectable position in society or a precarious one, depending on his luck, his skill, and the state of the economy.

Fayetteville also contained a group of propertyless workers. Clerks in mercantile houses comprised a small class of white collar employees. Some of these were young men of good family who were starting in business at the bottom. Others kept these jobs more permanently.[64] A more numerous group of manual workers included teamsters, porters, boat hands, sawmill hands, and day laborers. By 1840, eight cotton mills had opened in Cumberland County, giving work to a considerable number of white men, women, and children. White families of this kind were constant economic competitors

61. Fayetteville *North Carolina Intelligencer*, May 15, 1807.
62. Apprentice Bonds, 1820–50, in Cumberland County Records; Oates, *The Story of Fayetteville*, 830; Collection Description of Eccles Family Papers, in Southern Historical Collection; Fayetteville *North Carolinian*, January 27, 1844.
63. Fayetteville *People's Friend*, December 15, 1815; Fayetteville *American*, October 17, 1816.
64. Archibald McDiarmid, a rural minister's son and later state senator from Cumberland, appears as the recipient of a clerk's wages in a merchant's account book of 1816. Unidentified Merchant's Ledger, October 4, 1816, Account Book 341, North Carolina State Archives.

with slaves and free blacks. Boat hands were recruited from both races, and many day laborers were slaves who were licensed to hire their own time. The first cotton mill, moreover, had operated with slave labor. The later white mill workers had to face the epithet—uniquely derogatory in the antebellum South—that they were "factory slaves." That insult was naturally the provocation for a fistfight.[65] Poor white workers had to be constantly on guard lest their occupational status allow them to be reduced to the social level of blacks. The broadside of a Whig politician in 1836 denied defensively that he had ever flogged his white boat hands, although he boasted that he had "struck and whipped frequently some of the mulatto men whom I have had employed. I had good cause to do so, and may have to do it again."[66] The necessity for the denial is testimony to the sensitivity of whites on this issue, just as the credibility of the rumor is evidence of the social proximity of white and black laborers in the minds of some. The position of the poor white worker was thus marginal indeed.

Reports of crime in Fayetteville reveal that some poor whites crossed the color bar to mingle with blacks in an approximation of social equality. Stories of dramshop brawls, prostitutes' gossip, and a criminal's confession reveal whites and blacks drinking, whoring, and plotting crimes together. This activity was concentrated in Campbellton, the part of town which was "noted for its frequent disorders and breaches of the peace."[67] It was also the section where most of the town's free blacks lived. The unruly tendency of the poor of both races caused their more prosperous neighbors to view them with suspicion.[68] Social mixing of whites with blacks—especially for criminal purposes—might subvert racial discipline, according to some watchful whites, while it was probably the source of some ambivalence among the poor whites themselves.

Fayetteville's free black population was small but significant. Free blacks could vote in North Carolina until 1836. Their ballots often decided the outcome of town elections in the early nineteenth century. Free blacks shared the same skilled and unskilled jobs as poor whites, but they were subject to a stricter code of police regulations which was designed to prevent their leading racial revolts. Fayetteville leaders were mindful of the danger of slave uprisings and maintained one public and several private militia companies "upon

65. Fayetteville *Observer*, November 6, 1844.
66. D. G. McRae, "To My Fellow Citizens of the County of Cumberland," July 23, 1836 (Broadside in Rare Book Room, Duke University Library).
67. Fayetteville *Observer*, January 24, 1838; David Lowry Swain to S. W. Capers, *et al.*, May 29, 1834, David Lowry Swain to Henry Potter, n.d., MS copies in Governors' Letter Books, vol. 30, pp. 204–210, in North Carolina State Archives; Neill McPherson, "The Petition and Information of Thomas S. Ashe. . . ," March 27, 1847 (Broadside in North Carolina Collection).
68. Fayetteville *Carolina Observer*, June 21, 1826; Fayetteville *Observer*, May 10, 1837.

Table 3. Cumberland County Population, 1820–1840

	1820	1830	1840
Rural	11,030	11,966	10,999
decennial change		+8.5%	−8.1%
Fayetteville	3,416	2,868	4,285
decennial change		−16.0%	+49.4%
Total	14,446	14,834	15,284
decennial change		+2.7%	+3.0%

SOURCE: United States Manuscript Census Returns, Population Schedules, Cumberland County, North Carolina, 1820, 1830, 1840, microfilm copies in the North Carolina Collection, University of North Carolina Library.

which its citizens could rely in case of insurrections." In times of special danger, officials made use of "secret agents in the black community" to report any subversive activities.[69] But the county's black population made no concerted effort to challenge the status quo. Free black voters were not able to get a better price for their ballots than a yearly treat of whiskey and barbeque, while the slaves were limited to private resistance. Blacks were not overt political actors on their own behalf, but the presence of a black population was an essential component of the social and political landscape.

The inhabitants of Cumberland county were divided by residence, occupation, religion, ethnicity, and race. Substantial inequalities of wealth and social status existed among them. Given this disparity, it would not be surprising if county residents had different ideas about the world, different degrees of political influence, and different reactions to the events of the Age of Jackson. The party controversies that did erupt in Cumberland County were indeed affected by these differences. But the party system did not appear from a static pattern of social and cultural differences. Party development was also affected by an emerging problem that affected all residents of the county in one way or another.

The problem was a lack of growth. As table 3 illustrates, the population of Cumberland County barely changed at all between 1820 and 1840. In the 1820s, Fayetteville lost population substantially and rural Cumberland increased some; in the 1830s, Fayetteville more than regained its losses but the countryside declined. The net result was discouraging to local citizens who

69. Belden, "Traditions of Cross Creek," 10; Deposition of Lucretia Bass, November 24, 1810, Legislative Papers, Box 245; James Howard Brewer, "Legislation Designed to Control Slavery in Wilmington and Fayetteville," *North Carolina Historical Review*, XXX (1953), 155–66; Isham Blake to Edward B. Dudley, September 23, 1840, Governors' Papers, Box 93, in North Carolina State Archives; Louis D. Henry [Fayetteville Magistrate of Police] to John Owen, September 3, 1830, MS copy in Governors' Letter Books, vol. 28, p. 232.

compared the county to the rest of the nation. The United States' population increased 77.1 percent between 1820 and 1840, but this growth was not evenly distributed. Alabama grew by 361.8 percent in this period; Mississippi by 397.9 percent; Indiana by 366.0 percent. The West was growing rapidly and so were eastern cities. But nonurban seaboard states, especially those in the upper South, lagged far behind. North Carolina, South Carolina, and Virginia were all among the states which grew less than 20 percent between 1820 and 1840.[70] Evidently, the residents of these areas were emigrating in large numbers.

North Carolina's slow growth derived from its position in the regional economy and also from special local conditions. The antebellum South enjoyed a substantial economic growth rate and relatively high per capita income, but the prosperity of the region depended on high cotton prices and expanding cotton production. Rich new land in the Gulf states was the most effective place to grow more cotton, so young people coming of age in the upper South found prospects for making a living much brighter if they emigrated. Migration of whites and slaves from the Southeast to the Southwest was thus an inevitable feature of antebellum life.[71] Participants in the interregional slave trade profited from this movement, but southeastern town dwellers whose incomes depended on the volume of local commodity trade or farmers with an eye to their own land values suffered by comparison. In addition, families faced the emotional pressures of the choice between separation and financial sacrifice. The agricultural economy of the Southeast did not generate the urbanization, industrial growth, and diversification which might have offered underemployed residents an alternative to emigration.

These problems were common throughout the upper South, but they were especially severe in North Carolina. Shallow rivers and a treacherous coastline inhibited local commerce and agriculture and placed the state's citizens at a double disadvantage. The result was general economic stagnation. According to Hugh Talmage Lefler and Albert Ray Newsome, "during the first third of the nineteenth century North Carolina was so undeveloped, backward, and indifferent to its condition that it was often called 'the second Nazareth,' the 'Ireland of America,' and the 'Rip Van Winkle' state. . . . No state was less

70. *Preliminary Report of the Eighth Census, 1860* (Washington, 1861), 127–29.
71. Economic historians agree on the importance of migration to the economic well-being of the antebellum South, but they interpret the significance of this fact in very different ways. See Eugene D. Genovese, *The Political Economy of Slavery: Studies in the Economy and Society of the Slave South* (New York, 1965), 243–70; Robert William Fogel and Stanley L. Engerman, *Time on the Cross: The Economics of American Negro Slavery* (2 vols.; Boston, 1974), I, 247–53; Gavin Wright, *The Political Economy of the Cotton South: Households, Markets, and Wealth in the Nineteenth Century* (New York, 1978), 15–17, 89–97, 132–35.

developed or had more serious problems relating to agriculture, transportation, commerce, manufacturing, finance, education, and emigration than North Carolina." [72] Even as late as 1860, North Carolina had lower wages and higher illiteracy rates among native-born whites than any other state in the Union. The average value of North Carolina real property was $5.33 per acre in 1860, which placed it twenty-seventh out of thirty-four states. [73]

Economic backwardness created personal and family pressures for large numbers of North Carolinians. In 1833, Fayetteville's representative in the General Assembly composed a report which singled out family separation as the most damaging aspect of emigration for individuals and for the state. "The social relations of family connections evidently constitute the most lasting cement of the political permanency of any country," wrote James Seawell, chairman of the House of Commons Committee on Internal Improvements. "Indeed," Seawell asked, "what else is it but the social ties of family connections, when rendered happy and prosperous by their own industry, that stamps a value upon society?" State policy in North Carolina ignored this crucial fact, so "the devotion of the inhabitants to the interest of the state" consequently diminished.

> Go into any neighborhood [Seawell suggested] and inquire of the seniors or heads of families, "how many children they have raised, and in what State do they reside?" In nine cases out of ten, the answers will be, "I have raised some six or eight children; but the major portion of them have migrated to some other State;" and adds the parent, "I am anxious to sell my lands to enable me to follow them." Thus, it will appear that the lands of nine-tenths of the farmers of the State are actually in market. . . . Therefore, it is that all our farmers are land sellers, and no land buyers. [74]

One need not accept Seawell's statistics on demography or land turnover literally to see that emigration could be a crisis in any family and a blow to the property values of those who did not choose to move. It was also feared as a threat to the long-term social and political stability of the state. Ironically, even James Seawell himself met the hardship of emigration firsthand. His leg-

72. Hugh Talmage Lefler and Albert Ray Newsome, *North Carolina: The History of a Southern State* (3rd rev. ed.; Chapel Hill, 1973), 314.

73. Johnson, *Antebellum North Carolina*, 70; *Statistics of the United States (Including Mortality, Property, &c) in 1860* (Washington, 1866), 294–95, 319, 508. The six states which ranked lower than North Carolina were still at the frontier stage and contained vast stretches of wilderness land. The six states were Kansas, Arkansas, Texas, California, Florida, and Oregon.

74. J. Seawell, "Report of the Committee on Internal Improvements," *Legislative Documents*, 1833, reprinted in Charles L. Coon (ed.), *The Beginnings of Public Education in North Carolina: A Documentary History, 1790–1840* (2 vols.; Raleigh, 1908), II, 633–34.

islative efforts for Fayetteville failed and so did his personal fortunes. Within five years, he too had left the state and started life afresh in Columbus, Mississippi.[75]

On a more personal level, the tensions produced by the emigration dilemma appeared in the experiences of four brothers, the sons of Bartholomew Fuller, Baptist preacher and Revolutionary patriot of Franklin County. The oldest, Willie J. Fuller, remained on the land as a farmer. His three brothers, Elijah, Thomas, and Jones, migrated to Fayetteville to try their hands in business. Thomas died in 1832, while he was still a young man, but Elijah lived on to a successful old age. He was an active partner in the general merchandise firm of Hart & Fuller, and he later obtained an appointment as a veterans' pension agent. The job gave Fuller access to hard money, an advantage which he parlayed into the profitable business of "shaving notes." Elijah's brother Jones, however, found few rewards in business; his family and friends worried that he wasted his talents on drinking, gambling, and politics. The pragmatic Elijah was probably relieved when Jones sought a fresh start by moving to Mobile, Alabama, in the late 1830s.[76] Elijah's partner, James Hart, accompanied Jones, and soon afterward both men were writing Elijah urging him to follow them and leave Fayetteville forever. "I think it about the poorest place that I have ever seen, for a man to undertake to make a support," Jones declared, "and I do think you ought to get away from there as soon as possible." Hart later put the matter more strongly: "You are throwing your life away by staying there." Elijah Fuller agreed. Replying to Jones, Elijah admitted "you are correct when you say a fortune cannot be made here" and announced his wish to leave North Carolina as soon as he could get away.[77]

Business calculations, however, were not the only considerations that affected the decision. Mobile was far away and life was short. Men who moved to the fever country could not count on seeing their loved ones again. The farmer, Willie J. Fuller, thought that it was Jones, not Elijah, who was throwing his life away. He wrote to Jones in piteous tones, begging him to reconsider before it was too late. "In my last to you I was very explicit to you respecting the venturing of yourself in sickness and death for the purpose of making money. . . . This letter is to say to you leave Mobile and come home. Once more I say come home, your home is here if you have a home in this world. but sir for me to write and fear that I am writing to a dead man and that

75. James Seawell to Michael J. Kenan, November 18, 1838, in Thomas Kenan Papers, Southern Historical Collection.
76. Collection Description of Bartholomew Fuller Papers; Fayetteville *Carolina Observer*, July 31, 1832; O. P. Stark to Jones Fuller, May 25, 1838, Elijah Fuller to Jones Fuller, May 29, 1838, both in Elijah Fuller Papers.
77. James Hart to Elijah Fuller, June 1, 1838, James Hart to Elijah Fuller, July 11, 1838, Elijah Fuller to Jones Fuller, October 18, 1838, all in Elijah Fuller Papers.

man my brother. . . ." [78] Willie added that he was sick himself, so sick that he had been unable to write for a week. "In conclusion I must say to you please come back and let me see you one time more." [79] The message was unmistakable: emigration could extract an enormous price in family anguish and personal guilt, regardless of its pecuniary benefits. Jones resisted his brother's entreaties, but Elijah wavered. His business was not doing badly, he wrote, and a certain young lady did not find his attentions unwelcome. Besides, he admitted, "mother is much opposed to my leaving and I shall regret much to wound her already mortified feelings." [80] In the end, Elijah married and never left Fayetteville.

Restless young men like the Fuller brothers were natural constituents for a political program that would enable them to become prosperous and remain at home at the same time. Dilemmas like theirs, which pitted personal interest against family loyalty, must have pained thousands of citizens as they weighed the decision to go west. Many chose to stay home like Elijah, but others continued to leave in spite of the pain, thus maintaining what one writer called "the astonishing emigration from this state." [81]

Slow growth and emigration were problems that attracted a considerable amount of public discussion in Cumberland County and in North Carolina generally. As early as 1815, state senator Archibald D. Murphey of Orange County was warning that "within twenty-five years past, more than two hundred thousand of our inhabitants have removed to the waters of the Ohio, Tennessee and Mobile. . . . In this state of things our agriculture is at a stand; and abandoning all idea of getting rich, by the cultivation of the soil, men are seeking the way to wealth through all the devious paths of speculation." Judge Toomer even acknowledged that something was amiss in his welcoming speech to Lafayette. "We have neglected to improve our advantages," he admitted. "We have relied too much on the bounty of the Parent of eternal good." Even when Fayetteville's population was recovering in the 1830s, writers in the town's press continually bemoaned "the immense tide of emigration which is daily flowing from our State to enrich and populate the Western states." [82]

North Carolinians who wished to correct these conditions believed that the state's soil was fertile and that its economy should always be based on agriculture. If only shipping costs were lower, they argued, North Carolina farm-

78. Willie J. Fuller to Jones Fuller, October 5, 1839, in Elijah Fuller Papers.
79. *Ibid.*
80. Elijah Fuller to Jones Fuller, October 18, 1838, in Elijah Fuller Papers.
81. Fayetteville *North Carolina Journal*, November 11, 1835.
82. Archibald D. Murphey, "Report of the Committee on Inland Navigation," *North Carolina Senate Journal*, 1815, reprinted in William Henry Hoyt (ed.), *The Papers of Archibald D. Murphey* (2 vols.; Raleigh, 1914), II, 20; Brandon (ed.) *A Pilgrimage of Liberty*, 33; Fayetteville *Observer*, April 15, 1834.

ers could prosper at home. Reform-minded editors and politicians therefore supported "internal improvements," or transportation projects that would open up the choked harbors of the coast and penetrate the hilly backcountry of the Piedmont. River dredging, canals, railroads, and plank roads would make western lands more accessible to commodity markets and thus more attractive to restless eastern planters contemplating a move to the Gulf states. In addition, western farmers could expand their market production and purchase slaves to satisfy their needs for more labor, thus keeping more human property within the state. The probable result of an effective system of internal improvements would have been a westward extension of the plantation system from eastern North Carolina into the Piedmont. Such changes would have left the other disadvantages of the plantation economy undisturbed, but the flow of emigration to the southwest might have been alleviated.

These ambitious plans won the verbal support of most North Carolina governors and other senior politicians from Murphey's day down to the Civil War. A survey of thirty-nine opening messages to the General Assembly from governors of North Carolina between 1800 and 1860 found thirty which recommended increased attention to problems of transportation.[83] As Governor James Iredell admitted to the legislature of 1828, pleas for a system of internal improvements had already become "trite matters," but he urged the lawmakers to consider the subject anew. If "a judicious system of improvements [were] faithfully executed," he predicted, "a new life would be infused into every branch of industry; our agriculture would be relieved from a heavy burthen, which now oppresses it; our commerce would increase ten fold; the tide of emigration would be checked; and our population and wealth would advance with a rapidity equal to our most sanguine desires."[84]

Despite the promptings of Iredell and others, the General Assembly moved slowly. Capital for improvements was scarce and sectional arguments blocked consensus on which routes to develop first, so supporters of internal improvements had difficulty in translating verbal support into tangible results before the 1850s. Reformers also had to face the objections of opponents who rejected the concept of internal improvements altogether, especially when conducted at state expense. Established planters from the central coastal plain did not blame their problems on high shipping costs but on taxes, especially on federal tariffs that lowered demand for exported staples. Congressman Thomas H. Hall summarized their argument in 1831 in a letter to his constituents. "Let the money be applied to pay the public debt, and then reduce the

83. *North Carolina House Journals*, 1801, 1804, 1805, 1807–1816, 1818, 1822, 1823, 1825–60, *passim*.
84. *North Carolina House Journal*, 1828–29, pp. 136–37.

taxes—this will do more public good, than all this idle expense upon internal improvement, or anything else." [85] Led by the Old Republican Nathaniel Macon, these conservatives also opposed federal aid to internal improvements on constitutional grounds that were linked to their worries for the protection of slavery. As Macon warned a young protegé in 1818, "if Congress can make canals they can with more propriety emancipate." [86] Even when improvements were not sponsored by the federal government, the conservatives feared that high public expenditures and an activist state government would ultimately work to the disadvantage of the established order.

Supporters of internal improvements scouted the idea that their plans would undermine plantation agriculture. Improved transportation would encourage agricultural productivity and increase land values, so they believed the projects could easily be made self-liquidating. Moreover, they asked, what would be the consequence of continued stagnation? As early as 1815, Archibald Murphey was warning that "to delay this provision, is to postpone that national wealth, respectability and importance which follow only in the train of great internal improvements." [87] How safe would the plantation system be in the federal Union if the state or the region were lacking that position of strength? Two decades before secession, one North Carolina congressman was ready with an explicit answer. Edward Stanly wrote to Governor Edward B. Dudley:

> I have always felt and still feel the most anxious desire to see our Legislature observe some State pride, to encourage internal improvements, both by railroads and canals. We never can rival in prosperity our sister states, until this is done—it will increase our resources and advance our prosperity, as well as strengthen the bonds of our Union, in peace, and it will make us more respected and independent, if in the manifold changes, to which all things are liable in this world, we should cease to form a part of the Union—a thing not to be thought of, unless abolition forces [it] upon us. [88]

Such arguments gained persuasiveness as sectional tensions worsened. The governor who eventually led North Carolina out of the Union and into the

---

85. Tarboro *Free Press*, August 2, 1831.
86. Nathaniel Macon to Bartlett Yancey, February 18, 1818, in Edwin Mood Wilson, *The Congressional Career of Nathaniel Macon*, James Sprunt Historical Monographs, no. 2 (Chapel Hill, 1900), 47. I have explored the ideas of the conservatives more thoroughly in my article, "Squire Oldway and His Friends: Opposition to Internal Improvements in Antebellum North Carolina," *North Carolina Historical Review*, LIV (1977), 105–119.
87. Hoyt (ed.), *Murphey Papers*, II, 20.
88. Edward Stanly to Edward B. Dudley, April 16, 1838, in Governors' Papers, Box 84.

Confederacy was a westerner who had gained office as a sponsor of state-supported railroad construction.[89]

Most of the leaders of Fayetteville were not contemplating secession in the early nineteenth century, but they did have a special stake in transportation development. A well-planned system of improvements would build on natural advantages to encourage new production and to divert existing trade to strategic locations in eastern North Carolina. As Murphey had said, "If North Carolina had her commerce concentrated at one or two points, one or more large commercial cities would grow up."[90] Given the proven benefits of the Cape Fear River, why shouldn't one of those cities be Fayetteville?

When Campbellton was originally founded, the colonial assembly had hoped that "the trade of the counties of Anson and Rowan [i.e., most of the backcountry] which at present centers in Charleston, South Carolina, to the great prejudice of this province, will be drawn down to the said town."[91] Seventy years later, the assembly's expectations were only partially fulfilled. Fayetteville had an active trade with relatively nearby counties, but more distant farmers in the valleys of the Yadkin and Catawba rivers followed geographical advantages and continued to trade in South Carolina.[92] Hoping that the introduction of new transportation technology would stimulate business by enticing these farmers to Fayetteville, the town fathers supported any project that would improve their accessibility to the west. As might be expected, Judge Toomer expressed their ambitions in his welcome to Lafayette. "The spirit of Internal Improvement is, at length, awakened," he assured the general. "North Carolina may look forward with pride and pleasure to her destiny. . . . Roads will be made, rivers will be opened; our resources will be annually developed; and Fayetteville, at some future day, may be worthy of the distinguished name she bears."[93] The future of the town was therefore linked to the westward expansion of commercial agriculture. In this phase of the Transportation Revolution, the market town would be the natural ally of the plantation.

---

89. The man was John W. Ellis, a Democrat and a Piedmont cotton planter. See Noble J. Tolbert (ed.), *The Papers of John Willis Ellis* (2 vols.: Raleigh, 1964), I, lvi–lvii, lxvii, lxxviii–lxxxi, xcix–c.

90. Hoyt (ed.), *Murphey Papers*, II, 107.

91. McIver (ed.), *Laws of Fayetteville*, 2.

92. In the late nineteenth century, old-time Fayetteville residents remembered a heavy wagon trade extending from Fayetteville to east Tennessee and southwestern Virginia. Contemporary business records and political commentary suggest that extensive trade with such distant places was at best a memory of the past or a hope for the future in the 1820s and 1830s. Belden, "Traditions of Cross Creek," 2; [Duncan MacRae], "Fayetteville!" Fayetteville *Observer*, June 27, 1889, p. 2; Elijah Fuller Barter Book, 1833–38, in Elijah Fuller Papers; James Welborne to James Seawell, n.d., in Fayetteville *Observer*, July 9, 1829.

93. Brandon (ed.), *A Pilgrimage of Liberty*, 33.

As early as the 1790s, Fayetteville's hopes led to plans for a canal to the backcountry. Excavation actually began on the venture but ultimately nothing came of it.[94] In the 1820s a new burst of optimism prompted the town meeting to ask the legislature for a system of three major state roads that would funnel the traffic of western North Carolina first to Fayetteville and then down the Cape Fear River to Wilmington. The language of the townsmen's request revealed the character of their ambitions by listing the advantages of the proposed system. "It will bring down our rivers, the wealth of our mountains and valleys, open new sources of wealth, by giving stimulus to industry; concentrate the channels of our trade, and rear up a commercial emporium; strengthen the bonds of our social intercourse, by assimilating the manners of our people; and shed lustre and glory upon the state." [95] Translating these advantages into different vocabulary, we can see that the leaders of Fayetteville were asking for economic growth, urbanization, cultural change, and a boosted reputation. Their objectives were remarkably similar to those of the New South promoters who followed them two generations later. They wanted more than a road; in the language of W. J. Cash, they wanted Progress.[96]

Unfortunately for the ambitions of Fayetteville, Progress was a controversial goal in North Carolina and even in Cumberland County. Urban leaders described economic development as an unmixed blessing, but local farmers appeared more skeptical. As Gavin Wright has argued, these men could have expanded their production for the market in one of two ways. Either they could have shifted their efforts away from food production for the use of their families, or they could have added to their labor force by purchasing slaves.[97] Practically speaking, the second alternative meant going into debt. For the planter with ample capital, the risks of debt were not too onerous, but they might be overwhelming to the average yeoman farmer. Crop failure or a dip in market prices would inconvenience the large operator, but the overextended yeoman would be left with no cash to buy food and no means to pay his obligations. In an extreme case, bankruptcy or an inability to pay taxes would bring on personal disgrace, loss of the farm, destruction of the family's livelihood, and the chance of imprisonment for debt. The penalties for failure could be terrible.

---

94. William Barry Grove to James Hogg, March 17, 1791, in Kemp P. Battle (ed.), *Letters of Nathaniel Macon, John Steele and William Barry Grove, with Sketches and Notes*, James Sprunt Historical Monographs, no. 3 (Chapel Hill, 1902), 85–86; Agreement between the Cape Fear Navigation Co. and the Town of Fayetteville, 1837 (MS in Fayetteville Municipal Records, Miscellaneous Papers, Cumberland County Records).
95. Brandon (ed.), *A Pilgrimage of Liberty*, 33.
96. W. J. Cash, *The Mind of the South* (New York, 1941), 175–89.
97. Gavin Wright, *The Political Economy of the Cotton South: Households, Markets, and Wealth in the Nineteenth Century* (New York, 1978), 41–88.

The perils of commerce necessarily colored the farmers' perceptions of Fayetteville. Town was the place where the lucky yeoman could acquire the slaves and make the clever bargains that would lift him into the gentry. But not everyone who plunged into the game of market farming would win at it, and Fayetteville would also be the setting where the simple rustic would be cozened and foreclosed on by sharpers who were better at the game than he. After all, even Fayetteville merchants had to guard against the sharp practice of their fellows. "Take care of usury," James Hart wrote to Elijah Fuller. "There are men in and around Fayetteville who I know are capable of doing very mean things. And some too who stand high in society." [98] Even Judge Toomer, the preeminent spokesman for Fayetteville, betrayed some ambivalence over the moral implications of progress when he boasted of the town's simplicity and its freedom from "splendid arches, gilded spires, or gorgeous palaces." Outside of town, farmers who sold as little as a single bale of cotton were perforce involved with commercial agriculture, but relatively isolated country people did not necessarily thank merchants or townsmen for their role in linking rural producers with world markets.

Cumberland County farmers therefore faced a choice between the personal liberty they associated with subsistence farming and the hazardous allure of commercial production and urban markets. Small planter James Evans voiced their dilemma when he complained to his brother John, "negro hire is remarkably high consequently farmers who have to hire will do bad business this year. In fact there is little to be made by farming in this section of the country at any time, though it seems to be the most independent occupation a man can follow." Fortunately for the Evans brothers, their father, Josiah, had gambled on a commercial operation and succeeded. "Father says he made his fortune by farming," James continued, "but my opinion is if he had not had any stave timber or stream for saw mill he would have lived and died a poor man." [99] Slightly different experience could have enabled James Evans to substitute "bottom land for cotton" in place of "stave timber" without changing the essential principle: to exchange near-subsistence farming for more commercial activities was to give up a guaranteed independence for the mere chance of prosperity. Not unlike the people of classic peasant cultures, these countrymen had no love of poverty as such, but experience taught them that the certain risks of personal or communal ambition might well exceed their promised but elusive rewards. [100]

98. James Hart to Elijah Fuller, July 11, 1838, in Elijah Fuller Papers.
99. James Evans to John Evans, undated draft, ca. 1838, in James Evans Papers.
100. George M. Foster, "Peasant Society and the Image of Limited Good," in Jack M. Potter, May N. Diaz, and George M. Foster (eds.), *Peasant Society: A Reader* (Boston, 1967), 296–323.

Occasionally, pieces of doggerel or satire in the Fayetteville press expressed backcountry suspicions by contrasting city trickery with rural vulnerability. Using Scottish dialect, one rhymester had this to say about "The Fayetteville Merchant":

> Here ilka store keeps twa three rinners
> Whilk commonly are young beginners,
> These stand forever on the watch
> The honest kintra man to catch . . .
> Ilk ane endeav'ring for to get him,
> The rest as eager not to let him . . .[101]

According to the poet, the sly merchant who befuddled "the honest kintra man" with strong drink got his business. Another piece in a similar vein described a roving adventurer who won the trust of rural folk with smiling promises of love and high profits, but absconded with predictable results.

> The lady now mourns, the creditors fret
> He's got all their money, and left them to sweat,
> And now they cry out, he has ruin'd us, damn him,
> So this is the last of *Leny Bohannan*.[102]

One western correspondent, who called himself Timothy Trueman, Revolutionary veteran, reported a seemingly common attitude when he wrote to complain of irregular delivery of his newspaper. "Not a waggoner passed up from Fayetteville but I enquired of him for the 'People's Friend,'" he related. "Not one could tell me any thing about it. Some indeed positively assured me that there could be no such an individual in the place, for he found them all actuated by the same motive, *a desire of gain*." [103]

The farmers of Cumberland County were affected by economic decline, but internal improvements were not their only possible remedy. Declining population and notices offering farms for sale "for cash or young negroes" indicated that a common rural solution to the county's problems was to move to the Southwest where land was fertile and cheap. Those who remained might be tempted by the blandishments of Progress, but few of them endorsed it unreservedly. When farmers did not openly criticize Progress, their frequently complained-of "apathy" betrayed a doubt that internal improvements were as beneficial as spokesmen claimed.

When country people displayed what one editor called "the most extraordinary apathy that ever disgraced a free people," Fayetteville was deeply af-

101. Fayetteville *North Carolina Chronicle*, September 13, 1790.
102. Fayetteville *Gazette*, December 11, 1792.
103. Fayetteville *People's Friend*, December 15, 1815.

fected, because internal improvements could not be built without the farmers' support.[104] Canals, turnpikes, and railroads were all too expensive to construct without generous expenditures of public funds. The townspeople acknowledged this difficulty when they asked for public roads and not for a chartered turnpike company. Without the approval of the farmers who cast most of the votes in North Carolina and who held most of the seats in its legislature, internal improvements would never come.

Throughout the South, the promoters of internal improvements were dependent on public funding. James A. Ward found that 57 percent of southern railroad capital in 1860 came from public sources, whereas the proportion nationwide "was on the order of 25 to 30 percent." Ward does not believe that these figures indicate that the South had difficulty generating private development capital. "The South merely relied on the public coffers to a greater extent than did the rest of the country," he concludes, implying that southern developers could have chosen just as easily to conform to national patterns.[105] The governor of North Carolina would have disagreed. In his annual message to the legislature of 1834, Governor David Lowry Swain reported that "the experience of another year affords conclusive proof that individual associations never will, and never can accomplish any plan commensurate with our necessities and resources."[106] The state Board of Internal Improvements concurred. "No general system of improvement can be effected, in North Carolina, by incorporated companies," the board declared in 1833. "In old and wealthy communities, individual capital may be commanded for such objects," but not in North Carolina.[107] Capitalists there and elsewhere in the South could not or would not supply the liquid sums which were necessary for such expensive undertakings. Where private capital did not act voluntarily, each taxpayer would be compelled to contribute his mite.

The necessity for public funding of internal improvements perhaps made modernization of the economy a more explicitly political question in North Carolina than in states where the hidden hand was more forthcoming. The question of state support for transportation projects came up before the legislature repeatedly in the antebellum period. Candidates for office were asked to take a position on the matter, and every crossroads election was potentially a referendum on the economic future of the state.[108]

104. Fayetteville *Observer*, January 14, 1834.
105. James A. Ward, "A New Look at Antebellum Southern Railroad Development," *Journal of Southern History*, XXXIX (1973), 413.
106. *North Carolina Senate Journal*, 1834–35, p. 136.
107. North Carolina Board of Internal Improvements, *Report to the General Assembly of North Carolina* (Raleigh, 1833), 16.
108. C. C. Weaver, *Internal Improvements in North Carolina Previous to 1860*, Johns Hopkins University Studies in Historical and Political Science, Vol. XXI, Pt. 3–4 (Baltimore, 1903),

By bringing the farmer closer to the potential purchasers of his crops, internal improvements might have stimulated both rural and urban prosperity. Some rural voters supported internal improvements for this reason, but others thought progress would carry too heavy a price. Internal improvements were denounced as costing too much, as conferring unequal benefits among equal taxpayers, and as stimulating the destruction of rural isolation and superior agrarian morality. As eastern conservative Willis Alston reminded an audience of Halifax County farmers on the Fourth of July, 1824, riches bred luxury and luxury was fatal to republicanism. "A system devised in heaven, would fail to command the respect of a licentious and abandoned people," he warned. *"The tables of Sinai could not control the Jews—so* must the provisions of our Constitution, lose their influence over *us*, when we reject our simplicity of manners and our regard for virtue. So long as we remain true to ancient feelings and principles, we have nothing to fear: when we depart from them, our dignity and our prosperity will leave us. It is beneath a nation of freemen, to entertain an ambition for dominion and luxury." [109]

Religious spokesmen shared Alston's concern over the relationship between liberty, morality, and extravagance. Church leaders at an early period had been quick to attach sacred significance to the American republic. In the words of the Presbyterian Synod of the Carolinas, national independence was the means by which God "emancipated us from the anti-christian and unscriptural controul of earthly kings." [110] Political freedom, however, was also a source of concern for Christians, for liberty made it possible to forget religious restraints and indulge a variety of licentious appetites. Just as Presbyterians received pithy advice "to live within your incomes" and "contract no extravagant debts," Baptists cautioned one another against all sorts of excessive consumption. "Brethren, you have been called unto liberty," urged the Cape Fear Baptist Association in 1811. "Use not your liberty for an occasion to the flesh, but by your love, serve one another." The Baptists were especially concerned about competitive tendencies among their members which might lead to mutual destruction if unrestrained. *"Thou shalt love thy neighbor as thy self,"* the Association reminded its members, *"but if ye bite and devour one another, take heed that ye be not consumed, one of another."* [111]

23–29; J. Allen Morgan, "State Aid to Transportation in North Carolina: The Pre-Railroad Era," *North Carolina Booklet*, X (1911), 123–54; Thomas E. Jeffrey, "Internal Improvements and Political Parties in Antebellum North Carolina, 1836–1860," *North Carolina Historical Review*, LV (1978), 111–56.

109. Tarboro *Free Press*, July 9, 1824.

110. Presbyterian Church in the U.S.A., Synod of the Carolinas, *A Pastoral Letter, from the Synod of the Carolinas, to the Churches Under Their Care* (Fayetteville, N.C., 1790), 6, 10.

111. Cape Fear Baptist Association, *Minutes*, 1811 (Fayetteville, N.C., 1811), microfilm copy in North Carolina Collection.

The authors of the 1811 pastoral letter may not have been thinking primarily about material acquisitiveness and consumption, but the dangers of prosperity to a simple Christian community cannot have been far from their minds. In 1825, however, the association devoted its entire missive to a warning against the sin of covetousness. What these rural Baptists described as a sin was very much like what Alexis de Tocqueville and other foreign visitors to the United States described as Americans' most engrossing national pursuit. "Covetousness," the association declared, "consists in an inordinate desire of earthly things, or what belongs to our neighbours, and a dissatisfaction with what we have, an overanxious care about the things of this world, a rapacity in obtaining wealth, and a tenaciousness in keeping it." In an admonition which nicely expressed an attitude of ambivalence towards acquisitiveness and not a total condemnation of it, the association declared that the worst aspect of covetousness was "its near resemblance to virtue." "Lying concealed under false titles of industry and frugality, [covetousness] brings with it so many plausible reasons, and raises a man in the view of too many, to a state of reputation on account of his riches." [112]

The Cape Fear Baptist Association spoke most directly to the dozen or so rural churches which comprised its membership, and which were just beginning to grow beyond their origins among the obscure and powerless members of plantation society. Its message was relevant, however, to an entire nation of movers, shakers, and ambitious wheeler-dealers who may have sometimes wondered where their plans were leading the republic. The Baptists concluded by asking their brethren to supplant competitiveness with mutual support. As the earlier letter had expressed it, "we therefore beseech you, as the elect of God, to put on, holy and beloved, bowels of mercy, kindness, humbleness of mind, meekness, long suffering, forbearing one another and forgiving one another. . . . *Even as Christ forgave, so also do ye.*" [113]

Concern over the moral consequences of economic change also appeared among the advocates of development. Even Archibald Murphey worried about the fleshpots of Egypt, though his approach to economic problems was very different from those of evangelicals or conservatives. In the booming years that followed the War of 1812, Murphey feared that the unprofitable nature of agriculture was eroding North Carolina's virtue. "This perversion of things is gradually undermining our morality," he reported, "and converting the character which we bore of being industrious, enterprising farmers and thriving

112. Cape Fear Baptist Association, *Minutes*, 1825 (Fayetteville, N.C., 1825), microfilm copy in North Carolina Collection.
113. Cape Fear Baptist Association, *Minutes*, 1811 (Fayetteville, N.C., 1811), microfilm copy in North Carolina Collection.

mechanics, into that of shopkeepers and speculators." [114] Murphey was am-
bivalent in his attitudes towards trade, because his plans for North Carolina
would have made the state more dependent on shopkeepers than before. He
could denounce speculation in town lots and in virtually the next breath declare
that "the growth of our commercial towns is of peculiar importance to the
character of the state." [115] If such ambivalence could influence Murphey, North
Carolina's most thoughtful and original advocate of economic development,
how much more could it affect the mass of farmers and citizens who could see
the future much less clearly than he? At a time when even the president of the
United States feared for "the moral continuity of American history," it is not
surprising that lesser citizens worried that economic and social change could
undermine the moral foundations of the republic.

In the years ahead, it would take more than one reassuring civic ritual
to allay the citizens' fears. The objections of religious and secular leaders
to the moral implications of the future could be applied to more projects
than transportation improvements. All the agencies of nineteenth-century
Progress—banks, corporations, public schools, charitable asylums—could
be interpreted as departures from republican tradition. All over America,
these institutions were transforming the face of preindustrial society. Modern
changes had not hit Cumberland County with full force, but change was controversial there because some citizens proposed to import it. North Carolinians treasured republicanism but they interpreted its meaning in different
ways. Most of Judge Toomer's welcoming speech to Lafayette used political
traditions to justify continued material progress in the future. More nostalgic
portions of the welcoming ceremony, as well as the speech of Willis Alston,
used republicanism to question the course of innovation. The future of tradi-
tionalism was therefore a pressing cultural controversy as North Carolinians
faced the challenges of the nineteenth century. The challenge was basically
social and economic, but the citizens' response took shape in the political arena by the actions of political parties. The formation of Cumberland
County's party system expressed the community's struggle with the fundamental problems of the age.

114. Hoyt (ed.), *Murphey Papers*, II, 20.
115. *Ibid.*, II, 24.

II. A Frequent Recurrence to Fundamental Principles: Some Aspects of Prepartisan Political Culture

The citizens who rallied before Lafayette in 1825 and who divided into political parties a few years later did not face the challenge of social change completely unprepared. Even as they changed their political practices to accommodate new conditions, the citizens shared a set of values and expectations which explained what government ought to be and ought to do, who political leaders should be and how they ought to be chosen, what a man's civic duties were and how he should perform them. Social scientists call such values and expectations "political culture." The county's political culture was like a lens through which the citizens viewed the events of the Age of Jackson, magnifying some developments and diminishing others. It was also like an athlete's playbook, guiding the citizens as they faced a succession of contingencies. Finally, it was a source of inspiration, guiding the citizens in what they might reasonably hope for in the changing world of the 1820s and 1830s.

The emergence of the second party system cannot be understood without a review of the political culture which preceded it and which in many ways inspired it. Two aspects of the community's values in the 1820s had particular importance for political developments later. First, the regulations and attitudes which governed the citizens' willingness and ability to participate in politics were central to the formation of mass parties. Second and less obviously, the popular assumptions about which topics were legitimate subjects of political action or discussion played a crucial role in shaping the government's response to social problems.[1] On the eve of the second party system,

1. Walter A. Rosenbaum defines political culture at the "system level" as "the important ways in which people are subjectively oriented toward the basic elements of their political system." Political scientists generally investigate political culture in a system by collating large numbers of individual opinions; survey research is therefore their basic research tool. Rosenbaum also mentions political participation levels and the value content of political publications as important ob-

access to the ballot was relatively open, but political participation was low. Public opinion defined government as a moral enterprise and condemned the use of public power for all but the most restricted purposes. Both of these qualities would change dramatically as Cumberland County grappled with a new set of problems and opportunities.

The act of voting was the most important and most widespread form of political participation in North Carolina. By law, voting rights were broadly available after 1776, but in the colonial period, a fifty-acre landholding requirement had limited access to the ballot.[2] The state constitution of 1776 retained this requirement for electors of state senators, but any adult male who had lived in a county for a year and had paid public taxes could vote for members of the lower house, or House of Commons. Each county elected one senator and two commoners, and six towns could each send a borough representative to the lower house. Residents of these towns could vote for "town member" under the same franchise as rural residents, but freeholders in borough towns could vote in town elections whether they were permanent residents or not. Fayetteville was not one of the original six, but it received borough privileges in 1789. After the ratification of the U.S. Constitution, citizens eligible to vote for a member of the House of Commons could also vote for a U.S. congressman and a presidential elector. Eventually the sheriff, the clerks of court, and the governor were also chosen by popular election, but the landholding requirement to vote for state senator remained until 1857. As in most southern states, the county court exercised most powers of local government. Its members were justices of the peace or magistrates who were not elected, but appointed by the governor upon recommendation by the county legislators.[3]

For most offices, the North Carolina electorate included all free adult men, including free blacks until 1835. The tax-paying requirement was not a significant impediment to voting, because the constitution did not require that voters pay their current taxes before casting ballots. If he had ever once paid taxes, a free man who was otherwise eligible never lost his right to vote. The

jects of study in the analysis of political culture. These subjects are obviously more accessible to the historian than the unrecorded opinions of the average person. Patterns of voting cleavage reflect nonelite public opinion, as Lee Benson has observed, and these aspects of political culture are examined in Chapter III. Walter A. Rosenbaum, *Political Culture* (New York, 1975), 5, 9, 24–25; Lee Benson, "An Approach to the Scientific Study of Past Public Opinion," in Benson, *Toward the Scientific Study of History: Selected Essays* (Philadelphia, 1972), 105–159.

2. Chilton Williamson, *American Suffrage from Property to Democracy, 1760–1860* (Princeton, N.J., 1960), 13, 15.

3. North Carolina Constitution of 1776, articles VII, VIII, XXXIII, Constitutional Amendments of 1835, article III, Constitutional Amendment of 1857, Constitutional Amendment of 1789, all in John L. Cheney, Jr. (ed.), *North Carolina Government, 1585–1974: A Narrative and Statistical History* (Raleigh, 1975), 812, 814, 820–21, 816, 823.

principal taxes to be paid in North Carolina were an *ad valorem* tax on land and a per capita tax on "polls." A poll was any free man between the ages of twenty-one and forty-five or a slave of either sex between the ages of twelve and fifty. With a few minor exceptions provided by law, every free adult man under forty-five should have paid a tax on his own poll. In fact, few men who did not also owe taxes for land or slaves ever filed tax returns, and the county court did not bother to compel them. Young men who came of age between tax collection time and election day thus came forward to pay the poll tax once before assuming full citizenship rights, but no one else was subject to this minor inconvenience.[4]

The right to hold public office was not as widely available in North Carolina as the right to vote. The constitution restricted membership in the House of Commons and the Senate to the owners of one hundred and three hundred or more acres of land respectively. To be governor, a man's real property had to be worth a thousand pounds or more.[5] Harold J. Counihan has shown that North Carolina officeholders regularly exceeded these limits by a wide margin, indicating that informal requirements for officeholding were even higher. Ralph A. Wooster has found that North Carolina legislators in the decade before the Civil War were also prosperous men and, indeed, that the number of planters in the North Carolina legislature increased between 1850 and 1860.[6] Wealth and political office were closely associated by law and by custom throughout the antebellum period.

Cumberland County citizens exercised their rights to vote in large numbers in the first two decades after the ratification of the U.S. Constitution. Participation lagged thereafter but increased again in the 1830s. Popular voting reflected the higher interest in politics surrounding the first and second party

4. A congressional committee investigating charges of vote fraud in the Fayetteville district declared in 1804 "that the tax list of any year agreeably to the laws of North Carolina, are not a perfect record of those who are entitled to vote, because citizens who at anytime formerly had paid taxes, by the laws of that state appear to the committee to continue to enjoy the privilege of voting, though they might for many years have ceased to pay taxes." Comparison of census and tax records shows that many eligible men did not pay their poll taxes. In 1840, for example, there were 1,911 adult white males in Cumberland County. An estimated 450 men who were liable for the poll tax did not pay it. If these tax delinquent citizens had been disfranchised, no more than 1,461 votes could have been received in that year, even if all taxpayers voted. The records, however, show that about 1,573 men voted for a member of the House of Commons, 1,573 voted for governor, and 1,562 voted for president. "Contested Election of Samuel Purviance, A Representative from North Carolina," February 29, 1804, 8th Cong., 1st sess., in *American State Papers*, vol. 037, no. 176, p. 389; *Compendium of the Sixth Census*, 40–42; Cumberland County List of Taxables, 1840, in Cumberland County Records; Fayetteville *Observer*, August 22, 1838, August 18, 1840, November 18, 1840.
5. North Carolina Constitution of 1776, articles V, IV, XV, in Cheney (ed.), *North Carolina Government*, 813, 814.
6. Counihan, "North Carolina, 1815–1836," 22; Wooster, *Politicians, Planters, and Plain Folk*, 35, 40.

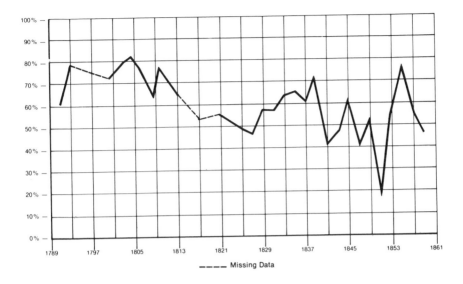

Figure 3. Cumberland County voting turnout, 1791–1859: percentage voting for Congress of those qualified by age, sex, and race.

Chart by Richard Volz

SOURCE: North Carolina Compiled Election Returns, 1790–1860, North Carolina State Archives; Published U.S. Census Reports for the First through the Eighth Censuses (see Bibliography for the complete citations).

systems. This cycle of interest appears clearly in figure 3, a graph of the voting turnout in congressional elections from 1791 to 1859.

Political participation was very high until after 1810. The 1804 contest to choose a successor to retiring veteran Congressman William Barry Grove brought out 84.1 percent of the free adult males in the county. In this particular election, the totals may have expanded because of ballot box stuffing, but J. R. Pole has found turnout rates exceeding 80 percent in many North Carolina counties during this period. Participation even exceeded 90 percent in some Maryland and New York counties.[7] These were years of sharp political controversy between Federalists and Democratic-Republicans and the congressional election was the principal occasion for citizens to register their opinions on questions of national importance. Turnout dropped at the close of the first party system, but it surged again in the Jacksonian period. By this

7. J. R. Pole, "Suffrage and Representation in Maryland from 1776 to 1810: A Statistical Note and Some Reflections," *Journal of Southern History*, XXIV (1958), 218–25, and "Election Statistics in North Carolina to 1861," *Journal of Southern History*, XXIV (1958), 225–28.

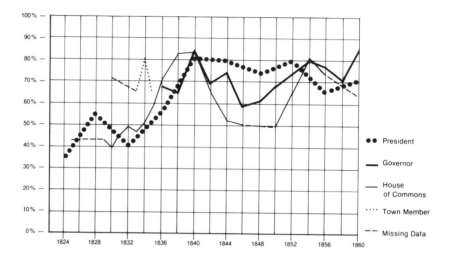

Figure 4. Voting turnout, Cumberland County, 1824–1860.
Chart by Richard Volz

time, however, popular voting for governor and president was well established. In 1842, moreover, Cumberland was placed in a new district where the Whigs were hopelessly outnumbered and the interest of both parties flagged considerably. Eventually, the congressional election became a minor, "off-year" contest, although a Know-Nothing candidacy revived interest briefly in 1855.

The political community expanded when noncongressional offices were being filled. A turnout of 50 percent, which was average in congressional elections, was about the minimum level in other races. Otherwise, figure 4 shows that the turnout for both kinds of elections reflected the intensity of political competition at any given time. Between 1834 and 1844, Whigs and Democrats were struggling to establish dominance over the state. During the 1840s, it appeared that Whigs would dominate, and participation slackened in both legislative and gubernatorial elections. After 1850 the struggle mounted again. Democrats captured the governorship and established their position as the majority party. As in the 1830s, each voter could believe that his ballot mattered and participation sharply increased. During the second party system, turnout rates for Cumberland County and North Carolina as a whole were very similar; from 1836 to 1860, participation in the governor's election was 72 percent statewide and 71 percent in the county.[8]

8. Pole, "Election Statistics in North Carolina," 225–28.

Voting in presidential elections followed a slightly different pattern from the governors' races. After a surge of enthusiasm in 1828, the level of participation in presidential elections lagged behind that in the state contests until after the Log Cabin Campaign of 1840. In all of North Carolina, voting in presidential elections trailed gubernatorial rates throughout the antebellum period. This did not stem from indifference to national politics. On the contrary, party lines between state politicians were uniformly attributed to differences over national questions, and the most important national question was the presidency. Ordinary voters, however, may have been more responsive to a direct appeal from an office seeker than to speeches and editorials about a distant presidential candidate. This almost certainly happened in 1827, when the turnout for the congressional election exceeded the presidential total for 1828 by two hundred votes, although the surviving literary evidence suggests that the congressional campaign was fought exclusively on the presidential question.[9] State politicians also observed that the "general ticket" system, which forced citizens to vote for a statewide slate of presidential electors instead of for a single elector representing his district, hampered popular involvement with the presidential election. "The people can never vote understandingly with the General Ticket," John A. Cameron objected. "They are unacquainted with the Electors—they have no guarantee that they will vote in pursuance to their wishes, and they cease to take a proper interest." The same objection came from other parts of the state. "Under the general ticket system the people will not attend the polls," worried one newspaper correspondent from Mecklenburg County. "They feel an unconquerable aversion to vote for men of whom they know nothing, or a cold indifference, which cannot be overcome."[10] Uneasiness over the method of electing the president did not end until the firm establishment of political parties in 1840. Thereafter, Cumberland County turnout in the presidential election usually exceeded state-level totals by a considerable margin.

Paradoxically, those same local elections which marginal voters later ignored were actually the first to feel the effects of partisan excitement. Initially, new voters responded to partisan appeals from legislative candidates while still hesitating to vote for unknown presidential electors. An effect of the campaign of 1840 was to bring these marginal voters into presidential elections. Their interest in state and local elections declined until the 1850s, when a renewed interest in state questions brought increased turnout in local contests.

9. John A. Cameron, "To The Freemen of Montgomery, Anson, Richmond, Robeson, Cumberland and Moore," Fayetteville, April 27, 1827 (Broadside reprinted in the Fayetteville *North Carolina Journal*, May 2, 1827).
10. Fayetteville *North Carolina Journal*, May 2, 1827; Fayetteville *Carolina Observer*, November 25, 1824.

Finally, figure 4 shows the level of participation in four of the last five elections for town member from Fayetteville, before the office was abolished in the reforms of 1835. This short line indicates that the level of political participation in town was generally higher than for the county. Townsmen had better sources of information about politics and may have had more motivation to vote than their counterparts in the country. Moreover, the simple act of getting to the polling place was much easier for the town dweller than for the rural resident.

Generally speaking, the political community of Cumberland County was defined by choice. A significant portion of the eligible voters declined to join at all, especially between 1810 and 1836, but in an exciting contest, voter participation approached 90 percent. Popular excitement was not entirely spontaneous. The people of Cumberland did not surge to the polls, catching local leaders by surprise, to demand the election of Andrew Jackson or anyone else. But when the issues that Old Hickory raised became the slogans of efficient party organizations, voters flocked to the ballot box.

The creation of party slogans was not a simple process. No matter how many objective causes made a party system logical, sensible, or even inevitable, what people thought about republican government limited politicians' imagination and affected what voters would accept. In the North Carolina of the 1820s, prevailing political ideology militated against political party formation. If the local press reflected public opinion accurately, Cumberland citizens regarded the American republic as a sacred instrument for the protection of liberty. Protecting the purity of the state was a more important task for political leaders than the use of state power to promote social goals. Excessive use of state power not only undermined liberty directly by restricting the citizens' freedom of action, it also corrupted the sacred republic by giving politicians an opportunity to promote their own private ends. Office seekers therefore protected their civic reputations by denouncing the desire for power. Any political combination with others was likely to belie these denunciations, so leaders were also quick to avoid any connection with the idea or practice of partisanship. On the other hand, if parties were necessary to mobilize the electorate, then antipower political culture did more to inhibit mass participation in politics than any legal restriction on the franchise.

Values and ideas which affected political development appeared in the rhetoric of candidates and in the language of Fayetteville's two newspapers. Each of these papers eventually became an effective party organ. The *North Carolina Journal* spoke for the Democrats and the *Carolina Observer* rallied the Whigs. In some other states party alignments grew out of conflicts in political values. In the realm of general political values, however, the *Observer* and the *Journal* showed more agreement than conflict. The opinions expressed by the editors, their correspondents, and candidates for public office in the state were undoubtedly those of an articulate elite, but the statements of local leaders were closely bound by what their audience wanted to hear. Public political language was almost certainly an accurate reflection of public opinion on the proper nature of American government.

The *Carolina Observer* was founded in 1817 but did not assume a stable character until after 1825, when Edward J. Hale bought it. The new editor was twenty-three years old. He remained with his new enterprise continually until March, 1865, when its press was destroyed by the troops of General Sherman. Although he was wealthy and well-born, Hale was a professional newspaperman. He learned the printing trade in the shop of Joseph Gales, Republican editor of the *Raleigh Register*. He also served a stint in the Washington offices of the *National Intelligencer*, whose two editors were Joseph Gales's son and son-in-law. Like his mentors in Raleigh and Washington, Hale supported William H. Crawford for president in 1824. When the Georgian lost, Hale was left politically homeless. A tepid Jacksonian who admired Calhoun, Hale eventually became one of the staunchest Whig editors in the state. He also became a bank director and president and half-owner of the Fayetteville Water Works. Retaining and augmenting his inherited fortune, Hale made his home a center of village society. His biographer noted admiringly that "splendid entertainments were given there, and his large income enabled him to spend three or four months each year in travel, taking with him all his family." As a landed heir who made a successful transition to urban sources of wealth, Edward J. Hale epitomized in his own career a tendency in North Carolina Whiggery towards enterprise, commercialism, and modernization.[11]

John A. Cameron was the editor of the *North Carolina Journal*. Like his Whig counterpart, Cameron was favored with wealth by birth and marriage. He was born in 1788, the younger son of an Anglican minister in Virginia. He received a bachelor's degree from the University of North Carolina in 1806 and a master of arts in 1809. The next year he represented Fayetteville in the House of Commons. Thereafter, Cameron's life was dogged by misfortune. He ran for Congress once as a Federalist, twice as a Jacksonian, and each time was unsuccessful. He was trained as a lawyer, but an illness contracted while commanding the state's forces in the War of 1812 destroyed his voice and ended his usefulness as an advocate. In 1817, Fayetteville obtained a branch of the second Bank of the United States and Cameron became its first president. He left that post and entered a mercantile partnership, but his ex-

11. John H. Wheeler, *Historical Sketches of North Carolina* (Philadelphia, 1851), 114; Ashe *et al.* (eds.), *Biographical History of North Carolina*, VIII, 179–84; Fayetteville *Carolina Observer*, November 15, 1827.

perience in that venture showed him to be extremely inept in business matters. His partner managed to accumulate over eighty thousand dollars in debts and to bankrupt the firm without Cameron's prior knowledge. Financially ruined and unable to practice law, Cameron was a desperate man. He wrote to his wealthy brother, Duncan, distractedly asking for advice about teaching school or becoming a minister. He even went to Washington to ask President Adams to appoint him commissioner under the Bankruptcy Bill.[12]

Disappointed in his search for patronage, Cameron returned to Fayetteville and turned his back on the Adams administration. Finding a financial backer, he began to publish the *North Carolina Journal*. During the next four years, Cameron never abandoned his search for a remunerative and dignified office. He ran for Congress twice in this period and made a second trip to Washington to seek appointment from President Jackson. In 1831 he finally received the consulate to Vera Cruz, and he left Fayetteville forever. He was able to remain in government service by later obtaining an appointment as a federal judge in the Territory of Florida, but bad luck dogged him to the end. He died in a steamboat explosion in 1838.[13]

The political loyalties of John A. Cameron experienced as many vicissitudes as his finances. Successively he was a Federalist, a petitioner of President Adams and perhaps his supporter, and finally a Jacksonian. A cynic might conclude that Cameron's opinions were perforce available to the highest bidder, but this may not have been so. Everything in his early background, including his wealth and family connections, suggested a Whig party affiliation. Cameron's repeated misfortunes, however, had left him a bitterly disillusioned man. In Cameron's opinion, he lost his first campaign for Congress because his opponent was "indebted for his success to such means as no gentleman would use." Years later he wrote to his brother, "I am sick and disgusted with the villainies of the world, and want to get out of its contact as soon as I can. . . . The world was not made for me nor I for the world."[14]

12. Ashe *et al.* (eds.), *Biographical History of North Carolina*, III, 46; John A. Cameron, "To The Freemen," April 27, 1827; Daniel Miles McFarland, "Rip Van Winkle: Political Evolution in North Carolina, 1815–1835" (Ph.D. dissertation, University of Pennsylvania, 1954), 68; John A. Cameron to Duncan Cameron, March 9, 1825, April 19, 1826, in Cameron Family Papers, Southern Historical Collection; John Haywood to Willie P. Mangum, March 24, 1826, Willie P. Mangum to Charity Mangum, April 16, 1826, in Henry Thomas Shanks (ed.), *The Papers of Willie Person Mangum* (5 vols.; Raleigh, 1950–56), I, 260, 275.
13. Fayetteville *North Carolina Journal*, March 17, 1826; Compiled Election Returns, "Congressional," 1827, 1829, in Miscellaneous Collections, North Carolina State Archives; John A. Cameron to Duncan Cameron, January 18, 1830, October 9, 1830, March 13, 1831, in Cameron Family Papers; Willie P. Mangum to Duncan Cameron, May 24, 1832, in Shanks (ed.), *Mangum Papers*, I, 547–48; Wheeler, *Historical Sketches*, 130.
14. John A. Cameron to Duncan Cameron, n.d. [May 12, 1813], March 9, 1825, in Cameron Family Papers.

Cameron's pessimism was not the result of momentary depression. Five years later the gossipy travel writer Mrs. Anne Royall complained of his pious melancholy by noting that "the Jackson Editor [in Fayetteville] is as thoroughgoing a long-face as any." [15]

The tone of his letters suggests that Cameron's unhappy state of mind stemmed from his conviction his bad luck was not fair, that in a just world a man of his family and background would not have to suffer his humiliations. His letters about office-hunting implied that he was not asking the government a favor, but that Adams and Jackson both owed him a position of dignity and comfort. He expressed shock when he discovered that "considerations of policy and mutual bargainings govern more [in making appointments] than any other [factor]," including his own sense of what he deserved. [16] In other words, Cameron blamed a wicked and topsy-turvy world for his misfortunes. He may have believed sincerely that only General Jackson's primitive purity could restore social order and save the country. Whether he believed it or not, Cameron's message in the *Journal* and on the stump became the current language in Cumberland County. His words and those of the other county leaders embodied the intense concern which early-nineteenth-century Americans felt for the character of their government.

Like the state in all western countries in the nineteenth century, the governments of Cumberland County, North Carolina, and the United States were powerful arrangements for punishing criminals, enforcing contracts, guarding private property, and protecting the existing social structure. No discussion of political culture should lose sight of the state's powers to remunerate some citizens and to repress others, but it is also true that the governments of the United States were more than social housekeeping operations. Rush Welter has expressed a common observation of students of American culture by remarking that "Americans of the Middle Period tended to see themselves as heirs of all the ages, who had at one and the same time put ancient ideals into practice and transcended the very best that had first given impetus to those ideas." [17] The governments of America were the principal manifestations of this great dual accomplishment because they had perfected a balance between liberty and power. Guided by Providence, the American people had learned to govern themselves with a combination of freedom and restraint, and had created a suitable tabernacle for the eternal verities of republican politics and reformed religion. The sacred character of the state gave American politics a ritual quality which transfigured its more mundane coercive functions.

15. Royall, *Mrs. Royall's Southern Tour*, I, 151.
16. John Cameron to Duncan Cameron, June 6, 1830, in Cameron Family Papers.
17. Rush Welter, *The Mind of America, 1830–1860* (New York, 1975), 5.

The fear that royal power would devour liberty and wreck the special character of the American experiment had inspired the American Revolution and had guided the Founding Fathers as they wrote the first state constitutions. By the antebellum period, the political theory that had explained the events of the eighteenth century had evolved into regional variants. In Alabama, J. Mills Thornton III has found that the presence of slavery encouraged a popular idea of liberty as the absence of personal restraint. In the Midwest, Eric Foner has shown that the prevalence of small farmers and shopowners stimulated the emergence of free soil ideology from the general principles of the American political creed.[18] In North Carolina, public spokesmen tended to emphasize the settled and perfect character of American institutions. In contrast to the fluid social conditions in frontier Alabama, North Carolina's economic and political elite was relatively stable, and most politicians did not stand to gain by denouncing their opponents as aristocrats. Slave-based society was much older than democracy in North Carolina, and slavery's influence on political culture was more to encourage political quiescence than political conflict. Writers in the press tended to suggest that conditions in America were already ideal and that controversy and agitation could only damage the quality of public life. This belief appeared clearly in 1824, when conflict over the presidency seemed to bode ill for the future. "Who are we?" cried "Brutus," an eloquent correspondent of the *Carolina Observer* in 1824. "What are we doing? What [is] our object?"

> We are citizens of the only republic on earth that can sustain itself without calling foreign aid. All free people, and all lovers of freedom, look to us as a light and a landmark, as a grand example for their imitation, and watched by the keen eye of despotism we exist as a free people, the last and only hope of the world. . . .
>
> And shall we by our petty quarrels for men continue to distract the country and lay the foundation of lasting feuds? Shall we do so much for the accommodation of the enemies of freedom; so much to ensure our own weakness and future division. Or shall this state of things be kept up to enable the intriguers of the country to make better bargains for themselves.[19]

"Brutus" called for a speedy resolution of the conflict, preferably before election day. He apparently hoped that public opinion would abandon the in-

---

18. Bernard Bailyn, *The Ideological Origins of the American Revolution* (Cambridge, Mass., 1967); Major L. Wilson, *Space, Time, and Freedom: The Quest for Nationality and the Irrepressible Conflict* (Westport, Conn., 1974); Eric Foner, *Free Soil, Free Labor, Free Men: The Ideology of the Republican Party Before the Civil War* (New York, 1970); Thornton, *Politics and Power in a Slave Society*.
19. Fayetteville *Carolina Observer*, July 8, 1824.

triguers and unite on one candidate. Balloting would thus have been a mere formality, as it had been in previous presidential elections.

A similar disapproval of political controversy came from editor Edward Jones Hale. "With us," he declared thankfully, "it is rare that either the public or private character of a candidate, his competency or incompetency, is the subject of newspaper discussion. . . . The public interest may sometimes suffer in consequence of the usual policy of silence on such matters, yet with so much disgust do we look upon the lengths to which it is carried in other States, the heart-burnings it causes, the injury to public morals, and degradation of the press, that we sincerely deprecate its introduction among us." [20] In spite of the fact that political conflict was sometimes bitter, prominent spokesmen continued to suggest that prolonged debate was regrettable or illegitimate.

Hostility to political controversy and satisfaction with things as they were did not encourage an activist philosophy of government. Visionary writers regretted that the state did little or nothing to promote intellectual or economic improvement, and one governor complained that the General Assembly spent more money for its own salaries than for any other item. In spite of these criticisms, defining and maintaining the moral tone of the nation attracted more interest than the chores of state government. The most important task in that process was to make sure that the national destiny not be entrusted to impure, selfish, or untrustworthy hands. As Samuel Dickins said when he was running for Congress in 1816, "the excellent constitution under which we live, I believe to be the best the world has yet ever seen."

> A scrupulous adherence to its principles will preserve to our beloved country, all those civil and religious rights and that plenty, tranquility and happiness for which she is now so far distinguished above other nations. We are indeed a favored people and it rests with ourselves whether we shall be so favored for ages to come. We have but little to apprehend from the hostile attacks of any external enemy. When we fall it will be by the fatal effects of our own folly and vices: I am therefore, hostile to every course of policy, which tends to sap the foundation of public virtue. [21]

A similar concern for political morality dominated the resolutions of the Republicans of Robeson County in their convention of 1828. "The Presidential election," they declared, "presents a question of more vast importance than any that has arisen since the formation and adoption of our Federal Constitu-

---

20. *Ibid.*, May 14, 1829.
21. Samuel Dickins, "To the Electors of the District composed of the counties of Wake, Orange and Person," Raleigh, July 6, 1816 (Broadside in the North Carolina Collection).

tion. It is one in which every American must and ought to feel a deep interest; for on its final issue will depend in a great measure the future happiness and prosperity of our country." The outcome of the election, the citizens continued, would decide whether the heritage of the Revolution would be preserved sacrosanct, or "surrender[ed] into the hands of corrupt and unprincipled politicians to promote their illicit and ambitious designs and to subserve party purposes." [22]

The importance of political morality made a declaration of purity much more important for a hopeful politician than a list of programmatic promises. A separate article of the state constitution's Declaration of Rights made this injunction explicit. "A frequent recurrence to fundamental Principles," read Article XXI, "is absolutely necessary to preserve the Blessings of Liberty." [23] Successive generations of antebellum editors and politicians obeyed this directive so faithfully that a preoccupation with principles and the honesty and consistency with which they were held was the most pervasive theme in all published political discourse. These principles were only rarely controversial. As he summarized it in 1829, for example, John Cameron's fighting creed was only a bundle of platitudes. "These principles consisted [when he last ran for Congress], briefly, in respect for the will of the people—in ardent attachment for the constitution of my country—in admiration for devotion to liberty and popular rights—in a fixed determination to support, as far as my influence could extend, the respective rights of the federal and several State Governments. Time and subsequent events have left me no cause to change my principles or my opinions, but have confirmed my faith in them." [24]

Every politician in the country would have given this statement a ringing endorsement, but these principles were much more common as political statements than assessments of the material payoff of various policies. Likewise, the most effective way to discredit an opponent was to question his moral or symbolic fitness for public office. Hear the editor of the *North Carolina Journal*, for instance, as he urged the election of a certain congressman in a neighboring district in 1829.

> A due regard to consistency, and to their own characters as politicians, will govern the voters. If they elect Mr. Rencher, they will give another proof of their confidence in General Jackson and his administration— they will put the seal of their disapprobation to those countless slanders

---

22. Fayetteville *Carolina Observer*, June 12, 1828.
23. North Carolina Constitution of 1776, Declaration of Rights, article XXI, in Cheney (ed.), *North Carolina Government*, 810.
24. John A. Cameron, "To the Freemen of Richmond, Robeson, Cumberland, Anson, Montgomery, and Moore," July 20, 1829 (Broadside in Edmund Deberry Papers, microfilm copy in North Carolina State Archives).

which are daily emanating from the opposition party against the administration—they will give their sanction to the measures of Reform, which under Jackson's administration, are infusing new life, vigor, purity, and strength into our political institutions; if they elect Mr. Long, they will manifest a want of confidence in Jackson's administration—they sanction the calumnies which are now in circulation against the administration . . . they will disapprove of the System of reform now going on—and they will sanction the abuses and corruptions of Adams' administration.[25]

The editor was making no plea for the material advantage to be gained to the district by one candidate or the other. The "Reforms" that Cameron praised in this passage were known by his readers to consist of replacing Adams supporters in the government employ with Jackson men and attempting to reduce the level of government services. He did not even seem concerned by the material support in the form of votes in Congress which Mr. Rencher might offer to these reforms. Rather, the most important question to be decided in the election was the affective condition of the new district. Would the voters "give proof of their confidence" for the forces of good? Would they "put the seal of disapprobation" on the machinations of evildoers? We see in this editorial the vocabulary of Christian witness, not the calculations of perceived self-interest which are more familiar to modern politics.

The kinds of transgressions that were most likely to disqualify a man for public service were those which betrayed a love of power. Like the eighteenth-century whig theorists, North Carolina politicians and editors believed that power had an insatiable appetite for liberty and that forceful exercise of state authority was subversive of America's most precious asset.[26] The existence of slavery undoubtedly encouraged the persistence of this special sensitivity, for North Carolina leaders showed acute anxiety over powerful interference with this institution. Edward J. Hale, for instance, felt that President John Quincy Adams' threat to send the army against the state of Georgia was an unconstitutional abuse of power which the president "had not a shadow of law or reason to justify." In 1826, the *Observer* endorsed Jackson for president, "who," it said, "if he does not possess the talents of Mr. Adams, has, as we believe, better principles, and will pursue a straightforward honorable course in which, if there be nothing splendid, there will at least be safety."[27] In his private communications Hale expressed the same sentiments. He was greatly alarmed by Jackson's behavior in response to the Nullification Crisis

25. Fayetteville *North Carolina Journal*, November 18, 1829.
26. For a discussion of antipower ideology at the national level, see James Sterling Young, *The Washington Community, 1800–1828* (New York, 1966), 60–61.
27. Fayetteville *Carolina Observer*, March 1, 1826.

in South Carolina, and he wrote Senator Willie P. Mangum that extreme measures, including secession, were the South's only defense against northern oppression. "Take that right [secession] from us and we shall be left without a protection against the exercise of any arbitrary power the Genl. Govt. may assume, it will then be necessary only for some *popular* President to pronounce to congress and the Judiciary that the Genl. Govt. is all Supreme and unlimited in its constitutional powers, and you will immediately find a host of implicit believers in the manufacturing States ready to prove by *constitutional technicalities* the truth of the absurdity." [28] To counter the doctrines of Jackson's proclamation, which he saw as "strik[ing] at the root and foundation of the republican principles of the States," Hale recommended a return to the "principles of 98–99," and failing that, "the contest must necessarily be settled by the sword." [29]

As the more committed opponent of John Quincy Adams, John Cameron was naturally more sweeping in his warnings of that president's attitude toward power. In his roundhouse blast at the president, Cameron struck most of the major themes of the opposition press throughout the country. He paid special attention to a famous gaffe in the president's Inaugural Address. Adams had dismissed potential opposition to his grandiose legislative program by urging Congress not "to proclaim to the world that we are palsied by the will of our constituents." Equally heinous, in Cameron's view, was Adams' accession to office by "bargain and management," his attempt to practice diplomacy without the advice and consent of the Senate, his desire to entangle the country in foreign alliances, his alleged use of federal appointees "to *electioneer* for his benefit," and his effort to dictate the choice of his successor. [30]

There was nothing unusual about this rhetoric. It was standard all over the country. Its only remarkable feature was the degree to which it resembled the language used by the enemies of Andrew Jackson and Martin Van Buren to assemble their own opposition coalition six to ten years later. These early Whigs (Edward J. Hale among them) made Van Buren notorious for "management" just as Van Buren's friends had done for John Quincy Adams and Henry Clay. Andrew Jackson's appointment of a mission to Turkey was denounced on the same grounds as Adams' abortive Panama mission. Whig opposition to the Jacksonian "spoils system" and to the successful attempt by Jackson to choose his successor is famous. Even Adams' alleged love of luxury found a later parallel in Martin Van Buren's gold spoons and French perfume. [31]

28. Edward J. Hale to Willie P. Mangum, January 30, 1833, in Shanks (ed.), *Mangum Papers*, II, 15.
29. *Ibid.*
30. Fayetteville *North Carolina Journal*, September 26, 1827.
31. Robert Gray Gunderson, *The Log Cabin Campaign* (Lexington, Ky., 1957), 101–107.

Antipower feelings were not limited to the enemies of President Adams. When the friends of Adams addressed the people of the county, they returned to the Jackson men the same weighty charge already directed at their own candidate: "Coalition." Jackson's friends had no common set of principles, they charged. As a result, "should such an administration be formed . . . they will be compelled to compromise . . . principle will yield and expedience become the cardinal doctrine." They went on to dismiss Jackson's appeal as "solely of a military character." [32]

Unworthy politicians could reveal their lust for power in various ways, but the most obvious and most damaging was to join or organize a party. Virtuous statesmen had no need to act in concert with others; they could see and follow the public good without group leadership. But the politician who desired to use the machinery of government for private ends would be forced to conspire with others equally low-minded. As one congressman wrote in 1813, "the existence of party generally presupposes that some deviations from true policy have been committed—Experience proves that these deviations will not only be more frequent and irregular, in proportion as party feeling is more violent and excessive; but also that neither party can arrogate to itself an exemption from error." Even at the height of the first party system, office seekers were often careful to deny their interest in party loyalty or membership. In 1810, Federalist William Gaston assured the voters of the New Bern district that "the man . . . does not exist who more sincerely deprecates the horrid consequences of factious divisions of our country, than myself." Likewise, Congressman Lewis Williams promised the voters of Surrey County in 1813 that "My politics are Republican, but absolute devotion to the Republicans as a party, is neither professed or acknowledged. I have . . . never failed," he boasted, "to condemn what appeared condemnable, and to applaud what seemed praiseworthy in the administration of any president." [33]

Hostility to party politics persisted strongly in the 1820s. Ronald Formisano has associated antiparty feelings with the elements which gravitated to the Whig party.[34] In Cumberland County, however, antiparty feelings were common among those who later became Democrats, as well as by those who later became Whigs. As one who had changed parties, John Cameron was predictably quick to stress that old distinctions no longer mattered. When an Adams editor assailed his principles in 1826, Cameron vigorously denied that

32. Fayetteville *North Carolina Journal*, December 12, 1827.
33. William Gaston, "To the Freemen of the Counties of Johnston, Wayne, Greene, Lenoir, Jones, Carteret and Craven," New Bern, July 24, 1810 (Broadside in the North Carolina Collection); Lewis Williams, "To the Freemen of the Counties of Wilkes, Surry, Iredell, and Ashe," [April, 1813] (Undated broadside in the North Carolina Collection).
34. Ronald P. Formisano, "Political Character, Antipartyism, and the Second Party System," *American Quarterly*, XXI (1969), 683–709.

the distinction between Federalist and Republican still had any meaning. "Genuine Federalism and genuine Republicanism," he proclaimed, invoking Thomas Jefferson by name, "are the same thing." On the other hand, Cameron did stress a new distinction based on the next presidential election. "The question," he said, "is not now between Federalists and Republicans . . . but is between the people, on the one side, struggling for their rights, and the Administration, on the other, struggling to retain power which has been obtained through management and intrigue." Concerning his own affiliations, Cameron made clear that he belonged to the opposition, or as he preferred to say, *"we are of the party of our country."* Later, when he was running for Congress, Cameron praised Andrew Jackson lavishly, but refused to join a Jacksonian party. "I must be distinctly understood," he insisted, "as not pledging myself to support or oppose, indiscriminately, the measures of any set of men. . . . My course in Congress shall be frank and independent." [35]

For his part, Edward J. Hale was even more censorious of party spirit than Cameron. He agreed that the distinction between Federalist and Republican had become meaningless. Moreover, he refused either to embrace the Adams administration or any of its prominent opponents as Cameron had done. "For ourselves [he wrote], while we would scorn the course of the Journal, we are equally averse to enroll ourselves in the ranks of an opposition. Mr. Adams never was our choice for the station he now fills; but since he has occupied it, we have not seen much to condemn in his course. If ever we should see aught of corruption, of a departure from a republican policy, it will then be proper to manifest opposition; but for the present, we adopt the liberal sentiment of Mr. Crawford, 'Let the administration be judged by its measures.'" [36] In the end, Hale's opposition to Adams' conduct of the Georgia Indian controversy caused him to support Jackson's election in 1828, but at the same time he vowed never to join a faction to pursue a political goal. [37]

The significance of this convergence of political rhetoric in opposite political camps is not simply that Hale aped Cameron in order to win elections, but that antiparty and antipower values were not peculiar to one faction or another. [38] In the political culture of the 1820s, hostility to "management," to active, powerful government, and to organized parties operating under distinctive party names found a ready response in every quarter. It does not deflate the importance of these themes, moreover, to observe a certain tension between professed ideals and practical politics. The men who denounced the

35. Fayetteville *North Carolina Journal*, November 8, 1826; John A. Cameron, "To The Freemen," April 27, 1827.
36. Fayetteville *Carolina Observer*, March 1, 1826.
37. *Ibid.*, March 15, 1827.
38. *Cf.* Lynn L. Marshall, "The Strange Stillbirth of the Whig Party," *American Historical Review*, LXXII (1967), 445–68.

office-hunger of politicians usually aspired to office themselves. The severest critic of faction and intrigue in the opposition usually hoped thereby to advance his own prospects and those of his friends. Popular attitudes, however, forbade a candid avowal of political ambition. Even the most eager and resourceful organizer, therefore, was forced to cover his moves with heated denials of self-interest and with bitter imputations of the same offense to his opponents.

The reality of political competition, in spite of official statements which deplored its existence, points to a final set of customs which affected the future of county politics. Since an officeholder's primary job was to serve the republic as a righteous individual, the most effective tactic for a rival office seeker was to attack his competitor's private reputation. The result was a marked tolerance, even a predilection for "gutter politics," or prolonged and intense campaigns of personal vilification, slander, and abuse of opponents by political activists of every stripe. This tendency was widely regretted, and the desire to avoid it lay behind many demurrers of partisan intent. William Gaston, for example, was aggrieved by a personal attack in 1810, and reminded the voters that "in presenting myself to your notice as a Candidate, I cautiously abstained from every remark and every expression which might rouse the furious passions of party." The typical editor promised in the opening number of his newspaper "never to wound the sensibility of private character." [39] In the heat of battle, however, these pledges were frequently forgotten. Extreme bitterness often erupted between politicians, sometimes from a loss of temper and sometimes as a deliberate campaign tactic.

Instances of the appetite for personal slander are not hard to find. Extended quotation from some of the newspaper and broadside wars of the period can help us to appreciate the quality of language that was used in these disputes and the intensity of emotion which they aroused. In 1827, for example, John A. Cameron accused Edward J. Hale of inconsistency. During the same generation, Ralph Waldo Emerson advised Americans that "a foolish consistency is the hobgoblin of little minds," but Editor Hale viewed the matter differently.

> With nothing to lose himself [Hale said of Cameron], he is the proper instrument to sully the character of others. Degraded to the lowest degree in the estimation of a virtuous community, among whom he once held the highest station, his character would afford a fit subject for the pen of a Milton to sketch a fallen Angel. We do not mean to sully our columns with a detail of the lights and shadows of his life—with a view

39. Gaston, "To the Freemen," July 24, 1810; Fayetteville *North Carolina Journal*, May 17, 1826; John Chalmers Vinson, "Electioneering in North Carolina, 1800–1835," *North Carolina Historical Review*, XXIX (1952), 171–88.

of what he was, what he might have been, and what he is. And we only alluded to his character now because he has dared to call in question our political integrity! He![40]

Hypersensitivity and a willingness to answer personal abuse in kind were not limited to editors. A quotation from a handbill of Charles Fisher of Salisbury illustrates the power of these qualities among candidates, and the process by which slander worked itself into a canvass. Fisher was running for the House of Commons in 1833. His first handbill, dated June 25, 1833, outlined a calm program for a constitutional convention, railroad construction, and a new state bank. None of these should have been controversial in Rowan County, but Fisher warned his readers that certain persons in Salisbury would attempt to malign him. He was not mistaken, and by the time his third circular appeared on August 6, Fisher was proving himself no amateur in the arts of counterdefamation. His special target was "that miserable creature, A. G. Carter."

> This intermeddling creature A. G. Carter attempts to justify his assaults on my character by saying that I have attacked him at public meetings; but he does not tell that he first commenced the work;—he does not tell, that without a single word of offense on my part, he took his horse, and scoured the county defaming and abusing me. Never until I was assured of this from many sources did I mention even the name of this heartless being, and even then I ask, who acted most like a man,—I who exposed his conduct in open day before public companies, where all could see and hear, or *He* who went about defaming me at private houses, and in secret places? This malignant creature commenced his dirty work against Jno. Giles; At Fulton Mr. Giles gave him before the people, a merited castigation, while I was more forbearing with him. Soon after in the spirit of a true spaniel, he licked the hand that inflicted the lash on his back, while he continues to growl at me, who treat him with more lenity.
>
> In his vulgar hand-bill, he accuses me of almost every offence he can think of, and as might be expected he has not told a single truth in the whole. The fact is, he wished to make me out very bad, and to do this, he had only to look on himself, and draw from his own picture.[41]

The same level of abuse could be found among the friends of political candidates as among the politicians themselves. In 1829, the supporters of Edmund Deberry for Congress said of his opponent that "it is not easy to speak of the character of Mr. Cameron in the terms of decency and moderation." John

---

40. Fayetteville *Carolina Observer*, October 18, 1827.
41. Charles Fisher, "To the Freemen of Rowan County," June 25, 1833, and "To the Freemen of Rowan County," August 6, 1833 (Broadsides in the North Carolina Collection).

Cameron's followers struck back by saying that Deberry's defender "has given indulgence to the most malignant passion of the human heart to gratify private pique and to revenge personal dislike. And vampire-like," they went on, "he fastens on his prey to glut his vengeance and glories in the destruction of reputation he is making." As Deberry and Cameron went on personally to accuse each other of vainglory and cowardice in the War of 1812, their friends fell to quarreling among themselves over which one was most guilty of "dirty insinuation" or "hyperbolical exaggeration." [42]

In examining the language used by publicists in any extended political quarrel in this period, one is struck by the extraordinarily "thin skin" of the several combatants. No rhetorical extravagance, however absurd, could be brushed off as "just politics." Every ridiculous charge, every unjust accusation, was painstakingly disproved, and, if possible, hurled back at the opposing side. And once the controversy began to grow hot, all participants were at their greatest pains, not to make rational arguments about policy, but, in the language of another handbill from Rowan County, "to support their designs by infamously traducing the character of [a] good man, by a false statement of facts and by erroneous representations." Indeed, the common theme of all these controversialists, aside from their general abusive tone, is their sensitivity to "the purest treasure mortal times afford—a spotless reputation." Charles Fisher took his greatest umbrage at his opponents' attempts "in prejudicing against me the minds of some of my honest Fellow Citizens whose good opinions I value much." [43] The friends of Deberry and Cameron each lunged for the "character" or "reputation" of the other, and similar concern is obvious in all the vast literature of prepartisan political scurrility.

This weakness for petty bickering and character assassination reveals internal tension in political activists. No matter how solemnly publicists proclaimed adherence to the official agenda of politics, their personal feelings were in many ways at war with the code. In spite of declarations to the contrary, the thirst for personal glory was obviously a very powerful motive for political activity. Indeed, judging by their common emotional reaction to political attack, the highest consideration at stake to the participants in these elections was "the estimation of a virtuous community." The true measure of victory was not the legislative program one obtained, or even the vindication of noble principles one achieved, but the respect and admiration one gained in the eyes of one's neighbors. How else can one explain the apparently sin-

42. Fayetteville *Carolina Observer*, July 2, 1829, July 23, 1829, August 6, 1829, August 13, 1829.
43. A Few Citizens of Rowan, "To the Freemen of the Counties of Mecklenberg, Rowan, and Cabarrus," [1810] (Undated broadside in the North Carolina Collection); Fayetteville *Observer*, September 5, 1838; Fisher, "To the Freemen," June 25, 1833.

cere description of electioneering as the product of "the most malignant passion of the human heart," or the fact that Deberry and Cameron continued their public quarrel for months after the election was over?[44] Any attack on personal reputation threatened the most important emotional goals of every public man. Accordingly, private character was simultaneously the most precious asset and the most vulnerable target of a prepartisan politician.

Awareness of the prickly sensibilities of leaders and activists can give a second perspective on the prominence of national issues in North Carolina politics and the reluctance to agitate questions of state and local policy. In spite of a ritual preference for disembodied principles, the emotional meaning of politics was so intensely personal that critics found it difficult to discuss state policy without implicitly deprecating the ability of specific leaders. By the same token, leaders found it hard to interpret such criticism as anything but personal attack.

Seen in this light, the concentration on national topics appears to have been a gentlemen's agreement among politicians to protect each other from their own worst impulses. Private reputation was still so precious that it demanded extraordinary defense, even to the death. Reflections on a man's ability or principles were physically as well as politically dangerous. From disparaging a man's character, it was a very short step to questioning his honor—a step which might lead to the dueling ground. Consequently, Hale's predecessor at the *Observer* was careful to point out that "we cannot give publicity to any thing personal. It not only lowers the dignity of a public journal, but tends greatly to destroy its usefulness, to descend to personalities; and while they cannot benefit the public, they will most certainly injure the publishers."[45] If most contests did not end in bloodshed, it was still possible that in a free-wheeling verbal brawl the reputation of the attacker might suffer as much as that of the one attacked. Rather than incur such a risk, it was often safer to mouth bromides about national politics and avoid any threats to one's position in the community. By denouncing remote or impersonal figures like the president or the tariffites or the abolitionists, one benefited from the fact that these targets could not or would not fight back effectively. On the other hand, if the character or ability of one's opponent seemed too vulnerable to ignore, many strategists decided to descend to the gutter immediately, where any personal discussion was bound to end up eventually, rather than to waste time fencing over taxes or internal improvements.

Prepartisan political culture was thus a serious stumbling block for those who sought state power to promote economic development or for those who

44. Fayetteville *North Carolina Journal*, September 23, 1829.
45. Fayetteville *Carolina Observer*, June 12, 1823.

sought to make politics their trade. The second party system would ultimately become the way around key obstacles for politicians of either tendency, but prepartisan ideology was hardly irrelevant to the system that they later constructed. As we shall see, creative political thinkers retained their beliefs about the sacred character of the state and the corrupting influence of power, but they were able to interpret the events of the 1830s as premonitory signs of power-hungry plots against republicanism itself. They persuaded themselves and their audiences that homeopathic doses of power, discipline, and management would be necessary to stave off a series of far worse abuses. In a nutshell, this was the argument that justified both party formation and also state aid to internal improvements. Key elements of the old political culture were thus employed to devise a significant alternative to it.

Party organization, however, was not primarily an intellectual task. The ideological aspects of party formation did not become ascendant until the second stage in the process. This step was not reached until the limitations of the older political system had appeared in a series of elections that did not fit the ideals of the newspapers or the handbills. In the middle to late 1820s, the preliminary stage of party formation began, as Cumberland voters divided along lines of social cleavage that were not sanctioned by the prevailing ideology. It became obvious that the legitimate agenda of political *discussion* did not always control the actual range of political *behavior*. Throughout its early history, conflicts had appeared in the Cumberland County voting record that transcended the personal rivalries of individuals and the formulae of official ideology. Under the pressure of economic challenges, some of these divisions became more severe. As they did so, the social components of the second party system separated from one another and took on their distinct political identities.

III. A Right to Vote for Who I Pleased
Political Alignments After 1772

The voters of Cumberland County did not always observe the standards of disinterested virtue prescribed by dominant cultural spokesmen. Throughout the prepartisan period, the voters divided over questions which editors and officeholders did not often see fit to discuss. These unsanctioned political controversies punctured the prevailing ideological unity and laid open the underlying divisions of the local social structure. The earliest incident in the county's recorded political history was an instance of such conflict.

Campbellton received the right to choose its first assemblyman in 1765. The charter made all adult white males who lived within two miles of the courthouse eligible to vote, although laws restricted voting in the rest of North Carolina to the owners of fifty acres of land or more. This provision of universal suffrage did not endure for long. Seven years later, thirty-four merchants, freeholders, and other leading men of Campbellton petitioned Josiah Martin, royal governor of North Carolina, to impose a property qualification for the right to vote in town elections. "In a trading Town like Campbellton," they complained, "the Men of property are the fewest in number which must ever throw the power of determining the Election in the Hands of transient persons, Boatmen Waggoners and other Laborers, and take it from their Employers, who are principally interested in securing or improving from their right of Representation, the property of the Town." [1]

Exactly how poor voters damaged property is unknown, but Governor Martin acted promptly to stop them. In his reply to "our faithful Subjects the principal inhabitants of our said town of Campbelton," Martin granted the petitioners' request to limit the franchise to freeholders and the owners of

1. William L. Saunders (ed.), *The Colonial Records of North Carolina* (10 vols.; Raleigh, 1886–90), IX, 79.

houses with chimneys attached.[2] In the next election, the gratified notables bestowed their Assembly seat on William Hooper, an active lawyer and an immigrant from Boston who had signed their original petition and who may indeed have drafted it. Campbellton's labor troubles in 1772 may have been associated with the Regulator uprising in western North Carolina which Martin's predecessor had crushed the year before. As an unpopular attorney in the backcountry courts, William Hooper had been a target of mob violence in the Regulator riot at Hillsborough in 1770.[3] It is also possible that dissident elite members in Cumberland County drummed up a lower-class following for their own purposes, making the challenge to class privileges more symbolic than substantive. In either case, social tensions clearly troubled frontier Campbellton, and men of wealth handled the situation forcefully. They did not rely on indirect methods like social consensus or voluntary deference to keep their employees well-behaved, but simply called on royal authority to strip the poor of political power. Manhood suffrage was no casual matter for the first citizens of Campellton.

Politics and group conflict were evidently coeval in Cumberland, in spite of prevailing values which encouraged citizens and leaders to act solely on the basis of their individual dedication to worthy political principles. In this case, voters divided over property and its perquisites, the ancient feud between the few and the many. The result was the temporary end of a democratic experiment. In the ensuing half century, other controversies would erupt to divide the county's citizens. Revolution, constitution-making, and nation-building impinged directly on the county and each brought solidarity and divisiveness to different groups of citizens. Ethnic rivalries and urban-rural hostility were important lasting forces in county politics. Each of these sources of tension persisted into the Jacksonian period, and each played its role in the creation of political parties.

Cordiality between Governor Martin and the leading men of Campbellton was even more short-lived than the first experiment with broad suffrage. Three years after the governor granted their petition, the townsmen heard of battles between minutemen and redcoats near Boston and of British efforts to array slaves against masters. They responded with the Cumberland Association, an avowal of their willingness to fight the king until the differences between him and themselves should be resolved. "The actual commencement of hostilities against the continent . . ." they declared, "the increase of arbi-

2. *Ibid.*, 80–81.
3. Samuel A. Ashe, "William Hooper," in Ashe *et al.* (eds.), *Biographical History of North Carolina*, VII, 233–44; *Virginia Gazette*, October 25, 1770, reprinted in William S. Powell, James K. Huhta, and Thomas J. Farnham (eds.), *The Regulators of North Carolina: A Documentary History, 1759–1776* (Raleigh, 1971), 252; Lefler and Newsome, *North Carolina*, 185–90.

trary impositions from a wicked and despotic Ministry, and the dread of in-stigated insurrections in the colonies, are causes sufficient to drive an op-pressed people to the use of arms."[4] The spectacle of these "oppressed people" rising up against "the dread of instigated insurrections" among their slaves may strike the modern reader as quaint or worse, but the townsmen were showing their knowledge of eighteenth-century whig theory. The king's legitimate authority did not permit him to become a despot, but the king's transgressions of a well-known catalogue of proscriptions indicated that he was attempting to do just that. Despotism would undoubtedly be oppressive, and subjects could properly resist it.[5] The Cumberland Association was their first step; a year later one of their number went a step further. As a North Carolina delegate to the Second Continental Congress, William Hooper signed the Declaration of Independence.[6]

When they risked their necks for the idea that "all men are created equal," William Hooper and his friends assumed a new relationship to the "Wag-goners Boatmen and other Laborers," to say nothing of their benefactor, Gov-ernor Martin. As in other states, patriot leaders in North Carolina wrote wider suffrage provisions into their new state constitution as part of the effort to attract popular support to the War for Independence.[7] When they regained the ballot in 1776, the laborers of Campbellton did not renew the quarrel with their superiors which royal prerogative had silenced in 1772. Nevertheless, the American Revolution divided North Carolina and Cumberland County deeply. The lower Cape Fear region and the plantation counties of the central coastal plain had supported the independence movement, but the towns and the northeast sound region, which drew their livelihoods from the export of naval stores, harbored many friends of the Empire. In the backcountry, sev-eral groups of outsiders looked to the British for protection from overbearing local majorities. These groups included the members of pietistic sects and some surviving malcontents of the Regulator movement.[8]

No group of backcountry loyalists were more numerous or more important than the Highland Scots of the upper Cape Fear. Centering in Cumberland County, these recent immigrants did not share the language, religion, or so-cial structure of their whiggish neighbors and showed little sympathy for their rebellion. During the war, the Scots were mostly loyalist and furnished hun-dreds of volunteers for loyalist regiments and militia companies.[9] The magni-

4. "The Association," June 20, 1775, in Cumberland Association Papers, Southern Historical Collection.
5. Bailyn, *Ideological Origins*, 55–93.
6. Ashe, "William Hooper."
7. Williamson, *American Suffrage*, 76–116.
8. Robert O. DeMond, *The Loyalists in North Carolina During the Revolution* (Durham, N.C., 1940), 34–61; William H. Nelson, *The American Tory* (London, 1961), 91.
9. DeMond, *Loyalists in North Carolina*, 50–52, 90–96, 124–52; Troxler, *The Loyalist Experi-*

tude of their response suggests more than indifference but indeed outright antipathy for Anglo-American settlers. For their part, many of the non-Scottish leaders in and near Campbellton had declared their willingness to fight the king in the Cumberland Association. Many of these townsmen went on to compile distinguished records of military service in the cause of independence. Those merchants who stayed home continued patriotically to accept state and continental paper money of doubtful value.[10]

The Revolution in Cumberland County was consequently an intermittent civil war. In 1776, the Highlanders formed a 1,400-man army to rescue Governor Martin, who had retreated to the safety of a British sloop-of-war in Wilmington harbor. The defeat of this force at Moore's Creek Bridge led to relative military calm in North Carolina until Cornwallis invaded the state in 1780. Military activities in the Cape Fear valley then assumed a pattern of escalating partisan outrages on both sides that did nothing to mitigate the bitterness which earlier fighting had exposed. During 1780, as many as one Cumberland taxpayer in four paid triple or quadruple taxes in preference to swearing an oath to the state or even to submitting a tax return. Authorities on loyalism in North Carolina estimate that between one half and two-thirds of the inhabitants of Cumberland County opposed the success of American independence.[11]

The Scots and the townsmen of Cumberland County had largely fought on opposite sides in the war, but their wartime experience led both groups to support the adoption of the United States Constitution. Patriot legislators expected to finance the war by continued issues of fiat money and by the confiscation and sale of tory property. These policies were equally injurious to the loyalist Scots and to the wary merchants of Fayetteville, who expected their wartime confidence in the state's promises to be upheld. By making the proloyalist clauses of the peace treaty binding upon the states and by forbidding the emission of paper money by the states, the proposed Constitution would outlaw both confiscation and deliberate inflation. Consequently, it is not surprising that most of Cumberland County's representatives supported the Constitution at North Carolina's two ratification conventions.[12]

ence in North Carolina, 5, 21–29; Leonard L. Richards, "John Adams and the Moderate Federalists: The Cape Fear Valley as a Test Case," *North Carolina Historical Review*, XLIII (1966), 17–20.

10. Lucile Johnson and Cathi Dixon, "The Men Who Wrote Their Names in Local History," Fayetteville *Observer*, June 22, 1975, sec. B, p.1. The diarist of the Moravian settlement at Salem in western North Carolina recorded numerous wartime expeditions to Cross Creek to "get rid of Congress money." See Adelaide L. Fries (ed. and comp.), *Records of the Moravians in North Carolina* (11 vols.; Raleigh, 1922–69), III, 1069, 1164, 1169, 1170, 1302–1304, 1325.

11. DeMond, *Loyalists in North Carolina*, 57.

12. *Ibid.*, 169–80; Louise Irby Trenholme, *The Ratification of the Federal Constitution in North Carolina* (New York, 1932), 29–37, 42–47, 141–43, 162–63; Walter Clark (ed.), *The State Records of North Carolina* (16 vols.; Raleigh, 1895–1905), XXII, 29, 48.

A similar pattern of interests also characterized support for the Constitution at the state level in North Carolina. Organizers of the fight for ratification were eastern attorneys with personal and blood ties to commercial and loyalist families. In the courts and in the legislature, men like William Hooper, James Iredell, Samuel Johnston, William R. Davie, and Archibald Maclaine sought to strengthen North Carolina's currency and to soften the impact of antiloyalist legislation. Ratification of the Constitution was a natural outgrowth of these conservatives' course in state politics. Although North Carolina's first ratification convention postponed action on the Constitution, the second gathered in Fayetteville itself and approved the document overwhelmingly. Appropriately, the friends of ratification and commerce met and won their victory in the town's newly-completed Market House.

The supporters of the U.S. Constitution were also the organizers of the Federalist party in North Carolina. Like its Republican or Democratic-Republican rival, the Federalist party originated in Congress and in the first cabinet of George Washington. There, the Federalist supporters of Alexander Hamilton and his policies fought against the Republican admirers of Thomas Jefferson and James Madison. Both parties searched out local supporters in the hinterlands as part of a struggle to settle important questions of national policy. The resulting pattern of political competition constituted the first American party system.[13]

The Federalists supported a strong central government, domestic policies geared to the interests of commerce, manufacturing, and rapid economic development, and foreign policies friendly to Great Britain. Federalists often exhibited a bias in favor of elitism in society and politics. Republicans, by contrast, supported agrarian interests and did not wish to stimulate the economy in novel directions. They tended to admire the achievements of the French Revolution and voiced support for egalitarianism in America and elsewhere. In the South, Republican commitment to equality did not extend to the subject of slavery, and many great planters found that the party's support of agriculture counterbalanced its challenge to the principle of social hierarchy. Eventually, Republicanism became so widely accepted and its particular policies became so diluted by compromise that the party lost its distinctive character. In the so-called Era of Good Feelings which followed the War of

13. Lisle A. Rose, *Prologue to Democracy: The Federalists in the South, 1789–1800* (Lexington, Ky., 1968), 18; DeMond, *Loyalists in North Carolina*, 162–66; Trenholme, *Ratification of the Federal Constitution*, 36, 119–23; Ashe, "William Hooper," 233–44; Saunders (ed.), *Colonial Records*, IX, 80; William Nisbet Chambers, *Political Parties in a New Nation: The American Experience, 1776–1809* (New York, 1963), 34–74. Some authors question whether political parties in the modern sense truly existed during the so-called "first American party system," but the term survives as an expression of convenience. See Robert E. Stalhope, "Southern Federalists and the First Party Syndrome," *Reviews in American History*, VIII (1980), 45–51.

1812, virtually all national politicians of consequence called themselves Republicans.

In North Carolina, the first party system did not lead to an advanced development of political partisanship. Certain politicians became known as Federalists or as Republicans, but others never adopted a party affiliation. Party identification was not widespread among the electorate and party organization was primitive. The very existence of parties was widely agreed to be a sign of political failure among the participants in the system itself. Nevertheless, the influence of Federalists and Republicans on subsequent developments was considerable. The two parties offered a contrast of policies and political styles that held special significance for the politicians who came after them. The experience of an abortive party system and the factors which gave rise to it were therefore very influential for the permanent development of parties in the next generation.

As in North Carolina generally, support for the Constitution in Cumberland County prepared the way for Federalism in the first party system. In 1791, the citizens of the county sent William Barry Grove, their legislator and pro-ratification convention delegate, to the second Congress. Grove defeated the incumbent Timothy Bloodworth, a Wilmington antifederalist and antiloyalist, by 866 votes to 38 in the county. Grove was the stepson of Robert Rowan, a local Revolutionary patriot and leader of Campbellton. Grove was also a wealthy planter and a friend of Fayetteville's commercial aspirations. As early as 1791, he was promoting a canal and other internal improvements to facilitate navigation on the Cape Fear River. Grove stayed in Congress until he retired in 1804. He began to support partisan Federalist measures in 1794 and remained a committed member of the party throughout the rest of his career.[14]

Grove's constituents frequently showed that they shared his sentiments. In 1796, they sent him resolutions from a public meeting approving his vote for funds to implement Jay's Treaty. In 1798, they sent resolutions to Grove and to President Adams praising their firm conduct in the course of the XYZ affair. In 1800, even a rival for Grove's seat proudly assured his audience, "I am what the phraseology of Politicians has denominated a FEDERALIST, or in other words, I am the friend of Order, of Government, and of the present Administration."[15]

14. Richards, "Adams and the Moderate Federalists," 22–23; William Barry Grove to James Hogg, March 17, 1791, in Battle (ed.), *Letters of Macon, Steele and Grove*, 85–86; Rose, *Prologue to Democracy*, 113; Compiled Election Returns, "Congressional," 1791.
15. Halifax *North Carolina Journal*, July 25, 1796; Fayetteville *North Carolina Minerva*, May 19, 1798; Samuel D. Purviance, "To the Freemen of the Fayetteville District," Fayetteville, N.C., July 1, 1800 (Broadside in the North Carolina Collection).

Federalism persisted longer in the upper Cape Fear valley than in any other section of North Carolina. Cumberland County almost always gave its votes to Federalist candidates for Congress and the Assembly until after the War of 1812. In 1808, Federalist presidential elector John Winslow defeated his Republican opponent by 704 votes to 34. When William Barry Grove retired, William Martin, Samuel Purviance, and Archibald McBryde were his Federalist successors. As late as 1816, a "Federal Republican" editor complained when Democrats dared to claim George Washington as one of their own. It was not until 1821, when Archibald McNeill defeated John Culpepper for Congress, that Cumberland County began an unbroken record of support for Democratic-Republicans.[16]

Precise explanations are elusive, but some evidence suggests that residual bad feeling stemming from the Revolution and Confederation periods influenced the persistence of Federalism long after the party's usefulness as a proponent of particular policies had ended. In 1802, for example, county militia officers defied their Republican brigadier and joined British merchants in Fayetteville on the king's birthday to toast the health of George III. In 1813, apathy over the second war with Great Britain led Fayetteville's Republican editor to complain that "this town and its environs were [only] PARTIALLY illuminated in celebration of Comm. CHAUNSEY'S victory on Lake Erie."[17] Apparently, some citizens still felt fondness for the mother country.

The Federalists of Cumberland County were not without opposition. In 1788 and 1789, three of the county's ten delegates to the ratification conventions had voted against the Constitution. The three antifederalists were large landholders and slaveholders from rural Cumberland who evidently felt no powerful ties either to townsmen or to former loyalists.[18] Subsequent opponents of Federalism presented themselves as American patriots, as friends of the Revolution, as admirers of republican government, and as enemies of upper class domination of politics. In the embryonic state of party development under the first party system, these candidates did not always call themselves Republicans or appeal to national political symbols. They were the nucleus, however, of a Republican tendency in politics that would ultimately displace Federalism in Cumberland County affairs.

In 1800, Jesse Potts came forward as a candidate for presidential elector. His rival William Martin was a Federalist pledged to vote for John Adams.

16. Compiled Election Returns, "Congressional," 1791–1821; Fayetteville *Carolina Observer*, 1816.
17. Raleigh *Minerva*, July 20, 1802; Raleigh *Register*, July 27, 1802; Fayetteville *American*, October 22, 1813; Richards, "Adams and the Moderate Federalists," 21.
18. William C. Pool, "An Economic Interpretation of the Ratification of the Federal Constitution in North Carolina," *North Carolina Historical Review*, XXVII (1950), 293, 457.

Publicly, Potts only promised to vote "according to the best information he could find on the subject," but he was actually an admirer of France and of Thomas Jefferson, the Republican candidate.[19] Jefferson won most of North Carolina's votes, but in the Fayetteville district Potts confronted a strong body of political conservatism and Scottish ethnic solidarity. William Boylan, the editor of the Raleigh *Minerva and Anti-Jacobin* passed on this report of the Fayetteville election to a prominent Federalist correspondent. "Martin will have ten-to-one in Cumberland," Boylan wrote. "It was after twelve [noon] before [Boylan's informant] left town & at that time the Scotch were flocking in from all quarters—Several hundred came parading in town following the *bagpipes*—and nothing but piping was heard in town all the morning—this scene was truly mortifying to Pottes Jacobins in that place."[20] Potts himself complained bitterly that he was defeated by "pipe and dance" and publicly declared that he could never win office in the district until he denounced France and Republicanism and called for a hereditary executive or at least a life term for the president. "Then huzza for British influence, British forms, and British laws in America," he concluded. "This done I shall expect to gain popularity in this district."[21]

The experience of another Republican illustrated how the Federalist coalition could occasionally break down and the lengths to which Federalists would go to retain office. Duncan McFarland was an American-born Scot and a Republican from neighboring Richmond County. Known as the "Stormy Petrel" of North Carolina politics, he was constantly in trouble with the law and frequently engaged in furious personal controversies with the respectable Federalist leadership of Cape Fear valley society. William Barry Grove referred to him as "this wretch . . . this beast" and threatened to leave the state if McFarland ever won election to Congress. A correspondent of the Raleigh *Minerva and Anti-Jacobin* declared that "in the low arts of dissimulation, &c., he has hardly his equal; but in the art of gulling he never had an equal." McFarland spoke Gaelic and used the language to entice the Scottish voters away from Federalists like Grove and Samuel Purviance. McFarland ran well against Grove in 1796 but he lost. He carried the county and the district in 1804 when other candidates split the vote against him; in 1806 he carried Cumberland County, but a Federalist from another county carried the district.[22]

19. Delbert Harold Gilpatrick, *Jeffersonian Democracy in North Carolina, 1789–1816* (New York, 1931), 118.
20. William Boylan to Duncan Cameron, November 5, 1800, Cameron Family Papers, Southern Historical Collection, quoted in Rose, *Prologue to Democracy*, 260.
21. J. Potts, "To the Citizens of the Fayetteville District," Raleigh *Register*, November 25, 1800.
22. William Barry Grove to John Steele, May 27, 1803, in H. M. Wagstaff (ed.), *The Papers of*

McFarland's appeal was to ethnicity and not to political ideology. A newspaper writer vainly urged the Scots to "let not personal respect nor friendship, the influence of connections nor the drowsy laudanum of Adulation swerve you from your principles." [23] The closest that McFarland came to a party avowal in his only surviving handbill was to describe the efforts of his opponents as "the late attempts by violent partizans in this district, to degrade the republican form of government." [24] He was very energetic, however, in denouncing his Federalist opponents as tyrannical elitists who kept power by fraud, perjury, and violence. While confined in the Fayetteville jail on assault charges stemming from a political street brawl, McFarland attributed his predicament to lies trumped up by his enemies.

> At the Congressional Election of 1804, it was discovered by a *party* in this district, that all their attempts by false reports, scurrilous libels, and handfuls of tickets, &c. failed. The mortification of this old ruling party in being thus disappointed is more easy to be imagined than described. In order to degrade the first representative who had proved successful in defiance of their opposition [*sic*]. Malice with its envenomed shafts meditated revenge, and any means which would answer that purpose might with safety be resorted to as many of themselves were opulent and in power, besides the advantages of a judicial connexion, no dread of punishment could be entertained. [25]

In a footnote, McFarland explained that by "handfuls of tickets," he meant that in the 1796 election between Grove and himself, the number of ballots counted greatly exceeded the number of voters.

The style as well as the substance of McFarland's accusations support his biographer's contention that he based his success on ethnic appeals and on "constantly agitating the poor against the rich." [26] Evidence from anti-McFarland sources suggests that Federalists continued to expect deference as their due and to fear any sign of insubordination from below. In 1803, one Federalist from the Fayetteville district wrote publicly "that altho' federalism does not make all Vicious men Virtuous, Democracy tends to make all Vir-

John Steele (2 vols.; Raleigh, 1924), I, 386; A Scotchman by Birth But An American By Adoption, "To the Electors of the Fayetteville Division," Raleigh *Minerva; or Anti-Jacobin*, August 1, 1803; Compiled Election Returns, "Congressional," 1796, 1804, 1806; Gilpatrick, *Jeffersonian Democracy*, 169–70.

23. Monitor, "To the Citizens of Fayetteville Division," Raleigh *Minerva; or Anti-Jacobin*, July 18, 1803.

24. Duncan McFarland, "Communication," November 30, 1805 (Broadside in the North Carolina Collection).

25. *Ibid.*

26. Daniel M. McFarland, "Duncan McFarland" (MS in North Carolina Collection).

tuous men Vicious." [27] Five years earlier, Congressman Grove, in the words of David Hackett Fisher, "gave way to a violent panic" over his opponents in a letter to the secretary of war: "In this part of the state . . . we have few grumbletonians and still fewer jacobins. I am persuaded you may with safety confide in us so far as to lend us some of those arms which are and must be useless in their present situation, and may eventually be wanting in the hands of active citizens to keep a certain class of people in order. . . . The arms would be as safe as they are in one of the arsenals, and might be of infinite service in keeping up a proper respect and confidence in the government." [28] It is not hard to believe that men who felt so strongly would not scruple to tamper with electoral processes for the sake of a higher good. At McFarland's request, Congress investigated his electoral defeats in 1803 and 1806, and found widespread abuses throughout the district. On both occasions, the Committee on Elections revealed that many inspectors had not sworn to conduct the elections legally and therefore may have felt no compunction against stealing votes. In 1803, the inspectors in Montgomery County had actually refused to take the proper oath. The abuses in 1806 were so pervasive that Congress vacated the seat and called for new elections. [29] McFarland's character was definitely unsavory in certain respects, but his charges of repeated improper conduct probably contained a strong element of truth.

The experience of Jesse Potts and Duncan McFarland suggests three generalizations about the first party system. First, voters usually divided along ethnic lines. Scottish preference for Federalism may have reflected a cultural affinity for its principles, but nonideological factors were equally important. Otherwise, Duncan McFarland would not have been able to divert the Scots to Republicanism so easily. Second, political debate was heavily influenced by class tensions, even though legislation favoring one class over another was not an important aspect of partisan conflict after the early 1790s. Republicans occasionally called on the hostility of the poor for those who were "opulent and in power," while Federalists appealed to the propertied "friends of order and government." Third, a complex mixture of voluntary deference and coercion marked relations between political leaders and followers. Federalists de-

27. Monitor, "To the Citizens of Fayetteville Division," Raleigh *Minerva; or Anti-Jacobin*, July 18, 1803.
28. William Barry Grove to James McHenry, August 20, 1798, McHenry Papers, Manuscripts Department, Duke University Library, quoted in David Hackett Fisher, *The Revolution of American Conservatism: The Federalist Party in the Era of Jeffersonian Democracy* (New York, 1965), 22.
29. "Contested Election of Samuel Purviance," 389; "Contested Election of John Culpepper, A Representative from North Carolina," December 17, 1807, 10th Cong., 1st Sess., in *American State Papers*, vol. 137, no. 234, pp. 652–54.

manded votes from their social inferiors as a matter of right. Usually these votes were forthcoming, but when they were not, Federalists were prepared to steal them. The use of party structures to attract supporters and to generate group loyalties was almost nonexistent. Evidence from a town election of 1810 throws more light on these suggestions and tends to support all three of them.

The 1810 election for Fayetteville's representative to the House of Commons pitted Henry Branson against John A. Cameron. In the surviving evidence on this election, neither candidate expressed a party affiliation. Cameron referred to himself as a Federalist in other situations, however, and his supporters were the leading Federalists of Fayetteville. Jesse Potts, the Jeffersonian candidate for elector in 1800, supported Branson, and other evidence on the election suggests that Branson was the candidate of a Republican coalition, even though he eschewed a party label.

Though they viewed the election from drastically different perspectives, supporters of both sides agreed that it was a fairly typical example of town elections in the early national period. As one Federalist insisted, "the late Election for Town Representative for the Assembly was conducted with as little bustle, and with as much apparent propriety as our Town Elections, generally, are, when there is any contention." Branson's friends believed that "the Election was carried by storm," but as Jesse Potts said, "I never saw a fair Election for a Town Member since I lived in Town for twenty years past." [30] The election is a good example of the bitter rivalry that could erupt in Fayetteville's early political system even though party structure and identity were extremely primitive.

Henry Branson was a moderate property owner on the way up, but his surviving autograph letters show that he was not highly educated. He thought of himself as a champion of the underdog, or as he put it many years afterward, "I hope I shall always feald for the opressed." He owned four slaves at the time of the election. Seven years later he was the owner of a riverboat and a sawmill and was the president of the Cape Fear Navigation Company, the local river improvement corporation. [31] Branson was not accepted as the candidate of Fayetteville's Federalist elite. This group supported the same man who later became editor of the *North Carolina Journal*, John A. Cameron. Since he was only twenty-two, it is not altogether surprising that Cameron owned no slaves and paid no taxes in 1810. He apparently met the property

30. Depositions of Duncan MacRae and John Shaw, November 10, 1810, and Jesse Potts, November 23, 1810, all in Legislative Papers, Box 245.
31. Henry Branson to Thomas Ruffin, November 28, 1829, in J. G. deRoulhac Hamilton (ed.), *The Papers of Thomas Ruffin* (4 vols.; Raleigh, 1918), I, 529; Fayetteville *American*, January 19, 1817, February, 1817, July 23, 1818.

requirement for officeholding with a pair of backdated deeds for land sold to him at a nominal price by William Barry Grove.[32] Cameron's lack of wealth did not deprive him of elite support; according to one Cameron supporter, "he was unwilling to offer himself as a candidate until he was almost compelled to do so by several of the principal men of the town who all promised to support his election."[33] Cameron's education, occupation, family connections, and possibly his personal qualities may have compensated for his modest economic circumstances. Cameron won the election of 1810 by 119 votes to 88. Henry Branson thought he had been cheated of victory and challenged the election before the House of Commons. The dozens of depositions which both candidates submitted as evidence to the House committee on elections are a rich source of information on early political practices in Fayetteville.

Branson made three principal charges. He complained that Cameron received votes from "British Subjects who refuse to do Millatary Duty and who have not taken the oath of Allegiance agreeable to the Constitution and Laws of North Carolina." Branson also alleged that ballots were taken from nonresident and underage persons and even from slaves. Most important, Branson claimed that "persons who aided in [Cameron's] Election used force and violence and Compelled a number of persons to vote Contrary to their wishes or intentions and that Printed Tickets and Private marks were made use of to effect their purposes which is Contrary to the spirit and meaning of the Constitution and Laws of this state."[34]

Branson was right about the private marks. The ballots cast in the election were included in the evidence; most of Cameron's tickets show a distinct pen stroke on the back. A Branson witness reported a meeting of Cameron's friends who discussed marking the ballots in order to keep track of promised votes as they were placed in the ballot box, and the suggestion was apparently carried out.[35] Branson was less successful in proving his other charges. He did not even present evidence of alien voting. For all the voters he challenged on grounds of nonresidency, a Cameron witness came forward to refute the charges or at least to confuse the issue. A similar pattern of testimony blunted Branson's efforts to prove physical intimidation of voters. A Branson supporter accused Simeon Belden, John Matthews, and Angus Murchison of dragging men upstairs to vote for Cameron, but Cameron witnesses all denied the charges. Economic reprisals against Branson voters were casually admit-

32. Certificate of Robinson Munford, November 24, 1810, in Legislative Papers, Box 245.
33. Deposition of Isaac Cushing, November 10, 1810, in Legislative Papers, Box 245.
34. H. Branson, "Mr. John 'A' Cameron take notice . . . ," September 28, 1810, in Legislative Papers, Box 245.
35. Ballots with Deposition of Robinson Mumford, Clerk of Court, November 19, 1810, and Deposition of Donald MacLeod, Jr., November 24, 1810, both in Legislative Papers, Box 245. A hand-drawn line appears on the back of 68 out of Cameron's 119 ballots.

ted, however. As John McMillan, a justice of the peace and a Cameron supporter, acknowledged, "I do not recollect having threatened any person previous to the day of the election, [but] I do afterwards in one or two instances conceive I had a right to give my work to whom I pleased." [36]

Ultimately, Cameron kept his seat. His friends' transgressions were apparently not flagrant enough to justify a new election. [37] But the picture of the election which emerges from the depositions is dominated by biased inspectors, drunken and possibly intimidated electors, diligent poll workers who guided every "safe" voter to the polls under close observation, and a propertied alliance in favor of John A. Cameron, the Federalist candidate.

Both sides asserted that Cameron's friends were the most powerful men in Fayetteville. Larkin Newby, for example, was a pro-Branson election inspector who accused Simeon Belden and David Anderson of interfering with the election. "I was repeatedly both interrupted and insulted while in the exercise of my duty," he complained. Branson's friends had also exceeded propriety, he admitted, but "Mr. Camerons friends interfered more than Mr. Bransons . . . [because] they were of that standing in society which they thought entitled them to dictate." [38] Isaac Cushing was more specific. He quoted Belden as boasting that he had worked harder and more effectively for Cameron "than most any other one as he was firstly one of the Wardens of the Poor and 2ly [secondly] a magistrate and was consequently acquainted with many of the low or poor classes of people—and further that he believed that by his influence . . . he had been the means of gaining 10 or 15 on Mr. Camerons side which would otherwise have voted against him." [39] Speaking for himself, Simeon Belden denied any impropriety but blandly acknowledged that "Mr. Cameron had the great proportion of men of standing & respectability in town on his side." But since Cameron's supporters included "men of much more influence than myself" they were the ones who would have twisted arms, not he. Besides, Belden asked, why didn't the ten or fifteen "coerced" voters come forward and speak for themselves? The only effective case of coercion Belden admitted seeing on election day concerned a free black man who wanted to vote for Cameron but did not after being threatened by his landlord and employer, Captain Alexander McDonald. [40]

The only readily available index for the wealth of the participants in this controversy is slave ownership. The 1810 census supports the impression that

---

36. Depositions of John Shaw, November 10, 1810, John McLerran, November 12, 1810, and John McMillan, Esq., November 10, 1810, all in Legislative Papers, Box 245.
37. "Report of Committee of Privileges & Elections on the Memorial of Henry Branson," n.d., in Legislative Papers, Box 245.
38. Deposition of Larkin Newby, October 11, 1810, in Legislative Papers, Box 245.
39. Deposition of Isaac Cushing, November 10, 1810.
40. Deposition of Simeon Belden, November 12, 1810, in Legislative Papers, Box 245.

Branson's friends were men of moderate property at most, while the leaders of Cameron's friends were wealthy. Larkin Newby owned two slaves, Jesse Potts owned four, John Shaw owned four, and Captain McDonald owned none. Isaac Cushing, a blacksmith employed by David Anderson, owned one. Simeon Belden only owned four slaves, but David Anderson owned twenty-eight, John McMillan owned thirty-six, and William Barry Grove owned twenty-two. Of the other Cameron supporters who were accused of impropriety, John Eccles owned twenty-two slaves, Duncan MacRae owned six, John Matthews owned twelve, and Dillon Jordan owned seventeen.[41]

Branson also challenged a number of Cameron voters on grounds of non-residency. These men were a motley collection of drifters and casual laborers who occupied an opposite position in society from the Cameron leadership. They included the boat hands "Little Hector." McDonald, Daniel ("Suza") McIntyre, and "Old Murdoch" McLeod. Daniel Chisholm, an occasional sawmill worker, William Godfrey, an army recruit, and Rasha Hammonds, a sharecropper, also voted for Cameron. None of these men had a firmly fixed address.[42] Another significant bloc of Cameron votes came from the free blacks and mulattoes who gathered behind Mallett's Mill on election day to enjoy spirits and roast pig at merchant John McLerran's expense and who then marched to the polls under white supervision to vote for John Cameron.[43] The Federalist's supporters came from the top and the bottom of Fayetteville's social spectrum; Branson's friends apparently clustered near the middle.

How did Fayetteville's elite attract the votes of their social inferiors? John McLerran's barbecue was one obvious answer, John McMillan's layoffs were another, and Simeon Belden's heavy hand as warden of the poor was a third. Historians of Federalism, however, have often pointed beyond treating and threats as sources of political support to the voluntary deference of humbler men to the natural leaders of society. Unanimous popular support for upper class leaders was not unknown in the upper Cape Fear valley; William Barry Grove's 886-to-38-vote win over Timothy Bloodworth in 1791, and John Winslow's 704 votes over Alexander Rowland's 34 in 1808 were two prominent examples of this phenomenon.[44] Indeed, Federalists have often been described as unbending aristocrats who would not stoop to vulgar vote-catching tricks, whether honorable or not, but depended almost entirely on deference

41. U.S. Manuscript Census Returns, Population Schedule, Cumberland County, North Carolina, 1810, pp. 235–40; Fayetteville *People's Friend*, December 15, 1815; Deposition of John Shaw, November 10, 1810.
42. Depositions of William Cook, November 9, 1810, Jesse Potts, November 23, 1810, Nathan Pearce, November 24, 1810, all in Legislative Papers, Box 245.
43. Depositions of Lucretia Bass and William Denton, November 24, 1810, both in Legislative Papers, Box 245.
44. Compiled Election Returns, "Congressional," 1791, 1808.

to maintain themselves as the heads of government and society. When younger Federalists attempted to recoup losses by imitating the electioneering appeals of their Republican opponents, it was already too late to salvage the party's withered strength, and Federalism perished before the hosts of the rising common man.[45]

The Cameron-Branson contest and other elections in the upper Cape Fear valley, however, revealed Federalists who did not plead for votes but who did not stand aloof either. They sought votes aggressively by methods that did not compliment the electorate's faculty for rational choice.[46] Either they beguiled the voters with music and whiskey, or they coerced voters with threats of economic reprisal, or in the last resort, they sometimes stuffed the ballot box. It is possible, of course, that Federalists would have won most elections without resorting to dubious methods. They had, after all, a strong fund of ethnic and wartime sentiments to draw on for support. But fraudulent practices could be costly, as John Culpepper's friends discovered when Duncan McFarland succeeded in having Congress overturn the results of the 1806 congressional election. It seems unlikely that such risks would be run without a conviction of their necessity. Nevertheless, voluntary deference was also a factor in Federalist success. The case of one disputed voter in the Cameron-Branson contest allows us to observe the process at work. Deference apparently existed, but its influence was strongly challenged by countervailing social pressures.

Miles Hussey was a literate white man between the ages of twenty-six and forty-five who had lived in Fayetteville for five years before the 1810 election. He owned no real property and paid no taxes, but he and his wife, their three young children, and an older white woman shared their home with a free colored person who was probably a tenant or a servant.[47] Hussey was neither an aristocrat nor a derelict. Henry Branson's friends may have felt they had a natural claim on his vote, but Miles Hussey wanted to vote for John Cameron. According to Simeon Belden, Hussey felt the need of a patron to protect his right to vote freely. "I saw him about sunrise on the morning of the Election," Belden recalled later. "He told me he would call at my Store about eleven oclock to go and vote for Mr. Cameron and begged I would be there to go with him as he was afraid he would otherwise be pulled and hauled about by Mr. Bransons friends."[48]

At eleven o'clock, Hussey did not find Belden at his store but met him at the bottom of the steps leading to the polling place. "Come let us go up and

45. Fisher, *Revolution of American Conservatism*, 179–81.
46. Rose, *Prologue to Democracy*, 260.
47. U.S. Manuscript Census Returns, Population Schedule, Cumberland County, North Carolina, 1810, p. 240.
48. Deposition of Simeon Belden, November 12, 1810.

vote," Belden said and led the way upstairs. At the top, Hussey remembered, "John Shaw took hold of me and said to me come go with me I want to tell you a secret. . . . He caught of me and was pushing me [and] I thought he wanted me to vote for Mr. Branson." Belden grabbed Hussey's other arm and the hapless voter became the object of a tug of war, the Republican hauling him one way and the Federalist hauling him the other. As slaveholders, Shaw and Belden were both Hussey's social and economic superiors. To whom should he defer? Hussey stood by his commitments; he resisted the Republican with the classic protest of a democratic individualist. "I told John Shaw I was a free man and had a right to vote for who I pleased." [49]

John Shaw did not give up until Belden intervened again. "He was extremely rude and insolent," Belden testified, but "I remonstrated sharply that I did not interfere with him or any of Mr. Branson's friends and begged him in future to desist from such conduct. I was not afterwards troubled by him." [50] Miles Hussey's vote was thereby saved for Federalism.

An observer of this incident with a taste for irony might have savored the fact that Miles Hussey claimed the birthright of an equal and independent free man in the context of his client-patron relationship with Simeon Belden, the storekeeper. Hussey's assertion of freedom indicated that the equalitarian ideals of the Age of the Common Man were already felt in 1810. John Shaw implied by his physical interference, however, that free choice was not universally accepted, even among Republicans. Hussey's defense of his freedom by appeals to a stronger patron testified to the continuing importance for some citizens of an enduring social hierarchy. What was true for Miles Hussey was surely true for others as well. Freedom of choice and political equality seem to have coexisted with hierarchy as models for the relationship between voters and leaders and between voters and each other. In Hussey's case, these contrasting ideals seemed to be operating at once in the same individual. The tussle over Hussey's vote was thus an expression of the transitional character of politics in the early national period.

In the years after 1815, North Carolinians and other Americans gradually lost interest in the battles of the first party system. No foreign wars forced the citizens to choose sides among European nations. Victorious Republicans adopted Alexander Hamilton's major programs, and new sources of economic conflict were slow to emerge. In Washington, stolid James Monroe presided over an Era of Good Feelings which featured rife competition between aspirants for the presidency but little controversy over fundamental principles of government. In Raleigh, Archibald D. Murphey attracted attention with his

49. Deposition of Miles Hussey, November 12, 1810, in Legislative Papers, Box 245.
50. Deposition of Simeon Belden, November 12, 1810.

dazzling plans for a network of internal improvements and a state-supported system of common schools. In both capitals, an antiparty ideology prevailed against the primitive institutions of partisanship and no new party system rose to replace the old one.

In Cumberland County, political activity followed developments elsewhere. A Fayetteville editor founded the *Carolina Observer* in 1816 to carry the torch for "federal republicanism," but his initiative found few followers. As the paper changed hands repeatedly, political discussion entirely dropped out of its columns.[51] The events of the preceding decades, however, had left enduring resentments which the end of organized opposition could not eliminate. Voters continued to divide in traditional blocs that would have crucial bearing on the next wave of party organization.

One obvious pattern of continued cleavage was geographical. The surviving congressional election returns for the seventh district, to which Cumberland County belonged, show that from 1791 to 1833, the majority of the county's votes went to a resident of Cumberland or the adjoining county of Moore in every election but two. For the most part, this geographical loyalty overlapped with ethnic and partisan loyalty. In the same period, Cumberland gave its votes to a candidate with a Scottish name eleven times; before 1821, almost all successful candidates for Congress called themselves Federalists.[52]

When Federalism began to lose popularity, geographical splits in voting patterns persisted. After 1806, John Culpepper was the favorite son of the western counties in the seventh district. Culpepper was a native of Anson County and a Federalist, but he was never popular in Cumberland. Scottish voters may have been repelled by the fact that Culpepper was a Baptist minister who embraced the Great Revival, while local Presbyterians still steered by the old light. Even in the heyday of Federalism, Cumberland voters had preferred men like William Barry Grove, Archibald McBryde, and Alexander McMillan, who were their neighbors, rather than Culpepper. After 1821, when Culpepper's opponents began to call themselves Republicans instead of Federalists, the county's support never wavered. The voters continued to oppose Culpepper and to favor his rivals by lopsided majorities. The transition from one party label to another was thus made easier by a continuity in geographical alignments and by the fact that Federalism had become identified with an unpopular individual. After Archibald McNeill, a Republican, defeated Culpepper in 1821 by 1,036 votes to 156, the county majority followed candidates of that party, and its Democratic successor, for the remainder of the antebellum period. Geographical alignments also persisted elsewhere in

51. Fayetteville *Carolina Observer*, August 22, 1816, and *ff.*
52. Compiled Election Returns, "Congressional," 1791–1833.

the district, as the western counties continued to support Culpepper the Federalist and later Edmund Deberry, a Whig from Montgomery County.[53] In 1829, a newspaper writer explained Deberry's unpopularity in Cumberland by the fact that "it is the wish of many people of the County, the expressed wish of not a few of them, *to break down the power of the Western Counties of the District*, and get a representative from *this* county."[54]

After the second party system was well established, Cumberland voters supported any Democrat over any Whig, regardless of residential considerations. Thus William Morris, a Democrat of Anson County who was a Baptist minister like Culpepper, carried Cumberland 918 to 426 against Deberry in 1839, only to lose in the district by 896 votes. In this election the citizens of Anson showed the same degree of partisanship as those of Cumberland by voting in their usual proportions for the Whig rather than the local candidate.[55]

The presidential election of 1824 was a further example of the influence of ethnicity and persistent loyalties from the first party system. When Andrew Jackson received North Carolina's electoral vote in that year, he benefited from a coalition of disaffected politicians who banded together in the so-called "People's Ticket," and ran as electors pledged to vote for whichever candidate would be most likely to defeat the front-running "caucus candidate," William H. Crawford of Georgia. Crawford's support in North Carolina came from Old Republicans in the eastern plantation counties. In the aftermath of the Missouri crisis, they feared the effects on slavery of any activist philosophy of government and favored Crawford's reliable stand on this question. Imitating their counterparts in Washington, the Crawford men in the North Carolina legislature nominated him in a Republican caucus. In the ensuing election, the state divided neatly on geographical lines. Crawford 'took the east, but the west and the numerical majority went to the People's Ticket.[56]

A vote for the People's Ticket in this election is usually interpreted as a vote for Jackson, but in some counties, this was not the case. In Cumberland, People's Ticket voters marked their ballots with a preference for John Quincy Adams or Andrew Jackson. Out of the 568 votes for the People's Ticket, Ad-

53. Catherine Barden Matthews, "John Culpepper: A Biographical Sketch," 1975 (MS in North Carolina Collection); *Biographical Directory of the American Congress, 1774–1971*, (Washington, 1971), 810–11, 841, 1357, 1389, 1392; Compiled Election Returns, "Congressional," 1791–1860.
54. Fayetteville *Carolina Observer*, July 23, 1829.
55. Fayetteville *Observer*, June 5, 1839; Compiled Election Returns, "Congressional," 1839.
56. Albert Ray Newsome, *The Presidential Election of 1824 in North Carolina*, James Sprunt Studies in History and Political Science, vol. 23, no. 1 (Chapel Hill, 1939), 73–75, 83–104, 160–64.

Table 4. 1824 Presidential Vote by Precincts with Indicators of Wealth and Ethnicity

Precinct name	Adams	Jackson	Crawford	Percent Scottish Names[a]	Wealth per Taxpayer[a]	Predominant soil type
Barbecue	42	12	1	77.3	$ 218.87	sandhills
D. Smith's[b]	54	0	3	82.0	225.75	sandhills
Christian's[c]	0	36	2	10.7	398.38	sandy loam
Newberry's[d]	6	19	1	2.7	458.62	sandy loam
Averasborough	33	14	34	15.0	735.46	sandy loam
Fayetteville	168	169	124	16.2	1,320.71	sandy loam
TOTAL	303	250	165	36.3	625.68	—

[a]These data are taken from table 2. Irregularities in nineteenth-century recording barred compilation of these statistics from the tax list of 1824, or from any closer year.
[b]Located in Quewhiffle district.
[c]Located in Buckhorn district.
[d]Located in Willis Creek district.
SOURCE: *Carolina Observer*, November 18, 1824.

ams got 303 endorsements and Jackson got 250. The remainder were scattered or showed no preference. The Crawford ticket received 165 votes.[57] Table 4 shows the distribution of votes by precincts.

The two Scottish precincts gave most of their votes to Adams, and two non-Scottish precincts gave their votes for Jackson. Fayetteville and the wealthy rural district of Averasborough divided their votes among the candidates. Strictly speaking, to conclude from table 4 that Adams voters tended to be poor Scots just because the Massachusetts candidate got heavy support from poor Scottish districts would be an example of the ecological fallacy. In this case, where the ethnic and political majorities were overwhelming, it is hard to escape the conclusion that Adams swamped Jackson among poor Scottish voters. These data controvert a venerable tradition in American political history, which links the interests and the votes of the "common man" with the antifederalists, the Democratic-Republicans, and the Jacksonian Democrats. In Cumberland County, we see small Scottish farmers living on some of the worst land in the state, supporting first the loyalists, then the Federalists, and finally the ex-Federalist, John Quincy Adams. As long as the Revolutionary experience itself remained the central point of reference for county politics, the ethnic divisions of the 1770s would persist. When new social and economic issues emerged to pit the country against the town, Scottish voters would find it easier to assimilate politically with their non-Scottish neighbors.

The election statistics do not suggest what divided Adams voters from Jackson men in the town of Fayetteville. Some surviving correspondence suggests, however, that the social resentments that divided voters in the town election of 1810 were still alive in 1824. In August of that year, William Cameron, the brother of John A. Cameron and the cashier of the Fayetteville branch of the Bank of the United States, wrote to his brother Duncan in Orange County. There were three candidates, he said, in the upcoming election for town member. They were "John Eccles, Jr., John Matthews, and Mr. Martin, a retailer of whiskey and onions in one of the shops on Hay Street." Eccles and Matthews were both Federalist veterans of the campaign to elect John Cameron to the legislature in 1810. William Cameron did not believe that such a person as Mr. Martin could aspire to official dignity on his own. He speculated instead that Martin had been put up as part of an upper class trick to draw votes away from John Matthews. "The respectable part of the community," he explained, "will support Eccles; but as they are unfortunately the smallest, it will not answer his purpose, unless he can get some of the other class to throw their weight in the scale." [58]

57. Fayetteville *Carolina Observer*, November 18, 1824.
58. William Cameron to Duncan Cameron, August 11, 1824, in Cameron Family Papers.

For his part, the snubbed "retailer of whiskey and onions" professed to see things differently. In a newspaper advertisement, John B. Martin connected presidential and municipal politics and based his candidacy on an appeal to artisans and other workers. "I am a candidate," he affirmed, "and I beg such of my friends as can read the newspapers, to name to their neighbor who can't read, particularly to the mechanic and laboring man, and to the friend of General Jackson, that if he wants a representative who knows his interest and will not be ashamed to come forward in support of it, that John B. Martin is at his service." [59] Martin's appeal was the first suggestion that the white workers in Fayetteville's mills and docks favored Jackson. The editor of the *Carolina Observer*, on the other hand, encouraged the notion that the upper classes would choose Adams. He quoted the Philadelphia *Gazette* that "a great majority of such of our citizens as may be truly styled 'the reading and reflecting part' prefer Mr. Adams." The editor added that the quotation was "applicable to almost every state of the union." [60] An alignment of illiterate laboring men against "reading and reflecting" elite members cannot be proved beyond question for 1824 even though such a pattern would conform to the long-standing tradition of political competition between classes that extended beyond the election of 1810 to before 1772. If presidential preferences did not follow class lines in this election, Cameron's and Martin's statements both suggest that recurrent resentments between rich and poor were still significant in municipal politics.

Although class feeling may have had some part in distinguishing Jackson voters from Adams supporters, it did not drive the two groups entirely apart. They remained together as allies against the caucus forces of William H. Crawford. Although he did not carry any precinct, the votes Crawford did receive came exclusively from Fayetteville and from the plantation village of Averasborough. His low tariff and strict construction program may have attracted votes from planters in both precincts who were hostile to any economic or constitutional threat to slavery. It is hard to be sure, because no friend of Crawford in the county left a record of the reasons for his support.

On the eve of the second party system, Cumberland County voters had no habit of expressing their differences in regular and organized competition between political parties. Persistent patterns of conflict did exist, however, which divided voters along geographical, ethnic, and class lines. These three traditional lines of cleavage would continue to be important in the emergence of mass political parties. During the 1820s, a fourth source of conflict emerged which eventually surpassed them in importance. This was a conflict between Fayetteville and the countryside. It first appeared clearly in 1829.

59. Fayetteville *Carolina Observer*, August 8, 1824.
60. *Ibid.*, July 15, 1824.

The country spokesman in this conflict was Archibald McDiarmid, who came from a distinguished Scottish family in rural Cumberland, and owned 1,999 acres of land in the sandhills district of Seventy-first. His father, Angus McDiarmid, had been a minister of one of the oldest Presbyterian churches in the county and a determined opponent of the revival movement that had flared at the turn of the century. His brother Daniel was clerk of the county court and later became one of the richest men in the county and state senator from Cumberland. In 1829, Archibald McDiarmid had already served two terms in the House of Commons and was running for his second term in the Senate. In time, he would be a leading member of the Democratic party, serving a total of four terms in the Senate. He died in a political duel in 1846. As a candidate in 1829 he was the bulwark of rural interests.[61]

As the champion of Fayetteville, James Seawell had a very different background. Although he later went bankrupt, he paid taxes in 1829 on sixteen slave polls, three lots in Fayetteville, and 3,380 acres of land in the county with an assessed valuation that totaled $3,800. He was the owner and builder of two steamboats, one of which was the first to operate on the Cape Fear River, and a leading incorporator of the Clarendon Bridge Company, which built and maintained a toll bridge across the Cape Fear. Seawell was also the president of the Cape Fear, Yadkin and Pedee Rail Road, which sought to connect Fayetteville with the town of Salisbury and the Yadkin valley to the west. He lived in Fayetteville and was serving as its magistrate of police (the equivalent of mayor) when he led the campaign against Archibald McDiarmid. Like McDiarmid, Seawell had supported Jackson in 1828, but by 1834, Seawell was a prominent leader of the Whig party in Fayetteville.[62]

Throughout his career Seawell was always a resourceful promoter. After bankruptcy he retreated with his family to Mississippi. Writing from Columbus to a Mobile banker, he confidently requested a loan of five or six thousand dollars with no security, on the grounds that he had conceived "a system of operations in the money relations of the country that cannot fail to produce without hazard a fortune of the greatest magnitude." He was writing in the fall of 1838, a time of severe monetary stringency.[63]

In the form and variety of his interests no less than in his ebullience, James Seawell represented progress and the town, and personally embodied all the bright promises and all the serious dangers of expansive commercial capital-

61. Cheney (ed.), *North Carolina Government*, 287, 289, 290, 292, 308, 310, 817; Cumberland County List of Taxables, 1829, in Cumberland County Records; Ernest Trice Thompson, *Presbyterians in the South* (3 vols.; Richmond, 1973), I, 315; Oates, *The Story of Fayetteville*, 623–24. The family name was also spelled "McDearmid."
62. Cheney (ed.), *North Carolina Government*, 243, 245, 246, 262, 264, 301, 303; Cumberland County List of Taxables, 1829, in Cumberland County Records; Fayetteville *Carolina Observer*, July 8, 1834; Oates, *The Story of Fayetteville*, 108, 178, 193.
63. James Seawell to Michael J. Kenan, November 18, 1838, in Kenan Papers.

ism. Seawell's kind of progress was threatening to rural Cumberland because it pointed the way to public debt, high taxes, and the consequent loss of civic and private independence. A quarrel soon erupted between the promoter and the preacher's son, even though their dispute was only incidental to the 1829 elections. McDiarmid was unopposed for the Senate. Seawell was running for the House of Commons, but he used his campaign as a vehicle to attack McDiarmid's voting record in the last year's session of the General Assembly.

In that session, western legislators had introduced a bill to construct a road at state expense from Wilkesborough, a foothills village in the northwestern part of the state, to Fayetteville, 176 miles away. Maintenance would be borne by the inhabitants who lived within three miles of the road. The state engineer estimated that the road would cost $63,200. Archibald McDiarmid objected strongly to the proposal, so the sponsors amended it to read that the road would extend from Wilkesborough all the way to the Cumberland County line and then stop. Presumably users of the road would continue their way to Fayetteville via the existing county roads. The exemption of McDiarmid's constituents did not satisfy the Cumberland senator. When the bill was taken up by the lawmakers, he moved to postpone its consideration indefinitely. In spite of opposition, the bill passed the Senate only to die in the House. It was McDiarmid's conduct in the episode that defined the major issue of the campaign.[64]

This debate over McDiarmid and the road was conducted on the hustings and also in a series of letters written by both candidates and their friends to the editor of the *Carolina Observer*. In its course several themes emerged which had bearing on political development in the county. On one level the argument between the two groups of writers dealt strictly with matters of economic interest. Fayetteville wanted a road that the country would have to pay for. McDiarmid, as the rural representative, refused to cooperate and the battle was on. On the second level the debate represented an introduction of new grounds for political dispute. McDiarmid, an old-fashioned man in many of his ideas and attitudes, was indignant at what he felt were the improper tactics of the opposition in holding him accountable for what he had or had not done to enrich his constituents. To offer the voters a financial reward in exchange for a term in the Senate resembled to him a species of bribery. "I have never been in the habit," he snapped, "of making a hobby of any measure for the purpose of obtaining a seat in the Legislature." On the other hand McDiarmid broke some rhetorical ground himself by introducing a charge which later Jacksonians would make a battle cry in the war against the "Monster Bank." "I viewed it [the road] as a violation of individual rights; unequal

64. North Carolina Board for Internal Improvements, *Annual Report* (Raleigh, 1823), 44; Fayetteville *Carolina Observer*, January 8, 1829, July 2, 1829, July 9, 1829, July 23, 1829.

and oppressive in its operation, and calculated to deceive the people." [65] To be sure, traditional grounds of debate were combined with the innovative economic arguments. McDiarmid struck back at Seawell by making insinuations against his character. This aspect of the quarrel moved parallel to the more modern debate about the road, and eventually rang with fervent references to "duplicity," "prevarication," "dissimulation," and "the foul dagger of vindictive falsehood." [66] Nevertheless, the charge which set off these outbursts was qualitatively different from the more routine forms of character assassination familiar from previous elections.

On a third level, the McDiarmid-Seawell debate bespoke the emergence of conflicting cultures in town and country. Several participants wrote as if McDiarmid's opposition to the town was a long-standing matter. In his original announcement of McDiarmid's vote, for example, Edward J. Hale professed to believe, with sarcasm too heavy to miss, that there must be some mistake. "Even if we could harbor the idea that the senator was inimical to the town of Fayetteville (which would be very extraordinary,) we could not believe him insensible to the importance of giving every facility to the planter for bringing his produce to market, or to the importance of drawing trade to our towns, which now goes abroad, and adds to the business and profit of our sister states." [67] McDiarmid's critics went on to charge that since he did not offer amendments to correct the road bill's defects, he was therefore "opposed to improvements, both internal and intellectual." McDiarmid replied by acknowledging that he was generally opposed to "all the visionary schemes projected by those who style themselves the friends of Internal Improvement." He denied that he made no effort to improve the bill. Instead, he had attempted to make the project a self-liquidating toll road that would eventually make a profit for the state. The sponsors refused to accept the idea, he said, because they were selfishly unwilling for the road's beneficiaries to pay its costs. McDiarmid claimed that he did vote to support "projects of general utility which have been commenced, and progressing [*sic*] with reasonable hope of their practicability," but he pointedly did not admit to supporting any new projects. [68] In his final letter of defense McDiarmid repeated his belief that the road as planned would have been unfair and offered as his ultimate justification that "I have not yet conversed with any person who lived beyond the limits of Fayetteville, who disapproved of my conduct."

In later years, acting in his private capacity, Archibald McDiarmid showed considerably more interest in internal improvements than he saw fit to reveal

65. Fayetteville *Carolina Observer*, July 2, 1829.
66. *Ibid.*, July 9, 1829.
67. *Ibid.*, January 8, 1829.
68. *Ibid.*, July 9, 1829, July 23, 1829.

in 1829.[69] Nevertheless his public persona in the contest with James Seawell represented a frame of mind that was very popular with the voters, yet has been generally ignored by historians describing North Carolina's movement away from the somnolence of the "Rip Van Winkle State." If McDiarmid's public statements in 1829 correctly reflected their views, these citizens were stoutly opposed to rapid development, to improvement, and to the social changes they sensed would accompany new economic growth. Moreover, barring federal aid or outside investment, development in North Carolina could be financed successfully only by transferring capital from the rural to the urban economy. McDiarmid probably understood this. By making the venture a toll road and thereby placing the cost of construction and maintenance directly on the merchants and their customers, he would kill the project, for the mercantile community could not support such an expense by itself. McDiarmid's sandhills constituents did not need the road for transportation of their own meager produce. The river and the county roads were sufficient for those purposes.

The senator's manner of opposition showed no conception on his part or on the part of his rural audience that a western road might offer country-dwellers more than transportation. He and they might have anticipated certain intangible benefits associated with a greater flow of people, information, and goods. They might have foreseen benefits like jobs, entertainment, and educational opportunities now associated with proximity to a growing city. If the possibility of these ancillary effects of a western road ever occurred to McDiarmid's supporters, it is quite possible that they regarded those "benefits" as dangers to be avoided, as threats to an agrarian world. In other words, they may have agreed with Thomas Jefferson that "the mobs of great cities add just so much to the support of pure government, as sores do to the strength of the human body." [70] In addition, McDiarmid's father, the stern antirevivalist, may well have bequeathed to his son and his flock a deep-seated suspicion of human projects to improve or profit a man or a community in the things that truly mattered. To such persons the flourishing commerce of Fayetteville and its ambitious entrepreneurs like James Seawell were enemies to be opposed, not fostered.

Interestingly enough, however, McDiarmid's hostility to the town and its culture was not seconded by the counties of the west, which were considerably more isolated and rural than Cumberland. As we have seen, some of these counties were traditionally opposed to Cumberland on political issues. Moreover, to these people Fayetteville was too far away to constitute much of

69. Fayetteville *North Carolina Journal*, February 9, 1837.
70. Thomas Jefferson, *Notes on the State of Virginia*, ed. William Peden (Chapel Hill, 1954), 165.

a threat. On the contrary, the western farmers needed Fayetteville's services as a market center in order to make their isolated rural life supportable. It was not unnatural at all, therefore, for western legislators to favor internal improvements and to fume at the "backwardness" of their eastern counterparts. The sponsor of the Wilkesborough Road, General James Wellborne, deplored the conduct of McDiarmid.

> Why is it that you send men here to represent you, who are so unfriendly to the only commercial town in our state that the Western People have. I would call the greater part of your representation narrow, contracted beings, who are opposed to everything that go to improve Fayetteville. Pray improve in sending men of liberal feelings, and who have a little State pride. . . . I am tired of legislating, and I had hoped that I should live to see the time, when Fayetteville would become a large commercial town, by turning all the *West*, as well as *East* Tennessee and *West* Virginia into our own markets; but God deliver me from *your* politicians.[71]

As matters eventually turned out, Archibald McDiarmid won his war against Fayetteville. He won reelection to the Senate and Seawell got a drubbing in his race for the Commons.[72] Moreover, the road to Wilkesborough was never built. Fayetteville did not get any improved route to the west until over two decades later when a plank road was built to Bethania, 129 miles away. By then, however, it was too late. The western trade turned permanently to the channels offered by the North Carolina Railroad, and Fayetteville's commerce dwindled.[73] This conclusion was not assured by the outcome of one election, however, and the struggle over progress in Cumberland continued to shape its politics in the years to come.

On the threshold of political party formation, Cumberland County government enforced the laws and regulations of its society, but political activity also expressed at least two other sets of concerns. Local notables sought office as a token of approval by their neighbors, and prominent social groups in the electorate vied with each other for superiority at the polls. The system functioned well enough as the expression of a stable pattern of personal and group rivalries, for dominant beliefs allowed little or no expression of a political mandate and office seekers promised nothing more than a preservation of political purity by the power of their personal examples. In other words, po-

71. Fayetteville *Carolina Observer*, July 9, 1829.
72. The totals in the Commons election were McNeill, 704 votes; Buie, 571 votes; Seawell, 271 votes; Massy, 234 votes. McDiarmid was unopposed. Raleigh *Star and North Carolina State Gazette*, August 20, 1829.
73. Robert B. Starling, "The Plank Road Movement in North Carolina," *North Carolina Historical Review*, XVI (1939), 1–22, 147–73.

litical losers had little to fear in the way of material deprivation at the hands of their victorious enemies. Competitions for office tended to become noisy exercises in character assassination which calibrated the status of feuding dignitaries but did little to foster group interests, stable political alignments, or a governmental response to social problems.

Substantial numbers of citizens were unmoved by these personality contests, and voting turnout dropped below the levels reached in the first party system. Only rarely did politicians permit themselves to articulate the geographical, ethnic, and class rivalries that might have stimulated broader popular enthusiasm. Evidence from voting behavior and scattered pieces of other evidence continue to suggest, however, that voters divided over questions that politicians did not always discuss. Cumberland County would not vote for the candidates of Anson and Montgomery counties, regardless of their ideological appeals. Scotsmen voted in a bloc, even though no surviving political appeal mentioned Scottishness as such after 1806. Signs of conflict between merchants and mechanics kept reappearing in 1772, 1810, and 1824.

When political leaders could combine the moral grandeur of national concerns with the immediate personal relevance of these neighborhood voting blocs, the second party system would emerge. The line of local cleavage which became most important in this regard was the dispute between the friends of Fayetteville's commerce and its enemies. The economic pressures which stimulated the emigration movement upset the stable arrangement of normal republican conflicts. Demands for governmental action on internal improvements and similar matters exacerbated rural-urban hostility and led to new insights about the relationships between events in Fayetteville and events on a larger national stage. Local disputes over the principles of political economy came to subsume other conflicts and brought county factions into conformity with national party alignments. This process did not reach its climax until after the election of Andrew Jackson had brought Cumberland County to the appearance of political unity. As local coalitions joined national parties, moreover, the language of politics would change. Antipower and antiparty themes, while never entirely extinguished, became muted under a new strain of partisan rhetoric, and party loyalty appeared strongly in the records of voting behavior.

IV. Andrew Jackson and the Will of the People: The Election of 1828

John Quincy Adams took office in 1825 with an impressive list of qualifications and high ambitions for the future of the nation. The fifth president wanted the federal government to be a powerful instrument for economic and cultural development, and his first annual message requested extensive federal initiatives in foreign policy, domestic affairs, internal improvement, and educational and scientific advancement. "Liberty is power," the president declared, and the conscientious Adams expected to exercise that power to the utmost.[1]

Adams' programs met massive political opposition. The president was already suspected of corruption as a result of his election by the House of Representatives and his subsequent appointment of Henry Clay as secretary of state.[2] If the manner of Adams' election threatened to corrupt the forms of republicanism, his ambitious use of government power pointed to the corruption of its substance. Orator after orator denounced the president and his program. They warned that large federal budgets would create chances for graft and, more important, that the economic changes which Adams envisaged might undermine republican society. Some of Adams' opponents were undoubtedly simple opportunists, but electoral results showed how much voters endorsed their conduct. Perhaps the most flamboyant of Adams' and Clay's critics was Congressman John Randolph of Virginia, who called their partnership a "combination of . . . the Puritan with the black-leg."[3] Most other southern politicians also resisted Adams' administration and joined the effort to defeat him for reelection.[4]

1. Richardson (comp.), *Messages and Papers of the Presidents*, II, 882.
2. Bemis, *John Quincy Adams and the Union*, 71–91, 126–51; Cooper, *The South and the Politics of Slavery*, 5–12.
3. *Register of Debates in Congress*, 19th Cong., 1st Sess., II, 402.
4. Cooper, *The South and the Politics of Slavery*, 5–12.

Andrew Jackson was the candidate of Adams' enemies. The general sought to avenge his defeat in the House in 1824, and charges of "bargain and corruption" dominated his campaign in 1828. Jackson remained silent about his plans for the presidency, but southern supporters agreed that the frontier general and large slaveholder would emphasize primitive purity, martial virtues, and limited government. Jackson appealed to voters all over the country, but especially to residents of the South. He became the only reasonable candidate for Old Republicans to support when William H. Crawford failed to recover his strength.[5]

North Carolina politicians accepted this logic gradually. The electorate had supported a Jacksonian coalition in 1824, but the state's congressmen had given North Carolina's vote to Crawford in the House of Representatives. The Old Republicans held themselves aloof during Adams' administration. In the *Carolina Observer*, Edward J. Hale reminded Crawford's friends that the Georgian had lost the last election "by an unholy alliance of the very parties which are now arrayed against each other, and which at that time had no feelings in common, any more than at present."[6] Former Crawford men like Hale hesitated to link themselves to an unpredictable popular hero, and they also balked at joining the upstarts who had defeated them four years earlier. Adams eventually frightened them far worse than Jackson, and by 1828, most of the Old Republicans stood by the side of Old Hickory. The conversion of the Crawford men left the remnant of Adams' friends isolated, and Jackson carried North Carolina 37,857 to 13,918. This represented a statewide increase in voting turnout of 43.3 percent over the 1824 election.[7]

Cumberland citizens shared the widespread interest in the presidential question. Adams had won the largest share of the county's votes in 1824, but in 1828 Jackson carried Cumberland with 71.6 percent of the vote. A simple coalition of Jackson and Crawford men did not account for the general's landslide, for the two candidates' combined shares of the vote in 1824 were only 58.7 percent. Either sizable numbers of Adams men defected to Jackson or the general attracted many new voters to his ticket. As it happened, county voting turnout increased from 34.6 percent in 1824 to 55.8 percent in 1828, making this election the most popular contest of the 1820s.[8]

The available evidence suggests that a Federalist alliance between Fayetteville voters and the rural Scots had dominated Cumberland County politics from the ratification of the U.S. Constitution to 1824. After 1828, this coali-

5. *Ibid.*
6. Fayetteville *Carolina Observer*, November 15, 1827.
7. William S. Hoffmann, *Andrew Jackson and North Carolina Politics*, James Sprunt Series in History and Political Science, XL (Chapel Hill, 1958), 6–25.
8. Compiled Election Returns, "Presidential Electors," 1828. See table 4 and figure 3.

tion never controlled the county again, and by 1840, all signs of it had van-
ished. With two ambiguous exceptions, no anti-Jacksonian candidate carried
Cumberland County for a state or national office for the remainder of the antebellum period. Nor did such a candidate ever represent the whole county in
the legislature, although Fayetteville sent a Whig to the House of Commons
in 1834.[9] The increased turnout and the accompanying realignment placed the
election of 1828 in Cumberland County in the category described by V. O.
Key as a "critical election." [10]

The struggle between Adams and Jackson concerned the citizens of Cumberland County so much that they took steps to prepare for it which they had
never taken for any other contest. The most politically active citizens in the
county organized themselves into two committees, one for each candidate,
and undertook a fervent and highly publicized canvass for the votes of their
fellow citizens. Previous political organizations, like the group who managed
John Cameron's victory in 1810, seemed informal and impromptu by comparison. Both committees took pains to reject the stigma of partisanship, but
each became the germ of a permanent political party. In an era of imperfect
national unity, the two parties became permanent institutions which linked

9. *Ibid.*, 1828–60. The names and party identifications of Cumberland representatives appeared
in the Fayetteville press every year during the second week in August, after every election.

In 1838, John Branch ran for governor as a Democrat against Edward B. Dudley, the Whig
incumbent. Branch had been a friend of Calhoun's while secretary of the navy in Jackson's first
cabinet. When Branch was forced to resign in the aftermath of the Peggy Eaton affair, he began to
organize opposition to Jackson in North Carolina. He maintained his states' rights credentials
intact, and by 1838 he had returned to the Democratic party as a supporter of Van Buren's Independent Treasury. He was not an official party nominee for governor, however, and several Democratic newspapers endorsed Dudley. The campaign was also complicated by the fact that Branch
had moved his family to Florida and appeared on the ballot in 1838 as a candidate for that state's
constitutional convention. Apparently alienated by such political and geographical inconstancy,
about three hundred Cumberland Democrats who turned out to vote for legislative candidates in
1838 boycotted the governor's election, and Dudley carried the county, with 51.9 percent of the
vote. See William S. Hoffman, "John Branch and the Origins of the Whig Party in North Carolina," *North Carolina Historical Review*, XXXV (1959), 299–315; J. G. deRoulhac Hamilton,
Party Politics in North Carolina, 1835–1860, James Sprunt Historical Publications, vol. 15, nos.
1–2 (Chapel Hill, 1916), 46–50; Fayetteville *North Carolina Journal*, July 18, 1838; Fayetteville
Observer, August 15, 1838.

In 1846, the gubernatorial nominee of the state Democratic convention declined before the
canvass began. Walter F. Leake of neighboring Richmond County then announced his candidacy
for the post. Leake was well-known and popular in Cumberland County. The Democratic State
Central Committee, however, gave its endorsement to James B. Shepard. Leake eventually accepted their decision, but some of his friends in Cumberland continued to feel that he had been
treated unfairly. Democratic turnout dropped by 369 votes over the previous election, but the
Whigs only gained 119 votes. These Democratic abstentions gave Whigs a majority of 21 votes in
the county, or 50.8 percent of the total. Hamilton, *Party Politics*, 104–106; Fayetteville *Observer*, August 13, 1846, August 6, 1844; Fayetteville *North Carolinian*, July 18, 1846.

10. V. O. Key, Jr., "A Theory of Critical Elections," *Journal of Politics*, XVII (1955), 3–18, and
"Secular Realignment and the Party System," *Journal of Politics*, XXI (1959), 198–210.

the feelings and interests of local voters to questions of national importance. When the efforts of the party organizers were multiplied thousands of times by similar actions in other communities, they had shaped the relationships between citizens and government in ways that they hardly guessed.

Cumberland's two committees did not emerge spontaneously or in isolation from similar occurrences elsewhere. The first movement for local organization in North Carolina in 1828 began in Beaufort, a coastal port and county seat of Carteret County. Like Fayetteville, Beaufort was an old center of commerce and Federalism, which hoped to bolster its trade by internal improvements. The programs of President Adams appealed to powerful interests and sentiments in the town, so the friends of the president began to prepare for his campaign almost a year before election day. On November 17, 1827, they met and asked for a statewide convention to nominate electors for North Carolina who would be pledged to the reelection of John Quincy Adams.[11] Their movement caught the attention of Edward J. Hale, who commented on the convention call in the *Carolina Observer*. "The reason of the adoption of the novel course proposed by the Carteret people, (novel in this State, at least) is evident," Hale remarked. "They know the Administration is in a lean minority in the Legislature, and they expect to make a better show of strength in this way."[12] A similar meeting assembled in New Bern in Craven County a few weeks later and echoed the appeal of the Carteret Adams men.

The leader of Adams' friends in New Bern was William Gaston, a distinguished Federalist lawyer whom President Adams had wished to make secretary of war. Gaston later dominated the Adams state convention and composed its *Address . . . to the Freemen of North Carolina*. The Adams leader had strong ties to Fayetteville. His sister and daughter lived there with their husbands, and his wife was a native of the town. She was the niece of William Barry Grove, and her uncle remained a close friend of Gaston's for many years.[13] It may have been at Gaston's behest that the Adams men of Cumberland County responded to the news from Carteret and Craven by calling their own meeting. On December 7, they gathered in the courthouse, passed a series of resolutions in which they endorsed the idea of a convention, appointed a committee of vigilance and correspondence, and issued their own address to the voters. In New Bern and Fayetteville, Jackson men responded to the Adams initiative by hurriedly calling their own meetings, which also formed committees and passed resolutions calling for statewide action.[14]

11. Hoffmann, *Andrew Jackson and North Carolina Politics*, 18.
12. Fayetteville *Carolina Observer*, November 15, 1827.
13. Joseph Schauinger, *William Gaston, Carolinian* (Milwaukee, 1949), 19, 23–24, 96, 117; William Barry Grove to William Gaston, March 12, 1804, in William Gaston Papers, Southern Historical Collection.
14. Fayetteville *North Carolina Journal*, December 12, 1827.

In a subsequent issue, the *North Carolina Journal* printed the minutes of the Fayetteville gatherings and informed its readers that "both meetings were highly respectable: that of the friends of General Jackson consisted of about 300 persons, and that of the friends of Mr. Adams between 110 and 140." [15] Louis D. Henry, a lawyer and frequently a state representative for Fayetteville, served as chairman of the Jackson meeting, and Dr. Benjamin Robinson, later chairman of the county court, presided over the Adams men. Subsequently, Dr. Robinson ran for elector on the Adams ticket. The Jackson committee had fifty-five members and the Adams group had twenty-five. Assuming that all committee members voted, roughly 7 percent of the electorate in November belonged to one of these committees.

The *Journal* did not say how the members were chosen nor what functions they performed during the campaign. Presumably the latter included a certain amount of personal canvassing, distribution of campaign materials, attendance at rallies, and financial support of the campaign. Perhaps one important function of the committees was simply to serve as a showcase for the number and quality of high-status adherents each candidate could attract to his side. Regardless of their specific duties, the committees both sought to mobilize county voters in support of their respective candidates. The literature which they distributed, the appeals they made in the Fayetteville press, and the speeches their members may have made on the hustings were the principal sources of political information for local voters. The written pronouncements of these two committees and their adherents are the best surviving guide to public opinion in Cumberland County in the critical election of 1828.

North Carolina historians have suggested that Jackson swept the state in 1828 because the public believed that Adams was unsound on the slavery question. [16] It is true that the existence of slavery had much to do with North Carolina's sensitivity to signs of expanding federal power. New federal authority, even for exemplary purposes, might create a precedent which would surrender control over slavery to a numerical majority with no direct stake in the outcome of their experiments. In 1820, the Missouri crisis had revealed a menacing northern tendency to interfere with the peculiar institution, while two years afterwards, Denmark Vesey's plotted insurrection in Charleston demonstrated what might happen frequently if the white South lost control over blacks.

Adams' position on slavery had been a source of some concern even before his election. In 1823, John MacRae, who was then editor of the *Carolina Ob-*

15. *Ibid.*
16. Henry McGilbert Wagstaff, *States Rights and Political Parties in North Carolina, 1776–1861*, Johns Hopkins University Studies in Historical and Political Science, ser. 24, nos. 7–8 (Baltimore, 1906), 48; R. D. W. Connor, *North Carolina: Rebuilding an Ancient Commonwealth, 1584–1925* (2 vols.; Chicago, 1929), I, 511; Lefler and Newsome, *North Carolina*, 343.

server and an Adams supporter, warned against "the unsound and dangerous doctrine advanced, that it can never be the policy of North Carolina to support a candidate for the Presidency from the nonslaveholding states." Mac-Rae sensibly pointed out that if the northern states followed the same policy the South could never elect a president and the Union would not endure.[17]

Edward J. Hale, the next editor of the *Observer*, also took note of the slavery issue. Hale had been a Crawford supporter but refrained from attacking the president until after Adams threatened to use the army to coerce the state of Georgia into compliance with a federal treaty with the Creek Indians. After Adams had revealed his insensitivity to states' rights, Hale publicly committed himself to Jackson.[18] During the election campaign itself, the North Carolina central Jackson committee mentioned in its *Address* that Jackson had been criticized as a slaveholder and asked voters, "Are you prepared to admit that every man who is the proprietor of slaves is thereby degraded from the rights of a citizen . . . ? Will you thus put your seal to your own infamy?" The committee sharply answered its own question, "We trust not." [19]

The slavery issue did arise in discussions of Adams' fitness for office, but it was not the most prominent theme in Jackson's campaign literature. Adams' loss of the West Indies trade through clumsy diplomacy with the British received more attention than slavery. The lengthiest and most conspicuous arguments did not concern slavery or export markets or any other material interest but focused on Adams' alleged corruption and his illicit thirst for power. Hostility to powerful central government and concern for the protection of slavery were closely related, but not necessarily identical. A certain constitutional sophistication was necessary for voters to interpret every criticism of corruption and broad construction as code words for racial fears. In this period, proslavery ideas as such would probably be most attractive to slaveholders, while the desire to protect republican government could appeal to almost everybody. If voters paid attention to the literal message of Jackson's followers, they rejected Adams because they concluded that he threatened the principles of republicanism.

In 1824, the most important argument used in favor of the People's Ticket had been that Crawford's nominations by caucuses in Raleigh and Washington destroyed the freedom of elections. Four years later, Jackson's supporters repeated similar arguments at every level of the campaign. When John Cameron, the Jackson editor, listed the reasons for his preference, the first one was that Adams "came into office in violation of the spirit of the

17. Fayetteville *Carolina Observer*, August 28, 1823.
18. *Ibid.*, March 15, 1827.
19. *Address of the Central Jackson Committee to the Freemen of North Carolina* (Raleigh, 1828), 15.

Constitution and in direct opposition to the will of the People." When the Jackson men of Cumberland County gathered to choose their committee of vigilance, they declared their belief "that the present administration came into office, through a system of management, bargain and intrigue, disgraceful to the country, ruinous to its liberties, and in violation of, and disregard to the will of the People—that it has widely departed from those republican principles on which our government was founded, and that its continuance will endanger our dearest and most invaluable rights." At the district convention in which representatives from five adjacent counties met to nominate a presidential elector, the delegates reminded voters that "In the last Presidential Election, the *Will of the Majority was disobeyed and defeated: the Constitution was violated in its spirit, if not in its letter. The elective franchise was poisoned and corrupted. A President was declared to be elected, who had received only a minority of the votes*." The state central Jackson committee repeated the same argument. "Jackson, the man of the people," they asserted, "was, at the last election, defeated . . . in order that Mr. Clay might be secretary of State, and heir apparent to the presidency. . . . North Carolina having voted for Jackson four years ago . . . she owes it to herself, to consistency, to the nation, to support him now." [20]

"The Will of the People," or its equivalent, was a phrase which recurred over and over in this literature. It is safe to assume that this slogan had a deep importance for the people of North Carolina, or the sensitive politicians who composed the pamphlets and addresses where it appeared would not have used it so tellingly. The supremacy of the majority seems to have been so significant to voters that rhetorically, it overshadowed Adams' actual performance in office and Jackson's specific intentions for his administration. The state Jackson committee had a simple explanation for this phenomenon. The committee reviewed the arguments for automatically electing the preferred candidate of the previous president and dismissed them with contempt. "Admit this, and your right to suffrage exists only in form; your Chief Magistrates cease to be elective, and you cease to be freemen." John Cameron expressed the same feeling more directly. "When the actions of public men shall pass unnoticed . . ." he avowed, "we shall no longer be *Freemen*, we shall be *slaves*." [21]

J. Mills Thornton III has reminded historians of the crucial significance of such language in states where slavery was not an oratorical abstraction, but

20. Fayetteville *North Carolina Journal*, November 8, 1826, December 12, 1827; *An Address to the Voters of the Electoral District Composed of the Counties of Anson, Richmond, Robeson, Cumberland and Moore* (Fayetteville, N.C., 1828), 3; *Address of the Central Jackson Committee*, 5.

21. *Address of the Central Jackson Committee*, 6; Fayetteville *North Carolina Journal*, November 8, 1826.

an ever present social reality. Free men apparently felt a powerful need regularly to assert and demonstrate their complete difference from slaves.[22] The accusation that a particular political movement tended to turn free men into slaves was potent rhetorical medicine, and the Jackson men took it up promptly.

Cumberland County's particular historical experience (which may not have been unique) suggests a second and complementary reason why Cumberland voters were jealous of their freedom. A half a century earlier, the grandfathers of some Fayetteville voters had lost the suffrage by the arbitrary action of a royal governor, acting in the interests of an overbearing elite. It had not been two decades since Miles Hussey had needed the friendship of a powerful merchant in order to vote the way he pleased and wealthy Federalists had boasted of their ability to control an election by manipulating employment opportunities and poor relief. Locally, the absolute freedom of elections was a symbol that those bad old days were past and that all white men stood equal in the eyes of the republic.

The desire to prohibit class distinctions among whites and the need to protect the superiority of free men over slaves were social and political pressures that clearly reinforced each other. The Jackson district convention's address, for example, moved easily and naturally from a denunciation of "aristocracy" to a demand for states' rights: "A mighty struggle is going on between the *many* and the *few*—between the *people* and their *rulers*—between *power* and *patronage* on one side, and *right* and *truth* on the other—between *Executive influence* and the *popular will*—between *construction* and *encroachment* and the *Constitution as it is*—between *corruption, extravagance, prodigality and waste* on the one side, and *purity, economy and responsibility on the other*—between the all powerful grasp of the *Federal*, and the rights and sovereignty of the *State Governments*."[23] The committee did not go further and explain directly that state sovereignty was necessary to defend slavery, but the inference was open for all who had the insight to make it. For those who did not, the call to defend republican equality was sufficiently arousing. Subsequent southern politicians would not be so reticent, and the notion grew that states' rights dogmas were necessary to prevent class distinctions among whites and to preserve caste distinctions between races.

The language of the pamphlet suggests a third reason why "the will of the people" had such intense significance. The convention's contrast between Adams' corruption and Jackson's purity made a strong appeal to the reader's sense of morality. The Jackson literature suggested strongly that Adams' po-

22. Thornton, *Politics and Power in a Slave Society*, 205–222.
23. *An Address to the Voters*, 3.

litical sins tended to pollute his private morals as well as his public performance. The Cumberland County committee of vigilance warned that "a system of corruption is extending its ramifications into every quarter" because of Adams' misfeasance and noted that "most of his life has been spent among kings and nobles, and . . . he has no sympathies for a plain republican people." John A. Cameron charged that Adams "took the bread out of the mouth of a poor widow, to glut the rapacious appetite of a professed libeller" and issued a call for "public servants who will disburse the public money wisely and economically, and not expend it in the purchase of billiard tables and dice-boxes." [24] Similar passages throughout the Jackson campaign documents evoked the feeling that the cause of General Jackson and the people was in some way a crusade of moral purification. In effect, this crusading tone was religious because of its link to the citizens' sense of the sacred. It was diffuse enough to address a community sense of right and wrong which could be shared by churchgoers and nonchurchgoers alike, but it was not so vague that it could not clash with religious appeals of a different nature.

John Quincy Adams had based his presidency on just such an appeal. His famous first annual message declared that "the tenure of power by man is, in the moral purposes of his Creator, upon condition that it shall be exercised to ends of beneficence, to improve the condition of himself and his fellow men." [25] Adams' justification of his administration clearly drew on the Puritan idea of office as a sacred trust which obliged the incumbent to pursue the purposes of the God who put him in power and who ordained human government as a type of his heavenly kingdom. This understanding of office had changed greatly since the seventeenth century; the younger Adams wished to use political power to promote secular progress and not a narrow Puritan version of the godly commonwealth. By the time Adams made this declaration in 1829, the religious world view of the Puritans had evolved into a general posture of support for human improvement and evangelical moral reform. Historians have also associated this tendency in American Protestantism with support for the Whig party. [26] Although this moral persuasion was not narrowly ecclesiastical by the 1820s and 1830s, it was not irreligious either, for it underlay many Americans' belief in the sacred character of their government.

The North Carolina central Jackson committee seized on Adams' moral legitimation of power and denounced it from a standpoint that derived from a different version of evangelical Protestantism. The committee quoted from Adams' message and acknowledged that "the people at large, derive the su-

24. Fayetteville *North Carolina Journal*, September 26, 1827, November 8, 1826.
25. Richardson (comp.), *Messages and Papers of the Presidents*, II, 882.
26. Benson, *The Concept of Jacksonian Democracy*, 191–207; Formisano, *The Birth of Mass Political Parties*, 102–127.

preme power from the moral Governor of the Universe," but they asserted that the community was not obliged to use this power for particular ends so long as they were "limited in its exercise by his benevolent purposes for their moral and intellectual improvement." Rulers of the people did not even have the right, much less the duty, to exercise power on behalf of the community, except as they were specifically delegated this power by the Constitution. According to the president's doctrine, the committee concluded, "it follows that the will of the people expressed in the Constitution is superceded by Mr. Adams' exposition of the will of the Creator." This deviation was more than illegal; it was "political heresy," for "how does this differ from the divine right claimed by Kings?" The committee did not deny that God had a moral design for the American future, but they insisted that the people themselves would perceive and follow the divine plan without the special mediation of magistrates.[27] This analysis elevated the expression *vox populi, vox Dei* to the level of theological literalism.

The historical relationship between religion and politics is not as well understood for the South as it is coming to be for New England and the Middle West. We do know that most white southerners who professed a religion were evangelical Protestants like most of their northern counterparts. But historians of the region's religion have pointed out that southern evangelicals originated as a persecuted minority, not as the inheritors of a moral consensus and a common conviction of historical mission. Donald G. Mathews has found, moreover, that evangelicals achieved cultural dominance in the South by successfully infusing the aspirations of plain folk for planter status with the dignity of moral purpose. Their former persecutions by the state left southern evangelicals skeptical that God's purposes for his people lay within the responsibility of government, while their ambitions for respectability in a slave society silenced their nascent impulses to bring in the Kingdom by reforming the institutions of this world. The crowds who thronged to southern revivals developed a strong preference for the separation of church and state, and little enthusiasm for secular crusades of moral improvement.[28] Thus Adams' justification of a powerful federal government offended religious sensibilities in North Carolina just as it violated the dominant political ethos. To the extent that religious beliefs functioned socially to reconcile community members to the existing social order, the religious and political objections to Adams were deeply intertwined.

In contrast to Adams' degeneracy, the committee of vigilance offered Andrew Jackson as the candidate outstanding for his democratic conviction, his moral purity, his physical courage, and his great public service. "General

---

27. *Address of the Central Jackson Committee*, 6–7.
28. Donald G. Mathews, *Religion in the Old South* (Chicago, 1977), 1–38.

Jackson *is one of the People*," they emphasized. "God and Nature, and not education, made him a great man. Without the advantage of birth or fortune to recommend him, he stands, as a shining example, of the proud height of virtuous eminence to which a great and vigorous mind, can elevate its possessor." [29] The committee reviewed Jackson's military career with lavish praise, defended him against the aspersion that his "talents are purely military," recited his civilian honors and services, and closed by stressing again the importance of the election and the moral distance between the candidates. They did not mention the social cleavages which had affected the last election, nor did they mention particular reforms or specific plans for Jackson's term in office.

The Cumberland County supporters of John Quincy Adams followed some of the same rhetorical themes that the friends of Andrew Jackson did. Like the Jacksonians, the Adams men viewed the upcoming election as crucial to the nation's future. "We believe the elevation of General Jackson to the Presidency," they resolved, "fraught with consequences the most dangerous to the happiness, peace, and future continuance of the government." Also like their competitors, the Adams men devoted more attention to the deficiencies of the opposing candidate than the merits of their own. They reminded voters that "General Jackson's claims (qualifications they are not) to the office to which he aspires . . . are solely of a military character." They feared that Jackson's experience predisposed him to an abuse of power and worried about the effects on republicanism if "one great military achievement become the passport to the highest civil office in the gift of the people." [30]

In accordance with conventional opinion, the Adams men preferred that political life be based on considerations of principle, but they did not see that any principles were at stake in the election. To them, "political principles" were convictions about particular government policies rather than commitment to the forms of decision-making. In their view, the Jacksonians showed no principles at all because their "unity of action" was not founded on "unity of sentiment in regard to political measures, but on discordant and even *adverse* views of public policy." They did not object to all "opposition and party spirit in a free government." Opposition was "useful when conducted with candor," but the absence of unifying principles among the Jackson men did not satisfy that stipulation. [31]

When it appeared several weeks after the resolutions of the Cumberland

29. Fayetteville *North Carolina Journal*, December 12, 1827. This description of the general, with its stress on God, nature, and a vigorous mind, fell rather neatly into the categories of Jacksonian virtue proposed by John William Ward: "Nature, Providence, and Will." Ward, *Andrew Jackson*, 207–213.
30. Fayetteville *North Carolina Journal*, December 12, 1827.
31. *Ibid.*

County Adams meeting, the address of the state Adams convention expressed the same thought. The convention maintained that in previous contests for the presidency, "the rivalry sprang from a difference in the *parties* who divided the Country. To the honor of the People, these parties were founded on measures and principles—not on men and a struggle for office. . . . The pending controversy exhibits no such dignity. It is not a conflict between opposing principles—but a conflict between opposing men and combinations of men. It is founded on no recognized differences about measures; but on competition for power and place." [32] The convention supported its claim that no difference of principle separated the parties by pointing out that Jackson's friends nationally included both the supporters and the opponents of internal improvements, the tariff, broad construction of the Constitution, and the other main policy issues of the day. Such diverse opposition could have no legitimate purpose, so the Cumberland committee concluded that "faction is abroad," and warned that "principle will yield and expediency become the *cardinal doctrine*." [33]

Under the rule of expediency, every presidential election would become a struggle for the perquisites of office and no president could expect more than one term before being toppled by a hungry combination of his rivals. The state convention predicted a sad result. "Let me enrich my family and friends—let me strengthen the power of my adherents during the short term of my office, would then be the natural suggestion of avarice and ambition." The consequence would be the very thing that the friends of Jackson professed to fear most—a calamitous abuse of power that would shatter the republic, if Jackson's military temperament had not already destroyed the restraints of the Constitution. [34]

Although the Cumberland County Adams meeting endorsed the democratic maxim that "all power emanates from the people," they failed to comprehend that the will of the people itself could be a political principle that transcended differences over policy. The address of the state convention shared the same blind spot. In the face of clamorous demands for the "Will of the People," the convention calmly maintained that "no usage can be more auspicious in its influence upon the tranquility of our Country, than the re-election for a second term of a President with whose Administration there is no well-founded and serious cause of complaint." [35] The Jacksonians were therefore able to throw the assertion that no principles were at stake back into the teeth of the Adams men and tout their own superior claims to political

32. *Address of the Administration Convention, Held in the Capitol at Raleigh, Dec. 20th, 1827. To the Freemen of North Carolina* (Raleigh, 1827), 4.
33. Fayetteville *North Carolina Journal*, December 12, 1827.
34. *Address of the Administration Convention*, 6, 13–14.
35. *Ibid.*, 5.

virtue. "*We* are not man-worshippers," cried the district convention. "We are contending for *principle* . . . [because] liberty is in danger. The Constitution is assailed. The republican form of Government . . . is sorely menaced by the proud spirit of Aristocracy." [36]

The accusation of the Jackson men could receive no surer confirmation than from the pen of the most prominent Adams supporter in North Carolina. In late February, 1828, William Gaston received a letter from his friend and former law student, Congressman John H. Bryan. Writing from Washington, Bryan reported that Gaston's address had made a good impression amongst the National Republican luminaries there, and he deplored the low tone of the Jackson campaign. [37] Replying to Bryan, Gaston vented his rage and frustration at the diverse combination which supported Andrew Jackson and his bafflement that men he respected could so forget themselves as to join with the worst elements in American politics. In the process, Gaston revealed his contempt for insurgent popular democracy and the ungentlemanly demagogues who expressed the people's will. "Heterogeneous indeed!" he exploded.

> Such men as [Louis] McLane & [Henry Moore] Ridgely, pure in principle, federalists in the legitimate sense of the term, representing a State [Delaware] so firmly attached to the Union and deeply interested in good order, united with the wildest disorganizers, the rankest antifederalists, and the crudest radicals!—McLane, who with such distinguished ability and admirable firmness, demonstrated the *right*—the *duty* of the House of Representatives—to select from among the candidates him whom in their deliberate judgment they deemed best qualified for the Presidential office—confounded in the ranks with those who shout forth as the fundamental primary principle of their opposition that Congress was bound to appoint him who had the plurality of electoral votes! Men, prudent sagacious refined, following after (those who are unworthy to loose the lachets of their shoes) the rowdies of the day who depend for their influence on appeals to the malignant passions of the vulgar and the prejudices of the ignorant! [38]

Gaston clung to his confidence that the Jacksonian coalition would disintegrate and the administration regain its former strength. "It is impossible that these gentlemen," he concluded, "should not discover how strangely they are misplaced, and with them to discover error must be followed by its correction." Gaston's denunciation of "the malignant passions of the vulgar" recalled the alarm of his mentor William Barry Grove in the late 1790s and his request for arms "to keep a certain class of people in order." Gaston still

36. *An Address to the Voters*, 3.
37. John H. Bryan to William Gaston, February 15, 1828, in Gaston Papers.
38. William Gaston to John H. Bryan, March 1, 1828, in Gaston Papers.

thought of himself and his fellow Adams supporters as Federalists. He did not feel bound by the will of the people, and he despised "the rowdies of the day" who did. He implied that most of Adams' friends were gentlemen like himself and he regarded the members of this group as the natural leaders of society. In Gaston's case, the Jacksonians' imputation of aristocratic and antidemocratic convictions to the Adams men was true.

Gaston's letter to Bryan spoke directly of the contrast between Jackson and Adams supporters at the national level, but his analysis of the election could be applied equally well to the state level. In his view, Adams supporters were Federalist survivors who were joined together by gentility and by common convictions on matters of government policy. This unity made the Adams men a legitimate political "party," according to the *Address* which Gaston wrote. The Jackson men, by contrast, represented a jumble of opinions and classes. They included some aristocrats who joined with plebeian dema-gogues for reasons unfathomable to Gaston. This collection of politicians had no common principles that he could see. Using the same logic, the Cumber-land County Adams meeting had branded their opponents a "faction." [39]

In an early preelection editorial, John A. Cameron presented the same analysis of the presidential contest, but connected it to a very different con-cept of legitimate political parties. Like Gaston, Cameron was an old Feder-alist of aristocratic origins, but he was among those who had gone over to the Jacksonians. Unlike Gaston, Cameron rejoiced in the breakup of the old party system. "The time has been when the terms Federalist—Republican—con-veyed a definite meaning. . . . But that time is now past." No important pol-icy questions divided the nation any more, so the parties had disappeared. The only remaining question was a conflict between the proponents of popular and elite rule. The Jacksonians represented the whole body of the nation and em-braced good citizens of all classes. This commitment to democratic social unity enabled Cameron to say, "we are of the party of our country," and to favor a definition of partisan legitimacy in which policy preferences and social hierarchy were largely irrelevant. [40]

The magnitude of Jackson's landslide suggests that he indeed captured voters from all classes, and the tenor of some campaign rhetoric supports Gaston's and Cameron's analysis of the social and political composition of the two sides. In their opening statements, the two committees seemed to fall neatly into stereotypes of cold, distant, and aristocratic National Repub-licanism and bumptious Jacksonian Democracy. Some of these differences stemmed naturally from the logic of the political situation. The Jacksonians were pushy and abrasive as befitted a group of challengers. The Adams men

39. Fayetteville *North Carolina Journal*, December 12, 1827.
40. *Ibid.*, November 8, 1826.

showed calm and pointed to the president's record as the supporters of incumbents are wont to do. These rhetorical patterns did not remain entirely consistent. Later in the campaign when the Adams men discovered the inadequacy
of their lofty poses, they experimented with more popular appeals. In the process, they showed themselves as equal to the demands of demagoguery as any
Jacksonian, and plunged into an intense personal quarrel between the committees reminiscent of the worst excesses of local politics.

In the spring of 1828, Adams campaigners began widespread distribution
of pamphlets favorable to the president. Congressman John Culpepper, who
had voted for Adams in the House of Representatives in 1825, was still representing the district, and he began the direct mail campaign by sending large
numbers of *Mr. Clay's Appeal* and the *Virginia Anti-Jackson Address* among
his constituents. The effort apparently backfired and several subscribers complained to John A. Cameron's *North Carolina Journal*. Culpepper had defeated Cameron for Congress only eight months earlier, so the editor was
happy to publish his readers' objections. One correspondent wanted to know
if Culpepper had dipped into public funds to pay for the documents. Another
tartly observed that Mr. Culpepper must have voted against a reduction in his
salary in order to pay for campaign literature. "I suppose the old gentleman
has sent them amongst us to convert us to the Adams faith," the letter writer
inferred, "but depend upon it, it wont do. We are 'Hickory' out and out. . . .
I really think it wrong that the public mails should be burthened with the
transportation of such immense piles of electioneering pamphlets: and . . . I
would say, that our member might be better employed in attending to his public business, than sending such things." The Washington *National Journal*
came to Culpepper's defense by asserting that Cameron's opinions in the matter were not to be respected because he was Culpepper's disappointed rival.
Edward J. Hale obligingly reprinted the defense for local readers, and thereby nourished the cordial animosity which existed between Cameron and
himself.[41]

A sharper controversy exploded over the distribution by the Adams committee of a lurid and scurrilous account of an incident in the Seminole War in
which six militia men under Jackson's command were executed for desertion
and mutiny. The pamphlet bore the title *An Official Record from the War Department of the proceedings of the courts martial which tried, and the orders
of General Jackson for shooting the six militia men, together with official letters from the War Department (ordered to be printed by Congress) showing
that these American citizens were inhumanly and illegally massacred.*[42] It was

41. *Ibid.*, March 5, 1828; Fayetteville *Carolina Observer*, April 3, 1828.
42. This was apparently not the famous Coffin Handbill, which was similar in content but carried
the title *Some Account of Some of the Bloody Deeds of General Jackson*.

the product of a national distribution system for Adams' propaganda. The local Adams men acknowledged that it "was originally published at Washington, and by the suggestion, direction, and aid of your Committee, republished at Raleigh." The local Jackson committee objected vehemently on the grounds that the pamphlet was "false and unauthorized" and was "intended to affect injuriously the reputation of a great public benefactor." [43]

Although the pamphlet did contain portions of a congressional report, and was designed to seem official to the credulous, the Adams committee was clearly within its rights to publish it. In their reply to the Jacksonians, they made short work of the objection of a lack of authorization. They improved the occasion by escalating the emotional battle for the county's vote which the pamphlet itself had begun. "Let our Fellow Citizens read the publication with attention and bring the case and the fate of the six militia men home to themselves," the committee urged. "*Is he a father*—he sees and feels, that the blood of the son is made to flow through the willfulness or ignorance of a victorious general. *Is he a son*—he mourns a father's counsel and a father's blessing when erroneous martial judgment writes the word '*approved*.' *Is he a brother*—he beholds the golden chain of affection broken to make an EXAMPLE, the guiltless doomed to suffer to prevent *future* crime." [44] This reply attempted to bring a political issue away from the market place and muster ground and into every family who read the newspaper—"home to the voters themselves." The Adams committee was deliberately manipulating family emotions as an instrument of political strategy. Though commonplace today, this cynical procedure violated all the proprieties of early-nineteenth-century politics. The public reputation of a political aspirant was a fair target for abuse, but the circle of the family was private and therefore sacrosanct. The committee was operating, moreover, at the behest of faraway agents in Raleigh and Washington to win office for a man their opponents identified as a power-hungry revisionist and the agent of threatening economic assault. The Jackson men were furious at the underhanded assault, and no wonder.

In this incident, the Adams men displayed a penchant for emotional inventiveness which does not gibe with their reputations as conservatives. The Jackson committee, by contrast, drew on traditional rhetoric and ideology to repel the assault. They defended their candidate by striking back at the private characters of his assailants. Moreover, their counterattack implicitly upheld the old assumption that character and reputation were the most important stakes in politics. The Jacksonians professed surprise that the friends of Adams, whom they had thought to be honorable men, would thus follow "the vocation of parasites and caterers, to labor in the kennels of party, and not to

43. Fayetteville *Carolina Observer*, June 12, 1828, June 19, 1828.
44. *Ibid.*, June 19, 1828.

scruple about means." When the pamphlet proved false, the Adams men would suffer "dreadful moral stigma." The Jackson men regretted that their opponents "without reflection, have launched their good names upon the reckless tide of party, which on its bosom bears along 'the feculence and dregs of every clime.' "[45]

The severest attacks of the Jacksonians were reserved for the spirit of the pamphlet itself. The work's worst feature was not its literal falsehood but its vicious attempt to destroy a national asset, the reputation of General Jackson himself. "The work as a whole," they stormed,

> misrepresent[s] and vilifie[s] the character and conduct of Gen. Jackson, with an appetite for slander, the rage and ferocity of which, has seldom had a parallel; which no oblations of his patriotism could appease—no considerations of a life devoted to his country could pacify—which neither feeding could slake, nor satiety gorge—but which, having devoured the living victim, hungers after the dead, and would feed like the vampire, on his character when he is gone, and leave it a dishonor to his country and a reproach to mankind. Yet this farrago, this medly pamphlet is styled "an official record," &c., "ordered to be printed by Congress." Mark reader! This pseudostyled pamphlet is anonymous!!! . . . Its author must be some *northern blue light or some leader of the Hartford Convention.*[46]

The factional difference which appeared in this quarrel contrasted sharply with the images derived from the two groups' opening statements. The Adams committee, the previous defenders of prudence and caution, spoke directly to popular passions. The Jackson men, on the other hand, drew much more heavily than did the Adams men on the traditional vocabulary of honor and reputation and suspicion of power. In the course of this campaign, the "conservatives" and the "radicals" appeared to have changed roles.

Some of this inconsistency stemmed from the fact that neither group was quite so different from the other as first impressions might indicate. Within limits, either could adopt a traditional or innovative stance as the occasion demanded. There is, however, a thread of continuity that ran through the works of both committees and tied them both to the substantive positions of their respective favorites.

The Jacksonians supported a frontier military hero, a man they explicitly likened to George Washington. Their bombastic appeals to popular prejudice were antiaristocratic, antideferential, and democratic in tone, but that should not disguise the fact that they most often looked to an idealized past for their political models and values. Even if the democratic tone of their speeches had

45. *Ibid.*, June 26, 1828.
46. *Ibid.*

never been heard in Cumberland County before, the speakers still justified that tone by references to the achievement of the Revolution, and not to some projected future equality. Jackson himself, moreover, became the president who rejected federal sponsorship of economic development in his vetoes of the Maysville Road and the Bank of the United States. Whatever the inclinations of his subordinates in certain states, the Old Hero himself stood for the world of the Founding Fathers.[47] It was not at all unnatural, therefore, for the new Jacksonian Democracy to appeal to old-fashioned virtues of honor, civic morality, and military renown.

The Adams men, by contrast, opposed the upstart hero from the backwoods. Their ideal presidential candidate was distinguished for his training, his experience, his skilled performance, and his urbanity. Adams stood for orderly management and controlled innovation in the economy and the general society. Having few hopes of establishing these values directly, the Adams men moved obliquely by dwelling on the dangers of the "military chieftain." When a placid recital of that danger was unavailing they turned to a demagogic statement of the same thing in their offensive pamphlet. Though the tone of this work was shrill, its appeal was to bourgeois virtues: to home and family, to order, to due process and respect for the forms of law. Ultimately therefore, it comported with the opening statement of the Adams committee.

The continuities between political program and political rhetoric were thus more important than the superficial differences between tone and substance. Nevertheless, the electioneering of the Adams committee and the Jacksonians' demand for proper decorum illustrate the difficulty of relying on campaign documents alone for an accurate understanding of political conflict. By themselves, the statements of the two committees do not prove whether Gaston's and Cameron's view of political alignments was correct. Fortunately, we can verify impressions collected from the campaign literature by examining the backgrounds of the men who composed the two committees.[48]

*   *   *

Louis D. Henry, the chairman of the Jackson committee, and Dr. Benjamin Robinson, his counterpart among the Adams men, were both former Federal-

---

47. A useful review of the points at issue between the "entrepreneurial school" of Jacksonian historians and their critics is Alfred A. Cave, *Jacksonian Democracy and the Historians*, University of Florida Monographs: Social Sciences, no. 22 (Gainesville, Fla., 1964), 54–82. My interpretation of the president's own thoughts and actions relies heavily on Meyers, *The Jacksonian Persuasion*.

48. Readers should be warned that the following section of this chapter depends exclusively on quantitative analysis of the property holdings of Whig and Democratic leaders. This section will begin and end with a row of asterisks; those who prefer to avoid a detailed technical discussion

ists. Two other Federalists followed Henry and one joined Dr. Robinson and his friends, but the previous political opinions of the other seventy-five committee members are obscure.[49] Gaston and Cameron were correct to some extent, for neither committee seems to have had an exclusive claim on the citizens' previous loyalties.

The property interests of the committee members are much more available than their political histories. The Cumberland County List of Taxables for 1828 contained important information on almost all of the eighty men who belonged to the Jackson and Adams committees of vigilance and correspondence. The list recorded each taxpayer's residence, the number of acres of rural land he owned, the assessed value of that land and its improvements, the number and assessed value of his town lots with improvements, and the number of his slave and free polls. Because men over the age of forty-five were exempt from the poll tax, the number of free polls a man paid for (with one exception, this figure was always "one" or "zero") was a rough indication of his age. The property holdings of several committee members could not be examined in this study. Either they could not be located on the tax lists, or their names appeared more than once, creating uncertainty as to which entry described the committee member and which described his namesake. After making these deletions, a population of seventy-five remained out of the original eighty; fifty-one men for Jackson and twenty-four for Adams.

The characteristics of these seventy-five men can help us distinguish the Adams men from the Jackson men in Cumberland County. They can also tell us about local political leadership in this period. First, were the members of the political elite representative of the electorate as a whole or did they share special qualities which set them apart? Second, what internal divisions existed within the seventy-five? Were there factors that distinguished Scottish members from non-Scots, for example, or less active members from more active ones? In the "Age of the Common Man," these two sets of questions both pertain to the degree of "openness" in the political system and, by extension, in the social structure generally. These two questions should be answered first because the candidate preferences of the elite members will be more meaningful when we understand their larger social context.

Some of the differences between committee members and the total elector-

---

may safely bypass these pages and rely on the summary of findings which follows them. A brief explanation of statistical methodology, especially of the concept of statistical significance as it is used herein, appears in Appendix II.

49. John A. Cameron and Dillon Jordan, Jr., were the two other Federalists who became Jacksonians. John Matthews was the other known Federalist who supported Adams. All but Robinson were veterans of the 1810 campaign between John A. Cameron and Henry Branson. Maj. Thomas J. Robeson, a Jacksonian, had commanded "Robeson's Republican Volunteers" during the War of 1812; no other Jeffersonian Republican appeared on either committee. Governors' Papers, vol. 30, p. 517.

Table 5. Committee Members and the Electorate, 1828–1829

	County population	Committee members
Support for Jackson	71.6%	68.0%
Percent Scottish taxpayers	36.3%	33.3%
	$N = 1,627$	$N = 80$
Fayetteville residents[a]	19.4%	46.7%
	$N = 9,081$	$N = 75$
Mean acres of land owned	419	1,750
	$N = 1,627$	$N = 75$
Mean assessed value of land	$423.64	$1,584.41
	$N = 1,627$	$N = 75$
Mean number of town lots owned[b]	1.8	3.3
	$N = 321$	$N = 35$
Mean assessed value of town lots[b]	$1,024.04	$1,508.00
	$N = 321$	$N = 35$
Mean value per lot [b]	$560.95	$456.97
	$N = 321$	$N = 35$
Mean number of slave polls	1.2	6.6
	$N = 1,627$	$N = 75$
Total mean assessed property value	$625.68	$2,355.48
	$N = 1,627$	$N = 75$

[a] Whites only.
[b] Fayetteville taxpayers only.
SOURCES: Compiled Election Returns, "Presidential Electors," 1828, in Miscellaneous Collections, North Carolina State Archives; Cumberland County Lists of Taxables, 1828, 1829, in Cumberland County Records, North Carolina State Archives; Fayetteville *North Carolina Journal*, December 12, 1827.

ate appear in table 5. The table shows that by at least two indicators, the leadership group was closely representative of the county as a whole. It contained roughly the same proportion of Jacksonians and Adams men and of Scots and non-Scots as the total electorate. On all other measures however, it is clear that the committee members led in more areas than in politics alone. They were more likely to live in Fayetteville than other inhabitants of Cumberland. As a group, they controlled many more slaves and much more land than the average county property owner. The only area where the total population approached the leadership group was in the value of lots in Fayetteville. Apparently Fayetteville property was so valuable that most lot owners were automatically wealthier than other inhabitants of the county. The average value of each lot owned by committee members who lived in Fayetteville was lower than the same value for all town dwellers. Informal inspection of the tax lists reveals that the leaders were likely to own inexpensive rental property and unimproved lots as well as their homes. Ordinary citizens were more likely to own a single home and perhaps a shop. The low *average* lot value among the leaders reflects this tendency. The superior economic position of the political leaders shows most clearly in the total mean assessed property value. This is a sum of the assessed land value and the assessed lot value, and it represents the dollar value of all a taxpayer's real property. The values of this variable show that the average member of a political committee owned almost four times as much total wealth as the average taxpayer in the county.

It is tempting to conclude from these data that affluence was somehow a requirement for membership in the political system. In literal terms, however, this was not strictly true. Many members of the committees listed no property at all on the tax lists, and a stranger to the county's politics might point to them as proletarian activists in the democratic process. In some cases, however, the apparent poverty of a member was merely an artificial product of the tax-reporting system. For example, Edward Lee Winslow, a leader of the Adams committee, reported no property at all in 1828 except a single slave. Winslow could hardly have been a poor man, however, because he was the son of a very wealthy merchant. Ten years later, he was chairman of the Bank of the Cape Fear, president of the Cape Fear Navigation Company, and a leading director of the projected Cape Fear, Yadkin, and Pedee Rail Road.[50] In 1828, Winslow had clearly not invested his wealth in real estate. Other "propertyless" men were actually in straitened circumstances but came from wealthy backgrounds. Such a one was John Cameron, whose enemies accused him of squandering two inherited fortunes (his own and his wife's) before making politics his profession.[51] The majority of the "poor" political leaders probably fell into one of the two categories suggested by the cases of Winslow and Cameron. Generally speaking, however, above average wealth was an informal requirement for political leadership in Cumberland County.

Even within this leadership group, there were varying degrees of activity and influence. Some men were appointed to committees but never took a conspicuous role in group activities, as those activities were described in published minutes. Others were quite active, serving repeatedly as chairmen of meetings, offering obviously prearranged resolutions, representing the county at district conventions, and so forth. These more active members were presumably a leadership clique within the larger group of political leaders represented by the general committee membership. In all probability, they organized the meetings, recruited other committee members, made informal decisions on campaign strategy, and relayed information from state and na-

---

50. Oates, *The Story of Fayetteville*, 857, 507.
51. Fayetteville *Carolina Observer*, July 30, 1829; John Haywood to Willie P. Mangum, March 24, 1826, in Shanks (ed.), *Mangum Papers*, I, 260–61.

Table 6. Committee Rank by Age, 1828

	Over 45 years[a]	Under 45 years[a]	Total
Passive Members	19 33.3%	38 66.7%	57
Active Members	5 27.8%	13 72.2%	18
Total	24 32.0%	51 68.0%	75

Corrected chi-square = .02271; p = .8801 (1 df)
[a] Age has been measured by whether or not the individual paid poll tax for a free poll in 1828.

tional leaders to the less active members. On the basis of this assumption, each committee member was assigned a political rank of "active" if his name appeared in the published accounts of group activities as a leader of any kind: chairing a meeting, writing or moving resolutions, serving as a convention delegate, or filling any similar position. Committee members who did none of these things received the rank of "passive." The degree to which exclusive criteria were requirements for membership in the active group is a further measure of the openness of the Cumberland County political system.

One obvious potential requirement for membership in the active group was age. It is possible that older men dominated positions of responsibility, or alternatively that the beginnings of party organization, as they appeared in the campaign of 1828, were undertaken by men who were younger, more vigorous, and more eager to innovate than their elders. We may cross-tabulate the active and inactive members of the committees by whether or not they paid poll tax to discover if age had any relationship to the degree of political involvement. This measure is crude, not only because it is based on a dichotomy between "under forty-five" and "over forty-five," but also because some men over forty-five may have paid tax for an adult son or an overseer or a squatter. The tax lists make no distinction in these cases, but judging by the number of men who paid tax on more than one free poll, these cases must have been rare. Table 6 presents the results of this comparison. The table shows that committee members of both degrees of activity paid the poll tax in roughly equal proportions. Men under forty-five were more numerous at both levels of leadership. Once within a political committee, age apparently had little or no relevance to one's degree of political activity.[52]

Residence is a criterion which may also have affected the degree of a com-

52. Conclusions from the contingency tables in this chapter are based on the significance level of the chi-square statistic. The .05 criterion has been used in most instances. Readers who are unfamiliar with this statistical device should refer to Appendix II.

mittee member's activity. Table 5 has already shown that committee members were more likely to come from Fayetteville than were other Cumberland residents. Town residence obviously made it easier to attend meetings, to hear political news and gossip, and to make oneself known to other political enthusiasts. Probably the same criteria operated within the committee itself, giving Fayetteville members greater opportunity to exercise leadership and hence greater access to the active group. Table 7 shows that this was in fact the case. Active members were more common in town, while passive members predominated in the country.

A third possible criterion for committee membership is ethnicity. We have seen that Scots belonged to the committees in proportions roughly equal to their numbers within the county. Did this equality also prevail within the committees? Scots may have been excluded from active positions from ethnic prejudice or some other reason, or they may have been overrepresented because of the eagerness of political organizers to court this important minority. Table 8 shows, however, that with only two Scottish activists in the two committees, Scots were clearly underrepresented at the higher levels of responsibility in spite of their equal membership within the larger leadership group.

Table 7. Committee Rank by Residence, 1828

	Country residents	Town residents	Total
Passive Members	34 59.6%	23 40.4%	57
Active Members	6 33.3%	12 66.7%	18
Total	40 53.3%	35 46.7%	75

Corrected chi-square = 2.82249; p = .0465 (1 df, direction predicted)

Table 8. Committee Rank by Ethnicity, 1828

	Non-Scots	Scots	Total
Passive Members	34 59.6%	23 40.4%	57
Active Members	16 88.9%	2 11.1%	18
Total	50 66.7%	25 33.3%	75

Corrected chi-square = 4.02961; p = .0224 (1 df, direction predicted)

It will be remembered from table 1 that few Scots lived in Fayetteville, which may be the reason for their exclusion from the higher-ranking circle. Certainly no ethnic discrimination was practiced against John Cameron, who as party editor and frequent candidate for Congress, was not outranked by any Jackson man in the county. Unfortunately, the small number of individuals at the two levels makes it impossible to test whether or not country residence accounts for all of the Scottish underrepresentation.

Wealth is a fourth criterion which may have affected the composition of Cumberland's political leadership. The members of political committees were, on the average, wealthier than other voters in the county. Wealth may also have created or supported differences in activity within the committees themselves. If high property ownership were the only criterion for political leadership, we would expect all categories of members to possess roughly the same amount of property. If special allowances were made for representatives of certain groups, however, we might expect certain classes of members to be less wealthy than others. Closer examination of the wealth of committee members can thus shed further light on the openness of the political system.

Age, for example, was not a barrier to leadership within the political committees, but wealth was a conspicuous requirement for entry into these groups. Ordinarily young men would be less wealthy than older men. Is it possible that young men were brought into the political system under lower expectations of wealth than older members? If so, the mean wealth of committee members who paid poll tax should be significantly lower than that of committee members who did not pay the tax.

Table 9 shows the results of a series of tests of whether there is a statistically significant difference between the average wealth of young men and old men. In table 9, no value of the "t statistic" meets the .05 criterion of significance.[53] The group of young men and old men in the Cumberland elite were much more like the second example in the preceding paragraph than the first example. Although there were differences in mean property ownership between the two groups, the dispersal about the means was so large that even a difference of over $500 as in lot value, is not significant at the .05 level. The "standard deviation" (shown as "$s = nnnn$" below each mean value) is a measure of the size of each variable's dispersal. We cannot conclude, therefore, that younger age was an occasion for lower entry requirements for the political committees. The system was just as closed in this respect as any other.

Ethnicity is a second characteristic for which a special relaxation of the entry requirements might have been made. Scots tended to live in the poorer

53. The use of the "t statistic" is explained in Appendix II. The .05 criterion has been used in these tests, unless otherwise noted.

districts. As a group, their property would have been worth less. Political leaders eager for Scottish votes may not have insisted that Scottish members be the financial equals of the more affluent non-Scots. Generally speaking, table 10 confirms this supposition. The Scots on the committees owned very little town property and fewer slaves than the non-Scots. The ownership of rural land, however, is an area of ambiguity in table 10. Certainly, Scots did not own fewer acres than non-Scots. If anything, they owned more. The observed mean value of this land was lower than the land of the non-Scots, but the difference in value was too small ($537.44) in relation to the variance of this variable and therefore did not show a conventionally acceptable level of significance. The figures on land acreage and land value suggest that the Scots owned large tracts of cheap land, probably in the sandhills. Because the Scots' property holdings were not padded with town property as well as rural land, their overall wealth was much lower than the non-Scottish committee members'.

This appears to be an area where the political system showed some flexibility. Even Scottish committee members were wealthier than the average voter in Cumberland County, and they were certainly wealthier than the average sandhills resident. But no one insisted that they be just as wealthy as non-Scottish members. It was apparently enough that the Scottish leaders were among the wealthiest members of their own community. The property requirements were therefore bent for their benefit but in a manner that reflected the generally elitist values of the political system. It was relative, not absolute superiority that counted.

It is possible that a similar adjustment was made between town and country residents, although it is difficult to predict the direction in which this adjustment would be made. Country-dwellers certainly ought to have owned more land, and town dwellers should have owned more lots. It is not easy to predict, however, which group should have had more total wealth, since previous information suggests large fortunes in both sections. Nor can we predict which group held more slaves, since slaves appear to have been as widely used in the commercial and manufacturing businesses of the town as in the plantations of the country. Table 11 shows that, as expected, committee members from town and country differed greatly in the sources of their wealth. Each class held slightly diversified property, with town dwellers purchasing some land in the country and country-dwellers investing in some town lots. The overall effect of this tendency is minor, however. In the categories of slaves and total wealth the groups show no significant difference. Though town and country leaders differed greatly in the sources of their wealth, the value of their total holdings was roughly the same.

Finally, there is the criterion of rank. Were the active committee members

Table 9. Property of Committee Members by Age, 1828

	Mean of those over 45 N = 24	Mean of those under 45 N = 51	t	df	p[a]
Acres of land	1853 s = 2409[c]	1701 s = 2839	.23	73	.411*[b]
Assessed value of land	$1429 s = 1359	$1658 s = 2818	−.47	72.92	.318
Number of town lots	2.6 s = 5.5	2.1 s = 3.7	.32	32.80	.375
Assessed value of lots	$1131 s = 2728	$ 602 s = 1112	.91	26.66	.184
Number of slaves	7.6 s = 8.1	6.1 s = 8.1	.75	73	.223*
Total assessed property value	$2560 s = 3401	$2259 s = 2984	.39	73	.350*

[a] Unless otherwise stated, all tests for differences of means in this essay will be one-tailed.
[b] An asterisk after any value of p will indicate, in this table and those in the rest of the chapter, that the given value of t and its significance level are based on a pooled estimate of the variance.
[c] The figure under each mean (s) is the standard deviation of that variable.

Table 10. Property of Committee Members by Ethnicity, 1828

	Mean of the non-Scots N = 50	Mean of the Scots N = 25	t	df	p
Acres of land	1640 s = 2939	1970 s = 2158	− .50	73	.311
Assessed value of land	$1764 s = 2902	$1226 s = 976	1.18	66.70	.121*
Number of town lots	3.0 s = 5.0	.6 s = 1.7	2.97	66.98	.002
Assessed value of lots	$1062 s = 2084	$ 190 s = 715	2.66	67.18	.005
Number of slaves	7.7 s = 9.4	4.4 s = 3.8	2.19	70.92	.016
Total assessed property value	$2825 s = 3635	$1416 s = 1160	2.50	65.45	.008

Table 11. Property of Committee Members by Residence, 1828

	Mean of country residents $N = 40$	Mean of town residents $N = 35$	t	df	p
Acres of land	2571 $s = 3029$	811 $s = 1889$	3.06	66.34	.002
Assessed value of land	$2321 $s = 2875$	$ 743 $s = 1451$	3.05	59.24	.002
Number of town lots	1.2 $s = 3.5$	3.3 $s = 4.9$	-2.06	60.96	.022
Assessed value of lots	$ 126 $s = 246$	$1508 $s = 2423$	-3.36	34.61	.001
Number of slaves	7.1 $s = 7.1$	6.0 $s = 9.2$	.57	73	.571*[a]
Total assessed property value	$2447 $s = 2903$	$2251 $s = 3358$	.27	73	.787*[a]

[a]These values are based on a two-tailed test.

Table 12. Property of Committee Members by Rank, 1828

	Mean of the passive members N = 57	Mean of the active members N = 18	t	df	p
Acres of land	1885 s = 2792	1320 s = 2376	.77	73	.221*
Assessed value of land	$1326 s = 1656	$2403 s = 3992	−1.11	18.88	.140
Number of town lots	2.2 s = 4.6	2.2 s = 3.4	− .04	73	.484*
Assessed value of lots	$ 742 s = 1890	$ 863 s = 1484	− .25	73	.402*
Number of slaves	6.1 s = 6.7	8.3 s = 11.7	− .79	20.62	.219
Total assessed property value	$2068 s = 2658	$3266 s = 4181	−1.15	21.51	.132

wealthier than the passive ones? The performance of the political system at the general committee level suggests that property was very important to the aspiring county leader. We would predict on this basis that inside the committees, higher wealth would continue to distinguish the active from the less active. Table 12 indicates, however, that there was no difference in the property holdings of active and passive committee members. There are indeed large observed differences between the two groups. These differences tend to belie the notion of equality, especially in the categories of land values and total assessed property value. However, the number of cases in the active group is so small, and their average figures are so greatly affected by a few extreme cases, that it is impossible to regard the observed differences as completely convincing.

Given the generally elitist character of political participation in Cumberland County, what is the meaning of specific political divisions within the group of seventy-five notables? While it is unlikely that either group was truly the spokesman of the common man, division between the groups was probably not random and their separating characteristics were important. Were there characteristic differences between the two groups which would explain why each group preferred the candidate of its choice? More immediately, was it the cause of Jacksonian Democracy that made the general's committee more open in its membership than the Adams committee? Within the limitations of an elitist system, how much did differences within the leadership class have to do with the general electoral cleavage of the whole county?

As in the preceding section, age is the first variable which may have influenced political preference. If the Jacksonians were truly more democratic, younger men may have been more welcome in their organization. On the other hand, the Adams organization was in some ways more innovative in its operations. Perhaps this reflected the influence of younger blood. Table 13, however, shows that age had no bearing whatsoever on political choice. As in the elite generally, young men were the majority in both political groups and in roughly equal proportions. Under the crude measurement offered by

Table 13. Candidate Preference by Age, 1828

	Over 45	Under 45	Total
Jackson men	15 29.4%	36 70.6%	51
Adams men	9 37.5%	15 62.5%	24
Total	24 32.0%	51 68.0%	75

Corrected chi-square = .18934; p = .68088 (1 df)

Table 14. Candidate Preference by Residence, 1828

	Country residents	Town residents	Total
Jackson men	30	21	51
	58.8%	41.2%	
Adams men	10	14	24
	44.7%	58.3%	
Total	40	35	75
	53.3%	46.7%	

Corrected chi-square $= 1.30236$; $p = .1269$ (1 df, direction predicted)

the poll tax records, age had no bearing at all on political behavior in Cumberland.

Residence may also have influenced political choice. If Jackson was indeed the favorite of the planters, he would have been more popular among residents of the country. This relationship may be distorted, however, because many of the wealthiest planters listed their residence as Fayetteville. In any case, table 14 shows that there is some reason to believe that Jackson was more popular among country-dwellers. Within the elite as a whole and within the active ranks of that elite, town members held more positions than one would expect given their proportions in the county. The same situation continues when the elite is divided by political preference. Town members were numerous in both groups. In the Adams group, however, the town dwellers were the slight majority, and in the Jackson group, the opposite proportions prevailed. Having predicted the direction of this table, we can state the significance of the value of chi-square as .1269. This probability level is insufficient to be very confident that residence was related to political preference. Jackson *seems* to have been somewhat more popular in the country, but given the limited size of the total group, we would need to find heavier proportions in each committee to be convinced of a real relationship. Nevertheless, the evidence in favor of a town party/country party split in political preference is very suggestive. A decade later, when the Democratic and Whig parties were firmly established, the residential differences between political groups became much more explicit. In the late twenties, however, the political distinction between town and country, as it was reflected in the membership of the two committees, was muted at best.

Ethnicity may also have affected party choice, although residential patterns may have confused the relationship.[54] Because Scots were more numerous

---

54. This potential relationship must be studied with caution. Approximately equal representation of Scots on each committee might not signify that ethnicity was unrelated to partisanship. Equal

Table 15. Candidate Choice by Ethnicity, 1828

	Non-Scots	Scots	Total
Jackson men	31	20	51
	60.8%	39.2%	
Adams men	19	5	24
	79.2%	20.8%	
Total	50	25	75
	66.7%	33.3%	

Corrected chi-square = 1.72335; p = .1893 (1 df)

in the country, and Jackson was probably somewhat more popular among country-dwellers, we would expect Scots to be slightly more numerous in his committee. Table 15 supports this prediction, without confirming it. The committees' Scottish memberships were not equal. The Jackson committee was able to attract a proportion of Scots that was almost twice as high as the Adams committee. The observed value of chi-square is slightly more significant than that of table 14, suggesting again that Scots may have been drawn to the Jackson side for other reasons than the simple fact of residence. This impression is also supported by a check of the two Scottish men listed as actives in table 8. Both were Jackson men.

While residence and ethnicity may have influenced political preference in Cumberland County, the factor which most historians cite as a distinct difference between Adams men and Jackson men is economic. Jackson's sweep of North Carolina in 1828 has been ascribed to a decision by eastern planters that with Crawford unavailable, their human property would be more secure under Jackson, a fellow slaveholder, than under Adams, a New Englander of doubtful sympathies. It may have been true that during the course of the Adams administration, planters generally concluded that his notions of broad construction and federal supremacy were too dangerous and came over en masse to Andrew Jackson. If this were true, then we would expect the general's supporters in Cumberland to be significantly wealthier, to own more slaves, and to have invested more heavily in rural land than their pro-Adams counterparts. On the other hand, if William Gaston and John Cameron were

---

proportions of Scots in each committee might be present in exactly opposite circumstances. If Scottish voters preferred Andrew Jackson on ethnocultural grounds, then organizers of the less favored candidate might be tempted to counteract by recruiting more Scots into their own committee than would have joined if no special efforts were made. In such a situation one candidate's committee would contain genuine community representatives. The other might contain an equal number of men with Scottish names who were atypical or politically eccentric in the Scottish community. Ethnic preferences in political choice would therefore be confused at best when examined in the committees' membership.

correct and Adams attracted the aristocracy, Adams men should have been wealthier than Jacksonians.

Table 16 shows that there did not appear to be any highly significant differences at all between Adams men and Jackson men. If there were any differences, they supported the ideas of Gaston and Cameron. The comparison of numbers of slaves suggests strongly that it was the Adams men and not the Jacksonians who were the larger slaveholders. The difference between the two means of this variable is the most significant in the strictly statistical sense of all the comparisons in table 16. In terms of property values, moreover, the Adams group mean uniformly exceeded the mean of the Jackson group. Although these differences do not meet the usual criteria of significance, they do erode a strictly economic interpretation of the turn to Jackson in eastern North Carolina. If masters feared for their slaves under John Quincy Adams, this fear did not spread to the largest slaveholders in Cumberland County, who would have had the most to lose.

There are features of table 16 which are bewildering on first inspection. Adams supporters were more likely to come from Fayetteville than Jackson supporters. Why then did they not own significantly more town property than the Jacksonians? Town residents were overrepresented in both sections of the elite. Why then did urban sources of wealth comprise such a meager proportion of the groups' total holdings? Of what importance is it that the Adams men and Jackson men held equal acreage but that the Adams men's land was more valuable? Some of this ambiguity results from the aggregation of town dwellers with country-dwellers in the table. By separating the committee members according to residence and repeating the tests, tables 17 and 18 relieve some of this confusion.

These two tables must be interpreted with caution. When the seventy-five subjects are divided into four unequal parts the size of the categories becomes small enough to cast considerable doubt on the validity of the various tests. Ten Adams men, for example, are a slender base to build a convincing model of rural National Republicanism, even in a smaller county than Cumberland. We should use the data of table 17 and table 18 as evidence of certain trends rather than as unassailable explanations of political preference. Even with this caveat in mind, we find that separation by residence makes the differences between the Adams men and Jackson men much clearer. Table 17 indicates, for example, that except in the category of town property, where both sides held so little that differences were inconsequential, Adams men who lived in the country were much wealthier than their neighbors who supported Jackson. This finding confirms the impression derived from table 16. In Cumberland County at least, political preference was not strictly a matter of economic self-interest. A protectionist president who may have been

Table 16. Property of Committee Members by Candidate Preference, 1828

	Mean of the Jackson men N = 51	Mean of the Adams men N = 24	t	df	p
Acres of land	1751 s = 2436	1746 s = 3232	.01	35.77	.497
Assessed value of land	$1349 s = 1652	$2085 s = 3582	- .96	27.71	.173
Number of town lots	2.2 s = 4.9	2.2 s = 3.2	.03	64.03	.488
Assessed value of lots	$ 723 s = 2022	$ 874 s = 1196	- .41	69.04	.343
Number of slaves	5.6 s = 7.9	8.7 s = 8.4	-1.56	73	.062*
Total assessed property value	$2071 s = 2950	$2959 s = 3393	-1.16	73	.126*

Table 17. Property of Rural Committee Members by Candidate Preference, 1828

	Mean of the Jackson men N = 30		Mean of the Adams men N = 10		t	df	p
Acres of land	2087	s = 2083	4023	s = 4094	−1.41	11.29	.093
Assessed value of land	$1543	s = 1567	$4653	s = 4455	−2.16	9.75	.028
Number of town lots	1.3	s = 4.0	1.0	s = 1.9	.32	32.86	.376
Assessed value of lots	$ 206	s = 240	$ 186	s = 266	− .89	38	.189*
Number of slaves	4.8	s = 4.9	13.9	s = 8.4	−3.25	11.16	.004
Total assessed property value	$1649	s = 1637	$4839	s = 4404	−2.24	9.84	.025

Table 18. Property of Fayetteville Committee Members by Candidate Preference, 1828

	Mean of the Jackson men N = 21		Mean of the Adams men N = 14		t	df	p
Acres of land	1271	s = 2342	120	s = 197	2.24	20.42	.019
Assessed value of land	$1072	s = 1767	$ 251	s = 516	2.00	24.82	.028
Number of town lots	3.5	s = 5.6	3.0	s = 3.7	.28	33	.392*
Assessed value of lots	$1603	s = 2959	$1365	s = 1363	.32	30.07	.376
Number of slaves	6.7	s = 10.8	5.0	s = 6.4	.59	32.63	.280
Total assessed property value	$2674	s = 4150	$1616	s = 1508	1.07	27.07	.148

"soft" on slavery perhaps posed an economic threat to the prosperous planters of Cumberland County, yet the rural supporters of John Quincy Adams appear to have been much wealthier than those of Andrew Jackson.

Differences between Adams men and Jackson men are also somewhat clearer among Fayetteville residents taken by themselves. Table 18 shows why the two groups, when residence was not controlled, seemed to hold equal acreage but not equally valuable land. The "equality" of the two groups, it appears, were merely an artificial product of the averaging process. Most landholders who favored Adams lived in the country and owned large amounts of land. There they greatly surpassed the Jackson men in acreage. Jacksonians were more moderate landholders who were generally split between town and country. In town, therefore, they were the largest landowners. The joint mean of the two groups as reported in table 16 disguised this difference.

Although the differences between Jackson and Adams town dwellers are most significant in the case of land and land value, they are suggestive in other areas as well. In Fayetteville the Jackson men appear wealthier than the Adams men in every respect. This is exactly opposite to the situation in the country. Some contributing factors to the difference in wealth between Jackson men and Adams men in Fayetteville seem to be accidental. A large part of the total group wealth of the Jackson town men, for instance, was owned by William Lord and John Kelly, two planters who were also interested in urban real estate. They listed themselves as residents of Fayetteville, but the configuration of their property holdings more closely resembled the patterns of country-dwellers than town dwellers. Between them, Lord and Kelly owned 73 slave polls, 9,482 acres of land worth $9,844, and 20 town lots worth $14,952. Clearly, these men would skew the direction of any small group they fell into. A comparable phenomenon bends the means of the Adams group in the opposite direction. We have already mentioned the "poverty" of Edward Lee Winslow, a prominent member of this group. A similar case is that of Henry A. Donaldson, an industrialist who owned two of the first three cotton mills in North Carolina. Only one of these was in Cumberland County, so Donaldson appears on the records as a moderate property holder instead of the wealthy man he actually was.[55]

*   *   *

Generally speaking, the political elite of Cumberland County was an exclusive group in 1828, for their average property holdings greatly exceeded

55. Cumberland County List of Taxables, 1828, in Cumberland County Records; Fayetteville *Carolina Observer*, June 21, 1826.

the wealth of most taxpayers. Within the committees, leadership positions were readily available to younger men and to men of moderate property, but committee members who lived in the country were less likely to lead than their associates from Fayetteville. This disadvantage especially affected the Scottish members, almost all of whom were rural residents who owned less property than the non-Scots. Otherwise, convenience, interest, and enthusiasm seem to have been the major limits on political involvement within the wealthier class of Cumberland voters. Outside these circles, the ordinary citizen hung back. Almost half of the time in the 1820s he did not even vote. He was welcome at the polls regardless of legal restrictions on the ballot, but his opinion was not sought in the councils of political leadership.

The majority of Adams men lived in Fayetteville and most Jacksonians lived in the country. The proportion of Scots who joined the Jackson committee was twice as high as the proportion who worked for Adams. Administration supporters who lived in the country owned many more slaves and much larger plantations than their neighbors who followed Jackson. Among townsmen, Jacksonians owned more property than Adams men, although quirks in the records make this finding somewhat ambiguous.

This quantitative evidence does not support the opinion that large slaveholders in Cumberland County stood with Jackson, their fellow planter, in order to protect their rights to human property. The tables lend more support to the analysis of contemporaries that Jackson attracted some citizens from the most propertied groups and others from those in more modest circumstances, while Adams represented a coalition of urban interests and large planters. Most Jackson men came from the country, but the richest Jacksonians came from the town. The Jackson men of Fayetteville were the townsmen with the closest ties to the rural community, the ones who invested heavily in farms and real estate. The Jackson men were the larger committee, and they contained a generous mix of diverse social elements. There were several very large slaveholders among them, a sprinkling of urban lawyers and merchants, some moderate farmers, and a considerable number of leading Scottish citizens. The Jackson committee did not duplicate the mythical average man of Cumberland County, but they could fairly present themselves as a relatively broad social coalition and the respectable embodiment of the will of the people.

By contrast, most Adams men lived in town, but the wealthiest Adams men lived in the country. They were the farmers with the largest commitment to commercial agriculture and the closest ties to urban business. They included Jonathan Evans, Josiah Evans, and Henry Elliott—the wealthiest planters, the shrewdest agrarian entrepreneurs, and the most successful operators in the market economy. They were also the members of a social elite and probably represented a convincing aristocracy to most of the dirt farmers of

Cumberland County. If they were desirous of economic development and a stronger federal government, they presumably remained confident that they could control the social changes that might result and continue in their positions at the top of Cumberland County society. Their ideological indifference to strict majority rule was not inconsistent with their social backgrounds.

From the standpoint of explaining why Jackson captured Cumberland County in 1828, the Scottish representatives were perhaps the most interesting element in the general's coalition. In 1824, a combination of Fayetteville and sandhills voters had given Cumberland's plurality to Adams. The available evidence suggests that a similar coalition had kept Cumberland County Federalist in the first party system. In 1836, the Democratic percentage in the sandhills was 55.5 percent. It rose to 71.3 percent in 1840 and remained relatively constant for the next twenty years.[56] No precinct-level election returns exist for the period between 1824 and 1836 which would identify exactly when the Scots changed their loyalties, but if the behavior of Scottish leaders was an accurate indication, the transformation began in 1828.

Other evidence also suggests that Jackson kept his 1824 supporters and added new ones from the sandhills and planting districts to build a broad popular alliance in 1828. In July of that year, Jackson carried straw votes in Neill's Creek and Christian's militia companies by a total of 273 to 11, indicating that these small-farm, non-Scottish neighborhoods were as overwhelmingly Jacksonian then as they had been four years earlier. The administration men had believed they would carry a majority in the plantation district of Lock's Creek, but Captain Plumer's men there went for Jackson, 35 to 19. Outside Cumberland County, a straw vote in the Richmond County Scottish neighborhood of Laurel Hill was 67 for Jackson, 5 for Adams. In a sandhills district of Moore County which was adjacent to the Cumberland Scottish districts of Quewhiffle and Barbecue, 91 of Captain Gaston's company voted for Jackson and 15 voted for Adams.[57]

It is also noteworthy that participation in the 1832 election was almost as low as in 1824, but the National Republican percentage in that canvass was almost half the size of Adams' proportion in 1824. In fact, if Adams' rural votes were subtracted from his total in 1824, his remaining share from Fayetteville alone would have been 23.4 percent, a figure in the same range as the National Republican percentages in 1828 and 1832.[58] In all likelihood, Adams and the National Republicans retained a small but relatively stable proportion

56. Fayetteville *North Carolina Journal*, August 18, 1836; Fayetteville *Observer*, November 18, 1840. See also figures 7 and 8.
57. Fayetteville *Carolina Observer*, July 31, 1828, August 7, 1828, July 17, 1828; Fayetteville *North Carolina Journal*, March 5, 1828.
58. Adams won 28.3 percent in 1828 and Clay won 21.9 percent in 1832. The county turnout rate was 34.6 percent in 1824, 55.8 percent in 1828, and 40.4 percent in 1832. See figure 3. Compiled Election Returns, "Presidential Electors," 1824, 1828, 1832.

of Fayetteville voters from 1824 through 1832. Jackson's gains in 1828 probably came from some newly mobilized voters and from significant defections
among Adams' former supporters in the sandhills.

The most plausible factors which might have led some Scots to prefer Jackson over Adams relate to cultural concerns. There is no reason to think that
the small Scottish farmers were not just as eager to demonstrate their freedom
as the other yeomen in the county. By all accounts, moreover, the Scots of the
upper Cape Fear were strictly Calvinist Presbyterians who resisted the op-
timistic revivalism of the Second Great Awakening.[59] If there was any connection between Arminian theology and faith in man's potential for material
self-improvement, then acceptance of predestination and innate depravity
should have made the Scots even less responsive to John Quincy Adams' confidence in government-sponsored reform than other southern Protestants. If
the earlier analysis was correct, moreover, the Scots had not supported Federalism because of an indelible affection for the party's principles, but because
of the hostilities generated by the American Revolution and its aftermath.
During the years of the first party system, no Federalist president summoned
them to worldly improvement, and their skepticism of progress remained un-
challenged. John Quincy Adams and the political movement he represented
were not so remote, however, and may have presented the Scots with a contradiction between their habitual loyalties and their community values. If so,
values seem to have prevailed. Old distinctions between country Scots and
non-Scots faded in importance beside their shared rural world view, and the
two groups joined in the cause of Jacksonian Democracy.

The election of 1828 elicited two different concepts of political partisanship. The Jackson men called themselves "the party of our country" because
they claimed to represent the great body of the people and stressed no common opinion on public policy except the principle of majority rule. Implicit
within their slogans was the Jeffersonian view that the people's interests and
the people's will were both unitary, that the only basic division in society was
between "the many and the few," and that parties in a republic would disap-
pear when the former group took control from the latter. The Adams men, on
the other hand, had accepted a Burkean notion of party as a circle of high-
minded men with common opinions on questions of public policy.[60] They accepted the idea that there would be other groups of men with other opinions,
and they did not object to the existence of opposing parties that were "conducted with candor," *i.e.*, that were consistent and sincere and were not

59. Boyd, *The Federal Period*, 191; Johnson, *Ante-Bellum North Carolina*, 349–50; Thompson,
Presbyterians in the South, I, 315.
60. Richard Hofstadter, *The Idea of a Party System: The Rise of Legitimate Opposition in the
United States, 1780–1840* (Berkeley, 1972), 29–33.

formed merely for the enjoyment of office. Privately, some Adams men accepted the Jacksonian division of society and thought of themselves as the righteous and genteel few.

The social composition of the two elite groups reflected their ideologies and their understandings of partisanship. The Jackson men represented diverse interests without a well-established consensus on policy issues, while the Adams men were a more uniform group of merchants and planters who were interested in promoting the market economy. Although the Jackson men claimed to represent no special interest except the will of the people, the tone of their rhetoric and their superior attractiveness to rural farmers betrayed their basically agrarian character. In their view, bargain and intrigue, elite rule, protective tariffs, broad construction, usurpation of power, and gambling devices in the White House were all corrupting influences in the traditional rural republic. The campaign thus dealt with the same issues of country versus town that the Seawell-McDiarmid quarrel did a year later. The presidential election, however, put the struggle on a national plane, and attracted more fervent interest and commitment. As a natural consequence, the turnout was higher in 1828 than any adjacent election, including the People's Ticket campaign of 1824. Saving the country's future from ruin was a worthier cause than even an anticaucus crusade could be, and the citizens of Cumberland responded accordingly.

The Jacksonian viewpoint triumphed in Cumberland County by 821 votes to 325. The victory was especially significant because, according to the *North Carolina Journal*, "The County of Cumberland and Town of Fayetteville . . . have been accounted Mr. Adams' *strong hold* in North-Carolina." [61] The Jackson men established that no group could obtain public office or control public policy without a vocal commitment to the will of the people. As an event in the evolution of political culture, the victory of Jacksonian democracy was therefore very substantial. Whether a simple commitment to majority rule sufficed to control public policy indefinitely remained an unanswered question. Events in the county in the following years would prove that the great body of the people could not remain unanimous for long. Paradoxically, the Jacksonians would be forced to shed some supporters in order to remain an effective local majority. As they did so, they became something more than a Jeffersonian consensus for democracy but still something less than a club of the like-minded. The Adams men and some erstwhile Jacksonians made a similar transformation. The two groups developed into the Democratic and Whig parties by a painstaking trial-and-error effort in the early 1830s.

As both sides formed their ranks, the relevance of traditional antipartyism

61. Fayetteville *North Carolina Journal*, December 12, 1827.

grew dimmer and dimmer. Posturing for the sake of one's honor was all very well in the context of homogeneous values, but when a community's basic vision of its way of life became a matter for debate and speculation, the practical outcome of politics assumed a wholly new importance. As the political divisions of Cumberland deepened, one heard less about the horrors of faction and the centrality of reputation, and more about the value of loyalty and the necessity for organization. With the coming of Jackson's Bank War, moreover, this somewhat amorphous local struggle took on concrete national meaning, and the citizens of Cumberland were ready for the challenge. They picked up the national labels and national symbols of their respective sides with little hesitation, and plunged into the second party system as soon as the tocsin sounded. Cumberland voters needed no gradual introduction to the second party system, for they had thoroughly rehearsed its issues in 1828 and 1829.

V. **Banners of Political Faith:** The Development of Party Platforms 1828–1834

Andrew Jackson's victory had established the fact that most Cumberland County voters would unite to defend the "will of the people." The election also divided political leaders into formal and competing organizations for the first time. For any local leader who could read the returns properly, the implications of these two developments were not lost. Whatever the office seeker's combination of motives—the simple comforts of patronage, community endorsement of his personal status, the achievement of a solid political program, or the moral gratification of public service—he could not afford to ignore the will of the people. On the contrary, activists had every incentive to keep this erstwhile sleeping giant awake, for any politician who could harness the people's will to his own goals was assured of personal success. And if the rudimentary committees of vigilance had had anything to do with the people's arousal, there was no reason on anyone's part to allow the electorate to slip back into its older tradition of unorganized independence.

The other questions faced by the citizens remained unsettled. Neither the Adams men nor the Jacksonians had made any attempt to link local controversies to the national presidential election. The Adams men had claimed to share common convictions on matters of national policy, and the pattern of their property holdings gave them a common interest in the market economy, but their defeat implied no inevitable verdict for local commercial interests. The Jackson men were more attractive to rural residents than the Adams supporters, but their victory did not necessarily mean a triumph for the enemies of development. The Jackson leaders had not even claimed to represent a common set of policies, and their interests and convictions were too diverse to form a governing coalition. James Seawell, the bridge builder and steamboat owner, rubbed shoulders in the Jackson committee of vigilance with Archibald McDiarmid, the Scottish farmer and opponent of new roads. In spite of their mutual dislike, Edward J. Hale and John A. Cameron spent an uncomfortable year as political bedfellows in the same group. These men could agree on very little except the importance of majority rule and the need for virtuous self-government.

This coalition could not remain stable. President Jackson took very vigorous action on divisive policy questions where candidate Jackson had kept silent. County leaders who could not support these actions had little choice but to leave the Jacksonian camp. Those who remained tended to be those who could reconcile their own desires for the local community with the president's intentions for the republic. These men solidified the Jacksonian coalition by finding ways to show voters that Jackson's battles in Washington were larger versions of struggles which concerned the citizens in Cumberland County. They created specific linkages between local and national controversies for the first time. In doing so they continued their homage to the will of the people as they broadened and formalized the temporary institutional structure of the committees of vigilance.

The men who could not continue to support Jackson gravitated to his longstanding opponents. Together, these two groups also pointed out the parallels between national and local events. They solidified a coalition that took the name Whig party. They hoped to unseat Jackson and his followers by showing that the president's policies harmed local needs and sensibilities. Each party created an intellectual and emotional framework for interpreting politics which allowed voters to recognize all local, state, and national events as unfolding aspects of a single struggle. These interpretative frameworks were the basic platforms of the Whig and Democratic parties. They gave to national political contests a sense of immediacy which previously they had lacked and redeemed local contests from triviality. When the two parties became firmly established, voter participation rates surged to previously unmatched heights, as every citizen came to recognize what the *North Carolina Journal* called "the banner of his own political faith." [1]

Fabrication of these banners challenged the abilities of Cumberland County leaders. If the polarization of the elite which occurred in 1828 was the first stage of party formation, the second stage was a search for explanations that would make the polarities clear and relevant for masses of voters. The leaders' search for connections between national and local events was decisively affected by important events outside the county. These new developments included a series of occurrences which heightened sensitivity on the slavery issue, a statewide movement for internal improvements, and the war between Andrew Jackson and the Bank of the United States. A brief survey of each of

1. Fayetteville *North Carolina Journal*, July 25, 1832.

these areas of political concern will clarify the subsequent intellectual development of the party platforms.

Andrew Jackson's first term in office featured a dramatic power struggle between the president and the vice president, John C. Calhoun of South Carolina. The dispute involved a factional struggle in the Democratic party, a constitutional debate over states' rights, and a sectional argument over the South's place in the national union. The controversy reached a climax in the Nullification Crisis, when Calhoun led the state of South Carolina to declare the tariff null and void within its borders and President Jackson threatened to send the army to enforce federal law in South Carolina.

William W. Freehling has shown that South Carolina's sensitivity to the tariff could not be separated from slaveholders' fears of their slaves and their uncertainty about the future of slavery.[2] Whites in Cumberland County shared these anxieties but not to the same extent as their neighbors to the south. In 1830, Fayetteville's Magistrate of Police Louis D. Henry reported to the governor of North Carolina that "in case of an insurrectionary movement of the coloured population of this place, the white community are in awful peril, from the manner in which the public arms are kept here." The arsenal was vulnerable to an axe or other small tool, Henry said, "and thus in a moment the blacks could arm themselves."[3] The next year, reports of Nat Turner's insurrection and a suspected conspiracy in adjoining Sampson County caused widespread alarm, but town officials kept their heads. They mobilized five companies of militia and sent reinforcements to Sampson but made no wholesale arrests of local blacks. Their attitude was summarized by a merchant who reported "great excitement" to his associate in Guilford County but concluded calmly, "I think it no harm to be prepared for danger even if it should not come."[4] In keeping with this cautious attitude, the *Carolina Observer* boasted that "in this place, there has been no interruption to business, and no undue excitement." A month later, editor Edward J. Hale endorsed a proposal for compensated emancipation with colonization of the freedmen without arousing any proslavery furor.[5]

At the height of the insurrection scare, prominent men of both town and country met separately and passed resolutions which denounced the tariff as "onerous . . . unjust . . . unnecessary . . . and inexpedient." They hastened to add, however, "that we value the Union as we value our individual happi-

2. William W. Freehling, *Prelude to Civil War: The Nullification Controversy in South Carolina, 1816–1836* (New York, 1965), 49–86.
3. Louis D. Henry to John Owen, September 3, 1830, MS copy in the Governors' Letter Books, vol. 28, p. 32.
4. John C. Latta to Robert C. Caldwell, September 14, 1831, David Franklin Caldwell Papers, Southern Historical Collection.
5. Fayetteville *Carolina Observer*, September 21, 1831, October 12, 1831.

ness and the happiness of our families . . . and as we value our National Independence, and the noble sacrifices that achieved it." They endorsed the proposed Free Trade Convention in Philadelphia and authorized delegates to it, but refused to encourage John C. Calhoun's presidential ambitions or his theories on state sovereignty.[6] When South Carolina acted on its threats and nullified the tariff in 1832, Calhoun's closest supporters in Fayetteville were dismayed and antinullification letters blossomed in the press.[7] At the same time, a number of former Jacksonians began to edge away from the president and to display a heightened sensitivity to states' rights. Several members of the president's 1828 committee refused to endorse Martin Van Buren for vice president in 1832 and backed Phillip P. Barbour of Virginia instead. No fire-eating speeches entered the press and no exaggerated denunciations of abolition appeared, but the Barbour supporters worried openly about "the present critical state of public affairs, when the constitutional rights of the Southern people are in danger of total usurpation."[8] The fear of conspiracy and the threat of the tariff had undoubtedly stimulated concern for the vital interests of the South.

The cause of internal improvements had more visible influence on the course of political development than questions relating to states' rights. In the years between 1817 and 1833, North Carolina spent $295,146.98 in state aid to internal improvements. At the end of this period, the Internal Improvements Fund was practically exhausted and the state had little to show for its contributions.[9] Poor planning and inexperience had produced what contemporaries regarded as a colossal waste of money, and sentiment ran high against any further experiments in this area. Discerning observers recognized two problems which had undermined early efforts. Poor planning and sectional competition had dispersed the available funds to numerous local projects, with the result that no comprehensive system had been possible. Most efforts had gone to improving navigation by river clearance and canals, but North Carolina's physical features limited the long-term feasibility of this approach.

In 1828, Joseph Caldwell, president of the University of North Carolina, began a series of newspaper articles over the signature "Carlton" which explained these difficulties and pointed to a solution. Later republished in pamphlet form, *The Numbers of Carlton* introduced North Carolinians to the idea of the railroad, a new invention which Caldwell believed could overcome the technical disadvantages of canals. He suggested that one central railroad

6. *Ibid.*, September 7, 1831, September 14, 1831.
7. *Ibid.*, September 11, 1832, September 18, 1832, October 2, 1832, October 9, 1832, October 16, 1832, November 6, 1832.
8. *Ibid.*, June 5, 1832.
9. "Report of the Board for Internal Improvements," *North Carolina Legislative Documents*, 1833, no. 7, p. 6.

which connected the mountains to the coast would stimulate the economy of the entire state, concentrate North Carolina's commerce in a single place, and reduce sectional jealousies.[10]

The Numbers of Carlton stimulated new interest in internal improvements among business and political leaders. Their interest increased further when Charleston merchants began to construct a railroad from their city to Hamburg, South Carolina. Charleston's project demonstrated that the railroad was indeed practical and might divert trade from one city to another if municipal leaders lacked the energy to compete. The first public meeting to call for a railroad in North Carolina met in Chatham County in 1828. The delegates asked for an experimental line which would run from the waterfront at Campbellton to the Market House in upper Fayetteville. Two years later, town leaders decided that the time was ripe to make this proposal a reality. The Fayetteville press reminded the citizens that "there is yet time to save ourselves" and asked, "shall we improve or neglect it?" [11]

This question had political overtones from the beginning. The *Observer* asked it in connection with a preelection appeal to the voters to support the candidate for town member who could do the most for local internal improvements. Without naming its favorite, the *Observer* urged support for the man who could make the most effective constitutional arguments for improvement, whose personal qualities would enable him to attract support from other sections, and whose personal involvement in Fayetteville's commerce linked his own interests more closely to the interests of the town. This candidate was evidently Louis D. Henry, a wealthy Jacksonian lawyer who had served several terms as magistrate of police. Henry was born in New Jersey and had graduated from Princeton, but he studied law in New Bern and settled in Fayetteville. He later became a senior Democratic politician in the state who served as Speaker of the House of Commons in 1832, commissioner to settle the Spanish claims in 1837, and the Democratic nominee for governor in 1842. In 1830, Henry defeated William Waddil, Jr., for Fayetteville town member, 173 votes to 127.[12]

When the legislature convened, a Fayetteville town meeting passed resolutions which requested state aid for a railroad to run from Campbellton to the commercial district in upper Fayetteville and from thence to the Yadkin River, about a hundred miles away. Failing a state subsidy, the meeting asked for a corporate charter to build the road privately with help from the town government. Henry supported this request in Raleigh, but all he obtained was a char-

---

10. [Joseph Caldwell], *The Numbers of Carlton, Addressed to the People of North Carolina, on a Central Rail-Road Through the State* (New York, 1828).
11. *Ibid.*, 231; Fayetteville *Carolina Observer*, May 13, 1830.
12. Oates, *The Story of Fayetteville*, 834; Fayetteville *Carolina Observer*, August 19, 1830.

ter for a railroad to run from the Campbellton waterfront to any point within Fayetteville. The town corporation received the right to buy all or part of the twenty thousand dollars of authorized capital.[13]

Undismayed, Fayetteville boosters argued that this small line would demonstrate the advantage of railroads and reduce the price of hauling local freight. They decided not to exercise the right of municipal ownership, and when the books opened, individuals quickly subscribed more than twice the allowed sum. Edward L. Winslow became the first president, and his brother Warren joined four other prominent merchants on the board of directors.[14]

After this promising start, the Fayetteville Rail Road faltered. The line was eventually completed from the river to the Market House, but poor design prevented it from operating successfully. Attention in Fayetteville soon shifted to grander projects. Within a year, Wilmington and Fayetteville merchants were asking for a railroad charter to run from the former town to the latter and then to the Yadkin River. The legislature granted a charter to the Cape Fear and Yadkin Rail Road Company, but the unwillingness of westerners to contribute to the project led to its demise. Given the shortage of capital, Wilmington wanted to connect the two towns first and penetrate the backcountry later, while Fayetteville's priorities were exactly the opposite. In December of 1832, a town meeting asked the legislature for a law permitting the town to borrow $200,000 for a railroad subscription and a petition from 112 prominent citizens supported the request. The petition succeeded over some opposition but the additional capital was apparently insufficient. The subscriptions of Wilmington investors were returned in May, 1833, and Fayetteville and Wilmington fell to quarreling over which town was responsible for the project's collapse.[15]

The lesson of the early 1830s seemed to be that private investment, even when supplemented by municipal bonds, could not generate the capital to meet North Carolina's needs. Urged on by Governor David Lowry Swain and other senior state politicians and businessmen, the Raleigh *Star* carried the internal improvements campaign a step further by calling for a state convention to develop new strategies. The convention met in Raleigh on July 4, 1833, a date which coincided with the cornerstone-laying ceremony for the new state capitol. James Seawell, then magistrate of police, called a meeting in response which named eleven delegates to the Raleigh convention. The group consisted of one judge, three practicing attorneys, two leading mer-

13. Fayetteville *North Carolina Journal*, December 15, 1830; Fayetteville *Carolina Observer*, January 6, 1831.
14. Fayetteville *Carolina Observer*, March 3, 1831, March 17, 1831.
15. Oates, *The Story of Fayetteville*, 94; Fayetteville *Carolina Observer*, December 21, 1831, February 21, 1832; "To the Honorable General Assembly of North Carolina: The Undersigned Citizens of the Town of Fayetteville . . ." December 28, 1832 (MS petition in Legislative Papers, 1832); Fayetteville *Observer*, May 7, 1833.

chants, the president of the Fayetteville Rail Road Company, a banker, and two editors, while three merchants, the town clerk, and the general agent of the Cape Fear Navigation Company served as a committee to collect information on the trade of Fayetteville.[16]

When the convention met, a full delegation of Fayetteville residents represented Cumberland County. The convention endorsed the so-called "two-fifths principle" that the state furnish two-fifths of the capital for any internal improvements project that lay completely within the state. The convention added that public money should only be spent for projects that directed commerce to towns in North Carolina, implying that the interests of merchants should prevail in a conflict with the interests of shippers. Robert Strange and Louis D. Henry, both Cumberland County representatives who later became major figures in the Democratic party, spoke in favor of this resolution, and no one from Cumberland spoke against it. Strange and Henry also served on a committee, chaired by Federalist William Gaston of New Bern, which prepared an address to the people of the state.[17]

The convention adopted no specific plan of improvement but called for numerous meetings which would collect information, educate the public, and instruct legislators on the subject of internal improvements. Fayetteville plunged eagerly into the business of organizing local meetings and spreading its ideas to adjacent counties. Louis D. Henry joined Edward R. Wilkings, a merchant, and Dr. Thomas N. Cameron, the brother of John A. Cameron, to produce a report to prove that the Cape Fear River, as improved by the Cape Fear Navigation Company, was superior to any railroad as an outlet to the sea, but that a railroad from Fayetteville westward was essential to open up the backcountry. They printed a thousand copies of the report and sent large delegations to carry its message to district conventions in Pittsborough, Salisbury, Wilmington, and Smithfield. Louis D. Henry and James Seawell played very active roles in most of these conventions and kept in close touch with Governor David Lowry Swain, who served informally as the statewide coordinator of the 1833 internal improvements campaign.[18]

The climax of their effort was a second convention in Raleigh timed to co-

16. Fayetteville *Observer*, June 18, 1833.
17. *Ibid.*, June 25, 1833; *Journal of the Internal Improvements Convention Which Met at Raleigh on the 4th of July, 1833, Together with the Address of the Committee of that Body to the Citizens of North Carolina* (Raleigh, 1833).
18. Fayetteville *Observer*, August 27, 1833, September 24, 1833, October 29, 1833, November 5, 1833, November 19, 1833; Raleigh *Register*, December 3, 1833; James Seawell to David L. Swain, September 22, 1833, Epistolatory Correspondence of David L. Swain, vol. 4, typed copies in Southern Historical Collection, made from manuscripts in bound volumes, Cobb loan, North Carolina Collection; Carolyn Andrews Wallace, "David Lowry Swain: The First Whig Governor of North Carolina," in J. Carlyle Sitterson (ed.), *Studies in Southern History in Memory of Albert Ray Newsome, 1891–1951*, James Sprunt Studies in History and Political Science, XXXIX (Chapel Hill, 1957), 67–68.

incide with the opening of the legislature. Forty-eight counties sent delegates to this convention. Governor Swain served as president and Edward L. Winslow acted as one of the secretaries. The final proposals of the convention were written by a committee chaired by John A. Cameron's brother Duncan, and the memorial of the convention to the legislature was composed by Judge Robert Strange. By a vote of forty-four counties to four, the convention adopted a plan for internal improvements based on two major thoroughfares "by rail road, river, or canal or by any two of them or all *united*," one from the ocean to the Tennessee line and the other from the Roanoke River on the northern border of the state to South Carolina. The key feature of the proposal called for exclusive state ownership of these facilities, to be paid for by loans of up to five million dollars.[19]

The legislature received the convention's memorial but utterly failed to act on it. To the intense disappointment of editors across the state, the legislators passed numerous charters for railroads without making any provision for public support or for a comprehensive plan of development. One of these charters went to the Cape Fear, Yadkin, & Pedee Rail Road and allowed this new company to build a railroad from Fayetteville to the west without making any connection with Wilmington. Fayetteville editors were not consoled by this sop. "The Legislature has not met public expectation," accused the *North Carolina Journal*, "and has, as we believe, defeated the wishes of a large portion of the people of the State, set at nought their recommendations through their Delegates in Convention assembled, and assumed to dictate to the people." In common with most of the state's press, the Fayetteville *Observer* was even more caustic. The legislature adjourned, Hale wrote, "not only without doing aught to improve the condition of the agricultural interests of the State, but actually having injured the cause by the utmost coldness and unconcern . . . [and] that the reliance of the people upon the Legislature, is fallacious." The *Observer* concluded with a call for political bloodletting: "At the next August elections, let the State Councils be purged of all who have proved unfaithful or unmindful of the high obligations imposed upon them." The *Journal* agreed: "It is time for reform."[20] The stage was thus set for a major political donnybrook, as the urban and commercial advocates of internal improvements confronted the silent but powerful opposition of eastern and rural defenders of the status quo.

As it happened, the August elections of 1834 never became a simple refer-

19. "Memorial of the Convention upon the Subject of Internal Improvement; Held in Raleigh, November, 1833, to the General Assembly of North Carolina," *North Carolina Legislative Documents*, 1833, no. 4, pp. 4, 5; Raleigh *Register*, December 3, 1833.
20. Fayetteville *North Carolina Journal*, January, 1834; Fayetteville *Observer*, January 14, 1834; Raleigh *Register*, January 14, 1834, February 4, 1834.

endum on internal improvements. The contest was complicated by the intrusion of another question that was equally significant to Fayetteville's future. If states' rights and internal improvements were two of the most important issues underlying party formation, the third and decisive controversy was Andrew Jackson's Bank War.

The second Bank of the United States was a mixed public and private corporation with headquarters in Philadelphia and branches in each of the states. It received a monopoly of the government's banking business and promoted a uniform national currency in exchange for this privilege. Under Nicholas Biddle, its last and most able president, the Bank followed a strict policy of returning the notes of all state banks promptly and demanding specie in return. This policy discouraged excessive note issue by the state banks and created more confidence in the notes they did issue. As a result, state bank paper circulated more widely and at less discount than before, and the interests of interstate commerce benefited accordingly.

Biddle's policies were popular among North Carolinians with an interest in finance. The state contained three banks during this period, the State Bank of North Carolina, the Bank of Cape Fear, and the Bank of New Bern, plus an office of discount and deposit of the Bank of the United States. All but the Bank of New Bern had offices in Fayetteville. During the 1820s, the North Carolina state banks had overissued their notes and had suspended specie payments repeatedly. North Carolina state bank notes circulated at a 12 to 14 percent discount outside the state and commerce suffered. When the Bank of the United States stepped in to referee note issue, the discount on state bank notes fell to 1 or 2 percent and specie payments resumed.[21] In the early 1830s, North Carolina merchants and commercial farmers were enjoying their first period of monetary stability in over a decade. To complicate matters, the charters of North Carolina's state banks were expiring and legislators and stockholders were having difficulty coming to terms over new charters. If the state banks were not rechartered immediately, banking customers expected assistance from the Bank of the United States in the period of transition.[22]

The charter of the Bank of the United States would expire in 1836, but the Bank's friends in Congress passed a bill to recharter it four years early in the mistaken belief that President Jackson would not dare cast a veto in an election year. Never one to shrink from a challenge, Jackson issued his veto on July 10, 1832. In his veto message, the president questioned the constitutionality of the Bank and objected vehemently to its privileges as a chartered monopoly. The veto message was a political and ideological masterpiece

---

21. Ralph C. H. Catterall, *The Second Bank of the United States* (Chicago, 1903), 435, 441–42; Jean Alexander Wilburn, *Biddle's Bank: The Crucial Years* (New York, 1967), 43, 51.
22. Boyd, *The Federal Period*, 130, 175.

which cast the Bank as the perfect symbol for economic forces which corrupted the republic and at the same time inhibited the average man. The *North Carolina Journal* praised the veto but the Fayetteville *Observer* mostly ignored it.[23] Hale was still a nominal Jacksonian in 1832 and may not have wished to jeopardize the Bank further by entangling its fate with that of Jackson's opponent, Henry Clay. Friends of the Bank may also have felt that the next four years would give them ample time to circumvent the president's objections.

Serious complaints about the Bank War did not begin in North Carolina until almost a year and a half after the veto. In the fall of 1833, Jackson shuffled his cabinet until he found a secretary of the treasury who would follow his orders and remove the public deposits from the Bank of the United States. Loss of the government's business naturally damaged the Bank's profits and stability and appeared to violate its charter rights. Some congressmen believed that the secretary of the treasury had no right to act as he did without the consent of Congress and that Jackson's orders were a usurpation of power. The Bank's major friends seem to have agreed that deposit removal threatened its existence far more seriously than the veto alone, and they reacted with fury. The Bank itself prepared for withdrawal by sharply contracting its discounts, which produced cries of pain from merchants and commercial centers all over the country.[24]

Biddle also fought back politically. He used his influence with provincial bankers and merchants to solicit petitions in favor of the Bank. The effort was very successful, perhaps beyond Biddle's expectations. Throughout the winter and spring of 1834, Congress received hundreds of petitions and memorials on deposit removal, some of which carried thousands of signatures. The Senate published seventeen messages from North Carolina, of which thirteen protested deposit removal and four supported it. The probank messages came from all parts of the state, principally from commercial centers like Fayetteville, New Bern, and Beaufort, but also from eastern plantation counties like Halifax and Lenoir and small-farm areas in the west like Mocksville and Wilkes County. Wake County and Edgecombe County in the eastern planting districts each produced two antibank petitions.[25]

Most of the North Carolina messages came in the form of resolutions passed by public meetings. Most of them laid dual stress on the ill effects of deposit removal and the alleged illegality of the president's actions. The resolutions from New Bern expressed a common viewpoint. "We look upon the

23. Fayetteville *North Carolina Journal*, July 25, 1832, August 1, 1832; Fayetteville *Observer*, July 24, 1832.
24. Catterall, *The Second Bank of the United States*, 298, 314–31, 335.
25. *Senate Documents*, 23rd Cong., 1st Sess., vol. 1, xvi, xix.

late alarming Executive encroachment on legislative and private rights, as dangerous precedent, and subversive of the constitutional liberties of the people. . . . The bank has established a sound circulating medium," the meeting declared, and "efficiently aided the enterprises of honest industry, and a renewal of its charter will be promotive of the best interests of the people." New Bern's resolutions might be dismissed as self-serving grumbles from merchants and diehard Federalists, but the lumbermen of Tyrrell County assured Congress that their petition in favor of the Bank was "*no political trick*, but . . . the deliberate expression of the opinions of men without distinction of party." Likewise, the Lenoir County petitioners stressed that "they are a community of plain planters; that they are not interested as stockholders or debtors in the bank, but they have a deep interest in the preservation of a sound circulating currency, and feel an unspeakable solicitude for a wise and honest administration of our Government and for the perpetuity of our constitution." [26]

The office of discount and deposit of the Bank of the United States in Fayetteville enjoyed particular support in North Carolina. Even John A. Cameron admitted "that the Bank of the United States has done some good—nay—much good," even though he insisted that all bank charters were unconstitutional. [27] The Salisbury memorialists informed Congress that "the undersigned take pride and pleasure in bearing testimony to the ability, integrity, and liberality with which the said bank in this state has been conducted." [28] Later that year, a Salisbury newspaper declared that "our own State Bank has devoured the poor man's substance with insatiate appetite . . . while at the very time the United States Bank at Fayetteville was relieving its debtors against its exactions. To North Carolina, this Bank has been a shield and a sanctuary." [29] Cumberland County inhabitants expressed similar sentiments. As early as June 6, 1832, citizens of county and town ("principally the former," according to the *Observer*) assembled to declare that "the continuance of the present Bank of the United States is demanded by the best interests of the country" and to urge Congressman Lauchlin Bethune to vote for its recharter. Col. Alexander Elliot, prominent planter and future Whig, chaired the meeting and William Murchison, townsman and future Democrat, served as secretary. When the *Observer* reprinted the minutes, the editor noted that two or three hundred citizens had signed the resolutions before they were sent to Bethune. He also remarked "that there probably was never an institution managed with more prudence and at the same time, liberality,

26. *Ibid.*, vol. 2, no. 120; vol. 4, no. 267; vol. 4, no. 293.
27. Fayetteville *North Carolina Journal*, February 3, 1830.
28. *Senate Documents*, 23rd Cong., 1st Sess., vol. 2, no. 54.
29. Salisbury *Watchman*, n.d., quoted in Fayetteville *Observer*, August 19, 1834.

than the Office of the Bank of the United States in this town" and reminded his readers that the Bank was responsible for making North Carolina money "as good as any Bank Notes in the Union." [30]

The business leaders of Fayetteville were therefore drawing on widespread and long-standing friendship for the Bank when they declared in their own petition to Congress in 1834 "that the removal of the Deposites by the Executive, is in violation of law, will result in loss to the Country, and the power, which has thus been exercised, and is claimed by the President, if recognized, and allowed, will ultimately tend to the destruction of the Constitution and the Government." [31] But the hesitation of state legislators to issue new bank charters after the state banks' poor performance in the 1820s and the appearance of antibank petitions suggested that anticommercial sentiment, though less articulate, was as widespread and deep-rooted as support for the banks. Like the questions of states' rights and internal improvements, the banking and currency issue had a joint impact on sensitive economic interests and traditional political fears about the abuse of power. All three issues were therefore ideal vehicles for popular mobilization.

An issue by itself would mobilize nobody. The ambitious politician who hoped to arouse the will of the people and to ride into office in connection with states' rights, internal improvements, or banks could not do so until the voters understood these issues properly. If he grasped this simple truth, the office seeker could attempt to mobilize voters by explaining each separate issue in the familiar terms of local political culture, or he might attempt something more radical. If he reworked popular concepts convincingly, voters might internalize new ways of looking at the world which would give meaning to a whole succession of previously unintelligible developments, without the need for repeated explanations and argument. As it turned out, this was the strategy that worked. In the new politics of the 1830s, rewards would go to the politician who could present the voters with the most meaningful new world view. Those who succeeded would enjoy the spoils of office and the satisfaction of serving the popular will. Increasingly, those who failed would not even enjoy the loser's consolation of being able to try again.

Eventually, county politicians created two alternative world views or intellectual frameworks which made the issues of states' rights, internal improvements, and banks intensely meaningful to the electorate. Those few who could not accommodate themselves to one viewpoint or the other dropped out of politics. These two world views amounted to the well-known Whig and Jacksonian "persuasions" or party ideologies. Each was a variant of tradi-

30. Fayetteville *Observer*, June 12, 1832.
31. *Senate Documents*, 23rd Cong., 1st Sess., vol. 3, no. 140.

tional republican political culture, and each enabled its adherents to identify with some version of the will of the people. Each formulation supported its own political program and provided certain answers to the questions of political economy that troubled the community and nation. Finally, each became the "banner of political faith" for a well organized political party. Creation of these frameworks was the second stage of political party formation.

The task of creation was not easy. In the first stage, the rupture of older patterns of consensus had followed more or less naturally from the pressure of outside events in politics and the economy. In the second stage, formulation of partisan ideologies called for more deliberative action, but many Cumberland County leaders had conflicting interests and attitudes on the major questions of the day. All factions of the elite made difficult adjustments to reconcile their local and national political views and to make the resulting packages comprehensible and acceptable to large numbers of voters. County leaders did not develop these platforms uniformly, nor were their thoughts independent from ideas in the national press and elsewhere. Their responses to the major events of the early 1830s generally paralleled the spectrum of their reactions to President Jackson, from enthusiastic acceptance through tortured indecision to thorough rejection. The parties finished their platforms at different times, but the process was mostly complete by 1834. The town election of 1834 capped the process of intellectual development and began the process of partisan advocacy.

The statements of John A. Cameron indicated the difficulty which many notables faced in linking local and national issues. In his private capacity, Cameron favored measures to encourage economic development. In 1824, he had served on a committee appointed by a Fayetteville town meeting to prepare a memorial to the legislature asking that body not to suspend improvements on the Cape Fear River, not to discharge the state engineer, and not to abolish the Board of Internal Improvements. As late as 1830, he had confirmed this position and even surpassed it. He had served on a committee to implement a resolution of a town meeting requesting state aid for a railroad from the Cape Fear River at Fayetteville to the Yadkin River in the western Piedmont.[32] These positions put Cameron on the urban side of the local town-country division. Cameron did not extend his urban orientation to his public role. As an editor, he was silent on the issue of internal improvement by the state. When he spoke about positive government programs on the federal level, he was vehemently opposed to urban values. To Cameron, industry was not a source of national prosperity. Measures to encourage it only debilitated

32. Fayetteville *Carolina Observer*, December 2, 1824; Fayetteville *Observer*, December 2, 1832.

the nation because they would "*create paupers* to work the Northern and Eastern manufactures . . . and . . . complete, if possible, the ruin, degradation and poverty of the Southern States." Agricultural expansion in the West, however, would increase the national welfare. "Policy and patriotism alike forbid the throwing of obstacles in the way of the growth of the new States," he claimed. "It is but adding to the strength of the whole, when by constitutional means, we encourage the growth of any member of the confederacy." The editor therefore opposed any limitation on the sale of the public lands. He opposed distribution of surplus revenue for internal improvements or any other purpose. The latter opinion was his only recorded difference with Jackson, who eventually acquiesced in the measure, though he disapproved of it. Cameron's position was thus more conservative than the president's.[33]

Cameron's mixed record of opposition and support to urban-oriented measures might have created problems of consistency for him as the second party system came closer to fruition. Before the system was fully mature, however, he was safely ensconced in Vera Cruz. Cameron was therefore never asked to explain why, if progress was a bad thing generally and if measures promoting it nationwide were also bad, measures promoting it in Fayetteville were good. This problem of consistency was particularly severe for leading Fayetteville Democrats like Louis D. Henry, Robert Strange, and Thomas L. Hybart, who wished to be urban-oriented in North Carolina and agrarian-minded within the nation as a whole. The inconsistency of local and national ideologies was the principal obstacle for Cumberland Democrats in linking political cleavages at the two levels. To rectify this difficulty was their major intellectual challenge in the early 1830s.

One approach to the problem was to renounce urban-oriented goals altogether. This was the position taken by Lauchlin Bethune, Cameron's successor as the perennial Democratic candidate for Congress. Bethune had served five terms in the state Senate in the 1820s. He first ran for Congress in 1831 and won. He ran three more times in the 1830s, but never won a second term. As a moderately wealthy planter who lived near the western boundary of Cumberland, he was further removed from urban influences than John Cameron.

Bethune began his congressional campaign in 1831 with a consistent rural orientation. He supported Andrew Jackson. He praised the opening of the West Indies to the products of North Carolina's farms and forests. He demanded the retirement of the public debt and a reduction of the tariff to the level of federal expenditures. Federal aid to internal improvements was usually unconstitutional, he said, and always unwise. Government lacked the

33. Fayetteville *North Carolina Journal*, January 27, 1830; James Parton, *Life of Andrew Jackson* (3 vols.; New York, 1861), III, 591–92.

"acuteness, sagacity and vigilance" of private enterprise, so all such projects should be left to individuals. With dubious logic, but with telling rhetorical effect, Bethune pointed to the "splendid abortion" in North Carolina's experience with internal improvements to prove that the federal government should not undertake such programs.[34] Bethune's rural appeal was successful in 1831. He carried Cumberland County and won in the district as well.

Lauchlin Bethune discovered the problem of ideological continuity in connection with banking policy, a subject he had not touched on in his 1831 circular. At the beginning of the 1830s he favored a national banking program that would preserve the advantages of the Bank of the United States but would eliminate the existing Bank's threat to the democratic process. Uncertain how to resolve these competing considerations, he tended to flounder when called upon to explain his banking policies.

In April, 1832, a constituent wrote Bethune to ask whether he would vote to recharter the Bank of the United States. The congressman began his reply by assuring his questioner that he was "intirely convinced of the necessity of some such Institution." The Bank was very useful in stabilizing the currency, handling the revenue, and assisting merchants and travelers. He went on to say, however, that the Bank's powers for good could easily be abused with grave consequences for the nation. The influence of the Bank might someday destroy the independence of the Congress, the courts, the president, the press, and the electorate. Its ultimate tendency would be to "add to the opulence & influence of the wealthy—oppress and grind the poor—Create a privileged order, and finally overturn the happiest form of Government ever devised." [35]

In the remainder of the letter, Bethune mentioned a variety of actions he would take or would like to take to balance the advantages and disadvantages of a national bank. He did not believe that any "moneyed institution should ever be rechartered." He would charter a new bank with proper safeguards. He would recharter the present Bank if it were "the wish of the majority of my constituents." He would delay the matter to a later session of Congress. These alternatives were hedged with conditions that made it difficult to be sure what the congressman's real plans were.[36] Either Bethune was honestly confused by a complex issue, or he equivocated to retain the friendship of his pro-Bank correspondent. To make matters more confusing, Bethune gave a different answer to the Fayetteville meeting which requested him to vote for

34. Lauchlin Bethune, "To My Fellow Citizens, The Freemen and Voters of Moore, Montgomery, Anson, Richmond, Robeson, and Cumberland," June 20, 1831 (Broadside in Deberry Papers, microfilm copy in North Carolina State Archives).
35. Lauchlin Bethune to Duncan McLaurin, April 22, 1832, in Duncan McLaurin Papers, Manuscripts Department, Duke University Library.
36. *Ibid.*

recharter. In his reply to this meeting, he said he had preferred to overturn the existing Bank's monopoly by creating two or three such institutions. However, he said, he now found that plan inexpedient. Nowhere in either letter did he intimate that a national bank was unconstitutional. When the bill to recharter the Bank reached its final roll call in the House of Representatives, Bethune voted with his anti-Bank colleagues not to order the bill to its final reading.[37]

At the time of that vote, Bethune might have been receptive to a moderate plan for a reformed national bank. The events of the next four years, however, led him to an extreme stand "against *a* Bank and *the* Bank." The steps by which he came to this position are hidden. By 1836, however, he had extended his antidevelopment opinions on other subjects to cover banking as well. In resolutions presented to a general meeting of Cumberland Democrats, Bethune declared that banks, corporations, and other institutions of "associated wealth" were the "main pillars and key stones of monarchies and aristocracies." The influence of banks, he maintained, would undermine the democratic process both in North Carolina and in the nation. At Bethune's urging, the meeting resolved unanimously "that we will vote for no candidate for the Legislature, who is a friend or in favor of admitting within this State, branches or agencies of the United States Bank or the circulation of its notes."[38]

The next year Bethune went even further. In his campaign circular for Congress in 1837, he denounced those who depended on banking and credit as parasites on the rest of society. They were "the agents by whom the fruits of the honest man's industry are to be transferred to the wealthy capitalist." They and their monied allies were the villains in "a struggle coeval with society itself . . . between the luxurious and idle on the one hand, and the frugal and industrious on the other." The Bank of the United States was therefore justly abolished. As for the state banks, the people themselves would soon pass on their "supposed utility." Furthermore, Bethune declared, Congress was not only unwise to establish any bank, but it had no constitutional power to do so. Nor, he said, did Congress have the "*right* of *regulating* the currency" beyond fixing the value of coins. For Bethune, the indispensable institution of 1832 had become an unconstitutional outrage five years later.[39]

Bethune was aware that his position had changed. He defended his incon-

37. Fayetteville *Carolina Observer*, June 26, 1832; *Register of Debates in Congress*, 22nd Cong., 1st Sess., VIII, 3454, 3852. When the Bank bill came to its first test vote in the House, some members sought to delay its consideration until the next session. Bethune voted with them but the effort failed.
38. Fayetteville *Observer*, July 26, 1837; Fayetteville *North Carolina Journal*, March 17, 1836.
39. Lauchlin Bethune, "To the Freemen of the Seventh Congressional District of North Carolina" (Broadside reprinted in the Fayetteville *North Carolina Journal*, July 19, 1837).

sistency by noting that "no party in this country has been perfectly consistent." Democrats should ignore the "artful efforts" which some would make "to shake our confidence in those whom we have trusted." [40] Nevertheless, Edward J. Hale gibed at Bethune's willingness to "surrender his opinions to the keeping of his party." He reminded his readers that Bethune had not only acknowledged a Bank's constitutionality in 1832, but had actually proposed to charter two or three similar Banks. "Had he never read the Constitution up to June, 1832," Hale mocked, "or was it necessary that he should read it through Gen. Jackson's spectacles to enable him to understand it?" [41]

By 1837 some such corrective had certainly done its work. When he replied to the *Observer*'s taunts, Hale's Democratic counterpart virtually acknowledged the fact. Why should not Bethune, the editor asked, "employ the *mental glasses* of the patriotic and honest Andrew Jackson . . . to aid him in arriving at a right conclusion [?]" [42] Bethune's new lenses must also have shown that equivocation could not keep probank and antibank votes in the same column. The events of the last five years had obliged him and other leaders to reconcile their individual views with national platforms. Moderation and indecision thus gave way and the useful Bank became a monster. By 1837, Democratic leaders in Cumberland had also abandoned the broad and ambiguous pro-Jackson consensus of 1828. Instead they found a smaller but more certain constituency by reinterpreting county conflicts in national terms. The local division between town and country thus became a "struggle coeval with society itself." All of these steps were part of the search for formulae that would make national and local cleavages congruent to the voters.

For Lauchlin Bethune, this search may have been easy. As he heightened the stridency of his speeches, he simply brought his bank policy in line with the tenor of his other views. For other Jacksonians the process was much more difficult. After a struggle, some became satisfied with a compromise that left their competing national and local loyalties relatively intact. Others felt compelled to break with Jackson altogether. Among the former group were Thomas L. Hybart and William F. Strange, John Cameron's successors as editors at the *North Carolina Journal*. Hybart and Strange were Fayetteville lawyers who served Jackson faithfully but who also believed in the future of Fayetteville. [43] They encountered particular difficulty in reconciling their support for Jackson with local developments in banking and internal improvements.

Unlike Bethune, Hybart and Strange never opposed all banks. From

40. *Ibid.*
41. Fayetteville *Observer*, July 26, 1837.
42. Fayetteville *North Carolina Journal*, August 2, 1837.
43. Fayetteville *Observer*, February 24, 1831.

March, 1831, when they bought the *North Carolina Journal*, to July, 1832, when they received Jackson's Bank veto message, they kept a prudent silence on the subject of a national bank. Even after the veto, Hybart and Strange praised the charter of four new state banks in 1834 to replace the institutions whose charters were expiring. In 1835, they supported the suggestion of "A Trader" that Fayetteville establish a bank for its own needs that was wholly owned by its citizens, with stock priced at twenty-five dollars a share to give men of small means the chance to invest.[44] Even on the subject of a national bank, Edward J. Hale later charged that "the Editors of the Journal were not opposed to the Bank until they sold themselves, body and soul, to party, for the sake of pelf."[45] The editorials of Hybart and Strange at the time of the veto virtually admitted the accusation, especially as it applied to the Bank in Fayetteville. "The management of the concerns of the Branch of the Institution is in the hands of men whom we personally respect," they acknowledged, "and in whose integrity we have every confidence." The Bank was thought to promote the town's prosperity, and "we have many private friends who have an interest in its continuance." They admitted that these considerations had influenced them not to criticize the Bank at first.[46]

But when the push from Washington came, the two editors did not hesitate. Previously, they said, "we have taken no part for or against this Institution." They had always believed, they claimed, that the Bank was unconstitutional, but had considered the matter settled by usage. Besides, "political and financial economy" were subjects too difficult for them to understand without assistance from the president's "gigantic strength of intellect." The appearance of the veto changed everything. Hybart and Strange recognized the document as a political masterstroke and expressed "the astonishment of those of his own party that their opposition to this political mammoth had not heretofore been more decided and zealous." They hastened to compensate for previous indifference by lauding Jackson for his "bold originality," "manly integrity of purpose," "true disinterested patriotism," and "sterling moral worth."[47]

The effect of fulsome praise alone might have been transitory. The most significant passage for the county's political evolution was the editors' forthright acceptance of the veto as an instrument for partisan polarization. "Let the friends of the Bank, construction and consolidation rally in all their force," they challenged confidently.

> It is what every sincere friend of his country must wish, to see every citizen arrayed in the approaching struggle under the banner of his own

44. Fayetteville *North Carolina Journal*, October 7, 1835, November 4, 1835.
45. Fayetteville *Observer*, June 13, 1836.
46. Fayetteville *North Carolina Journal*, August 1, 1832.
47. *Ibid.*, July 25, 1832.

political faith. . . . The National Republicans, Federalists, or by whatever they please to distinguish themselves may vilify Gen. Jackson as they please, and denounce him as the enemy to the general welfare. These ravings of disappointed ambition, these murmurs of unappeased avarice, will be understood by the real friends of their country, and we doubt not, that the Jackson and Van Buren Ticket will shew at the next election in the unexampled triumph which it will afford to the lately dispersed but now reunited and firm republican phalanx, that although error may prevail for a time, the final victory of truth is certain.[48]

Though the president's Bank policy may not have agreed entirely with their private views, Hybart and Strange thus rejoiced to see a firm national standard for all Democrats to follow. Whatever their previous opinions on banking, Hybart and Strange hastened to embrace the new orthodoxy.

The editors' policies on internal improvements were not so easy to make uniform. National party policy on this subject created no difficulty for them. They accepted Jackson's public view that federal aid to local projects was unconstitutional. Their problems over internal improvements arose over the question of state aid. Like several other urban Jacksonians, Hybart and Strange participated in the strenuous campaign for internal improvements which climaxed in the summer and fall of 1833. Hybart had served on the committee to implement the resolutions of the town meeting of December, 1830, which requested state aid for a railroad to the Yadkin. John A. Cameron and his brother Thomas had served on the same committee, as had Louis D. Henry. Hybart served as a delegate to the first Raleigh convention for internal improvements on July 4, 1833, as a member of the Cumberland committee of correspondence to publicize the convention's work, as secretary of a Fayetteville meeting on internal improvements in September, and as an initial shareholder in the Cape Fear, Yadkin & Pedee Rail Road Company. William F. Strange was less active, but he represented the county at an internal improvements convention in Wilmington in early November.[49]

Future Whigs outnumbered loyal Jacksonians on all these committees and delegations. Many Democrats shared Lauchlin Bethune's hostility to all state aid for internal improvements. Even strong Democratic friends of the movement occasionally faltered on the subject of state aid. As James Seawell reported to Governor David Lowry Swain, "it will require an effort from our friend L. D. [Henry]—to remove the doubts in our community as regards his views &c. upon the *two-fifths Principle*, his course upon that subject at Pittsb[r]

48. *Ibid.*
49. Fayetteville *North Carolina Journal*, December 15, 1830; *Journal of the Internal Improvements Convention*, 12–13; Fayetteville *Observer*, September 24, 1833, October 29, 1833, February 2, 1837.

has called forth enquiry &c. tho not formally." [50] While Hale rhapsodized on the blessings of progress in the *Observer*, Hybart and Strange mostly kept silent.

Occasionally this time-honored approach to divisive issues was not satisfactory and the editors gave economic development a modest endorsement. The legislative elections of 1831, for example, would affect the prospects for the railroad proposal which Hybart's committee had supported unsuccessfully in the last session. If the county delegation were hostile to the project, there could be little hope for a charter or a subsidy. The *Journal* editors broke precedent, therefore, and published a preelection editorial that was meant to affect the election's outcome. Their words were not addressed to Fayetteville voters, because Louis D. Henry sought the town seat unopposed. The county candidates differed on the issue of internal improvements, and the *Journal* supported the friends of the cause: "*Internal Improvements.*—The time of our elections is at hand, which must determine what is to be the character of our next Legislature. . . . When we look around and contemplate the untiring efforts which our sister states are making to improve their natural advantages . . . and when we draw a parallel between the condition of those states, and that of our own; the contrast is humiliating to every man, who is properly alive to those feelings of patriotism and state pride which should animate the bosom of every Carolinian." [51] By basing their argument on "patriotism and state pride" rather than on the concrete advantages of a railroad to Fayetteville, the editors clearly hoped to appeal to the widest possible rural audience.

Even so, they realized that even such a mild endorsement was offensive to many of their readers and they apologized in advance for any hurt feelings which might result: "We are aware that we have broached a subject, which from various causes has grown somewhat in disrepute, & consequently that our views must necessarily come into collision with the prejudices of some, and the settled despair of others. But . . . we hope that our suggestions on this subject . . . will receive that consideration which they are worth, from those liberal and patriotic citizens, who were ever ready to countenance any exertions, to promote the prosperity of that land, which is endeared to them by the purest and holiest feeling of the heart." [52]

The editorial did not name the men who would be more sympathetic to economic development, but the records of the next legislature made it obvious that the *Journal*'s favorite candidates had lost. The winners, John Bar-

---

50. James Seawell to David L. Swain, September 22, 1833, typed copy in Epistolatory Correspondence of Swain.
51. Fayetteville *North Carolina Journal*, August 3, 1831.
52. *Ibid.*

Table 19. The House of Commons Election of 1831

Candidate's name	Number of votes	1836 Party Affiliation
David McNeill	583	Democratic
John Barclay	572	Unknown
Alexander McNeill	370	Whig
Neill Johnson	332	Whig

SOURCE: Fayetteville *North Carolina Journal*, August 17, 1831.

clay and David McNeill, both voted against a bill on its second reading to aid the North Carolina Central Rail Road and Fayetteville's own Cape Fear and Yadkin Rail Road, and thereafter they voted in favor of indefinitely postponing the bill. They also voted to postpone indefinitely the consideration of two bank charters and in favor of resolutions endorsing the administration of Andrew Jackson. Barclay even voted for a bill that would render an application by one railroad for federal funds the same as forfeiture of its charter. Barclay and McNeill did not vote in favor of any legislation offering state aid to internal improvements.[53] The editors' tact and patriotic sentiments had been to no avail.

The outcome of the election of 1831 appears in table 19. The results of this election reflected the opinions of rural voters only, since Louis D. Henry was unopposed for town member and since Fayetteville residents could not vote for county candidates during the era of borough representation. Given the candidates' future party affiliations, the voting behavior of the winners, and the campaign issue raised by the *Journal*, the division of votes in 1831 probably represented the division between rural-oriented, anticommercial voters and urban-oriented, procommercial voters in the countryside itself. Although Whig and Democratic blocs appeared here in a local election, these blocs had no rigid connections to presidential loyalties in 1831. It was therefore possible for a Jacksonian paper to take a proimprovement stand without hopelessly compromising its party position. In the near future Hybart and Strange would show less latitude in what and whom they endorsed. As presidential politics became more closely tied to local events, the editors became unwilling to discuss internal improvements or endorse anti-Jacksonian candidates. Hybart, at least, never changed his mind about the economic value of internal improvements, but he relinquished their political value to the Whigs. The nature of his constituency gave him no choice. In the meantime, he and Strange dwelt on other issues.

53. *North Carolina House Journal*, 1831, pp. 192, 217, 220, 223, 240, 248.

One such issue was the question of economic and social inequality. The Bank War and conflicts over internal improvements paralleled divisions between town and country. They may also have been relevant to long-standing social tensions within Fayetteville itself. In at least one North Carolina county, a newspaper correspondent worried that "those incorporated companies for internal improvements, and manufactures, &c. are making the poor poorer and the rich richer" and warned that "those labor saving machines throw many of the poor laboring class of people out of employ or reduce their wages to a mere pittance." "Suppose for instance, the Central Railroad was completed," asked "Another Friend to Edgecombe" in his letter to the Tarboro *Free Press*. "What would become of the wagoners, wagons, and horses now employed in conveying the produce to market from the western part of this State?" [54] Licensed draymen in Fayetteville may well have asked themselves the same question, especially since supporters of the railroad from Campbellton to upper Fayetteville expected it to reduce municipal freight charges substantially. Teamsters in the western wagon trade and the blacksmiths, wheelwrights, harness makers, and wagonmakers who depended on their business may also have questioned the advantages of the iron horse. Even if they did not, Democratic leaders began to find that rhetorical attacks on business interests did not hurt them politically.

After the appeal of John B. Martin to "the mechanic and labouring man," the Jacksonians did not refer to social inequality for five years. The next use of this theme by a Jacksonian was entirely abortive. The effort was typical of the hit-or-miss search for serviceable issues in the second stage of party formation. The attempt occurred in the election of 1829, when "Fair Play," a supporter of John Cameron, recommended his favorite on the grounds that he was socially superior to Edmund Deberry, the pro-Adams candidate. "Fair Play" said of the latter, "that he is a plain farmer, and has been for several years a member of the State Legislature, we all know: and that he may have been raised to that honor from menial obscurity, I shall not dispute." The writer contrasted Deberry's low status with Cameron's "literary and practical acquirements . . . deep and profound legal and literary learning . . . his unbending integrity and unassuming honesty." [55] Deberry's friends quickly took advantage of "Fair Play's" snobbish indiscretion, warning the district against "the ruffle shirt party" of Jacksonian aristocracy. "Let that honest and most useful class of citizens, the farmers, such men as Edmund Deberry himself, see how they are designated by members of that class calling itself, ridiculously enough, 'good society.'" [56] Pro-Deberry writers roasted the Cameron

54. Tarboro *Free Press*, May 8, 1832.
55. Fayetteville *Carolina Observer*, July 9, 1829.
56. *Ibid.*, July 16, 1829.

side for the rest of the campaign for "Fair Play's" aspersions against the social dignity of farmers. After this blunder neither party was so foolish as to boast of its superior social position. In their continuing search for a platform, however, the Democrats were willing to take the opposite tack.

They approached the issue of inequality through the Bank War. Early Democratic rhetoric against the Bank was directed to its unconstitutionality and its threat to the democratic process. When spokesmen began to brand the Bank's supporters as aristocrats, however, they shifted the nature of their appeal. The first use of what might be called social arguments against the Bank appeared in the *Journal* only a month before the presidential election of 1832. The editors were criticizing the followers of Henry Clay for resembling the "combinations of wealth, power, and talents, struggling for mastery" in the election of 1800. The comparable combination in 1832, the editors told their readers, consisted of "the high Tariff party—the Bank party—the Nullification party." Their object in opposing Jackson was "the gratification of a mere heartless and sordid feeling—the few wish to rule the many." The tone of the editorial implied that these tyrannical forces were far from Cumberland. The businessmen of Fayetteville were not directly implicated in the crimes of their counterparts in Boston, Philadelphia, and Charleston. Nevertheless, Fayetteville millowners could not have been pleased to read that Jackson would reduce profits to save the country. "Is it not better," the *Journal* asked, "that manufacturers should languish, or at least that their profits should be curtailed—that foreign capital should be driven from our shores, and the wealth of our citizens should have no exclusive money privileges awarded to them . . . than that the Union should be jeopardized?" [57] Whether they were middling farmers or urban workers, lower-income voters may have found the prospect of diminished profits for businessmen psychologically satisfying. Most of the *Journal*'s declarations against "Bank aristocrats" were of this ambiguous kind. The people's enemies were distant actors like Clay, Biddle, and foreign stockholders. Virtually any reader could therefore see himself as among their victims if he so chose. Nevertheless, the criticisms were framed in such a way that the lower-income voter would be more likely to respond than a man of property.

Almost a month later, on the eve of the presidential election, the *Journal* returned to these themes in more lurid terms than before. "The same principles are involved in this contest," the editors declared, "as in the contest of 1800. . . . It is a struggle between the rich and the poor—the Aristocracy and Democracy of the country; the former are endeavoring to gain more power than the Constitution gives them, they want the power of a Bank monopoly—

57. Fayetteville *North Carolina Journal*, October 10, 1832.

they want by enormous tariffs to make the people, the labouring people, subservient to their will—they wish a splendid government, to be supported by taxes drawn from the pockets of the people. Shall these things be?"[58]

In spite of its highly colored tone, this bit of preelection hyperbole contains several conservative features. According to the editorial, "the Aristocracy of the country" did not rob "the labouring people" by expropriating profits at the workplace, but by imposing tariffs on consumer goods. This approach could appeal to farmers of every level, as well as other consumers. The editors continued to imply that the threats arose from outside Cumberland County, for they surely did not mean that any county residents favored high tariffs. That charge would have been absurdly false, even by the tolerant standards of antebellum journalism. Nor did anyone in Cumberland aspire to a Bank monopoly. Poor readers were not asked to assert their own interests in government, but to prevent the abuses of others. Nevertheless, the editorial foreshadowed more strident statements later in the 1830s.

Democrats sometimes stressed political consequences of inequality and neglected purely material disparities between classes. "Let the federal principle once obtain," warned the *Journal* in 1835, "and we shall then see the features of despotism abroad in our land, and men will then learn, by a practical application, what is the true meaning of the few governing the many." The editors predicted that a Whig victory would be followed by restriction to the wealthy of freedom of speech, freedom of the press, liberty of conscience, trial by jury, and the right to vote. "Beware how you commit your interests," the editors concluded, "to that class of politicians, who think there should be privileged orders in society—that none but such as they are pleased to term decent, talented or wealthy, should have any voice in the affairs of government."[59] There was no serious danger that Whigs might abrogate formal constitutional freedoms if they gained power, but the *Journal*'s warning may have reminded some voters of the reality of disfranchisement in the pre-Revolutionary generation.

Students of the Jacksonian workingmen's parties have found much imprecision in the use of "workingman" and the other terms that denoted class differences in Jacksonian America. As it was used in urban party battles, the word "workingman" did not refer exclusively to manual workers and did not evoke a sense of class consciousness in the classic meaning of that phrase.[60] Fayetteville voters were certainly no more discriminating in this respect than

58. *Ibid.*, November 7, 1832.
59. *Ibid.*, August 5, 1835.
60. Pessen, "The Workingmen's Movement of the Jacksonian Era," 434–35; Walter Hugins, *Jacksonian Democracy and the Working Class: A Study of the New York Workingmen's Movement, 1829–1837*, (Stanford, 1960), 51–53; Joseph Dorfman, "The Jackson Wage-Earner Thesis," *American Historical Review*, LIV (1949), 305–306.

their counterparts in New York, Boston, or Philadelphia. Nevertheless, Democratic leaders in the early 1830s found references to economic inequality to be natural and effective extensions of the platform they were building. Many antiurban overtures could be made to sound antiaristocratic as well. References to social divisions were a means for Democratic organizers to create an alliance between rural-oriented voters and some urban voters. Denunciation of inequality therefore entered the Democratic framework for interpreting political events and unifying local and national controversies.

While Hybart and Strange were struggling to find a balance that would keep rural and urban Democrats within the same Jacksonian coalition, some political leaders were deciding the balance could not be found. Having supported Jackson in 1828, these men discovered that their own political concerns could not be satisfied in the general's political camp. Some men drew this conclusion after personal disillusionment with Jackson's conduct in office. Others concluded that their own plans for the Fayetteville community could not be achieved while Jackson's coalition determined public policy. Many experienced a combination of these two influences when Jackson's veto of the Bank recharter forced a valuable local institution to close. Whatever their motives, the men who deserted Jackson seem to have found the decision hard to make. In a number of cases, their careers and backgrounds were not very different from others who felt the same cross-pressures but decided to remain with the Democrats. For the men who did change sides, the period of uncertainty in the early 1830s was a time of growing alienation from old friends and a search for common ground with old enemies. When these lapsed Jacksonians finally found a platform they could share comfortably with the former Adams men, the two groups organized as the Whig party.

One prominent Jacksonian who crossed over was James Seawell. As his 1829 donnybrook with Archibald McDiarmid illustrated, Seawell's convictions and associations were thoroughly sympathetic to economic development, and his stance did not change in the following years. He served as magistrate of police in 1829 and from 1831 to 1834 and as town member in 1833 and 1834. When the Cape Fear, Yadkin & Pedee Rail Road Company organized, Seawell was the natural choice for president. In the summer of 1833, he had worked harder for internal improvements than virtually any other man in Fayetteville. He chaired the town meetings, corresponded with political leaders, attended and participated in virtually every convention, traveled to the North in search of capital, and generally served as Fayetteville's leading advocate of state aid to railroads. In the legislature of 1833, he chaired the House Committee on Internal Improvements and prepared the report which cited family dissolution as the overwhelming consequence of state poverty and the emigration movement. Through his efforts, Fayetteville obtained a new charter for the Cape Fear, Yadkin, and Pedee Rail Road Company, but Seawell was not able to obtain state aid for the project. In 1834, his foremost objective in the next legislature was state approval of the two-fifths principle. In every aspect of his political career, Seawell was a friend of his town and its transportation needs. Moreover, when Fayetteville submitted its petition to Congress against deposit removal, Seawell's name headed the list of signatures.[61] When the Whig party took shape in the spring and summer of 1834, it was entirely natural that Seawell led the van as Whig candidate for town member.

Edward J. Hale was also a Jacksonian apostate. Unlike any of his colleagues, Hale left a record of his progress towards Whiggery in the columns of the *Carolina Observer*. Following his movements, we may learn something of the thoughts that animated other Whigs as well.

In some ways a contradictory figure, Edward J. Hale in the late 1820s and early 1830s held a mixture of "Whiggish" ideas on moral reform and positive government within a firm context of states' rights. When the Creek Indians were threatened with forced deportation, for instance, Hale declared that "every principle of a generous mind would revolt at the idea of expelling these poor people from the last remnant of 'the land of their forefathers.' "[62] Nevertheless, when John Quincy Adams attempted to use federal law to protect the Indians from the state of Georgia, Hale damned the president's nationalist principles "as not a whit better than the Alien and Sedition Laws of the first Adams."[63] Hale favored common schools and internal improvements, but he opposed the popular election of county officers, fearing that eventually "our Judges will ascend to office through the portals of a grog shop."[64] A supporter of John C. Calhoun, he could still call slavery an "evil" which the South would one day end if left alone by the federal government. He favored the Bank of the United States, but wished for modifications in its charter. A warm friend of progress, Hale admired Whiggish policies of economic development when pursued at the state level, but he privately supported the right of secession, even over the tariff, as the South's best defense against federal encroachments on states' rights.[65] Hale was the model of a strict constructionist who could join the Whig party at its birth over the issue of executive usurpation, and then grow in it without ever betraying a sense of inconsistency.

In 1828, Hale served on the Jackson committee of vigilance and correspon-

61. Oates, *The Story of Fayetteville*, 311; Fayetteville *Carolina Observer*, January 8, 1829, January 4, 1832.
62. Fayetteville *Carolina Observer*, June 9, 1825.
63. *Ibid.*, March 15, 1827.
64. *Ibid.*, January 12, 1826, August 29, 1830, December 4, 1832.
65. *Ibid.*, September 22, 1825, June 16, 1836.

dence. He was never entirely happy with the general, however, and for most of Jackson's first term, Hale reserved his warmest praise for Calhoun, the vice president. He remained loyal to Jackson only so long as Calhoun did. Although he specifically withheld praise of Jackson's patronage and banking policies, Hale expressed satisfaction with the administration and the president's hints of a second term in early February, 1831. When Calhoun published his hostile correspondence with Jackson three weeks later, Hale quickly changed his tune. He no longer showed pleasure in a second term for Jackson. But if Calhoun were to run, he declared, "we need hardly say, with how much real pleasure we should lend our feeble aid to a man of his brilliant talents, great experience, and unblemished private character." By the end of March, Hale was claiming that "there has never been a period since the formation of our government when so much corruption was tolerated." [66]

In spite of his support for Calhoun, Hale had never supported nullification except as it accompanied actual secession from the Union. When Calhoun favored nullification without secession in his Pendleton letter, Hale was suddenly without a political harbor. [67] He had cast off Jackson. He would not support Clay. He was reduced to calling for any "unexceptionable man" on whom "all good men" of the opposition could unite. Hale met with no response to this proposal except a witticism from the Oxford *Examiner*, whose editor remarked that "it looks very much like a 'bargain.'" Hale replied stiffly with a lecture on the value of compromise, reminding his colleague that "many political bargains or compromises have received the sanction of the American people, even in days of greater purity than the present." Hale asked for "no sacrifice of principle" in forming his proposed "union." Nevertheless, his suggestion evinced a drift towards partisanship and a growing pragmatic bent in political thinking. [68] When his call for a union of the opposition generated no further interest, Hale kept silent on the presidential question for seven months. When he finally spoke again, at the June, 1832, term of county court, he was the main supporter of the Cumberland campaign of Philip P. Barbour for vice president. [69]

This curious effort professed to be an attempt to keep Martin Van Buren away from the president's side and out of the presidential succession. It grew out of Van Buren's long-standing unpopularity. Even while he was still a first-term senator, the New Yorker had a reputation in North Carolina for corrupt intrigue. During the campaign of 1824, for example, "Lucius" wrote the *Observer* to question the motives of the Crawford press. "Do they wish to set up

66. *Ibid.*, September 3, 1829, February 3, 1831, February 24, 1831, March 17, 1831, March 30, 1831.
67. *Ibid.*, August 17, 1831, August 24, 1831.
68. *Ibid.*, October 19, 1831, November 2, 1831.
69. *Ibid.*, June 5, 1832; Fayetteville *North Carolina Journal*, June 13, 1832.

the Presidency and the higher offices of the nation at auction?" he demanded. "Do they wish that the business should appear undecided, til Martin Van Buren or any other man, can make the terms, and agree on his price? We hope not." [70] In 1832, suspicion of Van Buren's honesty was widespread, even among those who eventually voted for him. "A Citizen of Duplin" told why in a letter to the *North Carolina Journal*. "I am free to confess," he admitted, "that formerly I was much prejudiced against Mr. Van Buren." He recognized, however, that Van Buren had been slandered by his enemies "when I came to test his conduct by the immutable principles of right reason." Furthermore, said "A Citizen," the other voters in Duplin County felt the same way: "You may wish to know my reason for supposing that Mr. Van Buren will be the favorite candidate with us for the Vice Presidency at the next election, it is simply this, that the people have confidence in Andrew Jackson's word, and the testimony which he has given in his published letters of Mr. Van Buren's capacity and fidelity goes further with the people than everything which can be said against him." [71]

The friends of Judge Barbour, a states' rights supporter from Virginia, had less "confidence in Andrew Jackson's word" than "A Citizen." They claimed that their electors would remove Van Buren's "malign influence" by choosing Jackson for president and Barbour for vice president. The extent of the campaign's impact can only be guessed, because the Virginian withdrew at the last moment, and it is difficult to tell how much effect his action had on the small size of his total vote. In North Carolina, the Jackson and Barbour ticket won 4,255 votes to 4,538 for Clay and Sergeant, to 21,006 for Jackson and Van Buren. Its leaders in the state were both nullifiers and Clay supporters who hoped to whittle away at Jacksonism without making a frontal assault on the popularity of the Old Hero himself. [72]

In Cumberland County, the Barbour movement was a halfway house from the Jackson group to the Whig party. Of the seven men who were mentioned in the minutes of the Barbour meeting, six later became Whigs. Three of the six had served on Jackson's committee in 1828. None had worked for Adams. Of the six, five lived in Fayetteville. One was an editor, one was a judge, one was a lawyer, and two were both merchants and lawyers. [73] In other words, the

---

70. Fayetteville *Carolina Observer*, July 8, 1824.
71. Fayetteville *North Carolina Journal*, August 29, 1832.
72. *Ibid.*, June 27, 1832.
73. The seven men were Judge Henry Potter, John W. Huske, Edward J. Hale, Archibald McDiarmid, Alexander McNeill, William B. Wright, and Warren Winslow. McDiarmid had not been present at the meeting but was nominated as a delegate to the state convention of Barbour's supporters. He immediately declined the nomination and disavowed the Barbour movement. He was the only one of the seven who remained a Democrat in the future. The three Jackson committee members from 1828 were Potter, Hale, and McNeill. McNeill owned land in Flea Hill district, directly across the river from Fayetteville. The other five lived in town. John W. Huske and Warren Winslow were both lawyers and merchants. William B. Wright was a lawyer only. Fayette-

Barbour men were almost completely urban in residence and occupation. They claimed to support Jackson for president, but their backgrounds and outlook were incompatible with the president's more rural-oriented supporters. The editors of the *Journal*, as spokesmen for orthodoxy, recognized their basic anti-Jacksonian bent. "We have reason to believe," they charged, "that there was not one decided Jackson man who took part in the Barbour meeting." Moreover, said the *Journal*, "We understand that the meeting was composed mostly of the friends of Mr. Clay." [74] Cumberland's Clay men had their own organization in 1832, however, so the *Journal*'s charge may have been a calumny. It is at least as likely that the Barbour men were what they seemed to be: ex-Jacksonians looking for a home.

In making their appeals, Hale and the other Barbour men drew about equally on a widespread fear of Van Buren as a source of corruption, and on the charge that he favored the protective tariff. When the New York *Courier and Enquirer* hinted that Jackson preferred Van Buren as vice president, Hale fumed at this "attempt to direct and control the popular will." [75] In the Barbour group's address, they called for nominations by the people's primary assemblies and warned against the dictatorial influence of the national convention at Baltimore which had nominated Van Buren. Van Buren, the group concluded, had "aided and assisted in fastening the [protective] System upon the South, and continues to support the same," and therefore ought not to be elected. [76]

Conspicuous by its absence in the language of the Barbour meeting was any theme or set of themes that was identifiably urban or progressive in tone. Instead, all of its arguments were pitched in terms made famous by the Jacksonians in their successful campaign against John Quincy Adams. These included fear of the tariff, fear of corruption, suspicion of outsiders, and suspicion of change. Considering the backgrounds of Cumberland's pro-Barbour leadership, these themes were remarkable. Reading them, one is bound to suspect the Barbour leaders of insincerity. But before judging them harshly, we should reflect that like Hale himself, the other Barbour men may have had conscientious scruples against both Clay and Jackson. They probably felt that the old antiparty values were their only consistent ground for soliciting votes. Like so many of their peers, they were still searching for their bearings in the new political world of the 1830s.

---

ville *Observer*, February 25, 1836; Fayetteville *North Carolina Journal*, December 12, 1827, June 13, 1832; Fayetteville *North Carolinian*, June 13, 1840; Cumberland County List of Taxables, 1828, in Cumberland County Records; "List of Stores," Cumberland County Court Minutes, September Term, 1835, in Cumberland County Records; Royall, *Mrs. Royall's Southern Tour*, I, 147.
74. Fayetteville *North Carolina Journal*, June 6, 1832.
75. Fayetteville *Carolina Observer*, February 21, 1832.
76. *Ibid.*, June 5, 1832.

The tenor of the pro-Barbour literature does show clearly that traditional political values were still current in 1832. Leaders such as Hale apparently believed that at least some of the people could be won to a candidate by appealing to fears of backsliding republican morality. A writer to the Raleigh *Star*, whose letter was reprinted in the *Observer*, expressed this fear with special emphasis. The very existence of the argument that Van Buren should be vice president because he was the president's choice, wrote "A North Carolinian," was "a proof of how rapidly a considerable portion of our people are losing that high and lofty spirit of freedom which distinguished our ancestors." The writer deplored the alien influences which Van Buren represented and which might lead to the removal of principles from politics. "I consider the Baltimore Convention to be the first attempt, originating in New York, to extend to the whole Union the dangerous and corrupt system of politics which has so long degraded that State—a system which considers all political struggles not as combats for principle, but as a contention for plunder, and which regards offices but as the 'spoils of victory,' as avowed by a leading Senator from that State, in his place on the floor of the Senate." [77] A distaste for the methods of the Albany Regency was not a totally retrograde impulse. The fears of "A North Carolinian" nevertheless show that in spite of calls for "union," the future leaders of the Whig party were backing into partisanship hesitantly. At least they felt their natural constituency demanded a sense of such reluctance.

If the Barbour men found these antiparty values satisfactory grounds for opposing Andrew Jackson, the bulk of the voters did not. Barbour got only 58 votes in Cumberland County, while Van Buren got 593. Clay and Sergeant got 183 votes. [78] The total anti-Jacksonian proportion of the vote was virtually unchanged from four years before. After 1834, when the anti-Jacksonian leaders finally found a more usable issue than corruption, their popular support would be much larger.

Hybart and Strange and the Barbour men occupied the center in Cumberland's political spectrum. The group which lay furthest from the "locofocoism" of Lauchlin Bethune were the National Republican followers of Henry Clay. During the 1830s, this steadfast band showed the least amount of readjustment of its earlier positions. Nevertheless, these men were not exempt from the general tendency to find new bases for popular appeal as politics became more and more partisan.

Most of the adaptations which the Adams and Clay men made must be inferred from differences in their political remarks before and after the formation of the Whig party. Before that development, they repeatedly uttered sen-

77. *Ibid.*, September 4, 1832.
78. Compiled Election Returns, "Presidential Electors," 1832.

timents so insensitive to majority opinions that a partisan leader who hoped to win elections would never have made them. After the Whig party formed, the former National Republicans either changed their tone or allowed more flexible men to speak in their behalf. Their experience in the 1830s was an attempt to work with men less dogmatic than themselves.

The Clay men of 1832 who can be identified had been Adams men in 1828. They had never liked Andrew Jackson and the passage of time had not mellowed their opinions. Dr. Benjamin Robinson was probably representative of their point of view. Robinson had run as an elector pledged to Adams in 1828. Writing to his congressman in 1830, he was still echoing the sentiments which he had helped to distribute in the *Official Record . . . of the Court Martial Which Tried . . . the Six Militia Men.*

> I can not say [he wrote] that I am at all disappointed in the present Administration. They are doing as little evil (although they are doing all in their power) as I anticipated.
>
> You doubtless recollect that I predicted the downfall of Republican Government and Civil Liberty on the Election of General Jackson to the Presidency, when the good people of these U.S. were so completely deluded as to fill the Presidential Chair with a man of the General's stamp, totally incapacitated, my confidence in the permanency of our Political Institutions recd. a shock from which it has not recovered and I fear never will. . . . What are the relative prospects of the two aspirants, Van Buren and Calhoun? I sincerely hope they are flattering for neither.[79]

In his indignation the doctor did not bother to reconcile his forecast that Jackson would overturn the republic with his view that the Democrats "are doing as little evil . . . as I anticipated." What his letter lacked in internal consistency, however, it made up in sincere alarm and obvious alienation from majority opinion in Cumberland. Robinson's isolation from the county's mainstream may have reflected his birth and upbringing in Middlebury, Vermont. He must have been respected by his fellow Clay supporters, however, for they repeatedly called on him to chair their meetings. In 1832 he was the Clay electoral candidate for the seventh district.[80]

Before Robinson and the other Clay men could become effective partisans, they needed to minimize their personal hostility to Jackson. The Whig party lured wavering Democrats away from the president by pointing to specific official acts of his administration, not by aspersing his prepresidential charac-

---

79. Benjamin Robinson to Edmund Deberry, April 3, 1830, typed copy in Edmund Deberry Papers, Southern Historical Collection.
80. Fayetteville *North Carolina Journal*, December 12, 1827, June 13, 1832; Fayetteville *Observer*, June 3, 1834, March 10, 1836, September 15, 1836; Card Catalogue Entry for Benjamin Robinson Papers, Manuscript Department, Duke University Library.

ter. Whigs also drew on hostility to Van Buren, whom they represented as fundamentally different from the honest but misguided general. Neither of these more tolerant attitudes was apparent in Robinson's letter. The Clay men would also have to cultivate a little more respect for the vox populi. A party which hoped to win elections could not view the public as capable of complete delusion. The Whigs would have to adapt the same deference for the wisdom of the majority as the Jacksonians had. "The Republicans fear not to abide the struggle," wrote the *Journal*. "If overcome they must upon their own principles calmly submit to the will of the majority; but they doubt not of victory." [81]

There are other indications from the Clay literature that the National Republicans were hobbled by their own misunderstanding of political realities. A circular from the Anti-Administration Central Corresponding Committee in Raleigh to Clay's friends in North Carolina invoked the example of northern cities to infuse the Clay men with greater enthusiasm. "The cheering indications which have been exhibited at New York and Philadelphia, of a successful opposition to the re-election of Genl. Jackson, have encouraged us to reflect on the possibility of aiding their patriotic efforts in North Carolina." Only the extreme urban orientation of the Clay group could lead them to draw inspiration from quarters so foreign to most of North Carolina. Most state voters, moreover, would not like to think of their own "patriotic efforts" as merely auxiliary to those of New Yorkers and Philadelphians. The circular's next sentence however, reveals that the Clay men were indeed willing to believe that North Carolina's politics mirrored events in the metropolis. "The result [of Clay's northern victories] is a conviction, that our ability has been underrated by our opponents as well as ourselves." The sheet concluded by saying that if all the antiadministration men came to the polls, "success, though not certain, is by no means desperate." [82] This particular leaflet was not intended for general circulation, so it did not represent the central committee's notion of how to attract the average voter. Nevertheless, as long as the National Republican leadership was so completely urban-oriented that it forgot the world view of most North Carolinians, it could not compose an effective party.

A final area where the National Republicans needed to modify their rhetoric was the strength of their antiparty values. A certain amount of antipartyism was very useful to the Whigs in the early stages of their history. The successful Whig organizers walked a fine line, however, between a moderate antiparty stance that attracted votes and an extreme hostility to parties that

---

81. Fayetteville *North Carolina Journal*, July 25, 1832.
82. Joseph Gales, "To the Friends of the Anti-Administration Electoral Ticket in North Carolina," October 19, 1832 (Broadside in Cameron Family Papers).

obstructed political effectiveness. The latter attitude was common in the speeches of Edmund Deberry, the pro-Adams congressman from the seventh district: "As a friend of republican and liberal principles, I believe that a member of Congress should not devote himself and his high station to party views and party purposes [.] this is not only inconsistent with the nature of our free government but is a course altogether unworthy of the representative of freemen [.] He should make the great interests of his country and of the people whom he represents and not the particular interests of a party the object of his constant and untiring solicitude." [83] Deberry's opposition to discipline and organization may have been very popular among his neighbors in nearby Montgomery County, for they repeatedly gave him large majorities. Deberry never played a major part in forming the Whig party, however. He was its candidate but never its leader.

To lead them, the Whigs needed a more flexible man. He should be able to chide his friends for insufficient organization and blast the Democrats for an excess of it, all in the same breath. Edward J. Hale was making a step in this direction in 1834 when he republished a postelection editorial from the Raleigh *Star*. "The Whigs have been guilty of supineness," complained the editor, "and have acted without concert whilst the Regency, with a regularly organized corps, under the supervision of a grand Directory in this place, have united their energies, and strained every nerve to the utmost to sustain their sinking cause." [84] As the party system became well established, Hale showed more and more fluency in the language of organization. In 1837, his preelection editorial appealed to voters not on the basis of independent judgment, but of party loyalty and party discipline: "*To the Whigs of this District.*—We feel it our duty to make a solemn appeal to you in regard to the approaching Congressional Election. . . . To *all* we would say, recollect the lasting disgrace brought upon our State in November last, by the failure to go to the polls.—We had then the strength, as admitted even by our opponents, but were defeated. Let it not be so again. But if any of our readers was among those who then failed to perform his duty, let him now make what atonement is in his power, by doubling his exertions." [85] Two years later, in 1839, Hale could be pleased that "a watchful attention to the politics of the State never before exhibited to us, so exclusively a party conflict, so complete a marking of the party lines, as was apparent at the last election." [86]

83. "To the Freemen of the Counties of Robeson Cumberland Moore Richmond Anson and Montgomery" (Undated and unsigned draft of Reelection Circular, typed copy in Deberry Papers, Southern Historical Collection). Internal evidence shows that this draft was written by Deberry for his campaign of 1833.
84. Fayetteville *Observer*, September 9, 1834.
85. *Ibid.*, August 2, 1834.
86. *Ibid.*, January 23, 1839.

When the National Republicans joined with the Barbour leaders in the Whig party, their prickly characteristics began to subside. Under the leadership of men like Hale the Whigs were able to attract many more votes to the anti-Jacksonian cause than the friends of Clay and Adams had done. They were able to come together because the president's war against the Bank made executive usurpation and recklessness seem seriously threatening to the voters. Jackson's removal of the deposits gave them the best means by which to exploit overlapping cleavages in national and local politics. The same issue gave the Democrats their best opportunity to shape a permanent winning coalition. As they began to apply this discovery in 1834, both factions completed the second, or ideological stage of party formation and began the third and final stage of mobilizing voters behind the partisan standards they had raised. Fayetteville's participation in the Bank War was the galvanizing experience that brought the ideological developments of the previous six years home to the voters and showed a considerable number of them the close connections between local and distant events. The townsmen responded by forming permanently organized and self-described political parties for the first time. In consequence, the town election of 1834 had remarkable significance for the future of county politics.

On February 26, 1834, Edward L. Winslow forwarded Fayetteville's memorial against deposit removal to Willie P. Mangum, the U.S. senator from North Carolina who had broken with President Jackson. In his covering letter to Mangum, Winslow wrote that besides "many of the most respectable influential & wealthy of our citizens," the signers of the memorial also included "many of that class of our citizens, who are engaged in the different mechanical employments, there are others who are Farmers." [87] Winslow claimed that the list included both friends and opponents of President Jackson; Edward J. Hale repeated the assertion when he reprinted the petition and the names of its 262 signers. Winslow's statement was literally true, but primarily the memorial was a partisan document. Of the sixty-two signers whose party can be determined, only eleven were Democrats and the remainder were Whigs. [88]

Such rebuffs to Jackson were not accepted quietly by the state's Democratic leaders. Their plans for a counterdemonstration in support of the president were reported to Senator Mangum in a letter from James Seawell. "A great and desperate effort [he wrote] . . . will be made by the Administration Party in this State at the approaching election to gain the ascendency in the next genl assembly, their object is to test their strength by placing the election upon *Po-*

87. Edward L. Winslow to Willie P. Mangum, February 26, 1834, in Shanks (ed.), *Mangum Papers*, II, 105–106.
88. Fayetteville *Observer*, March 4, 1834.

litical [*i.e.*, partisan] *grounds.* . . . In this Town, their plans were convurted under the auspices of a caucus convened during our Supr. Court term,—Wm. H. Haywood Jr., from Raleigh was here and upon his return home became a candidate for Wake [County]." [89]

The possible outcome of this "great and desperate effort" had more than symbolic significance. The term of Bedford Brown, North Carolina's remaining Jacksonian senator, would soon expire, and the General Assembly of 1834 would have the responsibility of reelecting him or choosing a successor. A Democratic majority could return Brown to the Senate. By using the popular doctrine of legislative instructions, moreover, the Democrats could either cause the errant Senator Mangum to change his position on the Bank War or force him to resign. State leaders like William H. Haywood, Jr., therefore, were eager to win every possible seat for their party. The legislative election would also help them gauge the state of public opinion on the next presidential election, when Martin Van Buren would almost certainly be a candidate in his own right. [90]

It is not immediately obvious why the Democrats thought that running against the Bank would help them in Fayetteville. The economy of the town was mostly dependent upon commerce, and the Whigs could have argued plausibly that the death of the Bank could only be harmful to all residents. They did not make this argument, but dwelled instead on the moral, legal, and constitutional aspects of Jackson's act. The rhetoric of Whigs and Democrats both showed that the Bank issue was more than a matter of expediency. Like the road to Wilkesborough, the Bank of the United States was a symbol for the kind of country each faction wanted America to become. Unlike the road, however, the Bank was a national symbol of the future that engaged more than the interest and the local chauvinism of Cumberland voters. It aroused their patriotism as well. It was an issue which could speak to the concerns of the older republican values but could also speak to the most pressing and immediate social forces of the age. Knowing this full well, national propagandists had hammered at the question for months. Their efforts surely had great impact on the consciousness of Fayetteville's leaders, particularly in impressing the local Jacksonians with the idea that a seemingly innocuous or even beneficial institution of perhaps questionable constitutionality was in fact a monster to be crushed. [91]

The issue of internal improvements in 1834 was less clear-cut than the issue of deposit removal. Beneath a certain amount of obfuscation, however, the

---

89. James Seawell to Willie P. Mangum, June 1, 1834, in Shanks (ed.), *Mangum Papers*, II, 161.
90. Hoffman, *Andrew Jackson and North Carolina Politics*, 72–78.
91. Bray Hammond, *Banks and Politics from the Revolution to the Civil War* (Princeton, N.J., 1957), 326–68.

two parties were almost as polarized on this subject as on banking policy. Fayetteville's local controversy over internal improvements was not about whether or not to have a railroad charter. The charter already existed as an accomplished fact. Nor did the controversy concern whether railroads in the abstract were good or bad. As an abstract proposition, both parties claimed to be in favor of a railroad. Instead, the quarrel had to do with whether there ought to be a state subscription to the Cape Fear, Yadkin & Pedee, and whether an anti-Jacksonian was the best man to get it. In a larger, more symbolic sense, the question before the voters was whether getting a charter and promising a subscription made a man worthy of a term as town member, regardless of his presidential sympathies. In reply to this question, Fayetteville's Whigs answered "Yes," and the Jacksonians a resounding "No!"

James Seawell was the chosen leader of Fayetteville's "Bank or Whig party," while Thomas L. Hybart led the "Republicans." [92] The two men had both served on the Jackson committee of 1828, and both had worked in the internal improvements campaign of 1833. But events had driven them apart. Even while they were ostensibly cooperating in the internal improvements campaign of 1833, they were competing against each other for Fayetteville's seat in the House of Commons. Little is known of the 1833 election except that Louis D. Henry had held the seat in 1832 and had resigned in Seawell's favor. Henry was able to straddle the gap between Jacksonism and pro-improvement sentiment, but Seawell and Hybart were not. Seawell abandoned Jackson for the sake of economic development while Hybart did more or less the opposite. Each one ultimately accused the other of abandoning what was most important in favor of a paltry distraction. Seawell won the 1833 election, 197 votes to 105, but the material and emotional stakes had gone higher in the ensuing year. [93] When Hybart challenged Seawell again, he was entering a personal and political grudge match which polarized the entire electorate. "Party distinctions were strongly drawn," one participant testified later. "Few, if any men who voted at the election, left any doubt as to how they voted: each party had their public meetings, each expressed their sentiments freely, and on the day of the election each took their side." [94]

The two nascent parties laid out the issues of the election of 1834 in a pair of meetings in mid-June. Each group adopted a set of resolutions expressing its position in state and local affairs and making explicit connections between both sets of issues. These resolutions were equivalents of local party platforms.

Assembling as "the friends of James Seawell Esqr.," the Whigs began by

92. The Whig party name first appeared in depositions relating to Hybart's challenge of the election. Fayetteville *Observer*, January 20, 1835.
93. *Ibid.*, August 13, 1833.
94. *Ibid.*, January 20, 1835.

adopting opposition to deposit removal as their basic test of common identity: "Resolved, That the Freemen composing this Meeting cannot consent, by their influence, their example or their suffrages, to perpetuate the existence of the present party in power, neither can they sanction any act or admit the policy of any measure, however pure the motive which produced it, originating in violation of Law, and having a direct tendency to subvert the Constitution [*viz.*, removal of the deposits]." [95] The next three resolutions criticized Senator Brown and praised Senator Mangum and the pro-Bank congressmen for their several positions on deposit removal and "Executive usurpation." The fifth resolution introduced the subject of internal improvements by praising Seawell's record in the last legislature. "His devotedness to the cause of Internal Improvements," the meeting declared, "together with his ardent and unremitting desire to promote the general prosperity of this place, points him out as the fittest character to represent us again." The Whigs concluded by making explicit their conviction that Seawell's candidacy united their dual positions in banking and transportation. "Having confidence in the political opinions of Mr. Seawell, and believing that he will properly represent the views of this Meeting . . . we will give him, our hearty support at the Polls." [96]

A comparable meeting of "the friends of Andrew Jackson and T. L. Hybart," held at almost the same time, laid out an opposite position on the questions of the day. "We approve," the Democrats said, "of the course pursued by Andrew Jackson, as President of the U. States." They pointed to his banking policy as especially commendable and scored the "*grave and honorable Senators in Congress*" who abused him for it. Like the Whigs, the Democrats specifically thanked their friends and rebuked their opponents in the North Carolina congressional delegation. They next justified their preference for Hybart as town member in terms of his positions on national politics.

> *Resolved*, That we believe that our fellow citizen, Thomas L. Hybart, Esq. if elected to represent us in the next General Assembly, will vote for the re-election of Bedford Brown to the Senate of the United States, or for a successor of the same political faith. That he will vote in favor of instructing Mr. Mangum to change his course . . . or resign his seat in the Senate:—and in the latter event, that Mr. Hybart will vote for a successor who will place North Carolina in the desirable position of supporting (in the Senate, at least,) with undivided strength, her great political principles, for which the patriots of the revolution fought, bled, and conquered. [97]

95. *Ibid.*, June 24, 1834. The resolutions are reprinted in Shanks (ed.), *Mangum Papers* II, 299–300, although the editor has dated them incorrectly.
96. *Ibid.*, June 24, 1834.
97. Fayetteville *North Carolina Journal*, June 18, 1834.

In their next resolution, the Democrats appeared to duplicate the Whig stand on internal improvements. "As to local politics," they said, "we believe an enlightened and liberal system of Internal Improvement, is to North Carolina, of the highest importance." Their apparent support for the issue, however, was delusive. They did not mention the specific project most interesting to Fayetteville, namely the Cape Fear, Yadkin & Pedee Rail Road. Nor did they touch on the vital question of state aid.[98] The resolution might persuade the credulous that the Democrats were equal to the Whigs in their support for improvement, but it would not deeply offend any opponent of fiscal extravagance. For a committed friend of the railroad, the Democrats' general support of the idea of development was praise too faint to be satisfying. In spite of this surface straddling, therefore, the Democratic resolutions indicated that local and national issues were fused in that party as well as among the Whigs. Practically speaking, the party of Jackson would not be the party to deliver Fayetteville's railway, regardless of its theoretical merits.

In spite of the fact that state and national issues were tied together in the parties' platforms, the two groups did not emphasize the two areas equally before the public. As a matter of campaign strategy, Seawell's friends concentrated on the railroad, while Hybart's backers attacked the Bank. Each side accused the other of stressing the wrong set of problems.

As friends of Seawell, "Many" wrote to the *Observer* early in the campaign to deny that "our next Town Election is to rest on *political* [*i.e.*, partisan] grounds." Instead, claimed "Many," "*we* rest his [Seawell's] claims . . . upon a higher and more noble principle—we support him as the warm friend of internal improvements."[99] Whatever they thought of railroads, the Jacksonians could not agree that corporate charters involved "a higher and more noble principle" than the Bank War. Indeed, the blessing of higher principle was invoked for both sides. "They have not attempted, as the Bank party have done," replied one outraged Democrat, "to put their candidate on a rail road with the hope of riding him into the Legislature."[100] Speaking with the voice of authority, "the friends of Thomas L. Hybart, Esq." corrected "Many" sharply, and assured the readers of the *Observer* that "the town election is to rest on political grounds."[101]

Seawell was not the only leader who was anxious to avoid a "political" contest over deposit removal that might damage the town's interests in transportation development. At least one prominent Democrat agreed with him. Dillon Jordan, Jr., was an urban Jacksonian who was seeking one of the

98. *Ibid.*
99. Fayetteville *Observer*, May 20, 1834.
100. *Ibid.*, June 3, 1834.
101. *Ibid.*, May 27, 1834.

county seats in the House of Commons. Whigs described him as "the Lawyer that the Town People have put up to represent the County" in 1834.[102] He was still searching for a party platform that would enable him to remain a loyal Jacksonian without abandoning his active support for the western railroad. To this end he asked Seawell privately to use his influence to keep national issues out of the local elections. This attempt to belittle the importance of national party distinctions angered other Democrats. They seemed to assume that the chief value of the town election was its suitability as a theater to test their partisan strength. Jordan was forced to choose between his party and his railroad. He chose the former and retreated hastily from his offer of cooperation. He generated a noisy controversy with Seawell in the newspapers to hide his confusion.[103]

The Democrats forced the issue of the Bank War with a letter to both newspapers signed by "Many Voters." The letter posed three questions to the candidates for town member. The first two were phrased in such a way as to make a simple and direct, but intelligent response by an anti-Jacksonian impossible. The third was designed to neutralize Seawell's favorite issue. "*First—* Are you for or against the Administration of General Jackson? *Secondly—* Are you for or against the Bank of the United States? *Thirdly—*Are you in favor of prosecuting works of internal improvement in this State?"[104]

Hybart's answers were immediate and forthright. He was for General Jackson and against the Bank. He was also for internal improvements, though he had done less for the cause than Seawell, and he mentioned no specific plan or goal for development. Nor did he touch on the important question of state aid. He simply praised their benefits to "the Mechanic and all the laboring classes of society," thus deftly putting himself on the right side of this issue with some voters, while avoiding any commitments that might be offensive to his rural-oriented supporters.[105]

James Seawell preferred not to answer such a set of queries at all. The antirepublican implications of a refusal to answer constituents' questions, however, overwhelmed his reluctance. Eventually, he produced a set of answers that were as pompous as they were tardy. In his reply, he condemned the partisan trick of "Many Voters" to involve national politics in a local election. He reminded his readers that he had no political ambition, that he had been urged to run by friends of "both parties," and that he had agreed from a sense of duty. His disinclination for a partisan election was so great that he had been approached by a Democratic representative from the county who asked him

102. *Ibid.*, July 15, 1834.
103. *Ibid.*, June 18, 1834, June 25, 1834.
104. *Ibid.*, June 3, 1834.
105. *Ibid.*, June 10, 1834.

to keep national politics out of the local elections, in order not to distract attention from the cause of internal improvements. This representative was later identified as Dillon Jordan, Jr. In spite of these objections, however, Seawell would consent to answer "Many Voters." [106]

In reply to the first question, Seawell said that he had initially supported Jackson, but had become disillusioned by the president's incompetence and his abuse of power. He "most heartily disapprove[d]" of deposit removal and the discharge of Secretary Duane, but recharter of the present Bank was impractical. Instead, he supported the chartering of a new bank with greater public safeguards. As for internal improvements, he would say nothing. His opinions on this subject, he claimed, were so well known that no comment was necessary. [107]

Seawell became involved in a war of words with Dillon Jordan over the meaning of the allusion to the latter in Seawell's letter. In addition to the acrimony, letter writers of both persuasions bombarded the *Journal* and the *Observer* with partisan propaganda. Aside from the clash of personalities between Seawell and Jordan, the principal issue of the letters was not simply the Bank, but the idea of partisanship itself. Each party had embraced a different style of political advocacy, and the election would in some measure determine which style would prevail in the future. The Democrats, as the supporters of a single man and a concrete policy, found it easier to embrace the partisan idea than the Whigs. Their letters for the most part supported parties explicitly. "It has always been my opinion," declared Dillon Jordan, "that parties will exist where there is liberty, and that they help to preserve it." [108] Going further, "An Old Fashioned Republican" claimed that "in the nature of things there can be but two grand divisions of parties in this country," and he named them "Democratic Republicans and old-fashioned Federalist." However, said "An Old Fashioned Republican," "one of the surest tests of a republican is presented by the bank question, those who are opposed to the United States bank are as they have always been republicans; those who are in its favor are as they have always been, *federalists*." He urged all good Republicans to vote only for fellow Republicans, "for the Patriotic Jackson is warring for the liberties of his country." A strong Republican vote, even in the North Carolina legislative elections, would "strengthen his hands by sustaining his measures." The strength of party loyalty was so important for "An Old Fashioned Republican" that he professed more admiration for a candid and consistent opponent of the opposite party, than one who supported some Jacksonian measures but not other ones. "The vacillating feeling of the latter will beget

106. *Ibid.*, June 17, 1834.
107. *Ibid.*
108. Fayetteville *North Carolina Journal*, June 25, 1834.

contempt and distrust and ridicule and will certainly fail in the accomplishment of any important end." [109]

The Whigs, in contrast to the Democrats, followed Seawell's opening disclaimer opposing any emphasis on partisan distinctions. Replying to the challenge thrown down by "Many Voters," "J. B." denied that the public was ignorant of the opinions and qualities of the two men. The difference between Hybart and Seawell to this writer was not that each represented a rival party, but that the former was a partisan and the latter was not. Instead, Seawell was "a tried friend to the constitution and the laws, with intelligence to understand and firmness to maintain the great interests of his constituents." [110] Arguing in the same vein, "Civis" demanded to know *"Who are they*, Regardless of the interests of our town, both morally and politically, that have made the approaching election a question of party; at the same time to advance the prospects of their leaders, have endeavored to introduce the Van Buren system of political tactics, 'stop at nothing to promote your party?'" [111]

In spite of their distress over "Van Buren tactics," the Whigs stopped at very little themselves in their drive to get Seawell elected. Their efforts exposed some of the same social tensions that had appeared in 1810, but their use of class advantages to overawe the opposition was more subtle than the Federalists' had been. Under James Seawell's leadership as magistrate of police, the Whig majority on the town commission redrew Fayetteville's western boundary to include the fashionable residential neighborhood of Haymount. Democrats believed that these newly enfranchised voters cast ballots for Seawell. They claimed that the inhabitants who left town every summer for healthy retreats in the sandhills returned to Fayetteville in order to vote Whig. [112] At the other end of the social scale, Whigs recruited voters whom Democrats charged were ineligible. As Lewis A. Nixon, Democratic tavern keeper, said of one free black Whig, "I never knew of John White having a residence in the town of Fayetteville, except a few days at a time, when drunk about Campbellton, and last winter I saw him working at Sampson Boon's plantation on the East side of Cape Fear River, and I have also seen him frequently going as a hand on the River." [113]

For their part, Democrats claimed to be honest workingmen who toiled long hours for a modest competence. Defending his party against the accusation of midnight caucuses, "A Jackson Man" declared that "a large portion of the friends of the Administration in this place are men who get their bread by

109. *Ibid.*, July 30, 1834, August 6, 1834.
110. Fayetteville *Observer*, June 17, 1834.
111. *Ibid.*, August 12, 1834.
112. Fayetteville *North Carolina Journal*, July 9, 1834, July 30, 1834; Fayetteville *Observer*, January 27, 1835.
113. Fayetteville *Observer*, January 20, 1835.

the sweat of their brow, who, when the toils of the day are over feel themselves at liberty to meet and consult about the means of preserving their liberties." The Democrats met at night, "A Jackson Man" continued, because
"they hold no *salaried offices* which enable them to lounge away an afternoon
or attend public meetings to hear and make long speeches." [114] The writer's
claims for the occupations of Hybart's supporters cannot be verified, but it is
safe to say that Whigs would not have sought a public image as the special
party of manual workers. They were much more likely to complain, as
"Civis" did, that Democrats "have propagated reports calculated to array one
part of our community against the other, thus exciting the worst feelings of
our nature . . . and . . . despoil[ing] this great social fabric." [115]

Election day itself vibrated with tension and hostility which the abundant
availability of free liquor did nothing to dissipate. According to two Democratic participants, "early on the morning of the election, the Bank party distinguished themselves by wearing a Blue ribbon," while "the Republican
party adopted the pink ribbon." Robert Cochran Belden recalled later that "to
get rid of an uncertain element," the Whigs escorted a body of free blacks to
the polls early and flanked each one with a pair of whites as he gave in his
ticket. Later on, "large bodies of the voters of each party paraded the streets,
preceded by music." The parties marched to the Town House, where the voting took place. They entered by separate stairways, one of which was built
especially for the occasion, and divided on opposite sides of a strong railing
for speeches and reciprocal heckling. At one point, Louis D. Henry called to
the Democrats to keep order and in the process made stinging reflections on
the Whigs. Unable to contain himself, Edward J. Hale led his party in a cho-
rus of three groans, an action which Henry later described as "an insult . . .
gross and unprovoked." When Hale failed to apologize, Henry demanded
"that satisfaction which no gentleman can refuse to accord to another, under
such circumstances," and a duel between the two was only narrowly averted.
Before the day was over, a fight broke out over the ballot box itself. Leaping
from an overhead pulpit to join the fray, one Democratic pollwatcher landed
on the box and broke it. It was only understatement which led Edward J. Hale
to describe the election afterwards as "one of the most animated, we may say,
angry contests ever witnessed in this State." [116]

When the ballots were gathered off the floor and counted, James Seawell
had won by 200 votes to 184. Thomas L. Hybart challenged the result on the
grounds that Seawell did not meet the property qualifications for the House of

114. *Ibid.*, June 3, 1834.
115. *Ibid.*, August 12, 1834.
116. Belden, "Traditions of Cross Creek"; Fayetteville *Observer*, August 19, 1834, January 20,
1835, January 27, 1835; Fayetteville *North Carolinian*, April 25, 1840.

Commons and that the Whig election judges had used a double standard in accepting or rejecting voters with questionable qualifications. In the testimony accompanying these charges, activists in both parties admitted to creating new voters for the election by granting "freeholds" to committed but otherwise ineligible partisans. The House of Commons appointed a committee to investigate the charges. Their report pointed out that Seawell had once owned sufficient property to meet the qualification and that he still occupied the property, but that the title had passed to his brothers. The report also noted that if all of the questionable votes for Hybart were accepted and all the questionable ballots for Seawell were rejected, Seawell would still win the election by three votes. The House remained undecided in the case until it was revealed that one of Hybart's witnesses was a free black man. According to a correspondent of the *Observer*, this information "excited . . . a sensation of disgust, and turned the scales in favor of Mr. Seawell." [117] The House promptly tabled Hybart's challenge and Seawell kept his seat.

Fayetteville Democrats lost the election but they won a moral victory. Hybart had gained seventy-nine votes over his total in the last election while Seawell had gained only three. The next year, Hybart would defeat John D. Eccles, his Whig opponent, by twelve votes. In rural Cumberland, the Democratic victories were even more impressive. They swept the county offices against token opposition, except in the race for sheriff. There John McLean, the Whig incumbent, hung on for one more term to be replaced later by a succession of Democrats. The partisanship which the Democrats advocated, moreover, became the norm in Cumberland politics. Edward J. Hale professed to disapprove of excessive partisanship, but he described the state elections as a "great Whig victory" and asked exaltingly, "at what time since the war have [national] politics entered so much into our State Elections?" [118] By the late 1830s the Whigs had dropped the pretense of being nonpartisan and called for every display of discipline and loyalty that the Democrats had. While the Whigs remained a viable party in Cumberland, they attempted to match the Democrats in every index of partisanship.

Fayetteville voters were not alone as they split into rival parties. Throughout North Carolina, numerous local elections in 1834 turned on a combination of questions raised by banking, internal improvements, and national politics. The rhetoric involved in these contests frequently suggested that struggles for the symbols of authority between established leaders and less prestigious representatives were also at stake in these contests. In New Bern, for example, a meeting presided over by the intendant of police nominated

---

117. Fayetteville *Observer*, January 20, 1835, January 27, 1835, June 24, 1840; *North Carolina House Journal*, 1834, p. 200.
118. Fayetteville *Observer*, September 2, 1834.

M. E. Manly for town member in May. The editor of the New Bern *Spectator* rejoiced that municipal leaders had chosen a foolproof method for uniting behind a single candidate. "As every prominent citizen has an equal chance of being elected at such meetings," the editor concluded, "opposition to the approved candidate will rarely occur, and disagreeable electioneering contests, so greatly to be deprecated, will thus be banished from amongst us." The editor's complacency was afterwards disturbed by a tart notice that Charles Shepard, the incumbent town member, would fight to retain his seat, regardless of decisions made by smoothly arranged meetings. The notice was followed by a letter from Shepard which explained that the town's leading citizens opposed him because he had sponsored bank charter bills which restricted the corporations more than bankers wished. Shepard had also questioned whether a legacy left for the education of poor children was being properly administered and had originally run for office in opposition to a long-established and respected senior politician, probably William Gaston.[119]

Later that summer, the *Spectator* demanded that internal improvements and constitutional reform be the issues of the August election. The columns of the paper bristled with letters which denounced the district's representative in Congress for his opposition to the Bank and which called for town and county representatives who would vote for state aid to railroads. Nearby Pitt and Carteret counties divided over the same questions and in both places, candidates won who pledged support of internal improvements and opposition to President Jackson.[120]

Far to the west, Mecklenburg County experienced a similar conflict. Friends and enemies of the administration gathered in July and offered testimonial dinners to their respective favorites of North Carolina's two United States senators. According to the Jacksonians, the opposition meeting "was got up for the purpose of having an effect in the ensuing county election for the Legislature, as well as to have an effect on the next election for a Senator to Congress, and for the purpose of thwarting the views and policy of the present administration." Whig letters to the local newspaper likewise denounced Democrats for "bringing in matters so foreign in their nature, into county elections" as support for Jackson and opposition to the Bank. Each group charged the other with making improper links between county, state, and national politics, but neither backed away from the connections thus forged. The Jacksonian candidates carried Mecklenburg County on the strength of rural votes, but Whigs won a clear majority in the expanding vil-

119. New Bern *Spectator*, May 30, 1834, June 6, 1834.
120. *Ibid.*, July 18, 1834, August 15, 1834; Otway Burns to William J. Alexander, August 12, 1834, published in Charlotte *Miners' and Farmers' Journal*, August 23, 1834.

lage of Charlotte and in several rural precincts which may have been affected by the local gold mining industry.[121]

Perhaps the clearest parallel to the case of Fayetteville appeared in the Wilmington town elections. As the largest town in the state, Wilmington was a seaport, the regional marketplace for lumber, rice, and naval stores, and the county seat of New Hanover County. Commercial and slaveholding interests were both quite powerful and had clashed in past elections, but in 1834, merchants and planters had united enthusiastically in favor of railroad construction.[122] Support for state aid to internal improvements seemed to be even more widespread in Wilmington than in Fayetteville, although the Bank War was as controversial there as elsewhere. Friends and enemies of the Bank organized in 1834 to elect a sympathetic legislative delegation. Gen. Edward B. Dudley, later the first popularly elected governor of North Carolina, led the Whigs as candidate for town member while Daniel Sherwood opposed him as the choice of Democrats.[123]

As in Fayetteville, the Whigs of Wilmington called themselves "the friends of internal improvements" while administration supporters called themselves "the Jackson party." Whigs deprecated the introduction of national political questions into local politics and charged that Democrats were pandering to social rivalries. According to one letter writer, "there are some who are desirous to promote in this county a *plebeian* and *patrician* struggle for power," and proudly signed himself "A Patrician." Another Whig asked, "what is the object of electing a member of Assembly to represent the Town? Is it to represent a party? . . . Or is it to represent the Wealth, the Talent, the Respectability and the Interests of the Town?" Democrats retorted that "it is absolutely necessary to preserve the line of party distinction. Federalist and Democrat are terms as familiar now as ever, and they are as easily recognized, not withstanding the former has attempted a deception by disguising itself with a WIG."[124]

The Democrats attempted to draw these party lines by a series of questions which resembled the queries of "Many Voters" in Fayetteville. Was General Dudley a Jackson Man? Did he oppose recharter of the Bank and restoration of the deposits? Was he a nullifier? Would he vote for the reelection of Jacksonian Senator Bedford Brown? Unlike James Seawell, Dudley did not publish an answer to these questions, but he won the election, 133 votes to 91.

121. Charlotte *Miners' and Farmers' Journal*, July 12, 1834, August 16, 1834.
122. Wilmington *Cape Fear Recorder*, April 20, 1831, May 11, 1831, June 29, 1831, August 29, 1831; Wilmington *People's Press*, January through June, 1834, *passim*.
123. Wilmington *People's Press*, June 11, 1834.
124. *Ibid.*, June 25, 1834, July 15, 1834.

Thereafter, Whigs divided the votes of Wilmington evenly with their opponents, while rural New Hanover citizens voted exclusively for Democrats.[125]

North Carolina's division into political parties was not perfect in the summer of 1834. In New Bern, Charles Shepard withdrew from the contest before any votes were cast, and it was not until the following year that the New Bern *Spectator* described the appearance of party lines "after the most noisy contest which we have witnessed in many years." Elsewhere in the state, probank and proimprovements candidates ran unopposed in Salisbury and Hillsborough while partisan contests outside the major towns were hard to identify. Nevertheless, when the elections were over, the state press announced with confidence that antiadministration forces had carried the day, and most observers seemed to agree that questions of local and national politics had been commonly linked together.[126] The second American party system was beginning to emerge in North Carolina.

The adoption of the party system in Fayetteville was a painful process. Political polarization bruised friendships and threatened the town with violence. When Hale later aired both parties' dirty linen by publishing the depositions on the election challenge, "Timon" wrote the *Journal* to arraign his motives. Hale's purpose in reviving the ugly scenes of August, he charged, "was to prevent the subsidence of that storm of party excitement, which had so recently marr'd the harmony and friendship that were believed to have prevailed in our community. . . . It was to rekindle the animosity that had cruelly severed the ties of friendship with many, and implanted stings in the bosoms of some that would have rankled there till death in silence, but which may now burst forth into violence of action, that may produce consequences the most deplorable."[127] No new outbreak of violence occurred, but the personal rancor which "Timon" deplored apparently persisted for many years.

When Thomas L. Hybart finally won election as town member the following year, he served as Fayetteville's last borough representative. Constitutional amendments in 1835 abolished borough representation on the grounds that towns needed no special consideration in the General Assembly. Judge John D. Toomer defended the town's interests in the state's constitutional convention, but his lack of success brought no loud complaints in Fayetteville. Abolition of borough representation "has produced some surprize in this community," the *Observer* admitted, "but not so strong dissatisfaction as

125. *Ibid.*, June 18, 1834, August 20, 1834. Precinct-level election returns were collected for New Hanover County between 1836 and 1860 from Wilmington newspapers on microfilm in the North Carolina Collection.
126. New Bern *Spectator*, August 15, 1834, August 7, 1835; Salisbury *Carolina Watchman*, August, 1834; Hillsborough *Recorder*, August 20, 1834.
127. Fayetteville *North Carolina Journal*, January 28, 1835.

might have been expected." [128] The unpleasantness associated with borough elections was widely regretted throughout the state and probably influenced the convention in the decision to abolish them. A convention delegate from Orange County who was familiar with elections in Hillsborough may have spoken the private thoughts of many leading men in Fayetteville when he complained to the convention that "mechanics and others are excited by the parties interested in such elections, business is neglected, and the morals of the people corrupted." [129] According to the *Observer*, most citizens regretted the change in principle, "but we have not heard a single individual speak of it who did not feel that his individual comfort and peace would be promoted by the loss." [130] The new constitutional amendments also put an end to free black voting, a practice which highly embarrassed a society based on racial slavery.

Town member elections disappeared but the party system did not. The next January, both parties put up rival slates for magistrate of police and town commissioners. John D. Eccles led the Whigs to victory over Dr. Thomas N. Cameron and the Democrats, 161 votes to 136. Significantly, the *Observer* insisted that Democrats were outsiders in town government by labeling the two slates the "Regular Whig Nomination" and the "Opposition or Jackson" ticket. [131] Turnout dropped from the levels of August but partisanship did not. The organizations which solidified at the same time remained until the end of the antebellum period. County leaders had ended the searching for platforms which marked the first years of the 1830s. They were free thereafter to recruit mass adherence to the standards which they and national leaders had forged. In Fayetteville the recruitment process began in 1834. In the rest of Cumberland County it was not fully under way until 1836.

128. Fayetteville *Observer*, June 30, 1835.
129. *Proceedings and Debates of the Convention of North Carolina*, (Raleigh, 1836), 35, 36, quoted in Vinson, "Electioneering in North Carolina," 187.
130. Fayetteville *Observer*, June 30, 1835.
131. *Ibid.*, January 6, 1835.

VI. Aristocracy Against the Farmers
Party Growth and Social Composition
1834–1836

By 1834, political organizers in Cumberland County had selected formulae for linking local social divisions with national political controversies. Hostility to Fayetteville's commercial power, indifference or opposition to local internal improvements, dislike of banks in general and the Bank of the United States in particular, and admiration of Andrew Jackson became a coherent package of interests, symbols, and convictions which guided Democrats in their understanding of political issues. For Whigs, enthusiasm for economic development, desire for internal improvements, an appreciation of the credit system, and hostility to General Jackson became an equally consistent and attractive collection of attitudes. Not every political leader fully accepted the tenets of his party's creed; this was especially true among leading Fayetteville Democrats. For the most part, however, office seekers and party spokesmen conformed to their party's basic vision in their public addresses and appeared to recognize the party platform as their fundamental basis for attracting votes.

The party leaders began to use their respective platforms to mobilize voters in 1834. Whether they could do so indefinitely was problematical because the most important national issue to which local issues were linked was the character of President Jackson. When Old Hickory himself was no longer under review, the party system might conceivably have lapsed. The election of 1836 saw a largely successful attempt by Cumberland leaders to persuade the voters to transfer their personal attitudes for or against Jackson to more abstract and permanent institutions, the Democratic and Whig parties. That election also saw the spread of party behavior from Fayetteville into the surrounding districts. The party system began to maintain itself and to grow. In this sense, 1836 witnessed the final stage of political party formation.

Struggle over a new state constitution was a convenient bridge between the legislative elections of 1834 and the presidential election of 1836. North Carolinà had never revised the state constitution which its Provincial Congress had adopted in 1776. That instrument did not make legislative representation proportional to population, and western counties had long complained of malapportionment. They demanded a constitutional convention to correct the problem. By the early 1830s, dissatisfaction with the status quo was so intense that the Raleigh *Register* blamed the failure of internal improvements in the legislature of 1833 on the overwhelming sectional jealousy aroused by the convention question.[1] After 1833, leaders of eastern towns decided that they would never obtain their needed railroads until they met the demands of the west and reduced the power of eastern rural interests. In the local elections of 1834, candidates who supported internal improvements and the Bank also promised to press for constitutional reform. One participant in the Wilmington town elections of that year later recalled that they turned on "Jacksonism and Anti-Jacksonism, Convention and Anti-Convention," and Craven, Carteret, and Pitt counties showed similar alignments. Urban defections from the eastern phalanx turned the scale in favor of reform and the 1834 legislature called for a referendum on the convention question in February, 1835.[2] The referendum passed by a sectional vote and the convention to revise the constitution met in Raleigh on June 4, 1835. In effect, the state's electorate voted on the proposed amendments twice: once when they sanctioned the convention call itself and once when the convention had finished its work.

The legislature empowered the convention to propose a limited number of constitutional amendments for ratification by the people. The most important substantive change was to allocate seats in the House of Commons on the basis of federal population and in the Senate on the basis of taxable wealth. This amendment gave control of the House to the west and control of the Senate to the east. The most time-consuming and emotionally charged issue before the convention did not relate to representation, but to religion. The legislature had authorized the convention to alter Article XXXII of the old constitution, which provided "that no person who shall deny the being of God, or the truth of the Protestant religion, or the divine authority of either the Old or New Testament or who shall hold Religious principles incompatible with the freedom and safety of the State, shall be capable of holding any office or place of trust or profit in the civil department within this state." The article had never been enforced, prominent lawyers regarded it as legally meaningless, and no large body of non-Protestant voters clamored for its re-

1. Raleigh *Register*, January 14, 1834.
2. Harold J. Counihan, "The North Carolina Constitutional Convention of 1835: A Study in Jacksonian Democracy," *North Carolina Historical Review*, XLVI (1969), 338; *Proceedings and Debates of the Convention of North Carolina, Called to Amend the Constitution of the State, which Assembled at Raleigh, June 4, 1835* (Raleigh, 1836), 206.

peal. The desire for a change seems to have been a symbol of religious liberalism among certain members of the elite and a sign of respect to William Gaston, a Catholic who had just been appointed to the North Carolina Supreme Court. Nevertheless, popular opposition to repeal was bitter, and the convention settled for an amendment which substituted the word "Christian" for the word "Protestant." Other changes recommended by the convention of 1835 included the popular election of the governor for no more than two consecutive two-year terms, biennial elections of the General Assembly, abolition of free black suffrage and borough representation, and equalization of the poll tax for freemen and slaves.[3]

Cumberland County was generally regarded as an eastern county, but its leaders had long sympathized with the desires of the west for enlarged representation. John A. Cameron and John Armstrong, both future Democratic activists, had represented the county at an informal state convention as early as 1823 to request a revision of the constitution.[4] During the early 1830s, both newspapers regularly offered their sympathy for the western position. When the county supported the proposal for a convention by 558 votes to 207, Edward J. Hale was surprised only by the size of the opposition. He attributed the negative votes to "the mingling of politics and religion with the question, in some parts of the county."[5] The editor provided no further details, but he probably meant that some voters outside of Fayetteville objected to the mere possibility of a change in Article XXXII. These rural voters were likely to be Democrats, and their "political" objections to a convention may have stemmed from its parentage. The convention was the offspring of a coalition between westerners and eastern urban advocates of internal improvements. The same forces comprised a Whig coalition which would govern North Carolina from 1836 to 1850, and many Democrats may have anticipated the partisan effects of reform. When the amendments were submitted to a popular referendum, the Raleigh *Register* reported in shocked tones that "in Cumberland . . . the friends of Mr. Van Buren will go dead against 'ratification,' for no better reason than because the convention, which recommended the amendments to the people was WHIG to the core."[6] The *North Carolina Journal* criticized the amendments for retaining too many undemocratic features in the constitution. The referendum passed in the state, and Fayetteville voters approved it by 203 to 157, or 56.4 percent in favor. Turnout was light in the

3. Counihan, "Convention of 1835," 351–53; *Proceedings and Debates of the Convention of 1835*, 418–24.
4. Fayetteville *Carolina Observer*, September 11, 1823.
5. Fayetteville *Observer*, April 7, 1835.
6. Raleigh *Register*, September 22, 1835, quoted in Clarence Clifford Norton, *The Democratic Party in Ante-Bellum North Carolina, 1835–1861* (Chapel Hill, 1930), 47.

rural districts but the vote was 59.3 percent opposed. The amendments lost in Cumberland County as a whole by 331 in favor to 489 against.[7]

The Fayetteville press did not explain why the amendments failed to carry the county, but there is good reason to believe that the Raleigh *Register* was correct. Opposition to the amendments varied with support for the Democratic party. The correlation coefficient between the negative vote on the amendments and the Democratic vote for governor the next year was a moderately strong .5777 (see table 20). If the *Observer* was correct, opponents of the amendments had tried to persuade country voters that interference with Article XXXII was irreligious and that the overall work of the convention was prorailroad and anti-Jacksonian. Other voters may have followed the *Journal*'s suggestion and rejected the amendments because the provisions on free black voting, property representation in the Senate, and equalization of the poll tax were undemocratic in the modern sense. These arguments had limited effect before the convention met, but when the amendments themselves came before the people, they may have been responsible for defeating approval of reform in the county. Democratic politicians in Cumberland were taking advantage of the referendum to sharpen their organizing skills and to keep alive the notion that distant and familiar issues should both be understood through the same partisan framework.

In the same fall that Cumberland County voters defeated the amendments to the constitution, they supported Lauchlin Bethune for Congress in a partisan campaign against Edmund Deberry. The behavior of voters and the rhetoric of candidates in this election was not perceptibly different from previous encounters between these rival favorite sons.[8] A clearer picture of the emergence of partisan politics appeared in the elections of the following year.

As they did every four years, the people of North Carolina voted at two different times in 1836: on the second Thursday in August for the state posts, and on the second Thursday of November for the presidency. Because the amendments of 1835 passed at the state level, the voters themselves elected the governor at the August elections. Each party supported its own candidate for this office. Incumbent Governor Richard Dobbs Spaight of New Bern was the Democratic nominee and Gen. Edward B. Dudley of Wilmington was the Whig. In spite of this novelty, the attention of the press and of the county's political meetings focused on the presidential contest between Democrat Martin Van Buren and Whig Hugh Lawson White. White was a former Jack-

---

7. Fayetteville *North Carolina Journal*, November 4, 1835, November 18, 1835.
8. Edmund Deberry, "To the Freemen of the Counties of Anson, Richmond, Cumberland, Moore, and Montgomery," February 28, 1935 (Typed copy of Election Circular in Deberry Papers. Southern Historical Collection).

sonian senator from Tennessee who ran as a southern regional candidate. This preoccupation with national affairs was traditional. Besides, as the *North Carolina Journal* remarked, "The Governor of North Carolina has not as much power as a Justice of the Peace." [9] A successful candidate for the presidency, however, could reward his supporters and punish his opponents, so local politicians were very attentive to the interests of their declared favorites. The resolutions of each party's vigilance committee devoted only a few lines to the gubernatorial election but column after column to the presidential race. These electioneering statements on the presidential question are the sources for studying the issues between Whigs and Democrats in 1836. The distribution of party strength within the county, however, appears only in the governor's election returns, since the presidential election records were lost.

The campaign of 1836 took place under strong party management from the beginning. As in 1834, the Democrats were most active in this regard. In March of 1835, twenty-one months before election day, Cumberland Democrats were already appointing delegates to a district convention that would nominate a congressional candidate and send a delegate to the national convention in Baltimore. [10] Two months later, the district convention took place on schedule but only three out of six counties were represented. In spite of this limitation, the convention delegated the Honorable Robert Strange of Fayetteville to represent them in Baltimore, nominated Lauchlin Bethune for Congress, and issued an address to the voters on his behalf. The latter two functions had formerly been left to private initiative, but were thenceforth handled by party organization. Without expressing a preference for a presidential nominee they urged the district's Democrats "to sustain the nomination which the said convention may make." [11] When the convention made its nominations, the *Journal* urged Van Buren's election for his personal merits and his party services. The editors endorsed the vice presidential nominee, Richard M. Johnson, on the grounds of party regularity alone. A year later the party went through a second round of county and district conventions, and appointed a two-hundred-member committee of vigilance and correspondence. The *North Carolina Journal* boasted of the "truly Democratic character of this meeting . . . composed principally of the men who have hard hands and sound heads." Praise of party loyalty and regularity was a keynote of both proceedings. [12]

In contrast to the Democrats, the Cumberland Whigs lagged somewhat in party organization. They had no district convention in 1835, perhaps because

9. Fayetteville *North Carolina Journal*, September 22, 1836.
10. *Ibid.*, March 11, 1835.
11. *Ibid.*, April 29, 1835, June 3, 1835.
12. *Ibid.*, March 17, 1836.

they had no national convention to prepare for. In March, 1836, the Whigs did meet to plan a district convention that would nominate a district elector, attend to local campaign business, and communicate with other Whig groups. They also named a committee of vigilance of seventy-four members. When the district convention took place, the Fayetteville *Observer* bragged that every county in the district had sent delegates, twenty-two in all, and that there were "many spectators" in the courthouse to observe the proceedings, whereas the Democratic "convention" consisted of eight delegates from three counties only. In the fall the Whigs celebrated the victory of General Dudley in the governor's election with a "Whig Festival" or "Barbecue" that was held indoors in a Fayetteville tavern and featured speeches and toasts by local dignitaries.[13]

For most of the campaign the Fayetteville *Observer* did little explicitly to promote party spirit, though it was the principal Whig newspaper of the region. The editor, Hale, claimed "republican whig" was the label for his political affiliations, but just as often he used "republican" by itself.[14] Instead of stimulating party loyalty, he used antiparty values to cudgel the Democrats. "We should . . . exercise our independent reasons," he reminded his readers, "and remember that it is Martin Van Buren, and not Andrew Jackson, that we are called upon to vote for." Van Buren, he said, "is emphatically the *nomination* and *caucus* candidate."[15] If he were elected, the same kind of party machinery under which "the Northern States are this day labouring" would seize control of the government to the exclusion of the democratic process. He particularly criticized party meetings where "no discussion is permitted, resolutions are previously prepared, committees previously chosen, and the meeting called like a German diet to record the will of its masters." Moreover, Hale claimed that the majority of the people, being "agriculturists," could never come to political meetings so that county conventions were dominated by "politicians by trade, gentlemen of leisure, and those having business at the Court House and living at convenient distances."[16] These charges ignored the facts that Democrats were much more successful in recruiting middle-class rural farmers than Whigs, and that Hale himself had participated in his share of prearranged meetings.[17]

To the degree that Hale spoke for his party, the Whigs continued to voice antiparty values longer than the Democrats. Some authors have suggested

13. Fayetteville *Observer*, February 25, 1836, March 10, 1836, March 24, 1836. September 15, 1836.
14. *Ibid.*, June 16, 1836.
15. *Ibid.*, April 14, 1836.
16. *Ibid.*, September 15, 1836.
17. Most notably in 1832, but also in 1827. See Fayetteville *Carolina Observer*, June 5, 1832, and Fayetteville *North Carolina Journal*, December 12, 1827.

that nationally, the Whigs were more wary of party regimentation than the Democrats.[18] In Cumberland County, however, the Adams and Barbour campaigns had both been well organized, and the Whigs made facile use of partisan tools in the Log Cabin Campaign four years later. If the Whigs hung back from extreme partisanship in 1836, they may have had other reasons than simple antipartyism. The Democrats enjoyed the advantage of building party identification out of a strong preexisting loyalty to a heroic individual. They found the transfer of support and affection from Old Hickory to his appointed heirs relatively easy, given the fact that, as "A Citizen of Duplin" noted, "The people have confidence in Andrew Jackson's word." The Whigs, on the other hand, were forced to create loyalty to an impersonal and still inchoate institution whose initial justification had been hostility to "man worship." The Whigs of Cumberland and most of eastern North Carolina were a distinct minority. If they were to carry the region for White, they would have to win over restless Jacksonians, but they were less likely to do this successfully if they stressed their own exclusive symbols and identity.[19]

To a certain extent, therefore, the Whigs had no choice but to rely on antiparty values when the Democrats were flocking to the party standard with enthusiasm. Later, when the Whig party was more firmly established and had generated a group loyalty that surpassed simple anti-Jacksonianism, it effectively used party organization. When Hale denounced the Democrats for "caucus" organization, he may have been making a virtue of necessity.

Accusations that Martin Van Buren was unreliable on the slavery issue were also a favorite Whig weapon in the 1836 election. General Dudley attacked Van Buren for his support of Rufus King, the New York senator who had fought against the admission of Missouri as a slave state. "He is not of *us*," Dudley charged. "He is a Northern man in soul, in principle and in action, with no feeling of sympathy or of interest for the South. . . . He is an Abolitionist." [20] The Cumberland County convention in support of Hugh Lawson White picked up the same theme. The convention's resolutions of March 8, 1836, reminded voters that "we have been attacked by Northern fanatics with a violence which leads us to apprehend that they will not stop short of an effort to deprive us of our rights and property." In a time of crisis, the Whigs averred, only a southerner like Hugh Lawson White could be trusted as president, while Van Buren's questionable voting record and equivocal correspondence proved "that he is against us." Whigs also seized on the well-known

18. Marshall, "Strange Stillbirth of the Whig Party," 445–68; Formisano, *The Birth of Mass Political Parties*, 57–58.
19. Joel Silbey, "The Election of 1836," in *Crucial American Elections* (Philadelphia, 1973), 14–29.
20. Fayetteville *North Carolina Journal*, March 31, 1836.

fact that Richard M. Johnson, the Democratic candidate for vice president, and a slave woman lived together as man and wife. The Cumberland County Whigs referred to that relationship with scarcely veiled prurience, and described Colonel Johnson as "the candidate who has been selected to conciliate the favour of the Northern Abolitionists." [21]

The Democrats' principal issues in this election appeared in a set of resolutions that Lauchlin Bethune presented at the county meeting of March 9, 1836. Bethune praised Van Buren and easily defended him against Whig accusations of abolitionism by showing that real abolitionists were mostly recruited from Whig party ranks. Bethune's resolutions and the other Democratic campaign statements showed a keen awareness of the need to repel Whig charges on the slavery issue, but they do not indicate that slavery was the central issue in the campaign. Instead, Bethune's principal resolution made a concrete avowal of the economic basis of the Democratic party: "*Resolved*, That the time has arrived, when Democrats must take a stand against associated wealth. That money-corporations are so extensively growing up in these States, as to portend fearful convulsions to the country and to the establishment of an order of estate more powerful than the laws of government." [22]

Bethune warned that the Founding Fathers had abolished primogeniture and entail and other "monopolies and exclusive privileges" precisely to prevent the growth of "associated wealth" and "its power to overawe, oppress, and corrupt." He deplored the fact that "judicial construction" had done what the Founders had sought to avoid. Succeeding to the privileges of aristocratic families, corporations had been placed beyond legal control when their charters were held to be contracts, and now they would be able to subvert laws and the democracy which produced them without a check. "Thus a few men," Bethune concluded, "can do what a whole state cannot do or undo." [23]

In making his analysis, Bethune drew on the recent history of the Bank of the United States and the state banks of North Carolina for illustrative purposes. But his appeal was not a simple diatribe against the Monster Bank, nor was it a leveling attack on economic inequality. He referred specifically to "associated wealth," to wealth that transcended the abilities of a single man to accumulate, or to administer responsibly. As a large planter himself, Bethune presumably welcomed the opportunity of a private individual to make himself rich. When wealth was combined into a limited-liability corporation, however, it passed beyond the reach of individual responsibility—either financial or ethical—and became a monster indeed. Moreover, Bethune was

---

21. Fayetteville *Observer*, March 10, 1836.
22. Fayetteville *North Carolina Journal*, March 17, 1836.
23. *Ibid.*

not pointing particularly to corporations in the region around him. He expected his audience to be familiar with developments in other states where corporate organization had gone further than it had in North Carolina, and with the decision of the Supreme Court in *Dartmouth College* v. *Woodward*. He drew on the fears of his listeners of what might happen to their own state if the social changes brought about elsewhere by associated wealth were allowed to occur in North Carolina. He did not need to remind his audience that in Fayetteville itself there were those who sought the very changes which corporations would bring: merchants, stockholders, bank directors, even a railroad company. Republicanism was held to be in danger from these people, and Bethune asked Democrats to save it.

As they applauded his resolutions, the members of the committee of vigilance were not simply embarking on a "democratic translation of the class struggle." [24] They did not seek a rival system of economic favors from the state, nor did they ask for protection for their eroding class position. They were not opposed to wealth itself. If they had been, the affluent Bethune would probably not have been their spokesman. Instead they were expressing a fear about the future of their political system and the agrarian society which supported it. As a group, the Democrats were coming down four-square, not simply for the working class, but for their own understanding of democracy and the preindustrial world order they lived in. It remained for later generations to maneuver for benefits within the broker state. For the present, the Cumberland Democrats simply clung to their vision of republicanism and saw an "aristocrat" behind every effort to supplant it.

In addition to Bethune's analysis the party regaled itself with elaborate panegyrics of Jackson and Van Buren, with stirring denunciations of Federalism, nullification, Judge White's apostasy, and the dishonesty of Whigs for running three sectional candidates. They occasionally lambasted "the Bills making appropriations of millions of dollars by congress for works of internal improvement" and William Henry Harrison, "the ultra internal improvements candidate." [25]

Hostility to corporations and transportation development led quite naturally into general hostility to towns and their interests. The Van Buren central committee used an association with urban influences to smear the Whigs, declaring that "the villages of the state where the strength of the opposition is concentrated, will all be at the polls, and the people must meet them there." [26] The *Journal* described the "Whig Festival" given by the "FEDERAL, NULLIFY-

24. Seymour Martin Lipset, *Political Man: The Social Bases of Politics* (Garden City, N.Y., 1960), 220.
25. Fayetteville *North Carolina Journal*, March 17, 1836, October 13, 1836.
26. *Ibid.*, October 13, 1836.

ING, BANK PARTY OF FAYETTEVILLE" as having been "schemed and planned in Fayetteville, so as to operate upon the country, and to seduce the country people into the support of that apostate Judge White for the Presidency." [27] In their preelection editorial, the *Journal* editors bore down even heavier on the antiurban theme. At the same time they drew urban-dwelling workers within the coalition opposed to commercial urban culture. The result was the fiercest example of egalitarian rhetoric that the election produced.

> Look through our own state, yea, thro' out the union, and you will see nearly all the cities and towns, the banks, the brokers, stockholders, the rich and the arrogant all opposed to Van Buren and the People.
>
> It is the Aristocracy against the farmers, the mechanics and the laboring class. See the towns of Fayetteville, Wilmington, and Hillsborough, the Whigs headquarters, holding festivals to mock, divide and triumph over the people. Not an instance can be cited within the last 3 years where the Whigs have gained the elections in any town or city, but they have hurled every Democrat from office and persecuted the laboring classes in many instances by turning them from their employ, because they dared to vote against them.
>
> If they triumph over you in the election of a Governor, what will they do if they elect the president? Every town will send forth its drunken shout of triumph, *that the people have been defeated* and their insolence will persecute you in every walk of life. [28]

If these charges of social conflict were true, they were true in a different way than similar charges might be true in the twentieth century. What the Jacksonian editor meant to convey, and what his audience probably understood by his remarks, was not that Whig capitalists were determined to plunder the middle and lower classes and that, if elected, the Democrats had a plan that would stop them. Aside from the unconvincing complaint against Whig use of the spoils system, the Democrats did not predict that corporations would impoverish their constituents, but that the "monsters" would overturn certain values which the American republic was held to embody. The greatest danger of the corporation, in other words, was not that it was exploitative, but that it was corrupt. The truth of the editor's charges, therefore, depended not so much on whether economic developers would actually harm the middle and lower classes more than the planter aristocracy may have been doing already, but on whether a conflict over values was indeed going on in Cumberland and all over the United States between "the cities . . . and the People." In this sense, the Democratic charges were resoundingly true.

In spite of every effort or argument the Whigs might make, Van Buren

27. *Ibid.*, September 22, 1836.
28. *Ibid.*, November 3, 1836.

swept the county, 667 votes to 418. The turnout percentage was 56.6 percent, almost as high as in 1828. Van Buren's share of the vote was 61.5 percent, 10 percentage points lower than Jackson's proportion of four years earlier.[29] Although Whig Edward B. Dudley won the governorship with 53.2 percent of the vote in August, Whig abstentions enabled Van Buren to carry the state in November by 57.5 percent. The Democratic proportion of Cumberland County's vote hovered slightly higher than 60 percent for most of the next two decades. Evidently about 10 percent of the county's voters changed sides in the creation of the Whig party. Unfortunately, as in most of the elections which preceded it, the precinct-level breakdown is not available for the presidential election of 1836. It is, therefore, impossible to be sure where Van Buren's support came from, although the *North Carolina Journal* did claim that "we beat them at every precinct in the county."[30]

The record of the August elections does exist. The coefficient of correlation between the percent Democratic in each precinct in the gubernatorial and legislative elections is high (r = .7929), indicating a moderately large degree of straight-ticket voting. The Democratic percentage in the governor's election, moreover, was 61.6 percent—almost exactly the same as in November.[31] Because party regularity probably carried over from August to November, we ought to be able, with a certain amount of caution, to infer something of the support for Martin Van Buren from the distribution of votes for Richard Dobbs Spaight. Table 20 shows the precinct returns for that election, arranged in order of percent Democratic.

There are two important differences between the gubernatorial and presidential elections shown in the table. First, the turnout in the governor's race was 214 votes higher than the turnout in November. Second, the Whigs carried two small precincts in August, but they carried none three months later. The difference in turnout, therefore, was probably not distributed evenly throughout the county, as more county voters either stayed home in November or voted in their own neighborhoods instead of going to Fayetteville. For these reasons the resemblance between table 20 and a possible table of Van Buren's actual vote can only be approximate.

Nevertheless, the table does show an interesting pattern in the distribution of the vote. Though most precincts were Democratic, some were more Democratic than others. Sandhills and mixed precincts, particularly, are mostly clustered at the top of table 20, indicating lower support for the Democrats. These were also the precincts which, together with Averasborough and Fay-

29. Compiled Election Returns, "Presidential Electors," 1832, 1836.
30. Fayetteville *North Carolina Journal*, November 17, 1836.
31. *Ibid.*, August 18, 1836.

Table 20. Cumberland County Gubernatorial Election, 1836

Precinct	Spaight	Dudley	Percent Demo-cratic	Predominant soil type
A. Munro's (Seventy-first)[a]	17	47	26.6	sandhills
Murchison's Mills (Upper Little River)	16	25	39.0	mixed
Averasborough	66	62	51.6	sandy loam
Fayetteville	246	229	51.8	————
Barbecue	68	45	60.2	sandhills
Blue's (Lock's Creek)	54	33	62.1	mixed
Smith's (Quewhiffle)	30	10	75.0	sandhills
Flea Hill	65	18	78.3	sandy loam
Johnson's (Neill's Creek)	71	13	84.5	sandy loam
Newberry's (Willis Creek)	46	6	88.5	sandy loam
J. Munroe's	34	4	89.5	sandhills
Christian's (Buckhorn)	87	7	92.6	sandy loam
County total	800	479	61.6	————

[a] When a name is given in parentheses below the precinct name, it refers to the tax district corresponding to that precinct.
SOURCE: Fayetteville *North Carolina Journal*, August 18, 1836.

etteville, showed the least support for the Jacksonians in 1824. Much had changed in the twelve years since that election. By 1836, most of the county's voters were in favor of Jackson instead of against him. The old Adams and Crawford districts, however, showed a certain residual reluctance to embrace the Jacksonian cause. Ecological factors in those precincts certainly did not *cause* Whiggery—otherwise these districts would be mostly Whig—but something about the urban and sandhills electorate, whether memories of the past or social and cultural conditions in the present, made Whiggery slightly more palatable to them than to others. The evidence of the tax records may give us some idea of what those factors were.

Table 21 shows the coefficients of correlation between various items from the 1837 tax list and the returns of the 1836 election. Not surprisingly, the percentage of free polls (an inverse measure of the relative concentration of

Table 21. Correlations Between Social, Economic, and Political Variables Cumberland County, 1835–1837

	Percent voting for Spaight, 1836[c]	Percent voting against new constitution, 1835[d]	Ratio of free polls to all polls, 1837[e]	Percent Scottish names, 1837[e]
Percent voting against new constitution, 1835	.5777 (.040)[a] N = 10[b]			
Ratio of free polls to all polls, 1837	.5862 (.029) N = 11	.1015 (.390) N = 10		
Percent Scottish names in the district, 1837	−.3394 (.154) N = 11	−.4883 (.076) N = 10	−.0646 (.417) N = 13	
Total assessed wealth per taxpayer, 1837[e]	−.2880 (.195) N = 11	−.2172 (.273) N = 10	−.6486 (.008) N = 13	−.3985 (.089) N = 13

Coefficients of Multiple Correlation with "Percent Voting for Spaight, 1836"

	multiple R	multiple R^2	one-tailed test significance level
Ratio of free polls to all polls, 1837	.58615	.34358	.029
Percent Scottish names in the district, 1837	.64386	.41455	.059
Total assessed wealth per taxpayer, 1837	.66072	.43656	.117

[a]The figure in parentheses is the significance level, or value of p for the given correlation coefficient, or r.
[b]The letter N refers to the number of cases, or precincts, which were used to calculate the given coefficient.
[c]SOURCE: Fayetteville *North Carolina Journal*, August 18, 1836.
[d]SOURCE: *Ibid.*, November 18, 1835.
[e]SOURCE: Cumberland County List of Taxables, 1837, in Cumberland County Records, North Carolina State Archives.

slaves in a district) has a high negative correlation with total assessed wealth per taxpayer ($r = -.6486$). To a certain degree both of these variables were simply measurements of the same thing, namely, the general economic prosperity of a district. This was not altogether the case, however. The Scottish districts were poorer than the others, as shown by the negative correlation between percent Scot and wealth per taxpayer ($r = -.3985$). This relative poverty, however, did not necessarily bring with it a lower concentration of slaves, as the insignificant correlation between percent Scot and the percentage of free polls shows. Though all were relatively poor, some Scottish districts had many slaves and some had few. This variation may reflect different degrees of slave employment in the sandhills forest industries. A second source of noncorrespondence between total assessed wealth and percent slave polls appears in some of the "small farmer" districts like Buckhorn and Willis Creek. The inhabitants of these districts owned few slaves, but whether because of the intrinsic qualities of their soil, or because the larger concentration of farmers per unit of area caused their land to be more heavily improved and therefore more valuable per acre, their wealth per taxpayer was not as low as the low number of their slaves might lead one to believe.

A more important set of relationships for political analysis concerns those variables correlated with Democratic votes for governor. One variable that is closely associated with the percentage for Spaight is a purely political indicator, the vote to ratify the amended state constitution of 1835 ($r = .5777$). A second close correlation with votes for Spaight is the percentage of free polls within each district ($r = .5862$). The districts of Buckhorn, Neill's Creek, and Willis Creek scored very high on this variable. These districts were all far from Fayetteville, with a mostly non-Scottish population of small farmers. As table 20 clearly shows, these precincts all voted heavily Democratic. Precincts such as Fayetteville and Averasborough, with higher concentrations of slaves, were less sympathetic to that party. The negative correlation between percent for Spaight and total assessed wealth per taxpayer shows the same general relationship but more weakly. It is easy to imagine that these less wealthy districts with few slaves would be highly receptive to Democratic orators' ringing denunciations of aristocracy and the evil influence of urban culture.

The correlation of votes for Spaight and the Scottish percentage of a district ($r = -.3394$) is outside the usual limits of significance, but is nevertheless suggestive. Table 20 showed that sandhills voters tended to support the Democracy less strongly than those of other sections. Because the Scots were concentrated in the sandhills, this negative coefficient is not surprising. It is not clear, of course, that Scots themselves were adding the slight extra margin of Whig votes in these districts. But given the practically homogeneous Scottish population in several of these districts, it may be that a few Scots were returning to their earlier anti-Jackson stance. After the election the *North Carolina Journal* boasted of the Democrats' victory in spite of the fact that "religious prejudices were appealed to" by the Whigs.[32] This teasing reference to denominational conflict may reflect a Whig attempt to enlist conservative Presbyterian rectitude against the various forms of corruption rep-

32. *Ibid.*, November 17, 1836.

resented by Van Buren and Johnson. Study of the membership of the two committees of vigilance for 1836 may tell more about the possible continued relationship between ethnicity and voting.

The bottom of table 21 shows the multiple coefficients of correlation (multiple R) between the percent voting for Spaight and the socioeconomic variables of the table, listed in descending order of their importance to the overall relationship.[33] By itself, the percentage of free polls accounts for the largest single portion of the variance in the vote for Spaight. In other words, 34.4 percent of the change in percent Democratic from precinct to precinct can be predicted by knowing the concentration of slaves in that district. If one knew the percentage of Scottish names in the district as well, he would increase his ability to predict the percent Democratic to 41.5 percent. Finally, by taking the assessed wealth per taxpayer into account as well, one would increase the explained variance by a trivial amount (to 43.7 percent) while doubling the uncertainty of the overall relationship.

The interpretation of these results cannot be very precise. It is quite safe to say, however, that the simple affluence of a district, as measured by its assessed wealth per taxpayer, had little to do with its politics. Slaveholding, on the other hand, was very important in this regard. The concentration of slaves in a district does not seem to reflect the intensity of racial feeling among the inhabitants but the degree to which the citizens were involved in the urban economy. Even if he lived in the country, the large slaveholder, as a relatively sophisticated agricultural capitalist, was interested in markets, credit facilities, transportation opportunities, legal services, and the other commercial adjuncts of the town. He also probably read the newspaper more often, took more trips to town, and felt more at home when he got there, than the rural nonslaveholder. Even his nonslaveholding close neighbor may have acquired some of the urban sophistication of the large slaveholder by regular association with him. Many of the voters in these districts, therefore, could be expected to be less hostile to urban culture and more likely to vote Whig than the voters in remote, small-farm districts. Knowledge of a district's slaveholding pattern consequently goes a long way toward explaining its political orientation and its voting behavior.[34]

33. None of these combinations reaches a conventional level of significance. The number of precincts being studied is too small for us to be very confident that the observed correlations are not the result of some accidental variation in the election returns and tax lists. These are the best and most complete data on this event that we are ever likely to get, however. Sampling error, in other words, is not involved here. Putting aside questions of absolute significance, we may simply note that all three values of r are at least reasonably likely to be different from zero but that the likelihood declines as more variables (and hence more uncertainty) are added to the multiple correlation.

34. *Cf.* Alexander, *et al.*, "The Basis of Alabama's Ante-Bellum Two-Party System."

The meaning of the ethnic contribution to the overall pattern of voting is more difficult to explain. The findings suggest a residual cultural conflict between Scots and non-Scots but do not reveal its specific content. Without better knowledge of the meaning of ethnicity in the county in this period, the connection between the Scots' religion and the "appeals to religious prejudice" already mentioned can only be a surmise.

Finally we should note that a very large proportion—more than half—of the total variance in Democratic voting can never be explained by the information now available. Our measurements are too crude and the men who voted too individualistic for any reductionist model to be very successful. No variable can pigeonhole the Cumberland voter of the Age of Jackson. For the pivotal election of 1836, however, it does seem that the economic geography of a district, slightly modified by the ethnic composition of its electorate, does more than any other combination of measurements to explain the distribution of the county's vote. The same factors seem to have operated on individuals, as shown by the characteristics of the members of the two parties' committees of vigilance and correspondence.[35]

*　　　*　　　*

Cumberland County's grass-roots elite in 1836 was in several ways very different from the comparable group of leaders in 1828. In the earlier year, the elite consisted of eighty persons who came together for a single announced purpose: to organize and conduct a presidential election campaign. As purely *ad hoc* committees, neither faction of this elite could be called a true political party.[36] In 1836, however, the organizational framework of the elite had changed a great deal. The combined membership of the two committees was 274, an increase in size of 343 percent. The total voting turnout in November was 1,085, so in 1836 fully one quarter of the Cumberland County presidential electorate belonged to the political elite. To the extent that democratiza-

35. Readers should be warned that the following section of this chapter depends exclusively on quantitative analysis of the property holdings of Whig and Democratic leaders. This section will begin and end with a row of asterisks; those who prefer to avoid a detailed technical discussion may safely bypass these pages and rely on the summary of findings which follows them. A brief explanation of statistical methodology, especially of the concept of statistical significance as it is used herein, appears in Appendix II.

36. I have been guided by the definition of a political party offered by William N. Chambers in his essay "Party Development and the American Mainstream," in Chambers and Burnham (eds.), *The American Party Systems*, 5. "Stated broadly, a political party in the modern sense may be thought of as a relatively durable social formation which seeks offices or power in government, exhibits a structure or organization which links leaders at the center of government to a significant popular following in the political arena and its local enclaves, and generates in-group perspectives or at least symbols of identification and loyalty."

tion implies greater participation, the party system brought a considerable amount of democracy to county politics.

As true political parties, the two leadership groups in 1836 exercised many more functions than the organization of one campaign for the presidency. They ran party tickets for local and state offices, and they maintained their existence after an election was over. Each activity generated its own minutes to be published in the party newspaper, each with its own list of officers and major participants. Any man in the period from 1834 to 1836 who could thus be identified as a party activist was included in his party's elite group and ranked as an "active" member, regardless of whether he actually belonged to the committee of vigilance. In addition, any local candidate who carried a partisan endorsement or affiliation was counted as a member of that party. The ranking system of a simple dichotomy between "active" and "passive" members as used for 1828 was expanded by adding a third category for "candidates." This addition was made on the assumption that placing these men in office was a fundamental purpose for both parties and that candidates therefore outranked the rest of the party structure.

As in the case of 1828, some men could not be identified in the tax lists. The problem was compounded by the fact that the 1836 tax list is not extant and comparisons were necessarily based on information in the 1837 list. In the intervening year, relative economic standings probably did not change much, but a number of men had either died or moved away. Some missing subjects owned no taxable property at all and were thus never entered on the tax lists, but it has not been possible to identify these men accurately. The sample of party members who could actually be studied from all sources was therefore reduced to a group of 155 Democrats and 77 Whigs, or 232 men in all. Since the core of the Democratic group was a vigilance committee of 200 members, it is obvious that the greatest attrition took place in that party.

Like their counterparts of 1828, the men of Cumberland's vigilance committees in 1836 may be studied from two different perspectives. Taken as a whole group they can tell us something of the openness of the local political system. Taken separately by parties they can tell us something about the sort of person who was attracted into each party and what economic divisions, if any, paralleled the political cleavage of the county.

In table 22 social and economic characteristics of the combined membership of the two committees in 1836 appear beside equivalent figures for the whole county. When compared with table 5, table 22 shows some important continuities and changes between the positions of the elites in the two different years. In 1836, as in 1828, there was little difference between the leaders and the populace over political preference or ethnicity, although the Van Buren committee does seem to have been slightly larger in its membership

Table 22. Committee Members and the Electorate, 1836

	Electorate	Committee members
Support for Van Buren	61.5% $N = 1085$	73.0% $N = 274$
Percent Scottish taxpayers	33.6% $N = 1714$	36.6% $N = 232$
Percent Fayetteville residents	21.6% $N = 9050$	30.2% $N = 232$
Acres of land	382 $N = 1927$	1189 $N = 232$
Assessed value of land	$ 380 $N = 1927$	$1163 $N = 232$
Assessed value of town lots[a]	$1097 $N = 387$	$1788 $N = 70$
Number of slave polls	1.3 $N = 1927$	3.7 $N = 232$
Total assessed property	$ 500 $N = 1927$	$1704 $N = 232$

SOURCES: Compiled Election Returns, "Presidential," 1836, in Miscellaneous Collections, North Carolina State Archives; Fayetteville *North Carolina Journal*, March 17, 1836; Fayetteville *Observer*, February 25, 1836; Cumberland County Lists of Taxables, 1837, 1838, in Cumberland County Records, North Carolina State Archives; *Fifth Census or, Enumeration of the Inhabitants of the United States: 1830* (Washington, 1832); *Compendium of the Sixth Census.*
[a] Fayetteville residents only.

than its strength in the county would indicate (line 1). In this area and in others, the Democrats were more successful than the Whigs in generating popular participation. Line 3 of table 22 shows a very interesting difference between the elites of the two years. In 1828 there were almost twice as many Fayetteville residents in the vigilance committees as there were within the county as a whole. By 1836, the proportion of town dwellers in the elite had fallen dramatically. Table 23 is a cross-tabulation of town and country residents in the elite by the two dates. The value of chi-square for this table shows that eight years had brought about a very significant increase in the political participation of rural inhabitants.

The democratization represented by the larger committee membership and by the greater proportion of countrymen within the elite did not eliminate the radical difference in wealth between voters and elite members. The last five lines of table 22 show that the ownership of real property and slaves was much higher among leaders than among other citizens. The party system had

Table 23. Committee Members' Residence, 1828 and 1836

	Country residents	Town residents	Total
1828 elite	40	35	75
	53.3%	46.7%	
1836 elite	162	70	232
	69.8%	30.2%	
Total	202	105	307
	65.8%	34.2%	

Raw chi-square $= 6.7403$; p is less than .01 (direction predicted, 1 df)

clearly not equalized the relative standings of political leaders and political followers, and wealth was still an important entry requirement for joining an active political group.

It is possible, however, that the introduction of political parties had at least brought a lowering of the economic barriers even if it had not totally eliminated them. Inspection of tables 5 and 22 suggests that the elite of 1836 was less wealthy than the elite of 1828. Comparing the wealth of the two groups by means of the "t statistic" proves that this suggestion is correct. Table 24 shows the results of these tests.

In absolute terms table 24 shows that the 1836 elite was less affluent and therefore less exclusive on every variable measured than its counterpart of 1828. However, the reliability of these figures is mixed. For the most part the variables which were measured simply by counting articles (number of slaves, town lots, acres of land) show a significant difference between the two groups. However, the variables which are based on a monetary valuation for the most part show a less significant difference. The outcome of the tests on these variables probably has much to do with a change in the tax laws which went into effect in 1837. Before that date, each landowner essentially served as his own assessor, simply stating the value of his property, under oath, at each year's tax-gathering.[37] Not surprisingly, this system produced an ever-shrinking aggregate property valuation, and a dwindling supply of revenue to the state. In the case of Cumberland, the county's payments of the state land tax shrank steadily year by year, from \$410.41 in 1828 to \$356.81 in 1836. The system came under official attack in the 1830s, and in 1837, a new pro-

37. Henry Potter, J. L. Taylor, and Bartlett Yancey (comps.), *Laws of the State of North Carolina* (2 vols.; Raleigh, 1821), I, 454.

cedure which was based on independent assessment came into use.[38] The effect was a dramatic increase in assessed land values. Table 24 reflects this by the change in land values per acre (line 3) between the 1828 and 1836 groups. (*N.B.*, the latter group was measured by its position in the 1837 tax list.) There is every reason to believe, therefore, that if the 1836 group's property values had been assessed by the standards in operation in 1828, its observed levels of wealth would be much lower, perhaps by as much as 30 percent. Under these conditions, the differences of these variables between 1828 and 1836 would surely be significant at levels far below the level of .05. For this reason, it seems reasonable to conclude that the 1836 elite was probably much less wealthy than the 1828 elite, and that the arrival of the party system was accompanied by a considerable amount of relaxation of entry requirements into the leadership group.

It is also possible, as the Democrats' campaign rhetoric suggested, that the Democratic party was considerably more open than the Whigs. Tables 25 and 26 examine this possibility by testing the same difference of means as table 24, but separately for Jacksonians and anti-Jacksonians. Just as in 1828, the two tables indicate that the anti-Jacksonians of 1836 were wealthier than the Jacksonians. This relationship will be explored more fully below. At this point it is more important to note that starting from a lower position, the mean wealth of the Democrats in many categories fell further than Whigs in the eight-year period that separated the two elections. Using the .05 criterion, the Adams men/Whigs show a significant difference on only one variable, the number of slaves. On the value of town lots, the mean of the Whigs actually increased over time. Among the Jackson men/Democrats, however, there were significant differences in landownership, lot ownership, and slaves. If consistent measurements of assessed property values had been made, the Democrats would probably show much more significant differences on these variables than the Whigs. It is clear from these tables that the Democratic party relaxed its "entry requirements" even further than the Whigs in this period, although both sets of standards declined somewhat. In this respect at least, the party of Andrew Jackson was more than nominally democratic.

The introduction of true political parties not only affected the requirements for entry into the elite, but it also altered the expectations affecting rank

38. "A Statement of the Revenue of North Carolina," following "Treasurer's Report," bound in back of *Acts of the General Assembly of the State of North Carolina*, 1829 (Raleigh, 1830): "A Statement of the Revenue of North Carolina," following "Treasurer's Report," bound in back of *Laws of the State of North Carolina at the Session of 1838–39*; Fayetteville *North Carolina Journal*, November 26, 1834; Frederick Nash, James Iredell, and William H. Battle (comps.), *The Revised Statutes of North Carolina* (2 vols.; Raleigh, 1837), I, 519. Under the new assessment, the average value of Cumberland County land rose 30 percent over its 1828 level.

Table 24. Property of Committee Members, 1828 and 1836

	Mean of the 1828 committee members N = 75	Mean of the 1836 committee members N = 232	t	df	p
Acres of land	1750 s = 2694	1189 s = 2184	1.64	107.37	.052
Assessed value of land	$1584 s = 2440	$1163 s = 1901	1.37	105.14	.088
Value of land per acre	$1.07 s = 1.50	$1.52 s = 3.46	−1.56	279.75	.060
Number of town lots	2.2 s = 4.3	1.0 s = 2.6	2.31	91.48	.012
Assessed value of lots	$ 771 s = 1792	$ 548 s = 1650	.99	305	.161*[a]
Number of slaves	6.6 s = 8.1	3.7 s = 5.3	2.94	95.45	.002
Total assessed property value	$2355 s = 3103	$1704 s = 2562	1.64	109.10	.052

[a] An asterisk after any value of p will indicate, in this table and those in the rest of this chapter, that the given value of t and its significance level are based on a pooled estimate of the variance.

Table 25. Property of Anti-Jacksonians, 1828 and 1836

	Mean of the 1828 elite (Adams men) N = 24	Mean of the 1836 elite (Whigs) N = 76	t	df	p
Acres of land	1746 s = 3232	1190 s = 2559	.87	98	.193*
Assessed value of land	$2085 s = 3582	$1332 s = 2335	.97	29.42	.171
Number of town lots	2.2 s = 3.2	1.5 s = 2.5	.98	99	.165*
Assessed value of lots	$ 864 s = 1196	$1008 s = 2074	− .39	68.23	.328
Number of slaves	8.7 s = 8.4	4.9 s = 5.4	2.12	29.18	.022
Total assessed property value	$2959 s = 3393	$2340 s = 2867	.88	98	.190*

Table 26. Property of Jacksonians, 1828 and 1836

	Mean of the 1828 elite (Jackson men) N = 51	Mean of the 1836 elite (Democrats) N = 155	t	df	p
Acres of land	1751 s = 2436	1188 s = 1983	1.66	204	.050*
Assessed value of land	$1349 s = 1652	$1079 s = 1644	1.01	201	.156,*
Number of town lots	2.2 s = 4.8	.7 s = 2.5	2.16	59.54	.018
Assessed value of lots	$ 723 s = 2022	$ 320 s = 1342	1.33	65.09	.094
Number of slaves	5.6 s = 7.9	3.1 s = 5.2	2.16	64.99	.018
Total assessed property value	$2071 s = 2950	$1385 s = 2340	1.51	72.27	.068

Table 27. Party Rank by Age, 1836

	Over 45	Under 45	Total
Passive member	62 34.3%	119 65.7%	181
Active member	10 34.5%	19 65.5%	29
Candidate	5 22.7%	17 77.3%	22
Total	77 33.2%	155 66.8%	232

Raw chi-square $= 1.20038$; $p = .5487$ (2 df)

Table 28. Party Rank by Ethnicity, 1836

	Non-Scots	Scots	Total
Passive members	111 61.3%	70 38.7%	181
Active members	21 72.4%	8 27.6%	29
Candidates	15 68.2%	7 31.8%	22
Total	147 63.4%	85 36.6%	232

Raw chi-square $= 1.56691$; $p = .4568$

within the elite. According to table 27, age (as measured by payment of the poll tax) had no bearing on rank within the parties. Ethnicity had no bearing either, as table 28 shows. The latter was an important difference from the situation in 1828, when non-Scots sharply outnumbered the Scots. If the number of Scots in the middle rank lagged somewhat, then their community was compensated by the number of Scots endorsed as candidates for office. Party leaders were apparently learning the advantages of placing minority representatives in prominent positions of leadership.

One influence upon rank within the parties that did not change was the importance of town residence. Table 29 shows that the number of rural residents in the leadership structure had increased enormously by 1836. Almost all of these new recruits remained in the bottom rank of membership. To be an officer or a candidate, one still needed the convenience and connections that

Table 29. Party Rank by Residence, 1836

	Country residents	Town residents	Total
Passive members	144 79.6%	37 20.4%	181
Active members	10 34.5%	19 65.5%	29
Candidates	8 36.4%	14 63.6%	22
Total	162 69.8%	70 30.2%	232

Raw chi-square = 37.02281; p = .0000 (2 df)

Table 30. Party Rank by Residence, 1836
Controlling for Party

Democrats only[1]	Country residents	Town residents	Total
Passive members	113 85.6%	19 14.4%	132
Active members	3 25.0%	9 75.0%	12
Candidates	4 36.4%	7 63.6%	11
Total	120 77.4%	35 22.6%	155

Whigs only[2]	Country residents	Town residents	Total
Passive members	31 63.3%	18 36.7%	49
Active members	7 41.2%	10 58.8%	17
Candidates	4 36.4%	7 63.6%	11
Total	42 54.5%	35 45.5%	77

1. Raw chi-square = 34.52832; contingency coefficient =
   .42683; p = .0000 (2 df)
2. Raw chi-square = 4.19488; contingency coefficient = .22730;
   p = .1228 (2 df)

residence in Fayetteville could bring. Access to leadership positions was different in the two parties. By exhibiting the same information as table 29 but
controlling for party, table 30 shows that the Democratic leadership was much
more concentrated in Fayetteville than its Whiggish counterpart. Looking at
the two arrays in table 30 more closely, it is obvious the large increase in rural
participation came almost entirely to the Democratic party. Indeed, the two
parties had exactly the same absolute number of urban participants (thirty-
five), although the *proportions* of urban membership were quite different.
The new rural members of the Democratic party's committee stayed at the
bottom, making the party appear highly biased in favor of urban members.
The Whig party had a higher proportion of country members whom it placed
in leadership positions and supported for public office. Apparently, the sort of
rural inhabitant who became a Whig was a more presentable leader or candidate to his fellow Whigs than the average rural Democrat seemed to his own
peers. Table 17 shows that rural Adams men were much wealthier than rural
Jackson men. If the same patterns persisted in 1836, the special economic
position of the rural Whigs may have affected their availability for office. This
possibility will be explored in later tables.

    In 1828, the committees of vigilance included only those younger men and
country-dwellers who could match the same general pattern of property
ownership as the other member. If the party system had opened the elite group
somewhat, then the younger men and country-dwellers who joined the committees in 1836 would no longer be so exceptional. They would show the relatively lower financial status which we expect of such men. Table 31 shows a
test of this hypothesis for age and table 32 does the same for residence. The
younger men scored lower on all variables than their older fellow party members. Most of these differences are slight and insignificant, however. The difference between the two groups in total assessed property value approaches
but does not meet the .05 level of significance. Table 31 suggests that the
party system brought about some relaxation of the entry requirements in regard to age. The differences between the age groups which we observe, however, are not so great that we can have much confidence that the differences
were "real." We cannot be sure, in other words, that they resulted from a
genuine change of requirements and not from random variation in the committee's membership.

    In 1828 residence, like age, did not account for any significant difference in
the overall wealth of political leaders. Rural inhabitants naturally differed
from residents of Fayetteville in the kinds of property they owned, but the
total property values and the numbers of slaves in both groups were roughly
the same. In 1836 this was no longer the case. Urban and rural elite members
continued to differ in the sources of their wealth. But table 32 shows that the

Table 31. Property of Committee Members by Age, 1836

	Mean of those over 45 N = 77	Mean of those under 45 N = 154	t	df	p
Acres of land	1225 s = 2023	1170 s = 2266	.18	229	.429*
Assessed value of land	$1395 s = 2215	$1047 s = 1719	1.20	121.51	.116
Number of town lots	1.0 s = 2.4	.9 s = 2.7	.18	230	.429*
Assessed value of lots	$ 756 s = 2036	$ 445 s = 1415	1.20	113.62	.116
Number of slaves	3.8 s = 5.6	3.6 s = 5.2	.36	230	.359*
Total assessed property value	$2131 s = 3176	$1490 s = 2171	1.59	111.12	.058

Table 32. Property of Committee Members by Residence, 1836

	Mean of the country residents $N = 162$	Mean of the town residents $N = 70$	t	df	p
Acres of land	1522 $s = 2420$	406 $s = 1172$	4.72	225.36	.000
Assessed value of land	$1437 $s = 2085$	$ 490 $s = 1096$	4.46	211.95	.000
Number of town lots	.2 $s = .9$	2.8 $s = 3.9$	−5.42	72.05	.000
Assessed value of lots	$ 13 $s = 86$	$1788 $s = 2619$	−5.67	69.06	.000
Number of slave polls	4.0 $s = 5.4$	2.9 $s = 5.0$	1.36	230	.089*
Total assessed property value	$1450 $s = 2098$	$2327 $s = 3384$	−1.96	86.10	.027

Table 33. Property of Committee Members by Party Rank, 1836

	Mean of the Passive members N = 181	Mean of the leadership N = 51	t	df	p
Acres of land	1094 s = 1899	1530 s = 2998	− .98	60.26	.167
Assessed value of land	$1119 s = 1793	$1315 s = 2248	− .57	69.35	.284
Number of town lots	.6 s = 1.9	2.4 s = 3.9	−3.16	56.86	.002
Assessed value of lots	$ 271 s = 1203	$1534 s = 2468	−3.54	56.85	.001
Number of slave polls	3.3 s = 5.3	4.8 s = 5.3	−1.71	230	.045*
Total assessed property value	$1373 s = 2336	$2850 s = 2976	−3.27	68.72	.001

total property assessment of the rural members fell below that of the townsmen by almost nine hundred dollars. At the same time, the difference in slaveholding between town and country was proportionately greater than earlier. In other words, country-dwellers no longer had to match residents of Fayetteville in the total value of their estate. Residents of Fayetteville who did not own as many slaves as the rural farmers and planters had increased freedom to participate in the committees. Both changes reflect an increasing openness in the political system of 1836.

Rank within the committees of vigilance was at first closely related to residence but not to wealth. There was greater unity in the financial characteristics of rural and urban leaders in 1828 than later on, so that differences in residential patterns were not accompanied by differences in wealth between high-ranking elite members and lower-ranking ones. By 1836, the differences in financial characteristics between rural and urban elite members had broadened considerably while the urban concentration of higher-ranking members persisted. As a result, the high- and low-ranking members of the 1836 elites showed much greater financial differences than the same ranks showed in 1828.

These differences are shown in table 33. For the purposes of this test the three ranks of the 1836 elite were collapsed into a dichotomy, by combining the two upper ranks into one "leadership" category. According to table 33, landownership and land values did not greatly distinguish between leaders and followers in the 1836 group. Because they were chiefly townsmen, however, the leadership group owned much more, and much more valuable, urban property than the lower-ranking members. These differences contributed so much to the total property holdings of the leaders that the two groups showed a highly significant difference in total wealth. Moreover, the leadership group also owned a significantly higher number of slaves than the general membership. In other words, rank was closely related to wealth in 1836, much more so than in 1828.

This relationship seems paradoxical in view of the fact that the system of the later year seemed much more open in other respects than it had in 1828. The explanation seems to be twofold. First, the new openness of the political elite applied primarily to its lower levels. Secondly, most of the new and less affluent members also came from the country, where factors of distance and convenience sharply limited their ability to play leadership roles. Because wealth was linked to urban residence, and urban residence was linked to high rank, the higher-ranking members were much wealthier than their less active colleagues.

The exclusive character of both sets of party leaders guaranteed that the committee membership did not replicate the composition of either party's

Table 34. Party by Ethnicity, 1836

	Non-Scots	Scots	Total
Democrats	98 63.2%	57 36.8%	155
Whigs	49 63.6%	28 36.4%	77
Total	147 63.4%	85 36.6%	232

Corrected chi-square = .00698; p = .9334 (1 df)

rank and file. Nevertheless, the characteristics of the elite probably did reflect something of the predilections of the voters themselves or, at the very least, described the relative amount of openness within each party. By this standard, Whigs were wealthier and more exclusive than Democrats. Wealth was not the only characteristic which may have differentiated between the parties. Ethnicity, age, residence, and occupation may also have distinguished them.

One startling lack of difference between the two parties is the overall irrelevance of ethnicity to party choice. In 1828, ethnicity came much closer than age or residence to influencing an individual's presidential preference. In 1836, however, a very slight Whiggish tendency appeared in the Scottish districts. In the cross-tabulation of party members by ethnicity shown in table 34, ethnicity was completely irrelevant to party choice just as it was also irrelevant to party rank. However, when residence is controlled by preparing two tables, one for townsmen and one for country-dwellers, a clearer relationship appears. These two cross-tabulations are given together in table 35. The table shows that in town, party was entirely independent of ethnicity. In fact the distribution of Scots and non-Scots within the two parties was exactly the same. In the county, however, most Whigs were Scots and most Democrats were non-Scots. This hint of an association between party and ethnicity in the rural areas is counter to several other facts about the county in 1836. Ethnicity was totally unrelated to party choice in Fayetteville. The Whigs generally had very low appeal in the country. The Scots tended to prefer Jackson in 1828. To find a Whiggish bent among country Scots in 1836, therefore, seems substantively though not statistically significant. Perhaps their preference for the Jacksonians had derived mostly from the personal appeal of the president, and they were returning to the company of Adams men they joined in 1824. They may have been temporarily alienated by the moral image of Van Buren and Johnson. In any event, ethnic differences seem to have had some residual influence on Cumberland political preferences, even as late as 1836. Age seems to have some limited effect on party choice also, since table

36 shows that younger men may have shown more interest in the Democratic party than in the Whigs.

The influence of age and ethnicity on party choice was minimal at best. Residence, however, was a very important influence on party choice, just as the distribution of votes and the themes of party rhetoric would lead us to

Table 35. Party by Ethnicity, 1836, Controlling for Residence

Country Residents Only[1]	Non-Scots	Scots	Total
Democrats	69 57.5%	51 42.5%	120
Whigs	20 47.6%	22 52.4%	42
Total	89 54.9%	73 45.1%	162

Town Residents Only[2]	Non-Scots	Scots	Total
Democrats	29 82.9%	6 17.1%	35
Whigs	29 82.9%	6 17.1%	35
Total	58 82.9%	12 17.1%	70

1. Corrected chi-square = .86029; phi = .08703; p = .3537 (1 df)
2. Corrected chi-square = .10057; phi = .0; p = .7511 (1 df)

Table 36. Party by Age, 1836

	Over 45	Under 45	Total
Democrats	46 29.7%	109 70.3%	155
Whigs	31 40.3%	46 59.7%	77
Total	77 33.2%	155 66.8%	232

Corrected chi-square = 2.14274; p = .1432 (1 df)

Table 37. Party by Residence, 1836

	Country residents	Town residents	Total
Democrats	120	35	155
	77.4%	22.6%	
Whigs	42	35	77
	54.5%	45.5%	
Total	162	70	232
	69.8%	30.2%	

Corrected chi-square = 11.71288; p = .0006

believe. Table 37 shows the strength of this association. Town dwellers were evenly divided between Whigs and Democrats, just as the electorate of Fayetteville was equally divided in municipal elections. In the country, however, the Democrats attracted almost three times as many adherents as the Whigs. Their ability to recruit this group established the Democrats as Cumberland's country party. For the remainder of the second party system, the rural voters of Cumberland never wavered in their support for the Democratic party. Once formed, their loyalty was impervious to any device Whig talent could conceive. Whigs could never win countywide elections for this reason.

The economic characteristics of the two leadership groups reflected the rural preference for the Democrats. When we compare the two groups without controlling for residence (table 38), the results show that there were no significant differences between the parties in the number of acres owned or the value of those acres. Whig landholdings exceeded the Democrats' by a mere two acres, and the difference in values, while interesting, was not conclusive. The same pattern had prevailed in 1828. In keeping with their urban orientation, however, the Whigs far exceeded the Democrats in town property holdings. The Whigs also commanded the labor of more slaves and owned more total property. In the case of the latter four variables, the Whigs were much wealthier than the Democrats.

When the two sets of party members are divided by residence, as in tables 39 and 40, the economic patterns become clearer. The country Whigs owned much more and much more valuable land than country Democrats. They were more likely to own town property. They owned almost twice as many slaves. Finally, they were much wealthier in their total property holdings. The country Whigs, in short, were much more likely to come from the county's plantation aristocracy than the rural Democrats. This was just what Jacksonian orators had claimed. Here is the explanation for the fact that Whig leaders were more likely to come from the country than Democratic leaders.

Table 38. Property of Committee Members by Party, 1836

	Mean of the Democrats N = 155		Mean of the Whigs N = 77		t	df	p
Acres of land	1188	s = 1983	1190	s = 2559	− .01	120.56	.498
Assessed value of land	$1079	s = 1644	$1332	s = 2335	− .84	113.33	.200
Number of town lots	.7	s = 2.5	2.5	s = 2.5	−2.43	230	.008*
Assessed value of lots	$ 320	s = 1342	$1008	s = 2074	−2.65	108.55	.005
Number of slave polls	3.1	s = 5.2	4.9	s = 5.4	−2.43	230	.008*
Total assessed property value	$1385	s = 2340	$2340	s = 2867	−2.51	126.29	.007

Table 39. Property of Rural Committee Members of Party, 1836

	Mean of the Democrats N = 120	Mean of the Whigs N = 42	t	df	p
Acres of land	1398 s = 2113	1876 s = 3141	− .92	54.54	.182
Assessed value of land	$1215 s = 1675	$2071 s = 2894	−1.82	50.93	.038
Number of town lots	.1 s = .5	.5 s = 1.5	−1.92	44.36	.031
Assessed value of lots	$ 11 s = 89	$ 18 s = 78	− .43	160	.333*
Number of slave polls	3.2 s = 4.8	6.2 s = 6.6	−2.72	56.45	.005
Total assessed property value	$1226 s = 1675	$2090 s = 2930	−1.81	50.69	.038

Table 40. Property of Fayetteville Committee Members by Party, 1836

	Mean of the Democrats N = 35	Mean of the Whigs N = 35	t	df	p
Acres of land	468 s = 1221	342 s = 1133	.45	67	.329*
Assessed value of land	$ 569 s = 1434	$ 417 s = 650	.55	42.64	.294
Number of town lots	2.8 s = 4.8	2.8 s = 3.0	0	57.28	.500
Assessed value of lots	$1379 s = 2576	$2197 s = 2635	−1.31	68	.087*
Number of slave polls	2.7 s = 6.5	3.2 s = 2.6	−.48	44.76	.317
Total assessed property value	$1984 s = 3928	$2649 s = 2801	−.79	55.77	.217

Table 41. Cumberland Merchants by Party and Business Size, 1835

	$400–2,000	$2,000–5,000	$5,000–10,000	$10,000–15,000	$15,000 and over	Total
Democrats	5	6	3	2	1	17
Whigs	12	6	6	4	3	31
Unknown	5	6	10	2	4	27
Total	22	18	19	8	8	75

NOTE: The dollar sums at the top of the table refer to the amount paid by each merchant in 1835 for his stock in trade. These categories were fixed by law, and no more precise information on the size of any given business is available.
SOURCE: Cumberland County Court Minutes, September Term, 1835, in Cumberland County Records, North Carolina State Archives.

In spite of democratization in both parties, elitist values continued to operate in the higher reaches of the political system. By and large, only the rich occupied high office in the government of the party. Among the Whigs, candidates who met these requirements of wealth and prestige could be found in both town and country. Among the Democrats, however, country members were less likely to be affluent, so the party's higher ranks were filled more exclusively from the town.

When only residents of Fayetteville are compared (table 40), all of the financial contrasts that appeared so clearly among country-dwellers fade. In Fayetteville, there does not seem to have been a major difference between the parties on any of the six variables. The Democrats may have owned a bit more land and the Whigs, more valuable town lots. The Whigs also had higher mean overall property values than the Democrats, but none of the differences was statistically significant.

This apparent similarity is misleading. Other evidence on the social and economic position of the party leaders suggests that there were in fact marked differences between Whigs and Democrats, even in Fayetteville. The two sets of leaders may have owned equal amounts of wealth, but they earned it in different ways and occupied very different positions in the overall life of the community. Table 41, for example, is based on the list of persons who paid merchant's license fees in 1835. The amount of each merchant's fee or tax was graduated by the size of his investment in goods for sale.[39] The table does not show that small merchants tended to be Democrats and large merchants tended to be Whigs. On the contrary, the ratio of Whigs to Democrats was fairly even in every category. The table does show that Whigs greatly out-

39. "List of Stores," Cumberland County Court Minutes, September Term, 1835, in Cumberland County Records.

Table 42. Corporate Positions by Party

	Whigs	Democrats	Unidentified	Total
Directors	43	11	26	80
	53.8%	13.8%	32.5%	
Officers	15	3	11	29
	51.7%	10.3%	37.9%	
Total	58	14	37	109
	53.2%	12.8%	33.9%	

Raw chi-square $= 2.15$; $.5$ is greater than p is greater than $.3$ (2 df)
SOURCES: Fayetteville *Observer*, October 24, 1824, June 9, 1825, October 4, 1826, June 6, 1827, October 23, 1828, February 18, 1834, February 25, 1834, November 10, 1836, March 16, 1837, January 10, 1838; Fayetteville *North Carolina Journal*, June 6, 1827, October 18, 1827, June 4, 1828, October 27, 1830, May 30, 1832, June 6, 1832, June 3, 1835, September 30, 1835, November 4, 1835.

numbered the Democrats within the merchant class as a whole. Among the merchants with a known party preference in 1835, thirty-one out of forty-eight or 64.6 percent, were Whigs. In the next two elections, however, the Whig percentages of the county's vote were only 38.4 percent. This proportion remained roughly constant through 1860. The Whig party was much more attractive to the merchant community than to the voters as a whole.

Whigs also had greater ties than Democrats to local business corporations. These companies usually published a list of their directors and major officers every year in the *Observer* or the *Journal*. The names of the incumbents in 80 directorships and 29 offices were gathered from the lists which appeared between 1824 and 1838.[40] These 109 positions were shared by 33 persons. Of these, 7 were Democrats, 17 were Whigs, and 9 had no known affiliation. Table 42 shows that Whigs held the majority of all posts, both directorships and offices. Democrats who did join the corporate structure were not discriminated against, so the value of chi-square for the table is not significant. The absence of discrimination was surely less important to the voters than the overall domination of corporations by the Whigs.

A similar pattern appeared in several petitions and lists of supporters for the Cape Fear, Yadkin, & Pedee Rail Road. The names of supporters were found in two major sources: in the legislative act of incorporation, passed in 1834, and in the list of members of a committee to raise capital for con-

40. The corporations surveyed were the Cape Fear Navigation Company, the Rail Road Company, the Fayetteville branch of the Bank of the United States, the Cape Fear, Yadkin & Pedee Rail Road Company, the Fayetteville branch of the State Bank of North Carolina, and the Clarendon Bridge Company. Fayetteville *North Carolina Journal*, 1826–38, *passim*; Fayetteville *Observer*, 1824–38, *passim*.

Table 43. Timing of Railroad Support by Party

	Whigs	Democrats	Total
Early Supporters	24	10	34
	70.6%	29.4%	
Late Supporters	9	14	23
	·39.1%	60.8%	
Total	33	24	57
	57.9%	42.1%	

Raw chi-square = 5.17084; .05 is greater than p is greater than .03

SOURCES: *North Carolina Acts of Assembly*, 1833–34, pp. 82–89; Fayetteville *North Carolina Journal*, February 9, 1837.

struction, published in 1837. Altogether, 86 names were found. Party preference was determined for 57 of these. Of these 57, 33, or 57.9 percent, were Whigs.[41] Not only were Whigs more numerous than Democrats among railroad supporters, but they also declared their support earlier. Table 43 shows that Whigs outnumbered Democrats as the early supporters of the railroad by more than two to one. The value of chi-square for this table shows that party definitely had a significant relationship with the timing of the activists' interest in railroads.

The relationship between occupation and party choice was more elusive at the opposite end of the social scale. Democrats claimed that their party was more congenial to mechanics and laboring men, but in fact, manual workers were not conspicuous in the leadership of either party. The *North Carolinian* condescended to mechanics, even while praising the formation of the Fayetteville Mechanic Benevolent Association in 1839. "This class of citizens," the editor admitted, "when they respect themselves enough to become intelligent and moral, exert a controlling influence in the nation, which is irresistable." This influence was only latent in Fayetteville, the editor implied, but "the mechanic classes in the Northern cities are beginning to find this out, as they have long since in Old England, and France, and woe to the party whom they think proper to oppose in politics. We do not design these remarks as hints to our Democratic friends of the class of citizens we speak of, (though by the way it would be well for them to think of the thing)."[42] Apparently, the Democratic party had no settled policy of outreach to mechanics in 1839, nor were

41. Most of the twenty-five unidentified men appear to have lived in other counties, since their names are not on Cumberland's tax lists. Among the Democratic supporters of the railroad, Archibald McDiarmid had a prominent role. Fayetteville *Observer*, February 2, 1837; Fayetteville *North Carolina Journal*, February 9, 1837.
42. Fayetteville *North Carolinian*, April 20, 1839.

artisans a self-conscious and active group in their own right. It was nevertheless possible that one party was more popular among artisans than the other.

The officers and managers of the Mechanic Benevolent Society consisted
of three carriage and wagon makers, three saddlers, one hatter, one cabinetmaker, one confectioner, and three men of unknown trades. Of the twelve
leaders, five were Democrats, four were Whigs, and three had no known
preference. The even political division of the group may have reflected a disproportionate representation from the most substantial group of artisans. The
hatter and two of the carriage and wagon makers owned businesses which
later writers described as "factories," while one of the saddlers was a justice
of the peace.[43]

A clearer pattern of preferences emerged from a larger sample of artisans.
No systematic survey of occupations was compiled in this period, but the
county did keep careful apprenticeship records. Whenever a child was bound
out, the master filed an apprentice bond with the county court which stated
his name and trade and the conditions of the indenture. Some of the masters
were not artisans; many promised to teach their charges the trades of farmer
or of laborer, while C. P. Mallett the textile magnate solemnly promised to
teach one ten-year-old orphan "the art and mystery of a manufacturer of cotton."[44] After purging the list of obvious nonartisans, a group of fifty-five
white masters remained who had accepted apprentices in Cumberland County
between 1824 and 1848. This group was also skewed towards the more established and successful shopowners, but it was probably more representative of
all artisans than the officers of the Benevolent Association. Twenty-five of
these men were active in politics. They included five tailors, three carriage
and wagon makers, three carpenters, two coopers, two wheelwrights, two
shoemakers, a saddler, a printer, a confectioner, a hatter, a plasterer, a blacksmith, a cabinetmaker, and a tinner. Seventeen of the politically active masters were Democrats and only eight were Whigs. Democrats had no more
than a bare majority in Fayetteville during most of this period, but they enjoyed more than a two-thirds majority among these politically active mechanics. Unfortunately, no concrete information on the party preferences of unskilled workers can be found, but Whig observers complained that laborers
on the public works near town were solidly Democratic.[45] If they were, preference for the Democrats among skilled and unskilled workers probably helps
to explain why the party of urban and commercial interests was rarely able to
capture a majority in the town of Fayetteville.

43. Oates, *The Story of Fayetteville*, 359–60, 846; Fayetteville *Observer*, December 29, 1834.
44. Apprentice Bonds, 1824–48, Cumberland County Records.
45. John C. Latta to Robert C. Caldwell, August 17, 1838, in Caldwell Papers; Fayetteville *Observer*, August 22, 1838.

The membership records of Cumberland County churches also reveal differences between Whigs and Democrats which do not appear from the tax lists. Recent historians have directed considerable attention to the role of cultural factors, especially religion, in shaping the values, standards, and world views which affect political choice. In the case of the second party system, students of northern and midwestern states have found that individuals and communities who were strongly influenced by evangelical Protestantism tended to favor the Whigs, while Catholics and nonevangelical Protestants favored the Democrats. Evangelicals and Whigs, these historians argue, both looked favorably on projects for social improvement by government action, while nonevangelicals and Democrats suspected the power of government to improve mankind, especially a government controlled by evangelicals, and preferred to leave such matters to Providence and private initiative. Cultural or religious conflict between these groups was closely related to ethnic diversity, so that descendants of New Englanders in the Midwest found themselves ranged as Protestants and Whigs against Irish and Germans who were both Democrats and Catholics.[46]

We have seen that ethnicity had a marked impact on Scottish political activity in Cumberland County from the time of the Revolution through 1824 and that evidence of an ethnic influence on voting persisted in 1836. A similar phenomenon appeared in the case of Roman Catholics, Cumberland county's other white ethnoreligious minority. Catholics were a miniscule group compared to the Scottish Presbyterians, but the records of St. Patrick's Church in Fayetteville contained the names of eleven white male Catholics who were active in politics from 1824 to 1848.[47] Except for Henry Erambert, a tailor who probably came from a German background, most of these men had Irish names; several were positively identified as Irish in the records. Like their fellow churchmen elsewhere in America, Cumberland's Roman Catholics were overwhelmingly Democratic, in this case by a margin of ten to one. The Catholics' party choice was not a simple reflection of the poor economic position of immigrants, for Irish-born John Kelly and Dillon Jordan, Sr., were both quite wealthy Democrats. Their party took no clearcut pro-Catholic position in any North Carolina political conflict in this period, but it seems that the party's national openness to religious and cultural pluralism won it the support of Cumberland's tiny Catholic community.

Outside this group, connections between religion and politics were indirect. In two denominations, political preferences seemed to follow the social

46. Formisano, *Birth of Mass Political Parties*, 137–94; Benson, *The Concept of Jacksonian Democracy*, 161–207.
47. Parish Register, 1831–50, St. Patrick's Roman Catholic Church.

prestige of the membership more closely than culture or doctrine. According to Guion G. Johnson, the Episcopal Church was the most prestigious denomination in antebellum North Carolina. Speaking for the state as a whole, Johnson called it "far more influential . . . than its small number of adherents would indicate." She described its members as "merchants, planters, professional men, [and] government officials."[48] St. John's Episcopal Church in Fayetteville contained a generous number of wealthy and influential men; during the 1830s, twenty-one out of its forty white male communicants were active in politics. No other church in the county could match this proportion. Of these twenty-one, fifteen were Whigs. The parish register between 1819 and 1836 also showed that twenty-five white fathers who were noncommunicants still felt close enough to the Episcopal Church to bring their children there for baptism. Of these twenty-five, ten were Whigs and six were Democrats.[49] St. John's was clearly a church for Whigs.

A similar pattern characterized Presbyterians. According to Johnson, "the Presbyterian church in North Carolina, like the Episcopal church, enjoyed a prestige far out of proportion to the number of its followers."[50] The Presbyterian Church was the largest in Fayetteville, and relative to St. John's, fewer of its members were politically active. In 1832, its membership list contained the names of 136 white males. Of these, 24 became known Whigs and 21 became known Democrats. A second list was drawn up in 1837 and entitled "A List of Families in the Pres: Congre: Fay: requiring to be visited." This list apparently included regular worshippers at the church as well as formal members. Of the 66 white male family heads on the list, 19 were Whig and 13 were Democrats.[51] This church was also congenial to Whigs, but not so much as St. John's.

Outside Fayetteville, Presbyterians were much less likely to be community leaders. Membership records survive for three rural Presbyterian churches. The members of these congregations were mostly Scottish, and therefore probably poor. Only a handful of men in each group were active in politics. Of these, almost all were Democrats. Cypress Church, for example, listed fifty-two white male members between 1833 and 1836. Eight of these were Democrats; one was a Whig. Mount Pisgah Presbyterian Church named thirty-three white men in its session minutes between 1835 and 1840. Eight were Democrats and two were Whigs. Only Sardis Presbyterian Church was an exception to this pattern. Because it was patronized by the wealthy Elliott

---

48. Johnson, *Ante-Bellum North Carolina*, 346.
49. Parish Register, 1828–36, St. John's Episcopal Church.
50. Johnson, *Ante-Bellum North Carolina*, 348.
51. Session Minutes, 1832–58, First Presbyterian Church.

family, its twenty-one white male members contained four Whigs and two Democrats.[52]

The political contrast between urban and rural Presbyterian churches may have reflected the antievangelical leanings of the sandhills congregations. Alternatively, Whiggery may simply have been more popular in fashionable churches like Sardis and the congregation in Fayetteville. Poverty, obscurity, Scottishness, and theological conservatism were so thoroughly intertwined in the sandhills churches that it cannot be known with any certainty whether any of these factors had a more decisive influence on party choice than the others.

If wealthy and prestigious churches were more congenial to Whigs than to Democrats, the reverse proposition was less clear. We cannot be sure that poorer congregations preferred the Democrats. Part of the problem stems from a paucity of information. Useful records survive for the Methodist and Baptist churches in Fayetteville, but not for the numerous rural churches of these denominations.

According to Johnson, in Piedmont and western North Carolina, Methodism "at first made its greatest appeal to the yeomanry; in the East, especially in Fayetteville and Wilmington, the Negroes were the first to accept the faith. . . . constant evangelism was one of the cardinal tenets of the Methodist faith and it was by constant evangelism that the faith spread widely." Johnson described Methodism as "the religion of the common people" because of its emphasis on camp meeting revivalism and a "direct appeal to the emotions."[53] In a somewhat different interpretation, Donald G. Mathews has explained that the experience of the revival created a sense of community and self-worth among men and women who received no recognition in the world of the wealthy and powerful. Both authors agreed that Methodism and the other evangelical denominations were especially popular among middle- and lower-class whites and blacks.[54] In 1839, only fourteen out of the fifty white male members of the Hay Street Methodist Church participated in politics. Of these, nine were Democrats and five were Whigs.[55] Doctrinal sympathy for progress and benevolence did not make these evangelicals very receptive to the political friends of secular improvement.

Like the Methodists, Baptists in Cumberland County were devoted to revivalism and to evangelical improvement activities like temperance societies,

52. Session Minutes, 1833–54, Cypress Presbyterian Church, Cumberland County, N.C.; Session Minutes, 1835, Mount Pisgah Presbyterian Church, Broadway, N.C.; Session Minutes, Sardis Presbyterian Church, ca. 1835, Linden, N.C., microfilm copies, all in North Carolina State Archives.
53. Johnson, *Ante-Bellum North Carolina*, 344, 345, 348.
54. Mathews, *Religion in the Old South*, 35–38.
55. Lamb, *Hay Street Methodist Episcopal Church*, 33–34.

missionary societies, tract societies, Sunday schools, and so forth. Unlike the Methodists, Baptists showed no clear party preference. The most significant political fact about Baptists was the extremely small number of their members who took an active role in a political party. Political affiliations could be found for only six out of the forty-five white males who joined the Fayetteville Baptist Church between 1837 and 1850. Of these, three were Whigs and three were Democrats.[56] The names of twenty-six leading Baptist laymen from rural churches appeared in the annual minutes of the Cape Fear Baptist Association between 1825 and 1845. Three of these men were Whigs and three were Democrats.[57] The rest took no active role in politics, in spite of their demonstrated ability as leaders in their churches. Surely Baptists voted like other citizens and probably they supported their chosen parties faithfully, but few Baptists ever ran for office. Usually they did not choose or were not asked to sit on political committees, draft resolutions, or serve as delegates to local conventions. Among those few who did engage in these activities, neither party was more attractive than the other.

The political preferences of Cumberland County Protestants do not suggest that doctrinal issues guided their political behavior. If isolated rural voters had a sense that Whig ambitions for secular improvement were somehow presumptuous or defiant of Providence, this quasireligious conviction was not associated with any particular denomination, nor can it be disentangled from the very rational wariness of speculative enterprise which was also characteristic of these folk. It is more plausible that church members, like other voters, made their political decisions on the basis of conditions in the secular world.

The experience of the Rev. William Morris supports the impression that organized religion was not decisive in shaping political development in the upper Cape Fear valley. Morris was a Baptist minister from Anson County who ran as the Democratic candidate for Congress in 1839. Anson County was predominately Whig and Baptist; the Fayetteville *Observer* charged that Reverend Morris had received the nomination in order to attract his coreligionists of the other party. The editor predicted that the device would not work; "the Van Buren party will vote for Mr. Morris, just as they would do if he had no religion; and the Whigs will vote against him, with double zeal, to discountenance this attempt to make religion subserve politics, and because they would not convert a good preacher into a very indifferent Member of Congress." [58] The election returns showed that the editor had been correct; Whig incumbent Edmund Deberry carried Anson County by his usual mar-

56. Church Minutes, 1837–50, First Baptist Church, Fayetteville, N.C.
57. Cape Fear Baptist Association, *Minutes*, 1825–45 (Fayetteville, N.C.).
58. Fayetteville *Observer*, May 15, 1839.

gin, while Cumberland stood by the Democratic party as always. In spite of an all-out effort by the Democrats, Deberry carried the district and kept his seat.[59]

The clearest relationship between politics and religion had more to do with social status than theology. In the church as well as in the world, Whigs were gathered in the congregations of the mighty. Methodists and Baptists enjoyed less access to political preferment; among Methodists, relative uninvolvement accompanied a tilt towards the Democrats. This less pretentious church was thus more hospitable to the political opponents of aristocracy.

*   *   *

The eight years from 1828 to 1836 saw an important shift in the patterns of political leadership in Cumberland County. The introduction of political parties had created pressure on the local notables to increase popular participation in campaign activities, and at the same time had made campaigning more interesting and more important to a wider segment of the county population. As a result, both the Whig and the Democratic committees of vigilance in 1836 experienced a large increase in membership over the sizes of the Jackson and Adams committees which had preceded them. At the same time the mean wealth of political activists dropped considerably below the levels of 1828. In effect, the entry requirements of the political elite had been lowered to embrace a larger number of persons. This relaxation was more pronounced in the Democratic party than the Whig. Furthermore, the requirements had been lowered by different amounts to suit the needs of different groups. As before, the Scots were not expected to match the wealth of non-Scots. For the first time, however, younger men were admitted who were less wealthy than the older men. Country-dwellers joined who were less wealthy than townsmen, and townsmen joined who owned fewer slaves than the country-dwellers. In other words, a slightly different set of requirements was applied to different groups in the population in order to compensate for specific weaknesses in each group. All of these changes bespoke a definite process of democratization at work that accompanied the institution of political parties in Cumberland County.

In spite of these changes, however, there remained certain limits on the openness of the political elite of Cumberland. We cannot tell whether these limits stemmed from the apathy of lower-income voters or from discrimination by wealthy insiders, but it is clear that the political elite was wealthier than the bulk of county taxpayers. Within the elite itself, important barriers

59. *Ibid.*, August 14, 1839.

separated ordinary members from candidates and party leaders. Age and ethnicity did not prevent one from achieving high rank within one's party, but residence in Fayetteville was a considerable advantage. Wealth was also an advantage to those aspiring to high rank, but it is difficult to separate the impact of residence from the impact of wealth alone on rank. Broader membership in the committees clearly did not make the leading positions within them more attainable for ordinary voters.

Jacksonians boasted that their party was more open than the Whigs', and their claims had a basis in fact. Among the rural voters who constituted the large majority of Cumberland's electorate, Whigs were much wealthier than Democrats and much more likely to own large numbers of slaves. In Fayetteville, where most of the high-ranking party leaders lived, differences between Whigs and Democrats faded. Although urban Democratic leaders enjoyed a degree of taxable wealth that matched the holdings of the Whigs, other evidence points to clear differences between the two groups. Whigs outstripped Democrats in investments and in support for banks, railroads, and corporations. Most merchants were Whigs and most identifiable artisans were Democrats, while Whigs preferred the wealthy and more prestigious churches in Fayetteville. On a personal, as well as an ideological basis, Whigs were the party of progress, commerce, and the Transportation Revolution. Cumberland Democrats had good reason to think of the Whig leadership as a group set apart from their fellow citizens. It is not difficult to see why the *North Carolina Journal* could plausibly describe the emerging party system as a contest of "Aristocracy against the farmers, the mechanics, and the laboring class." [60]

In 1834, political leaders in Fayetteville found that linking local and national issues under partisan banners could elicit intense political enthusiasm among the voters. In 1836, voters all over the county subscribed to the same

60. Richard P. McCormick has found that North Carolina voters who owned less than fifty acres of land, which was the minimum required to vote for a state senator, showed the same party preferences as those who owned more than fifty acres. The foregoing information on property ownership and occupation, however, seems to suggest that economic considerations were not irrelevant to party choice in Cumberland County, at least among the quarter of the electorate which joined a committee of vigilance in 1836. A repetition of McCormick's tests has not shown that patterns in Cumberland County were substantially different from the distribution of votes in his sample of counties. Perhaps the discrepancy between these findings and McCormick's may be explained by the nature of the suffrage classes which the freehold requirement created. Nonfreeholders included genuinely poor men, substantial urban artisans and shopkeepers, and young men who had not received their inheritances. Land was cheap and infertile enough so that possession of a bare fifty acres was no guarantee of commercial orientation. Freeholders included speculators, lumbermen, and farmers of all kinds, from the wealthiest to virtually the poorest. Both suffrage classes were internally diverse, and the freehold requirement may not have been subtle enough to distinguish between economic groups of real political significance. See Richard P. McCormick, "Suffrage Classes and Party Alignments: A Study in Voting Behavior," *Mississippi Valley Historical Review*, XLVI (1959), 397–410.

party frameworks that the townsmen had endorsed earlier. Popular acceptance of party politics was the third stage of political party formation in Cumberland County. The stage was begun in 1836, but not completed. Election records indicate that voters did not find stable party homes until 1840. Several facts about the 1836 election indicate, however, why partisanship began to take hold at that time.

Hard work by political organizers cannot be discounted in explaining the formation of parties. Whether these leaders were moved by ideological conviction, or the hope of patronage, or a combination of the two, they strove increasingly to persuade their neighbors to join the party bandwagons. Numerous county meetings and district conventions stimulated party enthusiasm. Constant editorializing familiarized newspaper readers with partisan points of view. Events like the Whig barbecue offered food and good fellowship where subtle reasoning flagged in recruiting loyalties. Above all, the most active leaders went to great lengths to involve large numbers of voters in organized party activities. In the course of the 1836 campaign, earlier barriers to political participation sagged. Rural residents, less affluent men, and smaller slaveholders became more welcome on political committees. The Democratic party was especially successful in attracting the middle class of farmers, but both parties relaxed their earlier standards. Even outside the circle of committee membership, every voter who attended a rally, and every former nonvoter who came to the polls was another recruit to partisanship. The enlistment of these new participants owed much to the efforts of a handful of highly committed political devotees.

Their efforts would not have been effective, however, if the party platforms they sought to inculcate had not been credible to the voters. It had taken some awkward experimentation to construct these frameworks. By trial and error and by following the successes of others, Cumberland leaders found linkages between local and national events that rang true. It was logical that those who opposed the road to Wilkesborough should support the president who signed the Maysville Veto. In Fayetteville it was natural that those who believed in the value of commerce should support the Bank. These connections between events in Cumberland and events in Washington were not strained or wiredrawn. Party propaganda served mostly to reinforce a set of impressions that arose spontaneously. Political platforms, in other words, corresponded closely to popular perceptions.

A final reason for the success of party formation in 1836 was that the logic of the platforms comported with the circumstances of the voters' lives. Outwardly placid, Cumberland County society had nevertheless been touched by the Industrial Revolution. Social change had affected men's outlooks differently, according to their position in the county economy. Some leaders had discovered the value of commercial expansion and urban growth. Others who were situated differently saw reason to fear these changes. The ideological split between the Democratic and Whig parties arose out of this conflict. The economic and social divisions that affected the parties' members paralleled their intellectual disagreements. The leaders of both parties were wealthy, but their wealth tended to come from different sources. Men whose interests and occupations exposed them to the benefits of progress gravitated to the Whig party. Here were the railroad promoters, the successful merchants, the largest slaveholders and planters. On the other hand the more isolated and less sophisticated planters, or the town dwellers with greater ties to the country moved towards the Democrats. Both parties, moreover, maintained a core leadership in Fayetteville that differed very little in their economic characteristics. These individuals, men like James Seawell, Edward J. Hale, Thomas L. Hybart, and Dillon Jordan, Jr., were almost professional politicians. As such, they seemed to have as much in common with each other as they had with their constituents. In spite of similarities at the highest levels, however, the two parties drew the bulk of their leaders from different segments of county society. The social foundations of each party, moreover, would only grow stronger in the Panic of 1837.

VII. Exclusively a Party Conflict: The Panic of 1837 and the Election of 1840

Martin Van Buren had been president for only three weeks when portentous foreign news arrived in Cumberland County. In the *Observer* of March 25, 1837, Fayetteville readers learned that the booming cotton market in New York and Liverpool had suffered an abrupt collapse. Large business failures were reported in New York and New Orleans. The "flush times" of Jackson's second administration had given way to the Panic of 1837.

Falling prices quickly spread to Fayetteville. In the following weeks, the *Observer* reported that "turpentine, lumber, and timber, in which this part of the State is so largely interested, have fallen nearly fifty percent."[1] By mid-April, one Fayetteville merchant was writing to his backcountry correspondent in tones of great anxiety. "I suppose that the commercial world never was in so desperate condition as it is at present," wrote James C. Dobbin. "Everybody is failing. Our *particular* friend is entirely ruined."[2] In late May, Fayetteville's two banks bowed to a national movement and suspended specie payments. In an effort to keep the town's regional trade alive, a group of twenty-six merchants announced that they would continue to accept South Carolina bank notes at par. By mid-July, the policy had been largely abandoned. Banks all over the nation had suspended payment, and South Carolina notes were discounted 10 percent at New York. Fayetteville merchants had no choice but to follow the same standard.[3] The next year saw a modest recovery of prices. The banks resumed payments in August, 1838, but the resumption was only temporary. The renewed suspension of the Bank of the United States of Pennsylvania in October, 1839, forced all the banks south and west of Philadelphia to suspend also. New price declines accompanied this second phase

1. Fayetteville *Observer*, April 27, 1837.
2. James C. Dobbin to Solomon Van Hook, April 13, 1837, in Van Hook Correspondence.
3. Fayetteville *Observer*, May 24, 1837, July 19, 1837.

of the Panic, which was even more severe in Cumberland County than the first.[4]

Fayetteville's response to the Panic grew out of the town's experience with economic development, particularly in the critical areas of internal improvements, manufacturing, and banking. The citizens had supported constitutional reform in 1835 in hopes that a reapportioned legislature would look more kindly on their need for railroads. Fortuitously, the federal government deposited its surplus revenue with the states in the same year that the reformed legislature first met. Consequently, the state of North Carolina finally found the means and the willingness to support a system of railroad construction, and Fayetteville was not to be disappointed by the new regime.

At the end of the legislative session of 1836–1837, word arrived of a legislative compromise that applied the two-fifths principle to Fayetteville's railroad, now to be known as the Fayetteville & Western. If the town and its allies could raise $600,000, the state would supply $400,000 and the road could finally become a reality. The leaders of Fayetteville were so jubilant at the news that they fired a one-hundred-gun salute to celebrate. They completed the volley with four guns followed by six guns for the two-fifths principle, and one gun each for W. H. Haywood, the legislative sponsor of the plan, and Edward L. Winslow, the railroad's president and legislative lobbyist. Edward J. Hale reflected that the end of the session was "the first time . . . during our Editorial life, that we have had it in our power to express almost unalloyed satisfaction at the doings of the General Assembly." [5]

Over the next six months, Fayetteville slowly learned the painful lesson that state aid alone was not the magic answer to transportation problems. By June, the *Observer* was worried that Fayetteville had met its pledge of $150,000 but that the western counties had found only $60,000 for the project. Five months later, the newspaper repeated its complaint. Salisbury had done its duty, but if the other western districts did not follow suit, the dreams of the region must collapse. The *Observer*'s exhortations were of no effect. The Panic had begun and capital for investment had suddenly disappeared. The following year, Edward L. Winslow reported to the legislature that private investment of three-fifths of the cost could not be found and that the legislature must increase its support or doom the project.[6]

Obligingly, the Assembly agreed to assume three-fifths of the cost and the board of directors made a new attempt to recruit investors.[7] They dispatched the Rev. Simeon Colton, a Congregationalist minister from Connecticut and

4. See figure 5. For national effects of the Panic's second phase, see Peter Temin, *The Jacksonian Economy* (New York, 1969), 148–71.
5. Fayetteville *Observer*, January 26, 1837.
6. *Ibid.*, June 14, 1837, November 22, 1837, December 18, 1838.
7. *Ibid.*, January 16, 1839.

former principal of the Fayetteville Academy, on a fund-raising tour of the western counties. Colton could obtain only $46,000 in pledges, but he composed an extensive and perceptive report to account for his failure. Westerners would not subscribe to the railroad, he asserted, because of "the pecuniary embarrassment of the times, and a general belief that the money paid for the stock will prove an unprofitable investment." Colton concluded that the road would never be built unless the state supplied an even larger share of the capital.[8]

After this bleak assessment, Colton weighed some of the larger questions raised by the railroad's failure. He revealed that many westerners believed that the road would benefit Fayetteville exclusively and that Fayetteville alone should pay its costs. Colton scouted this opinion and explained that the initial impact of a western railroad would damage Fayetteville's interests, not further them. The road would carry imports and exports directly between the outside world and the backcountry, so farmers who had formerly driven their wagons to Fayetteville could begin to trade at country stores instead. Fayetteville's merchants might be limited to wholesale trade only. To make up their losses, Colton suggested that Fayetteville businessmen exploit the town's natural advantages for cotton manufacturing. "Making a proper use of these advantages, [Fayetteville] may attain to greater prosperity than she has ever done by trade." Anticipating the prophets of the New South, Colton suggested that Fayetteville could not escape stagnation without a basic reorientation of its role in production. If a shift away from reliance on staple exports were made, he predicted, "it is not unlikely that the town would also become the cotton mart for the State."[9]

Fayetteville boosters revived the idea of a railroad to the Yadkin from time to time, but the line was never built. The absence of capital, the indifference of outside investors, and petty jealousies among supporters in the town doomed the project. The private opinion of Elijah Fuller on internal improvements generally became an appropriate epitaph for the town's ambitions. Writing about the railroad and a proposed new line of steamboats, Elijah confided to his brother Jones in 1839, "very little stir is made about it. In fact I am of opinion that it will remain dormant. The Steam Boat Company has gone down as all other prospects of improvement in and about this place have done and must do and now sleeps the sleep of death."[10]

8. A. R. Newsome (ed.), "Simeon Colton's Railroad Report, 1840," *North Carolina Historical Review*, XI (1934), 206, 210, 211.
9. *Ibid.*, 214–15.
10. Elijah Fuller to Jones Fuller, May 12, 1839, in Elijah Fuller Papers. For backbiting among the railroad's supporters, see D. G. MacRae to Edward B. Dudley, October 4, 1839, and Doyle O'Hanlon to Edward B. Dudley, February 27, 1840, both in Governors' Papers.

Textile manufacturing as an alternative to continued reliance on trade attracted the attention of several men of property in Fayetteville. In spite of the Panic, eight tiny spinning mills were at work in Cumberland County in 1840. The millowners appear to have started on capital generated by mercantile businesses in Fayetteville, but at least some of them had sought public funds before the Panic had run its course. The Literary Fund, which was the endowment of the state system of common schools, and the Fund for Internal Improvement were two likely sources for state aid. While they were controlled by Whigs, the boards in charge of both funds were prepared to make loans "to incorporated companies for Roads, manufacturing, &c., in preference to any other purpose." [11] The state lending agencies were more useful to the mills than banks, which preferred to specialize in financing the sale of export staples, but dependence on political bodies exposed the mills to attacks from hostile Democrats.

During the administration of Governor John Motley Morehead, the Democratic Assembly sought to force the release of the names of borrowers from the Literary Fund and to prevent the future use of state funds for these purposes. The threatened action caused grave anxiety to at least one Cumberland county millowner. "At this particular crisis it would be of the greatest possible inconvenience to me," wrote C. P. Mallett to Governor Morehead. His operations were reeling from the renewed suspension of specie payments in 1839 and the resulting depression. If his loans from the Literary Fund were called in, Mallett informed the governor, it would "almost prostrate the enterprise which is just now being completed and likely to be creditable to the State, useful to the community and profitable to the Stockholders." Mallett continued his plea for help with a general denunciation of political interference. "At many periods of the last year I could scarcely say whether we were going ahead or not—having all the virulence of Loco foco party feelings arrayed against a Whig Corporation or Monopoly as they called it. In conclusion," Mallett pleaded to Morehead, "you must use your influence in my behalf upon my bond until I get 'out of the woods.' " [12]

In their private capacities, Governor Dudley, Governor Morehead, and their Whig colleagues on the Literary Board and the Internal Improvements Board were large planters and slaveholders as well as investors in banks, railroads, commerce, and mills. [13] While these Whigs ruled North Carolina, they

---

11. Edward B. Dudley to C. P. Mallett, March 6, 1837, in Governors' Letter Books, vol. 32., p. 52.
12. C. P. Mallett to John Motley Morehead, January 29, 1841, in Governors' Papers.
13. C. Alphonso Smith, "John Motley Morehead," in Ashe *et al.* (eds.), *Biographical History of North Carolina*, II, 250–58; Luther Nicholson Byrd, "The Life and Public Services of Edward Bishop Dudley, 1789–1855" (M.A. thesis, University of North Carolina, 1949), 5, 7–9, 94–106;

did nothing to discourage industrialization, but actively promoted it by loans from state funds. They also tried to protect Whig factory owners from Democratic harassment. Nevertheless, the experience of Mallett and his associates demonstrated that industrialization would be no easy answer to Fayetteville's persistent economic stagnation. The reliance of these antebellum capitalists on the state illustrated the financial and political difficulties which faced the entrepreneur who hoped to redirect a plantation-oriented economy. If he had no other interest in politics, Mallett's problems with the government guaranteed that he would maintain a lively interest in the vicissitudes of partisanship.

Conceivably, Mallett might have sought his capital from banks and thus have avoided the bother of political entanglements. The millowner believed, however, that "a Banking debt does not answer the purpose" of economic development.[14] His judgment was based on the weaknesses of North Carolina's banking system, a series of deficiencies which the Panic threw into bold relief.

After the Bank of the United States closed its Fayetteville office in 1835, the Bank of Cape Fear and the Bank of the State of North Carolina divided Fayetteville's business between them. Both institutions concentrated on what one board of directors called "the real business of the country."[15] In other words, the banks were conduits for funds from New York and Philadelphia to local wholesale buyers who spent the money to buy cotton, flour, lumber, tobacco, and other raw materials and who repaid it by shipments of these products to their northern creditors. It could be a very profitable business, but the stability of the system obviously rested upon steady or rising prices for raw materials, especially cotton. If the price fell between the time a merchant bought cotton from a farmer and the time he sold it again in New York or Liverpool, the merchant would be left with a debt to the local bank which he could not repay. The banks in turn would be pressed by their northern creditors and the general money supply would suffer a sharp contraction. This was what happened in the Panic of 1837. The local meaning of these international dealings appeared most clearly in the complicated dealings which tied together the fortunes of Warren and Edward L. Winslow, Jones and Elijah Fuller, and the Fayetteville branch of the Bank of Cape Fear.

The state of North Carolina owned slightly more than one-third of the paid-in shares of the Bank of Cape Fear, a fact which gave the governor a strong claim on intimate knowledge of the bank's operations. The Winslow family

---

David W. Roberts, "Edward Bishop Dudley" (Unpublished sketch in Charles L. Van Noppen Papers, Manuscripts Department, Duke University Library).

14. C. P. Mallett to Edward B. Dudley, January 7, 1840, in Governors' Papers.

15. J. D. Jones to Edward B. Dudley, June 10, 1837, in Governors' Papers.

of Fayetteville owned the largest bloc of the bank's stock in private hands. When the Panic began, Whig Governor Edward B. Dudley received bad news on the bank's operations in Fayetteville and reacted with barely controlled outrage. "I have examined the list of Bills of Exchange purchased at the Fayetteville branch of the Bank of Cape Fear with astonishment & regret," he wrote to the directors of the main bank at Wilmington. "The funds of the Bank appear to have been used with too much liberality for the accommodation of the Messrs. Winslow's without a proper regard to the safety of the Bank." Dudley charged the firm of E. L. & W. Winslow had received "2/3 of all the exchange business done at the Bank" and that their notes had not been secured by endorsements. The governor went on to excoriate the activities of these supposedly respectable businessmen: "The kind of business done by these Gentlemen if I understand it correctly (I think I cannot be deceaved) is that of Brokers dealers in exchange, buying & selling notes &c. They are Brokers & have been encouraged by these extrordinary accommodations in doing a 'wind business' to the injury of the regular business of the country & of the Bank." [16] Concluding, Dudley threatened to expose the management to the stockholders and the General Assembly if the debts were not reduced and better secured immediately. Subsequent investigation revealed that the Winslows owed the Bank of Cape Fear $220,000 which they could not pay. The most doubtful notes were those of Warren Winslow, who had shuttled between Fayetteville and Mobile, speculating on his own account in cotton and depreciated southwestern bank notes. His complete default would threaten the bank itself, so the parties agreed to a compromise. Edward L. Winslow, the more solvent partner, added his name to Warren's notes in exchange for extension of the loans. [17]

The compromise was a reprieve that taught no permanent lessons. Warren Winslow continued to get preferential treatment at the Bank of Cape Fear for his southwestern speculations, even though other Fayetteville merchants found credit almost unobtainable. One of Winslow's associates in Alabama saw the end coming three months before the second specie suspension in October, 1839. "H A [Hart Anderson] & Co. must fail this year," James Hart candidly informed Elijah Fuller, who was his Fayetteville correspondent. "And no doubt crush W. Winslow," Hart added, "as he is under heavy acceptances for them which I think they will not be able to meet." The Winslows survived until March, 1840, but Elijah Fuller expected the worst. "They will make a great crash here if they do fail," he confided to Hart. "Wilkings has

16. Edward B. Dudley to the President and Directors of the Bank of Cape Fear, May 18, 1837, in Governors' Letter Books, vol. 32, p. 85; "A List of Stockholders of the Bank of the Cape Fear, 1st October, 1838," in Governors' Papers, vol. 86, pp. 1923–25.
17. J. D. Jones to Edward B. Dudley, May 21, 1837, June 3, 1837, both in Governors' Papers.

stopped payment already and many others are badly frightened. The precious Banks are like a troubled Sea." [18]

Two weeks later, E. L. & W. Winslow stopped payment. The Bank of Cape Fear survived, but the Winslows' failure touched off a run on local businessmen who had had nothing to do with their activities. No public comment reached the newspapers, but Hay Street buzzed with gossip that Edward L. Winslow, railroad president and public benefactor, stood exposed as a common bankrupt. The two brothers ceased to speak to each other, and their lawyer launched on an alcoholic binge that lasted for days. The scandal was apparently intense. [19]

Elijah Fuller reacted to the Winslows' downfall with grim satisfaction. Fuller had engaged in the same kind of "wind business" that Warren Winslow had, and much of his correspondence in the 1830s dealt with his fast manipulations in soft southwestern currency. Fuller even nursed a private grudge against the local banks for not extending to him the same extraordinary credits that the Winslows had no trouble obtaining. Fuller's safety in the Panic probably owed more to the banks' earlier discrimination against him than to his own prudence, but when the moment of truth arrived, he held no sympathy for his overextended townsmen. "I do not know how a good many men in this place can get along," he wrote to Jones. "But you know that is no affair of mine.—I must look out for our Int[erest] first." In the succeeding months, Fuller was able to do that very handsomely, for his military pension agency had literally become a gold mine. "I do not care for a better market to invest a small capital than this," he boasted. "I sold a little exchange at 10 pr premium yesterday and could sell today at 12 but am holding up for 18 and expect to get it. You never saw people so lonesome as they are here at present." When interest rates reached 25 to 33 percent on six to nine months' paper, no locofoco caricature of moneylender's avarice could duplicate the emotions of this small-town Whig. [20]

The activities of men like Fuller and Winslow made perfect local ammunition for Democrats who blamed the Panic on the "wind business" of greedy

18. James Hart to Elijah Fuller, August 8, 1839, Elijah Fuller to James Hart, March 19, 1840, both in Elijah Fuller Papers.
19. Elijah Fuller to Jones Fuller, April 3, 1840, April 22, 1840, both in Elijah Fuller Papers; C. P. Mallett to John M. Morehead, May 27, 1840, in Governors' Papers. Jones Fuller had moved to Alabama for a fresh start in the early 1830s, where his family and friends hoped that the tutelage of James Hart would reform his weaknesses for personal profligacy and business imprudence. Contrary to Elijah's sternest warnings, Jones had dabbled in Warren Winslow's ventures, and he too was brought to the brink of ruin. In April, 1840, Jones's miscalculations came to light and (coincidentally) James Hart died. Elijah ordered his brother to return home and account for himself. The fascinating correspondence of Hart and the Fuller brothers thereby came to an end.
20. Elijah Fuller to Jones Fuller, June 28, 1838, James Hart to Elijah Fuller, April 6, 1839, October 17, 1839, April 3, 1840, all in Elijah Fuller Papers.

speculators. The experience of the Bank of Cape Fear illustrated the deficiencies of a credit system which was equally at the mercy of personal favoritism and a gyrating cotton market. It could be argued that speculative activities of dealers in exchange like Winslow and Fuller were necessary for interregional credit flows and that the Panic resulted from inevitable business fluctuations, not from fraud. Unfortunately, the impact of the Panic reached far beyond the circles of those who had dabbled in questionable practices.

The Panic's effect on the ordinary citizen depended on his involvement in the market economy. The Democratic newspaper correctly pointed out that "those who as it is said 'live within themselves,' making all that is needed for comfort and happiness, in their abodes of contentment and blessedness, feel this [depression] scarcely at all." If relatively self-sufficient farmers were not exactly living in "contentment and blessedness" after the Panic, they were not much worse off than they were before. On the other hand, as the newspaper also observed, "this loss falls heaviest on the merchants, and those, whose imprudent speculations and other frequent money dealings, require them to resort to Bank loans, and other liabilities to pay money."[21] In Cumberland County, these persons were concentrated in Fayetteville and tended to vote for the Whig party. The more self-sufficient lived in the sandhills and tended to prefer the Democrats. It is unlikely, however, that any class of voters was entirely untouched by the Panic of 1837.

Figure 5 shows that incomes in the Cape Fear valley as a whole received a severe jolt after 1837. The volume of cotton shipped down the Cape Fear River every year was multiplied by the prevailing regional price of cotton to arrive at the annual value of the region's cotton crop. The dark line in figure 5 represents these earnings for the years 1831 to 1840. Every inhabitant was not a cotton exporter, but cotton sales were still an important component of the area's annual income. The fine line in figure 5 is a crude consumer price index, based on the wholesale price of sugar and coffee. These articles were luxuries, but they were widely consumed by all classes. Since almost all consumer goods available in the Cape Fear country were imported, the behavior of this price index relative to the value of the cotton crop is a rough indication of changes in standards of living during the 1830s.[22]

21. Fayetteville *North Carolinian*, October 26, 1839.
22. In 1840, a Democratic merchant published a table in the *North Carolinian* which contained the average wholesale price during the month of May for the previous twenty-seven years for each of eight commodities, including cotton, coffee, and sugar. In the same year, the Cape Fear Navigation Company published a table showing the volume of traffic on the Cape Fear River from 1831 to 1840. The table showed the number of cotton bales which traveled downriver in every year except 1833. Assuming that all the cotton in the valley was transported on this river, and calculating the weight of every bale as four hundred pounds, the value of the region's cotton crop is simply the price per pound of cotton in the first table, times the number of bales in the second

These changes were substantial. Regional income was heavily influenced by boom-and-bust conditions in the world cotton market. The prices of coffee and sugar, however, were relatively stable during this period. If coffee and sugar were representative of other imports, then the income gains of the pre-Panic years were not vitiated by inflation of consumer prices. Real incomes rose dramatically.

After the Panic, the collapse of cotton prices was only slightly cushioned by adjustments in the price of consumer goods. To the extent that any citizen's income was affected by earnings from the sale of cotton, he inevitably suffered a corresponding decline in his standard of living. Nor was the initial sharp drop in prices followed by a steady recovery. Two years of stagnation succeeded the collapse, followed by another decline which increased the disparity between cotton earnings and consumer prices even more. By the time of the 1840 election, the average voter could not only look back on three years of hard times, but he had reason to believe that matters were getting worse.

Under nineteenth-century conditions, recurrent hard times were an inevitable feature of expanding capitalism. Conservative Cassandras had warned against the spirit of gain for exactly this reason, but during the season of rising prices, planters and merchants alike had happily accepted the blessings of prosperity. For many relative newcomers to the world of the market, the Panic of 1837 was now a shocking introduction to the unpleasant aspects of the business cycle. Other depressions had affected North Carolina before, particularly the Panic of 1819, but this slump was deeper, and nearly two decades of economic growth had widened the circle of those affected by market forces. Specie suspension and tight money were alien things, incomprehensible to many, the product of government meddling to some, outrages against common honesty to others. No one accepted depression as a normal if regrettable feature of the economy. Whatever their analysis, citizens assumed that the resources of republican government offered appropriate means to defend the community against this unnatural assault. Calls for political action were thus the common themes in all recorded responses to the Panic.

Whigs had experienced the 1830s as a period of heightened expectations

---

table, times four hundred. This method of studying regional income is more useful than studying price alone. In 1839, for example, cotton prices almost doubled over the 1838 levels. Cotton production was very low, however, because of poor yields. High prices were therefore simply a product of meager supplies, and not because of increased world demand. The value of the 1839 crop was therefore less than that of 1838, even though its price per pound was much higher.

Cotton was harvested in the fall and early winter. Very few farmers could hold their crops to trade at the higher May prices. Most of the cotton trading in May must have been done by speculators. Using May prices to calculate the value of the crop to the producers is somewhat misleading, but the available information allows for no convenient alternative. Fayetteville *North Carolinian*, May 16, 1840, June 13, 1840.

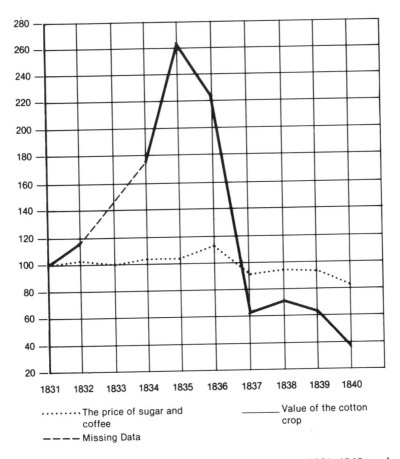

Figure 5. The value of the Cape Fear valley cotton crop, 1831–1840, and an index of the price of sugar and coffee. Index figures, 1831 levels equal 100.

Chart by Richard Volz

SOURCE: Fayetteville *North Carolinian*, May 16, 1840, June 13, 1840.

and intensified frustrations. The Panic appeared to them as a final blow to the hopes of Fayetteville and a demoralizing check to the potential growth of the nation. The Democrats left few private accounts of their reactions to the "flush times," but their political rhetoric expressed a fear that booming prosperity had been a moral snare. The presidency of Van Buren and the onset of the Panic appeared to each party as the confirmation of its suspicions about the economic policies of its opponents. The Whigs felt that the Panic showed the recklessness of the Democrats' currency experiments, while the Democrats felt vindicated in their efforts to diminish the power of the banks. Each party would need increased electoral support to implement its favored policies, so the Panic gave local leaders increased incentive to enlist the uncommitted. In addition, ordinary citizens whose lives were touched by the contraction or its attending difficulties became more sensitive to political explanations of private problems. These dual pressures on voters and leaders strengthened the party system. In 1839, Edward J. Hale declared approvingly that "in all our life . . . a watchful attention to the politics of the State never before exhibited to us, so exclusively a party conflict, so complete a marking of party lines as was apparent at the last [state] election." [23] The record-breaking turnout in the next presidential election reflected a similar phenomenon. The campaign of 1840 completed the process of party formation in Cumberland County.

According to Peter Temin, a recent historian of economic events in the 1830s, actions by Andrew Jackson and the Bank of the United States were not the principal causes of the specie suspensions of 1837 and 1839. Temin has explained that economic conditions responded to changes in the money supply and the balance of trade which had little or nothing to do with political decision-making. [24] Cumberland County leaders had access to an explanation of the Panic which was not unlike Temin's, but they did not accept it. After the second suspension, Hardy Holmes of the new Democratic paper, the *North Carolinian*, told his readers that apologists for the banks had identified two reasons for suspension. First, poor harvests had forced the British to buy grain on the Continent with specie. Second, a new policy by the Chinese government required British traders to pay for tea with specie and no longer with opium. The imbalance of trade between Britain and America drained specie eastward across the Atlantic to make up the resulting specie deficit in the Bank of England, and American banks were forced to suspend payments. [25]

The Democratic editor mentioned this explanation only to dismiss it. "Whether these causes be the real and true ones for the suspension or not," he shrugged, "it is quite certain that they are extremely remote." Banks were not subject to laws of nature, he reasoned; they were human inventions which "must be considered as entirely under our own control." He insisted on "a more *immediate* cause productive of the calamity" than events in China and Britain and proudly asked "whether the omnipotence of American legislation . . . has not in the majesty of its power some effectual remedy." He ridiculed the notion that an international balance of trade should dictate conditions in his own community and demanded that state legislatures "deal more rigor-

23. Fayetteville *Observer*, January 23, 1839.
24. Temin, *Jacksonian Economy*, 77, 78, 140.
25. Fayetteville *North Carolinian*, October 26, 1839.

ously with the Banks, and compel them to raise the credit of the currency, by prudent, but strongly coercive legislation." [26]

The editor voiced a refreshing confidence in the power of human agency over the mystifying "iron laws" of trade, but he was trapped by his overall commitment to the laissez-faire economy which surrounded him. Given that Holmes had no idea of disturbing the other features of the free market, his strictures against the balance of trade read something like the orders of King Canute. Holmes rejected an international and impersonal explanation of the Panic because it did not meet his political needs and did not fit in his ideological framework. Implicit in his discussion was the view that an unchanging world of yeoman farmers and other small producers could grow and flourish indefinitely, if only it were favored by the smiles of Providence and guided by the will of the people. The balance of the nineteenth century did not sustain the editor's optimism, but the age of steady deflation, trusts, combines, and Populism still lay in the future. For the present, Hardy Holmes clung to his Democratic faith in the power of men over money.

Private citizens also used their political convictions to guide their understandings of the Panic. James Evans, for example, left his impressions of the national and local economy in the draft of a cryptic and anonymous letter to his friend David Carver. Evans was an eccentric youth who liked to scribble snatches of empurpled rhetoric on the backs of old receipts and among the pages of his ledger. On this occasion, the young farmer outdid himself. "Fayetteville seems to be going down the hill as fast as the wheels of time can carry it," he prophesied in December of 1837.

> I find some folks are getting above themselves. Now, my dear Sir, if Martin Van Buren has become High Priest of Nature, Grand Master of the Supreme Mystics, & Emperor of the World, is that any reason why Petty Officers should be exalted [?] . . . Did the infatuated world only know all my calculations, or only a ten thousandth part of them!!! What Processions & Shoutings & Ringing of Bells & Dancing & Serenading with bands of music & firing of Canon should usher in the coming Year! The reign of terror is nearly over & when truth is triumphant Banks will become temples of Worship & then like a steam boat under a high pressure of Steam, the Earth will tremble with the Joy of its inhabitants. [27]

Evans' fantasies originated in an unusually turbulent imagination, but his composition only magnified the same fears and expectations which distracted the more prosaic minds around him. The status anxiety he felt undoubtedly arose from his own precarious toehold on the borders of the elite and from his resentment at Fayetteville's "exalted" contingent of new Democratic of-

26. *Ibid.*
27. [James Evans] to David Carver, December 23, 1837, in James Evans Papers.

ficeholders, but his worries also reflected Fayetteville's real position as a provincial backwater in a deepening recession. Evans' perception of Van Buren as an omnipotent enemy, his description of his present apprehensive state as a "reign of terror," his conflation of local and national experience, his association of relief with banks and steamboats, and finally, his millennial expectations for the election of 1840 only exaggerated thoughts which were common in Cumberland County. Whiggish gentlemen were indeed frightened by Jackson's and Van Buren's supposed usurpations, they fondly hoped that the populace would resume the proper reverential attitude to banks and the credit system, and they longed for technological solutions to their economic problems. James Evans' eccentricities were a faithful, though hypertrophied reflection of the emotional aftermath of the Panic. The apprehensions he shared with the soberer Whigs in Fayetteville made a lasting political impression on the leading men of the community.

Led by Edward J. Hale, orthodox Whigs were quick to blame the Panic on blundering Democrats. The Fayetteville *Observer* reacted to the first signs of collapse in New York and Liverpool by predicting the worst. "There is much reason to fear," the editor pointed out, "that the great calamity of widespread ruin and bankruptcy, which we have anticipated for a year or two past, is about to come upon our country." Two months later, when his predictions had been realized, Hale complained again of the "practical evils" of Democratic policies. "Let it never be forgotten," he reminded his readers, "that we owe them all to the late and present Administrations, whose tinkerings have destroyed the currency, broken down all confidence, and bankrupted the merchants, the Banks, and the Nation." [28]

In the succeeding months, the *Observer* elaborated its critique of Democratic currency policy by linking Van Buren's alleged monetary blunders to older themes in Whig doctrine. Not only did the newspaper complain that the president's Independent Treasury plan was deflationary and harmful, but Hale also connected it with Jackson's tendencies towards executive usurpation. "It would be more difficult to conceive of any mode," he wrote when the president submitted his proposal to a special session of Congress, "that more effectually surrenders the purse to the Executive; thereby uniting it with the sword, which is so justly calculated to excite alarm in the bosom of every patriot, for the safety of our Republican institutions." Hale also linked the Independent Treasury to the hated Democratic policy on the "spoils of office." "It will increase the patronage of the General Government to an almost unlimited extent," the editor warned his readers in September, 1837. A month later, he pointed out the contradictions of the Democrats' position under Jack-

28. Fayetteville *Observer*, March 23, 1837, May 24, 1837.

son, when they claimed that the government had no legal right to improve the currency, "though the same party had assumed to themselves without any authority of law the exercise of the fatal right of depreciating and destroying it. Such is the inconsistent course of a party," he concluded, "which has no other settled principle than the enjoyment of the loaves and fishes." [29]

In making his attacks upon the Van Buren administration, Hale did not propose a national bank as an alternative to the president's policies. Eventually he renounced the idea of a national bank, claiming that the advantages of such an institution were outweighed by the opportunity it gave for "demagogues . . . to rise by exciting popular clamor against the monster." [30] Instead of pinning his hopes on a single institution, Hale called for a return to the normal operation of an interrelated system of state banks. Normal operation of this "credit system" was prevented by administration actions and rhetorical attacks which paralyzed business confidence. The *Observer* called for an end to attacks on banks and for other symbolic steps which would lead to the return of confidence. The first and foremost of these steps, the *Observer* argued, was the election of Whigs at the state level.

> Now the administration has, by its specie-circular, its hard-money humbug, and other means, brought the Banks to their present condition, deprived them of the power to extend their usual accommodations, and obliged them to contract their circulation: whereby money has been made scarce and produce reduced to half its usual value. . . . When it was first attempted to cram that [hard money] system down the throats of the people, the country was in a high state. Now—but every man feels what is its condition now. . . . Will N. Carolina be behind her sisters in rebuking the spirit of interference which has brought distress upon her in common with the rest of the States? The glorious work was begun in August last, by the election of 8 out of 13 Representatives to Congress. It can be consumated in August *next*, by the choice of a like proportion of Whigs for the Legislature, and of our Whig Governor. [31]

Hale was not disappointed in 1838. The voters elected a Whig governor and a Whig legislature just as he had asked. Two years later, when the depression had still not ended, the editor used the same arguments to press for the election of William Henry Harrison. [32]

As editor of the party newspaper, Edward J. Hale was the foremost Whig spokesman on the Panic of 1837 and the lengthy depression which followed,

29. *Ibid.*, September 13, 1837, October 11, 1837.
30. *Ibid.*, July 9, 1839.
31. *Ibid.*, April 18, 1838.
32. *Ibid.*, February 19, 1840.

but Hale was not alone in his defense of the banking system. Most of Cumberland's Whigs would probably have agreed with James D. Pemberton, a man of some standing in neighboring Richmond County. Writing to his Whig representative in the state legislature of 1838, Pemberton insisted that "gold & silver alone cannot answer the purposes of currency in this widely extended and highly commercial country." He blamed the depression on the Democrats' refusal to provide a well-regulated paper currency to supplement the supply of specie. Speaking as a private citizen, moreover, and not as a political aspirant, Pemberton was free to call for the alternative he truly preferred. "The evils we have suffered for the two years past [cry] aloud for a remedy," he declared. "If no other and better mode can be devised than a Bank of the U.S. the people will have it or require it." He concluded by asking the Whigs in the legislature to instruct North Carolina's senators to oppose the Independent Treasury.[33]

Publicly, Cumberland Whigs showed some hesitation about endorsing particular policies purely and simply on account of their supposed economic utility. It was not until 1839, for example, that the local party spoke as a body on the issues raised by the Panic. In May of that year they criticized the Independent Treasury and defended the credit system. Their resolution took the high ground of constitutional principle, rather than pragmatism, as its basis: "That the Independent Treasury, being a divorce between the Government and the best interests of the People—being unsafe, insecure, and corrupting as a fiscal measure; placing the Revenue immediately under the control of the Executive instead of the legislative department of the Government, as wisely ordered by the Constitution, and being further an insidious blow aimed at the credit system, whose existence is the result and is co-extensive with free institutions— meets with our decided disapprobation."[34] The party based its opposition to other administration policies, including alleged executive interference with elections and with the actions of Congress, resistance by the executive to congressional investigations, and the practice of the spoils system, on similar constitutional grounds.

About a year later, the Whig party spoke in stronger terms. Meeting at the March, 1840, term of county court, the Whigs convened at the very moment when the Winslows' house of cards was tumbling and when so many of the party's most active supporters were facing financial disaster. Privately, the Whigs were confident that economic distress would lead the nation to the Whig camp. "Prices is an argument the simplest understand," wrote one merchant and lawyer. "As there is not the slightest probability of the condition of

---

33. James D. Pemberton to Duncan McLaurin, November 23, 1838, in McLaurin Papers.
34. Fayetteville *Observer*, May 18, 1839.

affairs being bettered—I look for the election of Harrison by acclamation." [35]
Publicly, the party placed heavier emphasis on the economic consequences of
Van Buren's policies, while continuing their legal and constitutional critiques
as before. "The present distressed situation of our country is truly alarming,"
they declared, "and has . . . been produced by the impracticable schemes of
the present administration, and its total disregard of the well known and well
defined principles of the law and constitution." The meeting supported this
resolution at length by citing the administration's hard-money policy and its
attempt to establish an Independent Treasury. More briefly, they charged the
Administration with an "avowed determination to *destroy credit . . . reduce
the wages of labor . . .* [and] *destroy paper currency.*" The resolutions concluded with a flourish by branding "the present administration as vicious,
corrupt, and impure" and promising to "spare no exertions . . . in overthrow-
ing an administration, *so regardless of right* and so reckless of principle." [36]
In joining their economic thrusts at the Democrats with their older charges of
unconstitutional abuses of power, the Whigs of 1840 set a pattern of rhetorical
continuity that persisted through most of the next decade.

Democratic response to the Panic of 1837 was relatively muted at first. Unlike merchants and speculators among the Whigs, Democratic farmers did not
record their reactions to the Panic in voluminous business correspondence.
For their part, urban Democratic leaders were silenced by long-standing difficulties of the party press. The *North Carolina Journal* had never been stable
financially. For most of 1837, the paper carried a "for sale" notice at the top
of its columns. The content of the paper deteriorated radically, as the editors
began to spend their time on other pursuits. Immediately after Van Buren's
inauguration, William F. Strange took a patronage job as clerk in the U.S.
Branch Mint at Charlotte, North Carolina, and Thomas L. Hybart returned to
his law practice. [37] Only rarely did any original material appear in the *Journal*,
which began to consist almost entirely of reprinted speeches and articles from
other sources. The silence of Hybart and Strange on the Panic, in other
words, was only a feature of their silence on every subject.

In June, 1838, Hybart and Strange were finally successful in selling the
North Carolina Journal. The new editor was one P. Gallagher, "a gentleman
of great experience and high qualifications in the management of an independent Press." The new editor withheld detailed discussion of the Panic, prefer-
ring to boost circulation by lower prices and sensational personal charges
against prominent local Whigs. [38] The new management of the *Journal* was

35. John W. Huske to Solomon Van Hook, February 15, 1840, in Van Hook Correspondence.
36. Fayetteville *Observer*, March 25, 1840.
37. *Ibid.*, March 23, 1837; Fayetteville *North Carolina Journal*, May 30, 1837.
38. Fayetteville *North Carolina Journal*, June 6, 1839.

not successful. Within six months, Gallagher abandoned the paper and the *North Carolina Journal* ceased publication.

Fayetteville was without a Democratic press from November 28, 1838, until March 2, 1839. The *Journal* then resumed existence under a new name, the *North Carolinian*, and a new editor, Hardy L. Holmes. Like many of his predecessors, Holmes was a lawyer. He was a newcomer to Fayetteville who was related to a prominent Democratic family of Wilmington and the lower Cape Fear.[39] Holmes did not last long as editor either, but he found an assistant who succeeded him and who finally made the Democratic press of Fayetteville a thriving institution. Holmes gave to the *North Carolinian* a scholarly polish to which the *North Carolina Journal* had never pretended.

In spite of the confused condition of their party organ, Cumberland Democrats did spread the message that the Panic of 1837 confirmed their earlier analysis of economic trends. Unlike the Whigs, the Democrats of the 1830s did not perceive the economy as a complicated system based on intangible qualities of credit and confidence. Instead, they described a straightforward world in which the labor of producers led directly to concrete values. Some Democrats found depression inexplicable except in terms of conspiracy by a powerful and unnatural force like the Bank of the United States. Andrew Jackson himself had endorsed this view in his message to the cabinet in 1833 explaining his position on deposit removal, and in his annual message later the same year.[40] Because the Bank had not been utterly destroyed by Jackson, these Democrats had predicted that it was bound to renew its battle for a recharter. "We are to have another 'PANIC,'" they had warned in 1835.

> The process for effecting it has already commenced, there has been another great EXPANSION of discounts by the Bank, (an increase of Fifteen Millions within the last five months) loans have been made with the payments thereof protracted to a period beyond that of the legal existence of its charter, thereby incircling more of the community within its POWER, and when the next canvass for the Presidency arrives, should any resistance be offered to its will, or any attempt be made to prevent it from making a President for us, we shall find ourselves again 'in the merciless grasp of another BANK CONTRACTION' far more afflicting than that we have already experienced.[41]

When another panic did arrive, P. Gallagher repeated the charge that it could only have resulted from an attempt by the Bank of the United States to coerce the people and the Congress. The depression, he said in 1838, was a

---

39. John H. Wheeler, *Reminiscences and Memoirs of North Carolina and Eminent North Carolinians* (Columbus, Ohio, 1884), 311, 411.
40. Richardson (comp.), *Messages and Papers of the Presidents*, III, 1224–38, 1250.
41. Fayetteville *North Carolina Journal*, April 29, 1835.

conspiracy by "that Monster, The Pennsylvania United States Bank, and a convention of other Banks, to distract the currency of the country. . .'. Those institutions," he said, were "uniting to create a panic, and suspending specie payments, contrary to all law and justice, for no other reason, than to goad the free people of this Republic into a compliance with their dominant will." The object of this conspiracy, Gallagher said, was to obtain a new national charter for the Bank.[42]

Other Democrats had a slightly more complicated view of the economy than Gallagher. They recognized that the process of production and the value of labor and property were not necessarily fixed, concrete, and independent of complex intangibles like credit and confidence. Instead, they argued that a simple economy was morally desirable, and that the Panic was produced by greed, fraud, and other moral failings. This view had been partially endorsed by Jackson also, when he explained that he had withdrawn the deposits "to preserve the morals of the people." [43] As soon as the Panic began, at least one Democratic merchant in Fayetteville expressed the view that the collapse was the fault of his own class. "I regret that the pressure and distress have reached you honest farmers," wrote James C. Dobbin. "It is the fruit of over trading— over Banking & mercantile extravagance. The policy of the Administration is all that can save the country." [44]

This explanation of the Panic was shared by Judge Robert Strange, a resident of Cumberland County who won election to the United States Senate in 1836. Strange was a distinguished lawyer who moved to Fayetteville from Virginia as a young man. Talent, family connections, and an advantageous marriage placed him in what his biographer called "a social circle of unusual excellence, embracing the Eccles, Toomers, Henrys, and other families distinguished for their culture and refinement." John Winslow, "who was at that time the most influential man in Fayetteville," had befriended Strange at an early stage of his career, but Strange never shared the Federalist or Whiggish inclinations of the Winslows and most of their friends and relatives. He was a firm Republican when he got to Fayetteville and he remained so. In 1821, he became Fayetteville's first Republican town member of the House of Commons and he served for three successive terms before his elevation to the superior court bench. In his last legislative term, Strange had attended the Raleigh caucus which endorsed the presidential candidacy of William H. Crawford. That fact, combined with Strange's roots in eastern Virginia, suggests very strongly that his politics as a young man were of the Old Republican school of John Randolph and Nathaniel Macon. The anticommercial

42. *Ibid.*, August 8, 1838.
43. Richardson (comp.), *Messages and Papers of the Presidents*, III, 1238.
44. James C. Dobbin to Solomon Van Hook, June 9, 1837, in Van Hook Correspondence.

attitudes of these old-fashioned Jeffersonians continued to shape Strange's public pronouncements for the rest of his career. Strange's legislative contacts and his service as a circuit-riding judge probably formed the basis for his election to the Senate, but his judicial office barred him from a public role in Cumberland County politics in the late 1820s and early 1830s. Strange's speeches in the Senate were widely reprinted in Fayetteville and reflected the views of Democrats back home like Gallagher and Dobbin.[45]

In a speech on the subtreasury bill in March of 1838, Strange declared that infallible public opinion made specie the only real money in the world. "In declaring that to be money which is not money [*i.e.*, bank notes], Government gives currency to a falsehood, and unsettles the sound foundations of public opinion." The results of this departure from the natural moral order were devastating, according to Strange, for "no man can see the consequences to which a falsehood may lead, which he has once labeled as truth." Moreover, he continued, "all values are created by the spontaneous production of the earth, by human labor, by animal procreation, or by some or all of these united. . . . Everything, therefore, which has the tendency to divert any considerable portion of a nation from agricultural pursuits, by turning them to speculation, professions, merchandise, or even to manufactures . . . has, as a general rule, the effect of diminishing the wealth of that nation." Strange drew together the conspiracy theories of Gallagher and the moral explanations of Dobbin by declaring that banks were a moral snare. Appealing to men's greed, "the paper system . . . [draws] them off from the cultivation of the soil to become speculators, bank officers, shop-keepers, and livers upon their wits." It was the duty of government, Strange declared, to limit the temptations offered by banks by separating the people's money from the "paper system."[46]

Like Strange, Lauchlin Bethune repeated the idea that banking derived from an unnatural and immoral departure from the prevailing agricultural system. "Look around you," he asked in his 1837 circular, "and see who are the most clamorous for this institution. Are they not either monied men who are not contented with lands and slaves as investments for their money, or men who have lived all their lives upon speculation, whatever calling they may have professed to follow?" "It is not much to be wondered at," he explained, "that the capitalist and the speculator who has nothing to loose, and risks the property of his neighbor that he may become rich; should be in favor

45. "Hon. Robert Strange, of Fayetteville, North Carolina," in *Biographical Sketches of Distinguished American Lawyers* (New York, 1852), 97–112; Samuel A. Ashe, "Robert Strange" (Unpublished sketch in Van Noppen Papers).
46. *Appendix to the Congressional Globe*, 25th Cong., 2nd Sess., 150; Fayetteville *Observer*, March 28, 1838.

of a system so admirably fitted for their respective views; but that the substantial man of industry should ever be found in favor of it, can only be accounted for by the mysticism in which the subject is involved." [47]

Other Democrats repeated the ideas of Strange, Gallagher, and Bethune. Some continued to berate the Bank of the United States itself as the cause of the nation's problems. A correspondent of the *Journal*, for example, declared that the "great issue" of the state elections of 1838 was "whether the people of these United States shall choose their own rulers, or whether a great national Bank shall do it for them?" [48] Others blamed the evils of the whole credit system. When he began to publish the *North Carolinian*, Hardy L. Holmes preferred the latter approach. Following a suggestion made by Senator Thomas Hart Benton of Missouri, Holmes proposed a plan to drive all paper money from the state and thus preserve North Carolina from "the abuses of the 'credit system.'" He stressed that "this vast bank machinery being the work of our own hands," it ought to be "regulated and strictly supervised by the wholesome checks of legislative enactments." Unlike Bethune, Holmes took care to stress that he wanted to control local banks, but not to destroy them. [49]

In 1840, Cumberland Democrats wrote Holmes's views into their county platform. "The fall of prices and the distresses of the country," they declared, "are the effects of the overtrading, frauds, suspensions, contractions and expansions of the currency by the banks of this country and in England." They went on to explain that these expansions and contractions were not the result of one institution's quest for a recharter but that they stemmed from the reckless desire for profits by all the major participants in the banking system. The Democrats recognized that the prosperity of the community depended on the soundness of "a mixed currency, composed of paper and specie." To protect the community's interests, they called for "a thorough reform in the banking system, so as to . . . make the Banks responsible to the people." The specific reform that Democrats usually mentioned was the president's plan for an Independent Treasury. [50]

For the rest of the campaign of 1840, the Democrats quietly insisted that their solution to the Panic was to reform the banking system, not destroy it. However, the popular appeal of radical attacks on all banks and especially the "monster" continued to inspire more sweeping denunciations from time to time. Thus H. L. Holmes could be brought to cry out violently, "WE ARE THE BOND SLAVES OF THE BANKS!" and Democratic orators took a similar tone on

47. Fayetteville *North Carolina Journal*, July 19, 1837.
48. *Ibid.*, August 5, 1838.
49. Fayetteville *North Carolinian*, June 15, 1839, June 22, 1839.
50. *Ibid.*, May 16, 1840.

the stump.[51] An antibank policy that was extremist in tone but moderate in its specific suggestions continued to characterize Democratic rhetoric throughout the 1840s.

The disparity between tone and substance in Democratic rhetoric may have stemmed in part from the fact that several of the men who gave the speeches and moved the resolutions had important personal interests in the very institutions they denounced. After Lauchlin Bethune branded banks, corporations, and "associated wealth" as the "main pillars and key stones of aristocracies and monarchies," Edward J. Hale publicized the business connections of several Democrats who had led the meeting. "Two of the presiding officers, who have sanctioned these bitter resolutions against aristocracies, Banks, Bank officers and Directors, are among our most wealthy citizens," Hale announced. "They are probably the very largest Stockholders in all this part of the State . . . they have been for many years Directors of Banks . . . one of them has been the regular Collecting Attorney for two Banks and doubtless the occasional attorney for others!"[52] Likewise, when Sen. Robert Strange predicted that "no one will attain to wealth or honor, who does not receive them at the hands of the bank aristocracy," the *Observer* hastened to make known that "he himself is a member of that 'aristocracy,' being a Stockholder, Director and BANK ATTORNEY!"[53]

The *Observer*'s charges were true on both occasions. In spite of his ideological commitments, Robert Strange had enjoyed a long and intimate association with the management of the Fayetteville branch of the Bank of Cape Fear. Louis D. Henry, the bank attorney who presided at the meeting which adopted Bethune's resolutions later admitted that he owned "some real estate, some negroes, some 12 or $15,000 of Ohio State Stocks, some Louisiana Bank Stock, some Raleigh and Gaston Railroad Bonds, some Cape Fear and Bank of the State stock, but that the chief part of his means was loaned out on bonds in the counties of Franklin, Warren, Cumberland, Sampson, &c &c., &c." John Kelly, a vice president of the same meeting, had once been a director of the Fayetteville branch of the Bank of the United States and the president of the Clarendon Bridge Company. Kelly owned thirty-six slave polls, $12,825 worth of urban real estate, and rural land valued at $7,309. Furthermore, Thomas L. Hybart, who addressed the meeting, had worked to obtain a new Fayetteville bank charter in the last General Assembly, and two members of the committee of vigilance had been mentioned as possible officers for "the monster in embryo." Lauchlin Bethune himself had been a charter stock-

51. *Ibid.*, March 7, 1840, March 21, 1840.
52. Fayetteville *Observer*, March 24, 1836.
53. *Ibid.*, March 28, 1838.

holder in the Cape Fear, Yadkin, & Pedee Rail Road, and in 1837 he presided at a fund-raising meeting for the same company.[54]

The comprehensive evidence on corporate leadership and party choice made it clear that these apparent cases of inconsistency were exceptional. Most leading Democrats were not as deeply enmeshed in banking and corporate enterprise as most leading Whigs, and most prominent businessmen were Whigs, not Democrats. In John Kelly's case, it was probable that his identity as an Irish Catholic immigrant had more importance in shaping his party choice than his economic success. Why men like Strange and Henry, however, should build their careers on a combination of service to banks and denunciations of banks remains something of a mystery. The *North Carolina Journal* replied primly to the *Observer*'s revelations that "the alleged inconsistencies of individuals do not affect the position assumed" by the party as a whole.[55] Insofar as political objectives were symbolic rather than substantive, the *Journal*'s answer may explain why Democratic voters were undisturbed by the presence of bank directors in their party's leadership.

The *Journal*'s defense does little to clarify how bank directors and bank attorneys could have willingly joined a party which regularly excoriated their existence. The possibility that these exceptional Democrats pilloried the "credit system" as a cynical posture for the sake of winning office is an explanation which cannot be ruled out. Some Whig observers firmly believed that wealthy Democrats were deliberate hypocrites. After Louis D. Henry delivered an exceptionally abusive speech in Orange County, one listener reported to a Whig merchant in Fayetteville that "many moderate and disinterested democrats openly winced at witnessing such an exhibition of demagoguism and buffoonery from a man of Mr. Henry's standing as a lawyer. Mr. H must evidently retain one prominent feature of his old Federalism in greatly undervaluing the intelligence and shrewdness of the plain farmers of our Country."[56] Marvin Meyers offered a more charitable explanation of Democratic inconsistency when he suggested that conscience and private interests pulled some Jacksonians in opposite directions, and that they handled their ambivalence by purifying government of involvement with institutions which they readily supported in private life.[57] It is also possible that the obvious popularity of attacks on banking and commerce was their only justifica-

---

54. "Hon. Robert Strange, of Fayetteville, North Carolina," 102; Fayetteville *Observer*, June 8, 1842; Fayetteville *North Carolina Journal*, May 30, 1832, February 9, 1837; Cumberland County List of Taxables, 1837, in Cumberland County Records.
55. Fayetteville *North Carolina Journal*, March 31, 1836. Strange, Henry, Hybart, and the other leading Democrats left no personal papers which would clarify their motivations in politics.
56. W. A. Norwood to S. W. Tillinghast, March 14, 1840, in Tillinghast Family Papers.
57. Meyers, *The Jacksonian Persuasion*, 12.

tion. Like James Fenimore Cooper's village politician, the leading Democrats of Cumberland County may have assumed sincerely that "it is impossible that everybody should be mistaken." [58]

Only one leading Democrat left enough evidence of his private convictions to give us some insight into how he combined contradictory commitments in his career and in his ideology. The father of James C. Dobbin was an unlettered man who supported Andrew Jackson in 1836 but who had also learned to turn a penny in the marketplace. He sent his son James to the University of North Carolina and afterwards enabled him to read law with Judge Robert Strange. In 1835, young Dobbin confided proudly to his friend Solomon Van Hook, a planter of Person County, that "our merchants have been making hansomely on cotton speculations—& I am pleased that Father is among the most fortunate thus far." Over the next two years, James C. Dobbin began to practice law, his father died, and the Panic of 1837 struck Fayetteville. He also married Louisa Holmes, of the same family as Hardy L. Holmes, the editor of the *North Carolinian*. Writing his friend again, Dobbin reported on the Panic's personal impact. "I am up to my very eyes in business—I am a Lawyer—Merchant—farmer—&c.—A heavy winters work lies before me—thirty or forty thousand to collect & pay out. I think I see my way pretty clear—and when I get all things straight here—in New York—& in Charleston—*then* you may look for me in Person—." In these letters, Dobbin presents the portrait of a conventional Whig—born in a mercantile family, interested in commerce, planting, and law, busy at suits and foreclosures in the midst of financial tumult. [59]

In spite of these interests, Dobbin kept the Democratic faith, even as his correspondent wavered. The legacy of his self-made father, the influence of Judge Strange, his Old Republican legal mentor, and his connection with the Democratic Holmes family may all have interacted to keep Dobbin in the Jacksonian ranks. From some source, he developed an especially acute sense of the importance of states' rights, which he cited as the basis of his own political preferences. In 1840, Dobbin wrote Van Hook in disbelief. "I am a little surprised at your politics: you ought to have imitated the magnanimous conduct of your former leader J. C. Calhoun. Dont you talk of States rights to me any more—and then *oppose* all the States rights measures of the country and advocate the most ultra measures of consolidationism. Shame! Shame! to one who professes to admire Jefferson!!!" Dobbin concluded his scolding on a personal note, but renewed his political warning. "My love to your wife,"

58. James Fenimore Cooper, *Home as Found*, (New York, 1872), 211.
59. Fayetteville *North Carolina Journal*, March 17, 1836; John Dobbin to Solomon Van Hook, November 15, 1831, James C. Dobbin to Solomon Van Hook, July 20, 1835, September 27, 1837, all in Van Hook Correspondence.

he wrote. "Tell her I say she must guard the little boys against their father's politics. However I have great hopes of you yet—as I presume you dont think of voting for Harrison." [60]

Van Hook's other papers suggest that he indeed became a Whig, but Dobbin's personal convictions overrode the influence of his business interests. A similar set of circumstances may have influenced Robert Strange, the Old Republican bank attorney. In any event, Dobbin's Democratic fidelity served him well. He won several terms in Congress, and in 1852, he broke the deadlock at the Democratic National Convention by nominating Franklin Pierce for president. After the election, Dobbin was rewarded with a seat in Pierce's cabinet as secretary of the navy. [61]

Regardless of their private motives, leaders of both Cumberland County parties confirmed and hardened their earlier public positions as they analyzed the causes and possible remedies of the depression. The respective arguments of the Whigs and the Democrats were readily adaptable to the positions they had taken earlier in regard to social equality and economic conflict. One effect of the Panic on political rhetoric was to prompt more appeals to social divisions among the electorate.

The Democrats were very explicit in their opposition to townsmen and commercial figures, though they were not always strident. They boasted, for example, that theirs was the "Farmer's Ticket," as distinguished from the so-called "Lawyer's Ticket" of the Whigs. [62] More often, writers flung social epithets with fervent abandon. In 1838, "A Voter" declared that the question in the election that year was "whether your rag and paper aristocratic banking institutions and brokers, swindling stock jobbers and privileged corporations, shall have the balance of power, or whether the true yeomanry of the country, the mechanics, manufacturers, planters, producers and laboring men shall have it." [63] In a similar vein, H. L. Holmes titled an antibank editorial of 1840 "Aristocracy or the Government and Oppression of the Few, with the Money Power, against the Democracy of the Will of the Whole People, Who are not Rich." He concluded the article by declaring, "This credit system, this paper money power, this horrid Aristocracy of wealth, enslaves this land." [64]

Most Democratic denunciations of aristocracy were based on generalities. Occasionally, a Democrat would accuse a particular Whig candidate of being too aristocratic or too involved with urban interests. When John McLean and

60. James C. Dobbin to Solomon Van Hook, January 28, 1840, September 16, 1838, both in Van Hook Correspondence.
61. John W. Huske to Solomon Van Hook, February 15, 1840, in Van Hook Correspondence; Oates, *The Story of Fayetteville*, 827.
62. Fayetteville *Observer*, July 22, 1840.
63. Fayetteville *North Carolina Journal*, July 18, 1838.
64. Fayetteville *North Carolinian*, March 7, 1840.

John Winslow ran for the General Assembly in 1838, "A Voter" asserted that "it is well known that the McLeans and the Winslows have been born under the *office* star." He assured readers of the *Journal* that "if you wish the sweat and labor of the poor man to enrich the fields of the rich man, then vote for Messrs. McLean and Winslow." [65] An editorial in 1840 belittled the qualifications of the Whig candidate for governor by complaining that "he has been too busy making money with his mills and farms, and workshops, and law suits, to attend to politics." [66] Eventually, these repeated blasts at the position of their opponents were accompanied by significant shifts in the social composition of the Democratic party.

In reply to the Democratic charges of aristocratic oppression, the Whigs tried to prove that lower-income voters were greater losers by Van Buren's policies than the rich. "The present times are the times for men who have money and can buy," declared Hale, "but they are grievous times for those who have anything to sell, or debts to pay." [67] No matter how logical their arguments may have been from an economic perspective, the Cumberland Whigs were not successful in persuading many farmers that currency inflation would be in their interests. The monetary nostrums that would thrill their Populist grandchildren left Jacksonian farmers unmoved, even hostile. Easy money arguments obliged the Whigs to defend banks, the hated credit system, and commercial institutions generally. Favorable views on these subjects could never prevail in rural antebellum Cumberland County. In that cultural climate, inflammatory demands for paper money would only have appeared ridiculous. Whigs continued to insist that hard money would benefit only the rich, but they seem to have made few converts.

Both publicly and privately, the Whigs deplored the Democratic tendency to excite economic jealousies. The *Observer* expressed relief that the Whigs had won the state election of 1838, even though "the most vile incendiary efforts have been made to array the poor against the rich." [68] After Harrison's victory in 1840, one Whig expressed the hope that since "it will be the interest of none to foment jealousies between the different classes of society— which has heretofore been the element of strength to the Democratic party— that the evil passions which have been so generally engendered by this strife will subside and good fellowship return." [69] Another Whig defended his organic vision of society with no little eloquence. "We are all one family," he wrote. "Those that sow tars of discord, and set the different elements of so-

65. Fayetteville *North Carolina Journal*, August 8, 1838.
66. Fayetteville *North Carolinian*, January 18, 1840.
67. Fayetteville *Observer*, February 12, 1840.
68. *Ibid.*, August 22, 1838.
69. John W. Huske to Solomon Van Hook, November 14, 1840, in Van Hook Correspondence.

ciety at variance with each other, are enemies to mankind. All should be mutual friends and helpers to each other, and who ever aids and assists his fellow men from good motives, by lending money, by affording employment by precept or example, is a benefactor to his fellow men. Those who trade on borrowed capital may and often do succeed and prosper, and in due time, retiring from business in turn, lend to others, as those who preceded lent to them." [70] No matter how well-intentioned, the paternalism of such remarks could never win votes. Nor could the professed benevolence of Whig capitalists quiet the fears Democratic farmers felt in the face of urban commercial society. Whig rhetoric was thus unable to reverse the social orientations of Cumberland politics.

As the leaders of each party staked out a position on the issues raised by the Panic, they also took steps to proselytize their views. They concentrated especially on perfecting the tools of party organization and popular excitement they had begun to develop in the middle years of the decade.

The most popular organizational measure of this type continued to be a general meeting of the party membership in the courthouse to listen to speeches and pass resolutions. This was an old device in Cumberland County, having been in use at least since 1828. Whigs and Democrats resorted to it several times in 1840, especially to promote party organization in the early stages of the campaign. Later in the year, both parties modified the basic format of this institution to make it more useful in soliciting uncommitted voters. The Whigs moved their meeting out of Fayetteville's courthouse and into the countryside in an effort to reach more farmers. These rural meetings sometimes concentrated on speechmaking. On at least one occasion, a barbecue for five or six hundred people was also included. In the fall, the Democrats began to hold weekly meetings in Fayetteville, featuring speeches by local orators, designed to arouse enthusiasm before Election Day.[71]

Nationally, the Log Cabin Campaign of 1840 was marked by the use of symbolic and emotional appeals at the expense of ideological debate. In Cumberland County, neither party was reluctant to use traditional means of propaganda, particularly the long, heavily argumentative speech or editorial in support of its candidate. The *Observer* reported, for example, that the Whig gubernatorial candidate visited Fayetteville in June, 1840, and addressed a rapt crowd at the Market House for four and a half hours. In addition to these devices, the Whigs experimented with the more exuberant methods employed by their friends across the nation. The departure of the Cumberland delegation

---

70. James D. Pemberton to Duncan McLaurin, November 23, 1838, in McLaurin Papers.
71. Fayetteville *North Carolinian*, March 7, 1840, May 16, 1840, October 17, 1840; Fayetteville *Observer*, March 25, 1840, June 10, 1840, July 1, 1840, October 2, 1840.

to the Whig state convention in 1840 took the form of a grand parade, accompanied by "a log cabin, [with] a coon or two on it, a cider barrel behind it, and . . . one or two clever old gentlemen [riding] in it."[72] The *Observer* reported that the cabin was decorated with "banners, inscriptions, &c." When they arrived in Raleigh, the delegates joined in another parade. The Raleigh *Register* gave the following account of their contribution: "We were delighted to see so imposing an array from Cumberland. . . . First came her noble Cabin, with the inscription on the door—'To rent after the 4th of March, 1841'—a Marten box, labelled 'O.K.'—Off to Kinderhook. Their beautiful Banner had the motto, 'Agriculture, Commerce, and Manufactures.' Reverse, 'No reduction of wages; the laborer is worthy of his hire. . . .' The Log Cabin was presented to the Tippecanoe Club of this City, and is now in their possession."[73]

The Democrats met these displays with indignation and ridicule. An editorial in the *North Carolinian* called the parade meaningless. "What argument is in it?" the editor demanded. "What means the coons and cider barrel?" He called on the voters to "show in November that this is all an insult to you and your good sense—that you are not the fools they think you are!"[74] Holmes was not content, however, to oppose visual imagery with words alone. He used a picture himself when he printed the only editorial cartoon found in any county newspaper during the period (figure 6). The cartoon depicted a deadfall trap, of the kind commonly used to snare small animals, in the form of a log cabin. The trap was decorated with a raccoon, the Whig party symbol, and baited with a barrel of cider. The caption reminded voters that they were rational men, not animals, and asked, "Are you minks, raccoons, wildcats, mere beasts and gulls to take such a bait, and be caught in such a trap?" Presumably banners, parades, and music were not entirely absent from the Democratic campaign either, since all of these devices had been used in the county before.[75]

The committee of vigilance was one electioneering institution which was not used by both parties. The Whigs organized a vigilance committee of fifteen members and a standing committee of a hundred members in March, 1840. Both groups were joined two weeks later by a Whig young men's committee of about forty members.[76] The combined membership of these bodies was far larger than earlier Whig organizations. The Democrats made no such efforts. The *North Carolinian* did not explain why a committee of vigilance was deemed unnecessary, but perhaps party leaders felt that their firm major-

72. Fayetteville *North Carolinian*, October 3, 1840.
73. Quoted in Fayetteville *Observer*, October 14, 1840.
74. Fayetteville *North Carolinian*, October 3, 1840.
75. Fayetteville *Observer*, August 19, 1834.
76. *Ibid.*, March 25, 1840, April 8, 1840.

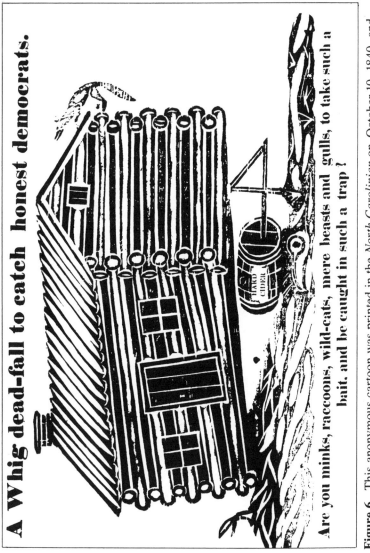

A Whig dead-fall to catch honest democrats.

Are you minks, raccoons, wild-cats, mere beasts and gulls, to take such a bait, and be caught in such a trap?

Figure 6. This anonymous cartoon was printed in the *North Carolinian* on October 10, 1840, and October 17, 1840.

SOURCE: From copy in North Carolina Collection, UNC Library, Chapel Hill.

ity position made that step superfluous. If the basic function of a published membership list was to show off the party's notables, Democrats may have thought their leading adherents were already sufficiently well known. In any case, neither party published a long list of members in the elections after 1840.

A final device which both parties used to attract a larger turnout was the simplistic or even demagogic appeal of the party press. Most of the campaign material in the *Observer* and the *North Carolinian* was complicated, even dense, discussion aimed at the fully literate reader. From time to time, however, each paper adopted a special tone that was meant to reach the poorly educated. The *North Carolinian* made such an effort when attempting to explain tariff policy to farmers and workingmen in May, 1840.

> Every man should be careful to study out well the nature of this Tariff, of which we have all heard so much, and about which, so few know anything at all, or at least very little.
>
> Do not suppose, because the *sheriff* does not collect this money as he does your State taxes, that therefore, the farmer never pays it. Every citizen pays this *tax*, as certainly as he pays his *"poll tax."*
>
> Let every man then be informed of the nature of this tariff. Let him study it Sundays, and when he quits work at night, as he would his *Bible*, in order that he may know what *taxes* he has to pay. Whenever the honest farmer does this, he will have but one rule to guide him in politics. He will vote for the man that is against this tariff, and he will vote against the man that is in favor of it.[77]

The tariff had been a subject of public controversy in Cumberland since at least 1824. This editorial suggests that sixteen years of discussion and criticism had not sufficed to acquaint every voter with a clear understanding of what the tariff *was*, much less of why it was objectionable. Public comprehension of complex economic issues was therefore dim at best. To the extent that most "honest farmers" did follow the Democratic party, it was not because they had itemized their economic interests, added them up, and voted according to the bottom line, but because the party's rhetoric accurately reflected the common sense reality they experienced in daily life.

H. L. Holmes's explanation of the tariff was an honest, if slightly condescending, attempt to present an issue rationally and without undue distortion. Not all appeals to simple readers were so candid. Holmes could oversimplify the issues until the facts were severely strained, and Hale could do the same. Carried away by their own propaganda, Whigs saw designs of executive tyranny in several issues where a calmer response was probably in order.

77. Fayetteville *North Carolinian*, May 16, 1840.

In May, for example, the *Observer* described a plan submitted by the Democratic secretary of war for a national militia system as a presidential attempt to impose a standing army on the country. "Mr. Van Buren intends to require every man in the U. States (except the office-holders and a few others) between the ages of 20 and 45 to go to the expense of furnishing himself with a musket or rifle, knapsack, bayonet, and belt, cartridge box &c., the whole of which will cost him probably not less than $15." Hale also implied that all men would be required to drill in distant states, under threats of heavy fines and imprisonment. The formation of a national militia system was mandated by the Constitution, and the Whig attempt to transform Secretary Poinsett's proposal into a project of despotism was a distortion. The Whigs' dire warnings were convincing to some voters, however. The *Carolinian* admitted that "the women, in many neighborhoods, where the people do not read much, have been alarmed by this whig humbug, and were actually in dread of their husbands being ordered off to Florida in the ranks of the standing army!" [78] The *Observer* also drew heavily on the famous speech of Congressman Ogle of Pennsylvania, who castigated the president's alleged extravagance in furnishing the White House. Hale also suggested that the federal census of 1840, which was the first to ask detailed questions about each family's property, was to serve as the basis for a direct tax. All of these charges were either misleading, unfair, or untrue. [79]

The perennial hobby of abolitionism was not absent from the rhetoric of either party in 1840. Southerners' anxieties over slavery were entirely genuine, and the preservation of slavery was a trancendent political objective for almost every white southerner. Both parties eagerly exploited this widespread concern and the demand for unanimity which it generated. In 1838, for example, the *Observer* defended the state banks on the grounds of states' rights and concluded its appeal with the evocative cry "let no man falter in his determination to put down a party that would destroy the institutions and rights of the States." Similarly, the *North Carolinian* reported in 1839 that "the late elections in every Slave-holding State (except Kentucky and Louisiana) shew that the voice of the people in solemn verdict is in favor to the present administration." The editor drew on an assumption that protracted differences of opinion were intolerable within the slaveholding states and asked, "IS NOT THIS SOLEMN VERDICT RIGHT?" He insisted that if the Whigs did not give up all their objections to the Democrats and accept the people's

78. Fayetteville *North Carolinian*, March 7, 1840, March 14, 1840, August 27, 1840; Fayetteville *Observer*, May 27, 1840.
79. Fayetteville *Observer*, June 24, 1840, July 20, 1840; Fayetteville *North Carolinian*, August 29, 1840.

decision at once, "all respect for the voice of the people is lost" and white solidarity would be dangerously vitiated.[80]

In 1840, Democrats used the slavery issue more regularly than the Whigs. Four years of Van Buren's presidency had rebutted Whig charges that he was an abolitionist, but William Henry Harrison's equivocal silence on the subject gave Democrats a chance to dose Whigs with their own medicine. Cumberland Democrats resolved that Harrison was "the favourite candidate of that united band of fanatics whose ultimate aim is the submission of *our* rights and the prostration of our peculiar institutions." Whigs struck back by publicizing the trial of Lieutenant Hooe of the navy, "a proceeding by which one of your own free white and gallant Virginians has been tried and convicted on the testimony of TWO BLACK MEN!" Whig speaker William McL. McKay combined the incident with references to the hard money policies of Senator Thomas Hart Benton of Missouri and the mulatto daughters of Vice President Richard M. Johnson to make a crowd-pleasing sally in a midsummer Fayetteville speech. "No No," the young activist gibed, "They may joke as much as they please about Benton's yellow boys [gold coins] and Dick Johnsons Yellow Girls But Martin Vanburens Black Boys is no joke for White men."[81]

Political insiders admitted privately that they appealed to racial fears with a certain degree of cynicism. Earlier in the 1830s, for example, North Carolina Democrats had accused Whigs of abolitionist sympathies because John Motley Morehead, Whig candidate for governor, had once presented an anti-slavery petition to the legislature from his Quaker constituents in Guilford County. The Democrats freely rang the changes on this information until Whigs revealed that Romulus Saunders, the Democratic candidate, had once submitted a similar petition to Congress. On receiving the news, Fayetteville merchant and banker John W. Huske gleefully asked a fellow Whig correspondent, "How do your democratic friends feel at being so snugly caught in their own trap with respect to Abolition[?] . . . Do they intend to support Judge Saunders?"[82] In truth, neither candidate sympathized with antislavery, but Whigs relished exposing Democratic insincerity on the subject. One North Carolina historian has concluded that "this practice came to be sort of a game between the Democrats and the Whigs," but beneath the spirit of play surged fearful and powerful emotions. William J. Cooper has tellingly shown how abolition-baiting and racist one-upmanship had devastating sectional

80. Fayetteville *Observer*, April 18, 1839; Fayetteville *North Carolinian*, November 30, 1839.
81. Fayetteville *North Carolinian*, March 7, 1840; Fayetteville *Observer*, June 24, 1840; William McL. McKay, Untitled Speech marked "Delivered at the Market House, Fayetteville, July, 1840" (MS in Elijah Fuller Papers).
82. John W. Huske to Solomon Van Hook, February 15, 1840, in Van Hook Correspondence.

consequences over the long run. In 1840, the obsessional defense of slavery still belonged to the future of Cumberland County politics.[83]

The electioneering of county leaders in 1840 successfully brought large numbers of new voters or formerly irregular voters to the polls. The total number of votes cast in November, 1840, was 1,562. This was almost 500 more than were cast in the same election in 1836. In August, 1840, the turnout in the governor's election was actually 11 votes higher than the total in November, and 274 higher than the total in August, 1836.[84] As figure 3 showed, participation in the presidential election exceeded 80 percent in 1840 and remained near that level for 12 years. This campaign brought a large new group of voters into the political community. Their entry completed the formation of the second party system in the county.

Most of these new voters came from the rural districts. Three hundred twenty-four more votes were cast in the 1840 governor's election than in the same election in 1836. Ninety-three of these were cast in Fayetteville, and 231 were cast in the country. Rural turnout thus increased 29.8 percent, while Fayetteville's increased by only 19.6 percent in this election. The rural precincts showed varying participation, but no common characteristic clearly distinguished the rural precincts with large increases from those having smaller ones.[85]

Although expanded participation was the most important innovation of 1840, there were also some changes in the provenance of the parties' votes. The correlation coefficient between the results of the 1836 and 1840 gubernatorial elections is $+.5307$, indicating that the sources of each party's votes were similar but not identical in the two contests. The correlation between the governor's and the president's elections of 1840 is almost perfect ($r = +.9848$), indicating that the parties' bases of support did not change substantially from August to November. The correlations between the governor's election of 1840 and those of 1842 and 1844 are also strong ($r = +.8861$ and $+.8306$, respectively). The bases of partisan support shifted significantly between 1836 and 1840, but very little thereafter. We should therefore like to

83. Norton, *The Democratic Party in Ante-Bellum North Carolina*, 64–68; Cooper, *The South and the Politics of Slavery*, 98–148.
84. Compiled Election Returns, "Presidential Electors," 1840, 1836, "Gubernatorial," 1840, 1836.
85. There are no precinct-level returns for the presidential election of 1836, so the proportion of rural and urban votes is unknown for that year. Discussion of changes in voting turnout over the four years must therefore depend on the governor's election. The August election in 1836 attracted 214 more voters than the November canvass, so the two elections were not strictly equivalent. It is probable, however, that the distribution of votes in August was not grossly different from the pattern in November. Fayetteville *North Carolina Journal*, August 18, 1836; Fayetteville *Observer*, August 19, 1840. See also Chapter VI, especially table 20.

Table 44. Changing Support for the Democratic Party in
Cumberland Precincts, 1836–1840

	Change in percent Democratic, 1836–1840[a]	Percent Democratic, 1840[a]
Lock's Creek	−30.6%	31.5%
Willis Creek	−25.5	60.0
Flea Hill	−25.5	52.8
Averasborough	− 8.4	43.2
Buckhorn	− 7.1	85.5
Fayetteville	+ 1.4	53.2
Neill's Creek	+ 2.7	87.2
Munroe's	+ 4.9	94.4
Quewhiffle	+ 7.1	82.1
Barbecue	+10.8	71.0
Upper Little River	+26.4	65.0
Seventy-first	+30.5	27.1
County aggregate	− 3.6%	60.5%

[a]Percentages are given for the governor's elections in 1836 and 1840. Precinct returns for the 1836 presidential election are not available.
SOURCE: Fayetteville *North Carolina Journal*, August 18, 1836; Fayetteville *Observer*, August 19, 1840.

know which precincts had the greatest tendency to change the degree of their support for the Democratic candidate in 1836 and 1840.

These precincts are identified in table 44. The table shows that rural party preferences were still in flux between 1836 and 1840. Democratic percentages within most rural precincts changed dramatically in this period. Fayetteville showed very little change, indicating that urban voters had settled on a party preference earlier than country voters.

The five precincts in which the Democrats gained the most in 1840 were all in the sandhills. With the exception of Flea Hill, the precincts where the Democrats lost the most were more prosperous precincts. Whigs found new adherents both in plantation districts like Lock's Creek and Averasborough, and also in small-farm districts like Willis Creek and Buckhorn. Precincts that became *more* Whig, however, did not become *mostly* Whig. The second column of table 44 shows that most rural precincts, regardless of gains or losses, continued to show a Democratic majority. Nevertheless, the main sources of Democratic strength had shifted. The sandhills precincts had shown a slight bias for the Whigs in 1836. Other precincts showed heavy support for the Jacksonians. The changes of 1840 softened these contrasts. In the future, a non-Scottish, small-farm district like Willis Creek would give about the same proportion of Democratic votes as the mostly Scottish, sandhills precinct of Upper Little River. Not all rural contrasts disappeared in 1840. The plantation districts of Lock's Creek and Averasborough became heavily Whig. Though they lived in the country, many of the voters in these districts were probably urban-oriented and thus sympathetic to Whiggery. The shift in the social bases of voting in 1840 amounted to a strengthened identification of each party with its rural-oriented or urban-oriented bloc.

Table 45 supports these conclusions more formally. The tendency to change support for the Democrats was tied most closely to percent Scot and the amount of landed wealth per taxpayer. If a district was rich, the Democrats tended to lose. High Scottish population and low wealth were characteristics of the sandhills districts. Ethnicity did not affect a district's actual percent Democratic in 1840, only the *change* in the percent between 1836 and 1840. The correlation between percent Scot and percent voting for Van Buren was not significantly different from zero. The 1840 election therefore saw a coming together of rural Scots and non-Scots. The same was not true of the rural rich and the rural poor. Wealth per taxpayer did make a difference in a district's support for Van Buren. The rural precincts which came together in

Table 45. Social and Political Variables in Rural
Precincts, 1836–1840 Correlation Coefficients

	Change in Percent Democratic, 1836– 1840	Percent for Van Buren, 1840	Percent Scot, 1838
Percent for Van Buren, 1840	.3418 (.167)[a]		
Percent Scot, 1838	.5875 (.037)	.0258 (.472)	
Wealth per taxpayer, 1838	−.5050 (.068)	−.5464 (.051)	−.1268 (.364)

[a]The figure in parentheses beneath each coefficient is the significance level of that coefficient.
SOURCE: Cumberland County List of Taxables, 1838, in Cumberland County Records, North Carolina State Archives; Fayetteville *North Carolina Journal*, August 18, 1836; Fayetteville *Observer*, August 19, 1840, November 18, 1840.

1840 were the sandhills and the small-farm districts. The wealthier districts aligned themselves more closely with the Whigs of Fayetteville. These new social and political alignments remained steady in the years after 1840.

The voting returns therefore suggest economic and cultural divisions among the electorate that parallel the stronger economic arguments in the Democratic press. The tendency to make economic and cultural divisions equivalent to political divisions appeared among party leaders in 1828 and 1836. Ordinary voters do not seem to have made the same connections between politics and economics that their leaders made until after the experience of the Panic. Even in 1840, however, the prosperity of a precinct did not determine its vote absolutely. At best, wealth per taxpayer explains less than 30 percent of the variance in rural voting.[86] Though not overwhelming, the relationship between party and wealth was stronger than it had been before. In the 1840s, the typical Democratic voter not only came from a rural district, but he came from a less prosperous district than the typical Whig.

The Panic of 1837 had brought momentous changes to the world of Cumberland County. Economic development and political reorganization had been under way for several years, but outside Fayetteville, earlier events and pronouncements had not led many citizens to change their political behavior. When the Panic struck, the private citizen suddenly learned that the dangers and opportunities described by the stump speakers had immediate relevance to everyday life, and he accepted mass politics as an expression of his individual hopes and fears. As prices sank lower and lower, Cumberland County Whigs saw a practical demonstration of the Democrats' wanton incompetence. As banks called in their loans and bankers curtailed their offers to buy, Democrats saw the stark reality of Whiggish villainy. Hundreds of voters who had never taken sides joined up with one party or another, and partisan arguments penetrated the countryside.

The citizens who joined the political community in 1840 were the last group of recruits to the second party system. When these new voters entered the political community, moreover, they came to stay. Participation in major contests remained constant throughout the 1840s, and most districts continued to divide their totals by the same predictable fractions. The Whigs of 1840 stayed Whigs; the Democrats stayed Democrats. In addition, the rhetoric and membership of each party showed a reasonable consistency. The Democrats called themselves the party of the average citizen, Democratic orators denounced the privileges of the rich, and Democratic voters tended to

---

86. The square of the correlation coefficient (r^2) denotes the proportion of variance in the dependent variable which is accounted for by the independent variable. In this case, $r = .5464$, so $r^2 = 29.9$ percent.

come from disadvantaged neighborhoods. Whigs spoke in favor of the credit system, and Whigs actually used its facilities more than Democrats. Behavior and ideology converged and then stabilized. For most activists, party organization was no longer a baneful sore on the republic; party spirit was at the center of political life and the focus of men's hopes for their country. For the remainder of the 1840s, Cumberland County politics were characterized by the routine operation of the second party system.

VIII. A Calm Quiet State of Things
Party Routine in the 1840s

At the September, 1842, term of Cumberland County Court, nineteen free-holders of the solidly Democratic precinct of Neill's Creek submitted an unusual petition to the assembled justices. These small farmers asked the court for permission to divert some of the hands and resources normally devoted to keeping the roads in repair to an attempt to make Neill's Creek navigable. The petitioners expressed the hope that improved transportation would enable them to float "tun timber" down the creek to the Cape Fear River and thence to distant markets.

The court appointed commissioners from the district to investigate the idea. They pronounced the job "entirely practicable" and justified the project in words that sounded novel in the mouths of habitual Democrats. "The time has arrived," the commissioners proclaimed proudly, "when this dark corner of your county intends no longer to submit to the shackels of ignorance and superstition, but will put on a spirit of interprise and laudable ambition and stear its course to eminence and virtue when instead of inumerating her resources by dollars and cents, it will be, by tens and hundreds." [1]

An anticommercial ethos was evidently waning among these isolated farmers. By the petitioners' own admission, the suspicion of luxury and speculation which ministers and politicians had both invoked in earlier decades could not withstand the allure of progress indefinitely. Even Democrats began to relegate wariness of economic change to the ignominious category of "ignorance and superstition" and aspired to "eminence and virtue," measured off

---

1. Petition from the Inhabitants of Neill's Creek, Cumberland County Court Minutes, September Term, 1842, in Cumberland County Records; Report of Commissioners Appointed to Determine if Neill's Creek Can Be Made Navigable, n.d., in Miscellaneous Papers, 1792–1869, Cumberland County Records.

in hundred-dollar quantities. As the depression receded and business conditions improved, farmers and forest owners tried their hands at lumbering and at the newly profitable business of making turpentine. By 1846, the *Observer* was reporting that "it is supposed that the Turpentine business will be so extended in this vicinity during the present season, as to require the appointment of Inspectors," and two Whig businessmen were accordingly elected. The cry went up again for improved transportation to remedy Fayetteville's persisting problems, and this time the idea of a western railroad received strong support from both party newspapers. The old dream of a railroad to the Yadkin never materialized, but the business community did receive state aid for a wide-ranging network of plank roads, the so-called "farmer's railroads." In the 1850s Fayetteville's railroad promoters settled for second best and began a western line to the newly-opened coal fields on Deep River, not far away. Capital was still scarce for such ventures, but a popular referendum approved a county subscription to the company's bonds. By 1860, 60.0 percent of the county poll tax and 33.0 percent of the county land tax were earmarked for the railroad.[2] The Whigs had won the argument for economic development, and an increasing number of Democrats had begun to see things their way.

Perhaps coincidentally, the county's demographic patterns began to change. After 1840, Fayetteville's population began a gradual advance that brought it to 4,790 inhabitants in 1860. This represented an 11.8 percent increase since 1840. Rural Cumberland grew 78.2 percent in the same period and reached 19,618 by 1860.[3] Ironically, new markets and new technology seemed to improve conditions in the country more than in the town, but the general stagnation of the 1830s had ended.

Not all Democrats gave up the faith of their founders. A portion of the party resisted the railroad subsidy bitterly on the grounds that it would benefit no one but the rich men of Fayetteville at the expense of rural taxpayers.[4] Anticommercial sentiment continued to appear in the press, though its proponents increasingly took on the tone of a beleaguered minority. In 1855, for example, the Fayetteville *Observer* received a letter from Jacup Jones, a Democratic farmer from Snow Camp, a rural crossroads in Alamance County. Jones's letter was a very significant expression of personal political sentiment from the sort of voter who was otherwise almost totally silent in the surviving

---

2. Fayetteville *Observer*, March 10, 1846, April 13, 1857, March 8, 1860.
3. *Population of the United States in 1860, Compiled from the Original Returns of the Eighth Census, Under the Direction of the Secretary of the Interior* (Washington, 1864), 358–59.
4. "Vote This Ticket, No Subscription," [1857] (Broadside in Duncan G. McRae Papers, Southern Historical Collection).

historical record. Amidst derisive remarks on Jones's spelling and politics, the editors of the *Observer* asserted that the letter was certainly genuine and not the product of feigned rusticity.

Jones wrote in reponse to a report in the *Observer* that a Democratic militia company in the backcountry had used a portrait of former President William Henry Harrison for target practice. Jones rejected the aspersion as an individual and in the name of his community. "Now I tel you jist what it is," he declared. "I dont bleve any sich a thing becase I dont bleve people would do sich" but "iff any off your Droted Whigs wus to show his face in thes parts he woud git his due if he went to medlin along with our musterin sertun." Jones went on to vent the resentment of commerce and the town which rural Democracy had long thrived on. "Now I hav bin to fayett and ive ben to raley [Raleigh], and Ive seen all your big works and I have never seen any of you whigs that I kerd a sent for never seed one that I axed a bit of odds." Moving easily from a statement of his personal outrage to the grievances of his community, Jones affirmed the dignity of Democratic Snow Camp against the grandeur of Fayetteville's Whigs. "Now I reckon there is jist as gud democrat papers as yourn is a whig and I mean to subscribe for won but it wont it be yourn case you is always making fun of the democrats and hard shel baptusts case they have sertain ways for themselves and case they bleve in the lord and do jist rite and case you hi flown whigs gits licked evry once and a while your awais a maikin things on us to injure our Karectors." The letter ended with a threat of boycott which not only stemmed from an old-fashioned suspicion that the "farmer's railroads" only benefited merchants, but also revealed his own perhaps unwilling reliance on the market. "We are a goin to quit goin to fayett," he warned, "and send our flower to Norfolk and you will not get to cheet us any more sartain nor have me up any moor about not whantin to pay toll on your Dratted plan Road[.] you see," Jones concluded, "we democrats up her aint gon to be runover no longer."[5]

The anticommercial sentiment which had riled Timothy Trueman in 1815 and "the honest kintra man" in 1790 still rankled for Jacup Jones in 1855. In Jones's case, the countryman's sense of economic exploitation merged with a larger cluster of complaints. It does not appear that Jones was a Democrat because he was a conservative Baptist or because he lived in a rural area or because he felt cheated economically. It seems more likely that being a Democrat was a way for Jones to express his membership in a community in which all these qualities naturally hung together. If the petition from Neill's Creek betokened a change in the attitudes of some Democrats, the letter of Jacup Jones affirmed their continuity among others. The pattern resembled an ex-

5. Fayetteville *Observer*, November 5, 1855.

panding ripple of commercialization, which menaced Neill's Creek yeomen in the 1820s and 1830s, won some of them over in the 1840s, and still threatened Snow Camp in 1855.

The economic changes that made the marketplace alluring to Neill's Creek did not bring small farmers into commercial production and then level off. Change went further and led to the successful rise of cotton mills in Fayetteville and surrounding areas of the sandhills. These mills were small and did not alter Cumberland County beyond recognition, but they did make the community more atypical of the region than it had been before their establishment. According to Frederick Law Olmsted, most of the workers in the mills were young women from Scottish families in the neighborhood. "In modesty, cleanliness, and neatness of apparell," Olmsted reported, "though evidently poor, they certainly compared favorably with the girls employed in a cotton mill that I visited near Glasgow, a few years ago."[6]

The female workers did not vote, but those who were male posed a challenge and an opportunity for county politicians. The male factory workers owed their jobs to the Industrial Revolution, but their roots were in rural poverty; their lives seemed to cut across the older division of Cumberland society that separated wealthier, urban, market-oriented men from poorer, rural, self-sufficient farmers. The mill workers had given up the personal independence enjoyed by farmers and had therefore lost one of the principal qualities of good citizenship as traditional republicans understood it. Their employers did not neglect the chance which this condition presented.

When the votes were counted on election night, 1844, Whigs discovered jubilantly that they had carried the Fayetteville precinct for Henry Clay. A Democratic crowd blamed their defeat on the mill workers employed by Charles B. Mallett's Rockfish Manufacturing Company and expressed their displeasure by offering "Three Cheers for the Rockfish Factory SLAVES!" The *Observer* reported later that Whig factory owners had told their Democratic employees that if the Democrats won and carried out their promised low-tariff policies, the factories would be forced to close. Thereafter "a proper desire to maintain the Tariff system, with which their Interests are so fully identified, induced many of [the workers] to vote for Clay at this election . . . without regard to former party predilections." The *Observer* also acknowledged the use of colored tickets which made secret balloting impossible. The newspaper declared that the workers in five Whig-owned mills voted Whig, while workers at the single Democratic mill voted Democratic as usual.[7]

The *North Carolinian* denounced the owners' actions. "It is illiberal—

6. Olmsted, *Seaboard Slave States*, I, 397.
7. Fayetteville *Observer*, November 6, 1844.

anti-republican—and unchristian-like, for men to use such means in electioneering," the editor asserted. Other Democrats blamed the defecting workers more than the dictatorial employers, and on the whole, the Democrats failed to defend the rights of these new actors in county politics. Campaign literature mocked "Factory Vagabonds" and one speaker had assured an audience "that he would rather see a child of his go to the grave, than to work in a Factory." The *Observer* rebutted these aspersions with an argument for the freedom of wage laborers that was typical of the defenders of early industrial capitalism.

> Why should a man, woman or child, remain at work in the Factories? Locofocism would fain persuade them all that they are horridly oppressed by these establishments. . . . They are free people,—free to go where they choose, and to labor at any vocation that may suit them. Surely if they are insulted, or oppressed by the proprietors, they ought not and would not remain. If they could earn more at any other work, they would not remain. . . . They have sense enough to see their own interest, and it is a gross insult to them, to tell them that they submit to be "dictated to," "brow-beat," "forced to vote," "dragged up in chains," "carried like sheep to the shambles," that they are "Factory Slaves," "Factory Vagabonds," and other such expressions used towards them by the leading Locofocos.[8]

It is hard to know what the workers themselves thought of this incident. Perhaps they followed their employers from honest conviction, but Democratic charges that the employers' statements were interpreted as threats of possible discharge ring true. If the workers responded unwillingly to employers' coercion, they may not have been willing to admit their loss of freedom to Democrats who still exercised free suffrage. Edward J. Hale, the editor of the *Observer*, appealed to the workers' manhood and predicted that "as long as [the charges] are remembered, they will prevent every man who has the spirit of a man, from voting with those who dare insult and abuse them." Some workers may have accepted the notion that the Democratic charges were more offensive to workers than to the employers. Thus, the Whig editor recounted that "we had to interfere to prevent the infliction of a drubbing on a Locofoco who had told one of these factory *Slaves* that he was compelled to vote for Clay."[9] Hale was grinding his own axe by reporting the incident, but it was not altogether unlikely that a mill worker would use violence to defend his reputation against the charge of weakness, dependency, and vulnerability to outside control, or in short, slavishness.

8. *Ibid.*, November 13, 1844.
9. *Ibid.*, November 6, 1844.

If the averted fistfight was typical of political culture in the second party system, the incident symbolized a subtle shift in the political life of the community. Although the county's economy and society had continued to evolve in new directions, political development had reached a plateau. The workers, the employers, and the party press all expressed in one way or another a republican ideal that had taken root in a society of independent yeoman farmers. The ideal did not quite fit the circumstances of early factory life, and the political system did not continue to change to meet the needs of cotton mill workers more directly and more explicitly. Neither political party made an effective defense of the workers' right to vote without coercion, nor did they address the questions of wages, hours, and working conditions which typically affect a first-generation factory work force.[10]

A lull in the pace of political change may have resulted from the anomalous position of Fayetteville's factories in the antebellum South. More likely it was part of a general American reluctance to stretch the republican doctrines of equal rights to meet the conditions of a new economy. In his report on his visit to a Fayetteville mill, moreover, Frederick Law Olmsted hinted that these workers faced a special inhibition to further political change. According to Olmsted, "a young man, employed in this factory, to whom the proprietor, having told me he was more intelligent and trustworthy than most of his class, had introduced me, finding that I was from the North voluntarily told me that Slavery was a great weight upon poor people here, and he wished that he lived in a Free State." [11] Olmsted was looking for such sentiments and his disclaimer of having elicited the comment is subject to some doubt, but he probably did not invent the incident altogether. It is not clear how many potential leaders of the poor disliked the influence of slavery, but Olmsted reported hearing similar comments throughout the South. Some planters opposed the introduction of cotton mills precisely because they feared that free soil ideology would spread among the operatives.[12] Some of the "Factory Slaves" may indeed have questioned the institution which conferred a disproportionate amount of power on selected individuals in a supposedly equal community of free whites. Hinton Rowan Helper was one young North Carolinian of the antebellum generation who developed a hatred of slaveholders, and there may have been others. Helper's personal experience proved the dangers of expressing such opinions, and the social pressures of white society militated overwhelmingly against their widespread dissemination or accep-

---

10. For a sensitive discussion of the possibilities and limitations of political action based on the doctrine of equal rights, see Alan Dawley, *Class and Community: The Industrial Revolution in Lynn* (Cambridge, Mass., 1976), 66–72, 220–41.

11. Olmsted, *Seaboard Slave States*, I, 397.

12. Genovese, *The Political Economy of Slavery*, 231–35.

tance.[13] If the mill workers were secretly receptive to ideas like Helper's, they found no vehicle for them in the second party system.

Other economic changes in the county took place in the context of political stability. The men of Neill's Creek continued to support the party of Old Hickory as they had done in 1824, regardless of their newfound interest in internal improvements. One month before they submitted their petition, Neill's Creek voters had given Louis D. Henry 92 votes in the gubernatorial election and only 11 votes to his Whig opponent, John M. Morehead. Two years later, the district supported the Democratic nominee for governor by 121 votes to 9 and the district's party loyalty did not waver in the years to come.[14] Regardless of shifts in opinion on certain issues, the spasm of institutional change had passed, and the dynamic period of party formation gave way to a period of party routine.

John C. Latta, a small merchant and diehard Whig, caught the prevailing mood well in a letter to his kinsman in Guilford County. "As to politicks," he remarked in 1843, "tho we have a contest [for Congress] . . . it seems to excite but little interest. Men in this section seem to have become tired of so much political controversy and are settling down into a calm quiet state of things." Two years later, Latta repeated his impressions. "Politicks has pretty much died away," he wrote. "The all absorbing matter with us here now is what can be done for the improvement of our Town—our trade has dwindled down very much to what it was in former years."[15]

Citizens did not lose all political interest in these years, although their participation in elections did drop slightly from the peak reached in 1840. It appears instead that they settled for a division of labor, and relegated day-to-day political action to the concern of specialists like editors and officeholders. After the political upheaval of the 1830s, these men made no attempt to change the basic institutions of politics or party identity, but stood by the proven formulae of the past. Year after year, each party harped on the same

13. Helper, the son of a small farmer in western North Carolina, lived in New York City and California as a youth. Although he was a virulent racist, Helper became convinced that slavery inhibited democracy and economic progress in the South and especially damaged the interests of nonslaveholders. In 1857 he published *The Impending Crisis of the South: How to Meet It*, a book which excoriated the economic effects of slavery and demanded emancipation for the sake of the nonslaveholding whites. *The Impending Crisis* was taken up as campaign literature by the Republican party and distributors of the book in the South faced prosecution for inciting slave unrest. Hinton R. Helper, *The Impending Crisis of the South: How to Meet It* (New York, 1857); Hugh C. Bailey, *Hinton Rowan Helper: Abolitionist-Racist* (University, Ala., 1965), 5–6, 57–59.
14. Fayetteville *Observer*, August 10, 1842, August 6, 1844.
15. John C. Latta to Robert C. Caldwell, June 29, 1843, February 17, 1845, both in Caldwell Papers.

set of issues in its rhetorical appeals. With minor exceptions, the men who led each party in the mid-1830s remained at the helm in the next decade. In every election, the voters in each precinct acted almost exactly as their predecessors had earlier. Political stability in Cumberland County was composed of these interlocking continuities in rhetoric, leadership, and voting behavior.[16]

The rhetoric of the two parties persistently focused on the national bank, the issue that originally divided them. Cumberland orators were not unlike national politicians in this regard. With no evident sense of anachronism, the Democratic editor could still maintain, ten years after deposit removal, that "the Democratic party are opposed to a United States Bank, the whig party are in favor; this is at present the *great question* at issue between the parties."[17] Indeed, long after Nicholas Biddle was dead and buried, and his Monster Bank had closed its doors forever, Cumberland politicians were still finding the currency question a familiar and comfortable stick to beat the opposition with. In 1842, for example, the Whig and Democratic nominees for governor debated before a large crowd in the Fayetteville town hall. "The burden of Mr. Henry's [the Democrat's] song was, the glory of Gen. Jackson's services, and a denunciation of Banks, of all sorts, State and National," the *Observer* reported later. "The Banks, Mr. Henry said, were corrupt; they were 'manufactures of rogues and swindlers,' they were rotten; political machines; lending their money to effect political ends; he himself had 'fallen among thieves' in having anything to do with them." Mr. Morehead, the Whig, replied by reminding the crowd that Henry had been a bank director himself and a bank attorney. "Strike down the banks," said Morehead, "and the creditors would swallow up the means of the debtors."[18]

Two years later, both parties returned to the theme in their official state platforms. Earlier, the *Observer* had abandoned the idea of a national bank as too unpopular. The Whig state convention of December, 1843, however, called explicitly for a national bank as "a convenient, proper, and necessary instrument" for regulating the currency and handling the revenue. The Democrats promptly responded in their own convention by labeling a national

16. William N. Chambers has also described a lull in political development after 1840 in "Party Development and the American Mainstream," in Chambers and Burnham (eds.), *The American Party Systems*, 21–23. In his study of the second party system in New York, Lee Benson likewise found that "group voting patterns crystalized in 1844." Benson, *The Concept of Jacksonian Democracy*, 123.

17. Fayetteville *North Carolinian*, July 29, 1843. "On a tour through northern Pennsylvania Buchanan tried countering the dangerous tariff issue by fulminating against the long dead national bank. This issue produced such a fine response that anti-Bankism became the staple of Democratic oratory in 1844." Charles Sellers, *James K. Polk, Continentalist, 1843–1846* (Princeton, 1966), 122.

18. Fayetteville *Observer*, June 8, 1842, June 15, 1842.

bank unconstitutional, "uncalled for . . . unnecessary, detrimental to our best interests, and dangerous to the liberties of the country." [19] That spring, the two gubernatorial candidates again met in Fayetteville, and each upheld his party's platform. The Democrat "was opposed to the Bank in all forms. . . . He would not give a straw for the liberties of the country if the whole money power were thus consolidated." The Whig, on the other hand, was in favor of "a National Bank, properly guarded. . . . A well-regulated credit system," he declared, "is as indispensable to the people as a supply of blood from the heart." [20] Fascination with banking continued to the end of the decade. In 1846, a Democratic candidate complained vehemently of the "hundreds . . . [of] instances in which paper money had turned to trash in the hands of the people." Later in the campaign, his Whig opponent defended paper money and the sound banks which issued it as the only purveyors of high wages and high commodity prices. [21] In the last presidential election of the 1840s, the Whig candidate for elector "still advocated a U.S. Bank." The Democrats were also still as firm as ever in 1848. "Major Jno. T. Gilmore," the *North Carolinian* reported, "is always ready, and walks into facts and figures without fear. [He] touched upon the U.S. Bank question, the subtreasury, the tariff, the war, and the acquisition of territory." [22] After so many years, new questions had begun to intrude in the debate, but still no partisan speech was complete that did not reaffirm the old familiar issues.

The questions of the protective tariff, federal aid to internal improvements, and distribution of the proceeds of the sale of public lands were all familiar companion pieces to the question of banking and currency. A Democratic district convention tied both protection and internal improvements to the bank question in 1840 and to the explosive subject of abolition: "Resolved, That we are in favor of the reelection of Martin Van Buren, because we believe, that in sentiment he is of the Jeffersonian Republican school; because he is opposed to systems of Internal Improvement by the General Government; because he is opposed to a Tariff of protection . . . and last though far from being the least, because on account of his solemn pledges to veto any movement of the Abolition party." [23] In 1843, the *North Carolinian* charged that Whigs showed zeal for Henry Clay solely from self-interest, those interests being "a National Bank . . . a Protective Tariff . . . a Distribution . . . [and] an assumption of the State debts." In 1845, a Democratic aspirant to Congress based the announcement of his candidacy on the same themes. "He ex-

19. *Ibid.*, December 13, 1843; Fayetteville *North Carolinian*, December 23, 1843.
20. Fayetteville *Observer*, May 29, 1844.
21. Fayetteville *North Carolinian*, April 18, 1846, June 13, 1846.
22. *Ibid.*, September 9, 1848, October 7, 1848.
23. *Ibid.*, April 4, 1840.

pressed his opposition to a protective tariff . . . [to] a distribution of the proceeds of the public lands, [and] to a U.S. Bank." [24] The linkage of this cluster of topics by the Democrats continued through 1848.

For their part, the Whigs generally defended the same set of issues. [25] There was nothing surprising about Whig support for banks, internal improvements, and distribution. Local support for a protective tariff, however, was a marked reverse from an older consensus in the county. Local opposition to the tariff was long-standing, even among businessmen. Edward J. Hale had advocated secession as a last resort if the North insisted on a tariff of protection. [26] When he was older, however, Hale gladly praised the Whigs because "they are in favor of encouraging the mechanics and laborers of our own country in preference to those of Europe." Whigs began vocal support of protection in 1842, when their gubernatorial candidate defended retaliatory duties against the imports of protected foreign nations. In 1843, the Whig state convention took the same position and added "that in adjusting these duties, such a discrimination ought to prevail as will . . . incidentally afford just protection to American industry." Having broached the topic, Whigs at both state and local levels continued to support incidental protection for the rest of the decade. [27]

An additional topic in the Whig anthology of issues was the alleged abuse of power by the president. Executive usurpation, proscription, and corruption appeared in Whig criticisms of Democrats from 1834 onwards. In 1837, the *Observer* declared it the Whig purpose "to oust the corrupt crew who have so long had possession and fattened upon the 'spoils of victory;' . . . who have set themselves up above the Legislative and Judicial departments of the government; whose doctrines and practices are as thoroughly monarchical and tyranical, as any advanced or acted upon in any of the despotisms of the old world." [28] Eleven years later, Hale was still sounding the same note of moral superiority. The election of Zachary Taylor, he said, was a "great victory over all the arts and appliances of the Office Holders, who have boldly entered the field in the struggle to maintain their hold on the Spoils." Taylor won, Hale said, because some Democrats had finally seen the light: "We honor them for their voluntary aid. They saw the Executive usurping the rights of the People, and concentrating all power in the hands of one man. . . . They saw corrup-

24. *Ibid.*, November 11, 1843, June 7, 1845.
25. See "The Whig Creed," Fayetteville *Observer*, April 24, 1844 and succeeding issues to the November election. See also Fayetteville *Observer*, May 18, 1839, January 15, 1840, April 13, 1842, February 3, 1846, February 29, 1848, September 26, 1848.
26. Edward J. Hale to Willie P. Mangum, January 30, 1833, in Shanks (ed.) *Mangum Papers*, II, 15.
27. Fayetteville *Observer*, September 26, 1848, June 15, 1842, December 13, 1843, February 3, 1846, February 29, 1848.
28. *Ibid.*, November 14, 1848.

tion stalk abroad in the land, without even an effort to hide its hideous face. They saw all this and nobly rushed to the rescue." [29] By recurring to the theme of executive corruption, the Whig party kept contact with its roots in the struggle against Jackson. The Democrats met the accusations of corruption with denials. As a nostalgic tie to the past, however, the issue of abuse of power had no exact counterpart, unless it was the memory of Old Hickory himself.

The defense of slavery was one item from the catalogue of conventional issues which underwent significant alteration in the 1840s. The two parties had reasons to agree and also reasons to disagree over slavery, and a variety of circumstances dictated whether amity or conflict would predominate at any given time. Both parties supported the institution without reservation, so on substantive matters, there were minimal grounds for debate. As before, however, editors and politicians were tempted to accuse each other of insufficient proslavery zeal or to suggest that antislavery elements had contaminated the northern wing of the opposite party. In the early 1840s, circumstances encouraged them to resist that temptation, especially around election time. Later in the decade, intense agitation of the issue became unavoidable if not entirely welcome in political debates. The contrasting treatment of slavery in the presidential elections of 1844 and 1848 illustrates how partisan use of the issue could change.

In early January of 1844, the Fayetteville *Observer* reported that Congressman John Quincy Adams of Massachusetts had submitted to the House of Representatives certain resolutions passed by the Massachusetts legislature which called for an end to the allocation of seats in the House of Representatives on the basis of a state's free population plus three-fifths of its slave population. Southerners regarded the preservation of the three-fifths principle as a vital sectional interest. Editor Hale accordingly seized the opportunity for partisan advantage and trumpeted that Adams' resolutions "WERE PASSED BY A LOCOFOCO LEGISLATURE OF MASSACHUSETTS, and by their order sent to Mr. Adams for the express purpose of being laid before Congress!" William H. Bayne of the *North Carolinian* refused to accept Hale's version of the story and began a correspondence to discover the facts. In the meantime, he retaliated by reviving an old remark of Ohio's abolitionist congressman, Joshua Giddings, who had urged Liberty party supporters to vote Whig on the grounds, as Bayne put it, that "WHIGS WERE DOING MORE FOR THE ABOLITION OF SLAVERY THAN LIBERTY MEN WERE." [30] This was a typical example of how party rivalry kept the slavery issue before the public and stimulated popular fears of northern hostility to southern interests.

29. *Ibid.*
30. Fayetteville *Observer*, January 3, 1844; Fayetteville *North Carolinian*, January 20, 1844.

By the time a full account of the Massachusetts resolutions trickled southwards, the details were flattering to neither party, for the resolutions had been passed twice by two successive assemblies. The *Observer* summarized the situation succinctly. "The Locofocos can make no capital out of these Massachusetts resolutions, except by falsehood or suppression of the truth," Hale concluded. "They were first presented to a Locofoco legislature by a Whig, and passed unanimously. They were next presented to a Whig legislature by a Locofoco, and again passed unanimously." Under the circumstances, each pot could only call the kettle black. "This shows," Hale snorted, "with what impudent mendacity it is that Southern Locofoco prints pretend that Northern Locofocos are the 'natural friends' of the South." William Bayne of the *North Carolinian* pointed out that the Hartford Convention had passed an identical resolution and declared that "it shews too plainly that Northern whiggery of 1843 is synonimous with Northern federalism in 1815. Would it were not so."[31]

If the origins of this editorial quarrel typified the ease with which slavery entered the partisan debate, the standoff which ended it demonstrated the difficulty which the parties faced in actually putting the issue to good use. As Hale and Bayne both admitted, the northern wings of both parties were somewhat tainted with antislavery sentiment. When all was said and done, moreover, the southern wings of both parties were equally proslavery in principle, although they disagreed on the best means to protect the institution over the long run. Swapping charges on the slavery issue might serve to keep partisan excitement alive between elections, but to summon the voters to the polls most effectively, political spokesmen had to emphasize the differences between the parties, not their similarities. So while slavery remained a highly sensitive issue, the white community's underlying solidarity on the subject stood in the way of its effective exploitation by political ideologues in the early years of the second party system.

Fayetteville editors diverted their readers with tales of abolitionists among the northern opposition in the winter of 1844, but when the summer and fall elections approached, the squabble over slavery subsided and the old party landmarks reemerged. The tariff was the principal issue in that election, and the *North Carolinian* and the *Observer* devoted long columns to the analysis of its merits and defects, and more especially, to the inconsistencies on the subject which were preached by the opposite side. In May, the two party candidates for governor began their canvass of the state at Fayetteville and spoke for one five-and-a-half-hour stretch at the Market House. They discussed distribution, the tariff, the banking system, and Texas annexation, but not slavery. Three months later, when the two candidates for presidential elector met

31. Fayetteville *Observer*, February 7, 1844; Fayetteville *North Carolinian*, February 17, 1844.

for their quadrennial debate, the subject of abolition did not come up. According to the *North Carolinian*, the Whig candidate began the encounter, and "proceeded to discuss, or, rather, detain his audience with incoherrent remarks about a United States Bank—the Tariff—the distribution—Veto Power and Texas." The latter topic had profound implications for the future of slavery, but if these were discussed explicitly, the newspaper did not mention it. Instead, the Democratic speaker replied briefly to the issues raised by the Whig and kept silent about slavery itself.[32]

In the final weeks before the elections, even economic details dropped away, and editors appealed only to the sentiments of party loyalty and the memories of electoral battles long past. "Democrats of Cumberland!" cried the *North Carolinian*. "The first Thursday in August is approaching! On that day you will have presented, once more, an opportunity of evincing to the world your consistent and steadfast adherence to the principles long cherished and ever dear to Americans . . . . Watch for the enemy—believe none of his stories—*remember the tricks of* 1840. Let every man who regards his country—who feels a deep concern for the perpetuity of our free institutions—who cherishes the good republican principles of the patriotic Jefferson and Jackson, once more go to the polls and vote to save that country, those institutions, and those principles." The tone of the *Observer* was the same. In late October, Hale addressed his more distant readers across the state for the last time before the presidential election. He identified respect for the Constitution and the laws as the fundamental principle of the Whig party and its basic point of difference with the Democrats. "Upon the present election," he warned, "will probably depend, for many years, the prosperity of the country, and for all time, the maintenance of the Constitution and the Laws. Come forward, then, all who feel an interest in good government, and common honesty in public and private affairs, and do your duty, and your whole duty."[33] Neither editor made the slavery issue itself the center of local political debate during the 1844 election campaign.

Four years later, the issue of slavery could not be kept out of county politics. By 1848, the Mexican War had been fought and won, immense territories had been added in the West, and the Wilmot Proviso had thrown open the explosive question of slavery in the territories. Whigs and Democrats in Cumberland kept the old issues before the electorate, but no party rally was complete without a searching examination of the opposing party's stance on the slavery expansion issue and a defense of the sponsoring party's proslavery credentials. Internal differences of opinion and crosscutting sectional alliances frequently made these partisan attacks and defenses very difficult ma-

---

32. Fayetteville *Observer*, May 29, 1844; Fayetteville *North Carolinian*, September 7, 1844.
33. Fayetteville *North Carolinian*, July 20, 1844; Fayetteville *Observer*, October 23, 1844.

neuvers to execute. Col. Samuel J. Person of Moore County, the Democratic candidate for presidential elector, actually urged moderation on the slavery expansion issue. A hostile account in the *Observer* reported that "Col. Person says 'that the South is too violent in its opposition to the Wilmot Proviso! That we ought to be kind, and appeal to the fraternal feeling of our Northern fellow citizens; that if WE continue to be so violent and intemperate, we shall arouse the angry feelings of the North, but that if we abandon the hostile position we have assumed, and trust to their friendship, that they are men like ourselves, and will do us justice.'" Three weeks later, one speaker at a local Democratic rally called for reliance on the North and for the election of Gen. Lewis Cass of Michigan as president, on the grounds "that if ever the Missouri compromise was to be secured to the south, it must be done by a northern man."[34]

These and other Democratic excuses for the northern wing of their party met the scathing reply from Edward J. Hale that "the South has been forbearing and patient to a fault." Nevertheless, Whigs faced the disadvantage that North Carolina Whig Senator George E. Badger had been one of the few southern congressmen to vote against a territorial bill which omitted the Wilmot Proviso and would have left the question of slavery in the newly acquired territories to the federal courts. Badger explained on the stump that the courts would inevitably rule against the South on this question and therefore could not be trusted, though he opened himself to Democratic charges that he was a very poor southern advocate if he believed "that we of the south have no rights." Whigs were also saddled with a vice presidential candidate, Millard Fillmore of New York, whose views on slavery were suspect. Former Congressman Edmund Deberry reassured his fellow Whigs that "of his personal knowledge, he knew him [Fillmore] to be entirely free from any taint of abolitionism and altogether as sound on that subject as any Northern man within his knowledge."[35] The latter description must have sounded like rather faint praise in 1848, but both parties found their northern associates increasingly difficult to defend as the sectional crisis worsened.

The slavery issue was no party humbug, for it was central to all southern interests and convictions, and the parties had been dedicated to its preservation from their beginnings. Insofar as structural weaknesses of the slave-based economy may have intensified the regional controversy over state aid to economic development, it could be argued that the need to shore up the economic viability of slavery had lain beneath the drive to create a party system in the first place. When they discussed the subject explicitly, each party in-

34. Fayetteville *Observer*, September 12, 1848; Fayetteville *North Carolinian*, October 7, 1848.
35. Fayetteville *Observer*, September 12, 1848, October 24, 1848; Fayetteville *North Carolinian*, October 28, 1848.

sisted that its own economic policies provided the safest guarantees for the future of slave society. Democrats maintained that a geographically expanding and agriculturally based society would best protect the interests of slaveholders and nonslaveholders alike, while Whigs expected that a developed and diversified regional economy would diminish southern dependence on the North and protect the South from all outside interference. The issue of slavery was highly charged emotionally, and it remained available as a potent political weapon.

While the defense of slavery was implicit in each party's program, prolonged popular agitation of the slavery controversy was not conducive to the normal operation of the party system in Cumberland County. A popular orator could attract much attention by decrying abolition in the enemy's camp, but experience proved that he who did so could easily be hoist by his own petard. Politicians who fell into this trap made their own party look indistinguishable from the competition, thereby vitiating their own followers' enthusiasm and defeating their original purpose. The older economic controversies held no such disabilities, but stirred up sharp contrasting images of style and substance and aroused the fiercest party loyalties. Consequently, these issues were preferred under ordinary circumstances. Many North Carolina Whigs, Edward J. Hale among them, had opposed the Mexican War precisely because they feared it would arouse a controversy over slavery which could do their party no good and which might dissolve the Union. The future proved them right. Even as late as 1858, when slavery had engulfed national politics, the *North Carolinian* mourned that recent elections had not "turned on some great political question, as for instance, the Tariff, the United States Bank, the Sub Treasury, or even the Distribution of the Proceeds of the public lands . . . or any other question upon which two great political parties might differ, and still claim for themselves a willingness and an ability to guard, protect, and defend from wrong, every interest, and every section." [36] In Cumberland County, attacks on the proslavery soundness of the opposing party were not a regular feature of published electioneering rhetoric in the early 1840s and entered local debates only after national events made further silence impossible.

As the Whigs and the Democrats consolidated positions on the Bank and the tariff and the other components of their platforms, two other themes which had been present in older political rhetoric quietly dropped from view. The first of these was the connection that the earlier parties had made between local and national issues. Both parties continued to appeal to different seg-

---

36. Fayetteville *Observer*, February 29, 1848, September 12, 1848; Fayetteville *North Carolinian*, October 23, 1858. The overall development of the slavery issue in southern politics has been carefully explored in Cooper, *The South and the Politics of Slavery*; Thornton, *Politics and Power in a Slave Society*; and Michael F. Holt, *The Political Crisis of the 1850s* (New York, 1978).

ments of county society. It became unnecessary, however, for the parties to discuss immediate local problems for the voters to understand these social divisions in larger national terms. What remained of local references were changed from radical conflicts of principle to milder differences of emphasis. In 1844, for example, both party papers favored a turnpike from Fayetteville to the west. The *Observer* regretted the legislature's inattention to state improvement "while our people are moving away, and the *grass is growing in the principal streets of our towns*, and the roads of the state are becoming impassable [emphasis added]." The *North Carolinian*, by contrast, declared that "*the first duty of a wise and good government is to make good roads—and thus foster its* agricultural interest." [37] Urban and rural orientation appeared only in the contrasting reasons the editors gave for supporting the same turnpike. Other differences between Whigs and Democrats over local issues in the period were of the same character. The exploitation of local controversies had been a temporary agency that fostered national loyalties.

Antiparty values also lost much of their former power. Citizens who found the notion of strict party regularity distasteful always felt more comfortable among the Whigs than the Democrats, but no self-conscious party leader could persist in the extreme antipartyism of the early republic. Both Whigs and Democrats eventually called for support explicitly on the grounds of party loyalty, and the superiority of the party's interests to the preferences of individual members. In 1840, Hale demanded that North Carolina Whigs abandon their favorite, Henry Clay, and accept William Henry Harrison, the nominee of the 1839 national convention: "The Whigs, *as a party*, pledged themselves to abide by the decision of a National Convention comprised of delegates chosen by themselves. That Convention has made its decision; its fiat has been promulgated to the country as the will of *the party*, and as such, let all hail and support it." [38]

The *North Carolinian* used an identical justification in a similar situation six years later. The editor was trying to summon support for a locally unpopular nominee for governor: "It remains now for the democratic party in North Carolina, to throw aside every feeling of disappointment, and to unite their strength, upon the man who stands forth before them as the *democratic candidate*, made so by an authority which the democratic party itself created. . . . We therefore look upon it as the duty of every democrat, to vote for Mr. Shepard for Governor of North Carolina." [39]

Antipower values and the disdain for expediency declined along with anti-

37. Fayetteville *Observer*, September 4, 1844; Fayetteville *North Carolinian*, September 7, 1844.
38. Fayetteville *Observer*, January 22, 1840.
39. Fayetteville *North Carolinian*, July 18, 1846.

partyism, as the Whigs demanded that the president offer to Congress "some specific plan for the relief of the country from the great distresses" brought on by the Panic of 1837. The Democrats deplored the proposed Whig remedies for the depression, but they did not hesitate to advance their own alternatives.[40] Democratic opposition to the "Mammoth Regulator" might be interpreted as an expression of antipowerism. But the party was not opposed to using state power to accomplish what they thought the Bank of the United States, a private corporation, incapable and unworthy of doing. Specifically, they demanded state laws to compel the banks to pay specie. They also proposed a government agency, the Independent Treasury, to handle the nation's revenues. Neither party passed much legislation to promote positive government, but categorical opposition to such a thing gradually dropped from their platforms.

The principal political values which survived from the prepartisan era to the 1840s were the concentration on national issues and the predilection for personal mudslinging. The former quality was not incompatible with the second party system. On the contrary, preoccupation with national issues was the lifeblood of political parties. Personal abuse survived in a limited form, mostly in a perpetual series of feuds between Edward J. Hale and his Democratic counterpart. A change of Democratic editors brought a brief cessation of hostilities, but Hale never remained on good terms with his rival for very long.[41] Aspirants to office rarely stooped to vilification any longer. Ordinarily, they had no need to. Under the new system, they stood for office as party representatives, and not exclusively on their personal merits. Private reputation was no longer all-important, and wanton defamation of character declined correspondingly.

The positions of Whigs and Democrats on all the rhetorical issues of the second party system grew out of their general stands on commerce and urban versus rural orientation. Whether they were merchants or planters, Whig spokesmen praised an expanding capitalist economy, and they hoped to concentrate more and more of the nation's business in the markets of towns like

---

40. Fayetteville *Observer*, September 13, 1837; Fayetteville *North Carolinian*, May 11, 1839, May 16, 1840.

41. When H. L. Holmes began to publish the *North Carolinian* in March, 1839, he sought Hale's good will by saying, "We cheerfully and earnestly recommend to our political friends to take his paper, and read both sides." Three months later, Hale was routinely referring to Holmes as a "Tory," and Holmes was struggling to retain his composure. "We cannot, and we will not consent," he wrote, "to get into the gutter and throw dirt with the editor of the Whig press in this place." After a year of bickering, Holmes insinuated that Hale showed cowardice in avoiding a duel, while Hale referred to the *Carolinian* as "that wretched compound of stupidity and falsehood." Such exchanges were typical in Hale's relations with the Democratic press. Fayetteville *North Carolinian*, March 9, 1839, June 8, 1839, April 18, 1840; Fayetteville *Observer*, June 6, 1839, April 22, 1840.

Fayetteville. Equally interested in success, the Democrats nevertheless feared the consequences to rural society and values if the center of society was displaced from the country to the town. As the Democratic editor explained in 1845, the ideological controversy between the parties was epitomized by their contrasting reactions to a very common phrase, "the credit system." "Ever since we knew anything about the democratic party," William H. Bayne declared, "they have been battling against the credit system, as conducted by the federal party, with its Banks and brokers and like concomitants, while the federal party have invariably maintained that the credit system was the only system upon which business could be done in this extended country; that to curtail the credit system would ruin the 'dear people,' of whose interests whiggery pretends to be tenacious." [42]

The editor's analysis was correct. The Whigs favored *credit*, that is, a concept of value based on abstractions, contracts, and banks. They favored an economic *system* that would involve intimately the shops and farms of Cumberland with operations and conditions all over the country and all over the western world. The Democrats showed fear of both these concepts. Their constituency believed in concrete values, in property that could be held in the hand or plowed with a team, and which always carried a constant value in gold. They enjoyed the prosperity that access to export markets gave them, but they feared too deep an entanglement with foreign economies. Ultimately, they feared the greed and unchecked growth to which the system pandered. Their suspicion of credit was not based on hostility to paper money per se, nor simply on its threat to their self-interest, but on their fear of its moral consequences. "Encourage that credit system that may be the hand-maid to prudent enterprize and honest industry," wrote "One of the People."

> But away with the present system, the parent of extravagance, of dissipation and wide spread ruin. Give the people gold and silver in their ordinary transactions, and give them a circulating paper currency with a specie basis to facilitate larger commercial transactions. Check the wild propensity to plunge into visionary speculations, and return again to the plain and honest path of Republican simplicity. Our country will then present to the admiring world the spectacle of a happy and contented people. The age of revulsions and panics will pass away, and peace and plenty will smile on her borders. [43]

The mythical agrarian past for which this Democrat sighed did not "return" to Cumberland County. The longing which the writer expressed, however, captured the imaginations of a majority of the county's voters. By using that

42. Fayetteville *North Carolinian*, March 1, 1845.
43. *Ibid.*, April 4, 1840.

longing as the basis of its rhetorical appeal, the Democratic party maintained its majority position for the duration of the second party system.

Not only were the messages of political speaking and writing mostly constant through the 1840s, but the same group of men continued to deliver them. The leaders who had dominated the Whigs and the Democrats in 1836 continued to do so in the next decade. The two parties did not publish comparable membership lists after 1836, so it is impossible to make precise comparisons between the two leadership groups. Reports of party meetings in the press, however, name the men who led each party every year. These lists reveal the durability of the county's political leadership.

Between 1838 and 1848, thirty-four Whigs were mentioned more than five times in the *Observer* in connection with party activities. These individuals were the leadership core of the Whig party. They were called on repeatedly by their fellow Whigs to serve as delegates to state and district conventions, to serve on resolutions committees, and to speak at party rallies. Of the thirty-four, twenty had been active in 1836.[44] Of the fourteen who had not been active, most appear to have been newcomers in the 1840s or previously underage. The concentration of authority was even more striking at the highest levels of the leadership group. The name of Edward J. Hale, for example, appeared nineteen times in party leadership positions between 1838 and 1848. He was a delegate to every district or state convention, and was virtually indispensable as a member of resolutions committees. Archibald A. T. Smith was another popular leader. A lawyer and the county's clerk and master in equity, he was a fixture at every Whig gathering, serving repeatedly as a chairman of meetings, composer of platforms, and delegate to conventions. Dr. Benjamin Robinson, a leader of the Adams, Clay, and White presidential campaigns, was likewise a repeated chairman of meetings in the 1840s. The Whig party leadership was essentially the same group in the mid-1840s as it had been in the mid-1830s. No major defections or accessions occurred to disturb its membership. Under the direction of men like Hale, Smith, and Robinson, the Whigs had become a stable body.

The leadership of the Democratic party showed even less variation than the Whigs. Twenty-five Democrats were mentioned five or more times in the Democratic press between 1838 and 1848. Twenty of these men were also active in 1836.[45] The most active Democrat was Dr. Thomas N. Cameron, a physician in Fayetteville and the brother of John A. Cameron, the former editor. Dr. Cameron was constantly employed as a Democratic chairman, as an author of platforms and as a party delegate. He was usually joined by James

44. Fayetteville *Observer*, 1838–48, *passim*.
45. Fayetteville *North Carolina Journal*, 1838, *passim*; Fayetteville *North Carolinian*, 1839–48, *passim*.

Table 46. Party Leaders by Residence, 1838–1848

	Town Residence	Country Residence	Unknown Residence	Total
Whigs	17	16	1	34
Democrats	11	12	2	25
Total	28	28	3	59

SOURCES: Fayetteville *Observer*, 1838–1848; Fayetteville *North Carolina Journal*, 1838; Fayetteville *North Carolinian*, 1839–1848; Cumberland County Lists of Taxables, 1839–1848, in Cumberland County Records, North Carolina State Archives.

C. Dobbin, a very popular orator, and William H. Bayne, the new editor of the *North Carolinian* and a reliable secretary for party meetings. Former officeholders like Lauchlin Bethune and Archibald McDiarmid also continued in leadership positions. Drift away from Jacksonism never plagued the party after 1834. Like the Whigs, the Democrats had found stability.

The leadership groups of both parties showed mutual differences and similarities. Fayetteville residents were overrepresented in both parties. As table 46 shows, neither party was clearly more urban than the other in residence at the highest levels of leadership. According to table 47, moreover, the leaders of both parties were scattered within a fairly small number of prestigious occupations.[46] But if the material in table 47 is consolidated by counting lawyers, merchants, physicians, and editors as "professionals" and farmers and planters as "agriculturalists," then fifteen Whig leaders would fall in the professional category and thirteen would be agriculturalists. Among Democrats, only eight would be professionals, while twelve would be agriculturalists. In spite of certain similarities between the leadership groups, therefore, Whig leadership tilted towards the town while Democrats inclined towards the country.

The same pattern appeared below the highest levels of party leadership. In 1843, for example, ninety-two persons can be identified as merchants from

46. Knowledge of elite occupations came from a variety of sources. Practicing lawyers' names appeared in the Execution Docket of the county court. Merchants paid annual license fees and their names were entered in the County Court Minutes every September Term. Physicians were identified by their title as "Doctor." Agricultural occupations were inferred from residence and landholding, but the distinction between farmers and planters was arbitrarily based on the number of slave polls declared in the tax lists. Both farming and planting categories probably contain some men whose principal source of income came from sawmills, gristmills, or forest industries, but these could not be isolated from the others. One lawyer and one physician were listed as planters because their great holdings in land and slaves made it difficult to believe that they could have practiced their professions regularly. The men were Benjamin F. Atkins, a Democratic lawyer, and Dr. John McKay, a Whig.

Table 47. Occupations of Party Leaders, 1838–1848

	Lawyers	Merchants & Businessmen	Planters[a]	Farmers[a]	Physicians	Editors	Unknown	Total
Whigs	5	6	8	5	3	1	6	34
Democrats	3	3	9	3	1	1	5	25
Total	8	9	17	8	4	2	11	59

[a] "Planters" were arbitrarily defined as rural landholders who declared ten or more slave polls in 1843. "Farmers" were rural landholders who declared fewer than ten slave polls.

the county license-tax records. Of these, thirty-four were Whigs and seventeen were Democrats, the rest being unknown.[47] Whigs appear to have outnumbered Democrats two to one among all merchants, even though the occupations of the highest Whig leaders do not betray this bias by the same proportion. Whiggery was also more popular among those who were interested in railroads. Internal improvements by the state were supported by both party newspapers in the 1840s, but only the Whigs volunteered in large numbers to serve on prorailroad committees. In August of 1846, nineteen men were chosen to represent Fayetteville at a railroad convention in Cheraw, South Carolina. Twelve were known Whigs and only four were known Democrats. Two months later, a similar convention was held in Fayetteville. Thirty-four of the town's representatives were Whigs, thirteen were Democrats, and four were unknown.[48] While running for the state Senate in 1846, Dr. Cameron probably spoke for his party when he declared "he was a friend to Internal Improvements, but he should vote against the application of a single cent of State funds to any scheme of improvement for any purpose."[49]

The continuity of leadership which both parties achieved was expressed and maintained through a variety of organizational measures. The forms that were established and expanded in 1840 as devices to get out the vote were retained through the decade. The same meetings that served to whip up popular enthusiasm also served to maintain a corps of leaders. Other institutions, especially district and state conventions, served party leadership almost exclusively. District conventions were usually held annually, at varying dates. State conventions were usually held biennially in advance of gubernatorial elections. These conventions nominated candidates for congressman, governor, and presidential elector. The delegates usually passed a set of resolutions to stand as the party's platform, and strengthened measures of party organization. Presumably the leaders also coordinated regional campaign strategy at such meetings.[50]

The Democratic county convention was a third institution for the party leadership. Supporters of conventions hoped that they would unite Democrats behind a regular slate of candidates for the legislature. These hopes

47. "Taxes Collected from Jewelers, Wholesale Retail and Commission Merchants in the County of Cumberland for the year 1843," Cumberland County Court Minutes, September Term, 1843, in Cumberland County Records.
48. Fayetteville *Observer*, August 25, 1846; Fayetteville *North Carolinian*, October 31, 1846.
49. Fayetteville *Observer*, June 9, 1846.
50. For district conventions, see Fayetteville *Observer*, June 12, 1839, July 14, 1839, March 25, 1840, November 15, 1843, May 29, 1844, June 27, 1848; Fayetteville *North Carolinian*, June 22, 1839, April 4, 1840, November 23, 1843, August 3, 1844, April 19, 1845, August 18, 1848. For state conventions, see Fayetteville *North Carolinian* June 6, 1840, June 27, 1840, January 15, 1842, December 23, 1843, March 18, 1848; Fayetteville *Observer*, October 14, 1840, April 13, 1842, April 20, 1842, December 13, 1843, February 29, 1848.

were frustrated. When a convention nominated regular candidates, other Democrats insisted on running against them in the general election. In 1846, quarreling between the friends of the convention slate and an independent candidate was very bitter. The dispute led to a duel in which Archibald McDiarmid lost his life. After this tragedy, the idea of a county convention was abandoned. The Democrats' refusal to accept the discipline of party regularity in legislative elections shows the limits of party development in antebellum Cumberland.[51]

For the most part, the Whigs made no attempt to hold plenary county conventions. Their problems were not to keep candidates from crowding the field, but to recruit candidates who were willing to assume the burden of running for office. After about 1842, Cumberland Whigs became resigned to the fact that their neighbors were incorrigible Democrats. No Whig, however popular as an individual, could ever hope to win a county election. Thereafter, Whig challenges to the Democratic candidates for the legislature were rare. The Whigs reacted with similar apathy in congressional elections of the 1840s, when gerrymandering made their efforts to elect a representative useless. In presidential and gubernatorial elections, Whig votes in Cumberland were as good as votes cast in the staunchest Whig County in the state. In those contests, especially during presidential election years, the Whigs were very well organized in a Tippecanoe Club or the equivalent.[52]

Durable platforms and experienced, well-organized leaders were joined by a loyal electorate as pillars of Cumberland's party system. After 1840, there was virtually nothing about any individual campaign that could deflect the men of Cumberland from their accustomed voting pattern. In every election between 1836 and 1860, the proportion of the vote going to each party was almost always constant. Furthermore, the social base of each party remained constant throughout the 1840s.

51. McDiarmid had figured in an early, prepartisan attempt to limit self-nominations by the action of a convention. This movement was also unsuccessful. See Fayetteville *North Carolina Journal*, April 6, 1831, May 16, 1832, August 22, 1832. For county conventions and other attempts to impose party regularity on the Democrats, see Fayetteville *North Carolina Journal*, March 7, 1838; Fayetteville *North Carolinian*, December 12, 1840, November 13, 1841; Fayetteville *Observer*, August 3, 1842; Fayetteville *North Carolinian*, July 13, 1844, April 8, 1845. For the duel between Archibald McDiarmid and Benjamin F. Atkins, see Fayetteville *North Carolinian*, February 14, 1846; Fayetteville *Observer*, June 9, 1846, July 21, 1846. Democrats in other states were more amenable to party discipline. See Michael Wallace, "Changing Concepts of Party in the United States: New York, 1815–1825," *American Historical Review*, LXXIV (1968), 453–91.

52. The *Observer* mentioned two Whig county conventions, one in 1840 and one in 1844. These gatherings were not much different from ordinary party meetings since there was no effort to guarantee equal representation from every precinct. Fayetteville *Observer*, June 10, 1840, July 10, 1844. For the Tippecanoe Club, see Fayetteville *Observer*, March 25, 1840. For the Clay Club and the Taylor Club, see Fayetteville *Observer*, January 31, 1844, and June 27, 1848.

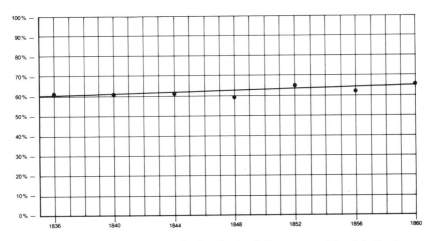

Figure 7. Percent Democratic in Cumberland County presidential elections, 1836–1860, showing the least-squares regression line. Intercept (a) = 54.3; slope (b) = +.15804; significance (p) = .05942

Chart by Richard Volz

SOURCE: Compiled Election Returns, "Presidential," 1836–1860, in Miscellaneous Collections, North Carolina State Archives.

The points in figure 7 represent the percentage of the vote going to Democratic candidates in all presidential elections from 1836 to 1860.[53] The line lying between these points is the unique line that comes closest to all the points simultaneously. It is called the regression line, and it shows both the regularity of Cumberland's vote and the trend of that vote over time. This regression line is very close to the points in figure 7. Evidently, Cumberland voters did not deviate far from their trend between 1836 and 1860. Another way of saying the same thing is that the percent Democratic correlated closely with the passage of time (r = +.6436).

The slight upward slope of the regression line (b = +.15804) suggests a slight drift in the electorate in favor of the Democratic party. The line's slight tilt may also represent random variation in the returns more than any real change in support for the Democrats. The chances are greater than 5 percent that the latter explanation is correct (p = .05942).

The more likely explanation for the slope in figure 7 is that a few more

53. In 1855, northern Cumberland County was split off from the south as Harnett County. The two counties continued to vote together in most elections and to report their votes jointly. Percentages for 1856 and 1860 are based on the sum of votes cast in Harnett County and Cumberland County proper. The percent Democratic in 1860 is based on the sum of votes cast for John C. Breckinridge and Stephen A. Douglas. Douglas, the northern Democrat, received only scattered votes in both counties. Compiled Election Returns, "Presidential Electors," 1856, 1860.

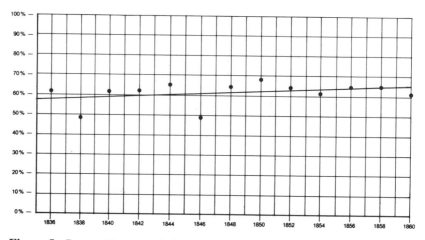

Figure 8. Percent Democratic in Cumberland County gubernatorial elections, 1836–1860, showing the least-squares regression line. Intercept (a) = 48.8; slope (b) = +.3022; significance (p) = .08316

Chart by Richard Volz

SOURCE: Compiled Election Returns, "Gubernatorial," 1836–1860, in Miscellaneous Collections, North Carolina State Archives.

voters in every election preferred the Democrats than had done so in earlier years. This trend was independent of the electioneering practices of any single campaign. Whigs may have had a slight tendency to defect to the Democrats. Young voters of the 1850s may have found the Democratic party more attractive than it had been to their elders. The important feature of this trend was not its cause, but its meagerness. If the trend really existed, it was very slight. For the most part, the Democratic and Whig parties attracted the same proportions of the vote every four years.

Gubernatorial election returns were mostly stable, but they varied more than presidential returns.[54] Figure 8 shows that in 1838 and in 1846, the Democratic percentage deviated so strongly from normal that a Whig carried the county. In each of these elections, however, there was some controversy as to whether the Democratic candidate was in fact the legitimate representative of his party.[55] These controversies resulted in enough Democratic abstentions in Cumberland to give the Whigs a narrow majority. These two exceptionally low percentages in the first ten years of the time series create most of the

54. As in figure 7, the votes of Cumberland and Harnett were summed before calculating these percentages. There was no Whig candidate for governor in 1858, but a Democrat who favored distribution challenged the regular Democratic nominee. The number used in figure 8 was the percentage of votes going to the regular Democrat.
55. See Chapter IV, *n.* 9.

pressure for a positive slope to the line. If the 1838 and 1846 elections were not considered, there would be little or no slope to the line in figure 8. Even so, the variability among the elections is so great that the reported slope ($b = +.3022$) is not significantly different from zero ($p = .08316$). In other words, the apparent drift to the Democrats is less consistent and less convincing among gubernatorial elections than presidential elections. In addition, unique factors, such as an irregular nomination in 1838 or 1846, could have more impact in the state elections than in national ones.

The aggregate returns suggest that Cumberland voters were very faithful to their parties. The precinct returns show that after 1840, each party continued to take its support from the same geographical areas of the county. To the extent that the geographical sections of the county represented social divisions in the electorate, the two parties retained the same social composition throughout the 1840s.

Table 48 contains the correlation coefficients between percents Democratic in the four presidential elections between 1840 and 1852. The correlations are all strongly positive and significant. There is a weaker correlation between the election of 1852 and the elections of 1840 and 1844, indicating some decay in old party loyalties over time. For the most part, however, Cumberland precincts at the end of the 1840s were voting much as they had at the beginning of the decade. The party loyalties formed in the Bank War and the Panic had endured, though the particular events inspiring them had passed.

Table 49 contains similar coefficients for gubernatorial elections. This table shows the same pattern of coherence among elections in the 1840s as table 48. In addition table 49 shows the fluidity of party support in the period

Table 48. Intercorrelations of Percents Democratic Among Twelve Cumberland County Precincts: Presidential Elections 1840–1852

	1840	1844	1848
1844	.7817 (.001)[a]		
1848	.7489 (.003)	.7325 (.002)	
1852	.6531 (.011)	.6776 (.005)	.7357 (.001)

[a] The figure in parentheses below each coefficient is the significance level of that coefficient.
SOURCE: Compiled Election Returns, "Presidential," 1840–1852, in Miscellaneous Collections, North Carolina State Archives.

Table 49. Intercorrelations of Percents Democratic in Gubernatorial Elections, 1836–1848

	1836	1838	1840	1842	1844	1846
1838	.4477 (.072)[a]					
1840	.5306 (.038)	.5024 (.048)				
1842	.4576 (.067)	.5933 (.021)	.8861 (.001)			
1844	.4660 (.063)	.5137 (.044)	.8306 (.001)	.8072 (.001)		
1846	.6948 (.006)	.6265 (.015)	.6728 (.008)	.8592 (.001)	.6640 (.007)	
1848	.5637 (.028)	.6423 (.012)	.7060 (.005)	.8979 (.001)	.8248 (.001)	.9070 (.001)

[a]The figure in parentheses below each coefficient is the significance level of that coefficient.
SOURCE: Compiled Election Returns, "Gubernatorial," 1836–1848, in Miscellaneous Collections, North Carolina State Archives.

before 1840. The correlation between the elections of 1836 and 1838 is not significantly different from zero at the .05 level. Every other pair of adjacent elections shows a strong positive correlation. Voting behavior in these two elections was therefore remarkably dissimilar. Some of this variation must stem from the exceptional character of the 1838 election. The uncertain state of the parties, however, was also responsible. Irregularities in the party identities of the gubernatorial candidates were themselves symptoms of volatile party alignments in the state at large. Within Cumberland County itself, neither party had yet gained a firm hold on the loyalty of many voters. The election returns therefore varied widely between the two years. The elections of 1836 and 1838 correlate better with the elections in the 1840s than they correlate with each other, but these associations were still weak compared to the strong relationships found after 1840. Voting behavior in the 1830s only approximated the pattern of the mature second party system.

When that system became well-established, regularity in governor's elections became even stronger than in presidential elections. Coefficients in the third through sixth columns of table 49 are mostly higher than the correlations between presidential elections in table 48. Disregarding the election of 1846, all but one of the coefficients for the pairs of elections after 1840 exceed .8000. The greater party regularity of gubernatorial voters probably resulted from the fact that they were a more select group than the presidential electorate. Figure 4 showed that turnout for presidential elections far surpassed turnout for the governor's race in the 1840s. The voters who showed up in August were more committed to political participation and less fickle in their opinions than the voters in November. Their record over time was therefore more consistent. The voting regularity which they displayed was the behavioral keystone of the second party system.

During the years that Cumberland County voters developed their routine pattern of partisan political activity, other North Carolina voters were establishing similar structures. As in Fayetteville, scattered local candidates had first used the Whig party label in the August elections of 1834. The following year, avowed Whigs captured seven of the state's thirteen congressional seats. In 1836, Gen. Edward B. Dudley, the Whig candidate, became North Carolina's first popularly-elected governor. His party kept the governor's chair until 1850. Whigs also carried the presidential elections of the 1840s, but after 1850, Democrats became the majority party and continued to dominate the state until the early years of the Civil War.[56]

Within North Carolina, competition between Whigs and Democrats was close and keen. The Whig share of the vote in the gubernatorial elections of the 1840s averaged 53.1 percent statewide. During the years of Democratic victory which followed, that party took 53.8 percent in the average gubernatorial election. When the second party system was in its national heyday from 1836 to 1852, the mean Whig proportion of the vote in presidential elections was a slim 51.5 percent in North Carolina.[57] When the electoral balance swung from the Whigs to the Democrats, the change reflected a relatively small shift in the overall distribution of votes.

As in Cumberland County, moreover, most districts in North Carolina exhibited the same pattern of political preferences year after year. Generally speaking, North Carolina Whigs were strongest where frustration over the lack of economic growth ran the highest. Their votes came largely from the northeastern counties bordering on Albemarle Sound and from a broad band of Piedmont counties arching northwesterly from the fall line to the Blue Ridge. Democrats claimed the plantation counties of the central coastal plain, most of the tobacco-planting districts on the Virginia border, and a cluster of cotton-growing counties in the southwestern Piedmont. This overall distribution of party strength showed very little permanent change before secession. Marc W. Kruman has found that the correlation coefficient between percent Democratic in the 1840 and 1860 gubernatorial elections was a substantial .79. After 1840, the correlation coefficients between all pairs of

56. Kruman, "Parties and Politics in North Carolina," 321.
57. Cheney (ed.), *North Carolina Government*, 1320–22, 1384–89.

gubernatorial elections ranged from .83 to .97. Kruman has also calculated that no more than 5 or 6 percent of the voters ever split their tickets in a state election.[58] The voters of Cumberland County were not unusual in their steady devotion to their chosen parties.

Although the division between Whigs and Democrats in North Carolina was almost even in the aggregate, the same was not true at the local level. Cumberland County kept a very strong preference for the Democrats. In the gubernatorial election of 1836, which was the first statewide contest of the second party system, Democrats took 61.6 percent of Cumberland County's vote. The county was twenty-second out of sixty-three counties in percent Democratic, and kept this general position for the remainder of the antebellum period. Just as Cumberland gave a large, reliable majority to the Democratic party, most other counties supported one party or the other by a relatively lopsided margin. In 1844, for example, the Whig candidate for president, Henry Clay, carried North Carolina by a close margin of 52.4 percent, but most individual counties were much less evenly divided. The typical county gave 68.0 percent of its vote to its favorite candidate. More precisely, an average of 35.9 percentage points in each county separated the winner's proportion of votes from the loser's. In 1844, the winning and losing presidential candidates came within 20 percentage points of each other in only twenty-two counties out of seventy-one in North Carolina. In this context, Cumberland County was more nearly competitive in 1844 than most counties. Clay's opponent, James K. Polk, took 61.0 percent of Cumberland's vote that year and exceeded Clay's fraction by 22.0 percentage points.[59]

The tendency of counties to divide unevenly had important implications for the second party system. The "typical" county was clearly no miniature edition of the state itself, with the same general balance of political or social forces. On the contrary, the pressures for political conformity must have been high in many communities. In the 1844 presidential election, Edgecombe County in the heart of the eastern plantation section gave 1,503 votes to Polk and 126 votes to Clay. The same year, Clay carried Stanly County in a poor and hilly section of the Piedmont by 520 votes to 48. The winner's proportion in each was 92.3 percent and 91.7 percent, respectively. In an even more extreme example, Old Trap precinct in Camden County in the northeast sound region reported 282 votes for Whig John Motley Morehead in 1840 and no votes at all for his Democratic opponent.[60] It is not necessarily true that all

58. Kruman, "Parties and Politics in North Carolina," 30.
59. *Ibid.*, 29; Cheney (ed.), *North Carolina Government*, 1388–89, 1322–23.
60. Cheney (ed.), *North Carolina Government*, 1322–23; New Bern *Spectator*, August 15, 1840.

282 voters in Old Trap had identical incomes, occupations, religions, or other relevant characteristics, or that political unanimity among them was the product of social uniformity. It is quite likely, however, that pressures for community solidarity in that precinct overrode all potential sources of disagreement.

Political homogeneity was not uncommon in the second party system. Commenting on unanimous counties in Alabama, J. Mills Thornton III has concluded that "election returns from those counties . . . can be studied to little purpose by one who seeks to discover the foundations of party division." [61] The problem of unanimous areas has not been fully studied, but one suspects that places such as Edgecombe County, Stanly County, and Old Trap precinct were examples of the rural oligarchies described by Whitman H. Ridgway in which eighteenth-century social relationships persisted well into the nineteenth century. [62] In these counties, a combination of personal, cultural, and material interests guided a unified local elite into one party or another, while the bulk of the citizens deferred to the decision of the notables. In addition, the extreme isolation of poor counties such as Stanly, may have restricted the flow of political information and discouraged the emergence of diverse points of view. Whatever the correct explanation, the presence of many unanimous counties in North Carolina will probably prevent the discovery of a uniformly applicable social demarcation between Whig and Democratic voters.

If party development in these communities depended on elite decisions, then for the most part, the leaders' choices were not capricious or arbitrary, but consistent with an overall pattern. Edgecombe County was surrounded by plantation counties with an almost equally high level of support for Democrats. Other counties in the northeast sound region gave Whig majorities that approached the unanimity of Old Trap precinct. Influences which transcended county lines and the possibly haphazard inclinations of individual elite families usually guided political developments within regions, even when these influences produced the same effect among virtually all varieties of voters.

In his work *The Loyal and the Disloyal*, Morton Grodzins made observations on patriotism which may also help to explain the basis of political party loyalty, both in the unanimous counties and in those which tended to divide their votes. Grodzins suggested that "populations are loyal to nation as a by-product of satisfactions achieved within nonnational groups, because the nation is believed to symbolize and sustain those groups. From this point of view, one is loyal not to nation but to family, business, religion, friends. One fights for the joys of his pinochle club when he is said to fight for his coun-

61. Thornton, *Politics and Power in a Slave Society*, 41.
62. Ridgway, *Community Leadership in Maryland*, 20–43, 127–35.

Table 50. Mean Percent Whig in North Carolina County Seats and Rural Precincts, Gubernatorial Elections, 1836–1842

	1836 N = 33	1838 N = 30	1840 N = 35	1842 N = 33
County seats	59.9	72.5	64.4	59.5
Rural Precincts	53.2	66.7	55.2	48.9
Difference	+6.7	+5.8	+9.2	+10.6

try." [63] It is unlikely that the impressive levels of voter participation and party loyalty described by Walter Dean Burnham could have been achieved in the nineteenth-century United States without the operation of a similar process of identification between citizens and political parties.[64] Presumably, Whigs and Democrats developed loyalty to their respective organizations as the parties came to embody the satisfactions which voters derived from primary groups and communities within their geographical localities. Of necessity, the structure and appeals of the successful political party were mirrors of the values of the primary groups which composed it. Political party conflict, moreover, reflected the rivalries and tensions of the society which supported it. In politically unanimous counties, party development gave the appearance of local solidarity behind community leaders and a spirit of defiance to forces outside the county. In politically divided counties, at least one basis for party competition appeared in the distribution of votes between the various precincts.

A search for precinct-level voting data in North Carolina has produced information for at least one gubernatorial election between 1836 and 1842 for each of fifty-three counties, yielding a sample of thirty to thirty-five counties for each election, not including Cumberland.[65] Table 50 displays the voting

63. Morton Grodzins, *The Loyal and the Disloyal: Social Boundaries of Patriotism and Treason* (Chicago, 1956), 29.

64. Walter Dean Burnham, "The Changing Shape of the American Political Universe," *American Political Science Review*, LIX (1964), 7–28.

65. Full or partial returns were found for the following counties: Anson, Ashe, Beaufort, Bertie, Bladen, Brunswick, Buncombe, Burke, Camden, Caswell, Chatham, Cherokee, Chowan, Columbus, Craven, Davidson, Davie, Edgecombe, Franklin, Gates, Granville, Johnston, Lincoln, Mecklenburg, Montgomery, Moore, Nash, New Hanover, Northampton, Onslow, Orange, Pasquotank, Perquimans, Person, Pitt, Richmond, Robeson, Rockingham, Stanly, Stokes, Tyrell, Wake, Warren, Washington, Wayne, Wilkes, and Yancey. The returns were located under the appropriate years in the "Election Records" file for each county in the County Records Section of the North Carolina State Archives, in the Secretary of State's Papers and the Legislative Papers, also in the North Carolina State Archives, and in the August issues of the following newspapers: Fayetteville *Observer*, Tarboro *Free Press*, Salisbury *Western Carolinian*, Charlotte *Journal*, Raleigh *North Carolina Standard*, Raleigh *Register*, New Bern *Spectator*, and Greensboro *Patriot*.

pattern found in these samples. In each election, the average Whig percentage of the vote in the county seat precincts exceeded the Whig share in rural precincts. Whig strength in the towns grew, moreover, when economic conditions worsened after 1839. By 1842, a large majority of town dwellers were voting Whig while a smaller majority of countrymen were voting Democratic. North Carolina was a rural state, but the villages which served as county seats were the local centers of trade, government, and communication. Whiggery was not a predominately urban phenomenon in these counties, but the party's additional attractiveness to village residents was substantial. A division between rural and village communities was evidently one pattern of primary-group rivalries which was relevant to the shape of the second party system in almost every North Carolina community, regardless of its geographical location or the particular details of the local economy.

Within this context, the experience of Cumberland County seems broadly representative. Like most North Carolina counties, Cumberland's electoral statistics showed a large majority for one of the two parties, but its Democratic fraction was not so large as to exclude Whigs altogether. As in the other counties for which data exist, Whigs were more plentiful in the county seat than outside it. Beneath the statistical details, Cumberland shared a deeper experience with other communities. Over the course of two decades, the citizens had wrestled with the demands and contradictions of an expanding market economy. They had worked out some of their responses privately, outside the political arena, but they had also drawn on republican traditions to defend or assert their visions of the ideal future. In the process, they had formed a set of political parties to express their sense of the struggle between competing ways of life.

Their efforts had climaxed in 1840. Thereafter, the ideas and practices of party government were widely accepted. "The will of the people" had become the acid test of community policy, and however fraudulently it was obtained, popular approval had become the *sine qua non* of American as well as of local politics. Republican political culture had been radically recast since Lafayette's visit, but the 1840s brought no fundamental change to the structure of party government. A cycle of political invention had closed.

IX. Conclusion: Cumberland County and the Second Party System

On December 4, 1860, the citizens of Cumberland County gathered in Farmer's Hall for yet another community ritual. As they had done so many times before, the participants selected a chairman and secretary, appointed a committee to report resolutions, and listened to clamorous rhetoric until the resolutions were complete. Like other such meetings in the antebellum period, this was an attempt to establish and demonstrate popular unity in the face of perceived external attack. Unlike the others, the meeting of December 4 was called to spell out the terms upon which the local citizens would agree to remain part of the United States of America.

A month before, Abraham Lincoln had been elected president. The issue of slavery had swallowed up all others in national politics, and the Republican party had come into power. As Cumberland County interpreted the outcome, "the recent election has resulted in the success of a sectional party whose past history is written in a determined and persistent aggression upon the interests of the South." Following their state constitution's exhortation, the citizens responded to this attack on their interests by another "recurrence to fundamental principles." The "*avowed* policy" of the Republican party, they declared, "is totally inconsistent with the preservation of our most sacred rights obtained by force of arms and solemnly guaranteed to us by a Constitution, binding alike upon the whole country." A secessionist minority thought the election's affront to southern rights so severe that North Carolina should leave the Union forthwith, just as neighboring South Carolina was then doing. The majority of participants rejected this course, and concluded that Lincoln's mere election was no cause to secede, but that "any attempt on his part to carry out the policy of his party will meet with our determined resistance." The majority made it clear that the rights and liberties they regarded as sacred were more precious than the Union itself. "While the Union of these States is dear to us as a heritage bequeathed us by our forefathers," their resolutions insisted, "dear to us by every tie which can bind a people to a government, best for us as a nation, and to mankind as an example, so long as its terms are faithfully adhered to; yet . . . our lives, our liberties, and our honor are dearer to us, and for the preservation of these we must, if the direful necessity be forced upon us, surrender our adherence to it."[1] The citizens' evocation of "our most sacred rights" emphasized that if compelled, they would secede in order to preserve the same republican values for which, as far as they were concerned, the Union had been established in the first place.

Four and a half months later, Fayetteville held a second meeting. News had arrived of Fort Sumter's surrender and of President Lincoln's call for seventy-five thousand volunteers to suppress the rebellion. In the words of the Fayetteville *Observer*, "The President's Proclamation is 'the last feather that breaks the camel's back.'"[2] The community's terms for remaining in the Union had been decisively violated. Fayetteville responded with a renunciation of Jacksonian-era politics and a bitter leave-taking of the old republic.

Mayor Archibald McLean asked five of Fayetteville's most senior and respected citizens to draft the meeting's resolutions. The aging Edward J. Hale acceded to the mayor's request and joined several of his former enemies in a statement that demanded an end to the second party system and rejected the government that the system had sustained. According to Hale, "it was the saddest public duty he was ever called upon to perform." "Resolved by the people of Fayetteville in Town Meeting assembled," the declaration read, "that the exigencies of the times require every loyal son of North Carolina to bury past political animosities, and forgetting past political contests to unite hand and heart in resistance to sectional rule, and to take all proper steps to maintain, secure and defend the rights of North Carolina as one of the Southern States." The citizens asked the governor to summon the General Assembly in emergency session, and to take all necessary steps for the military defense of the state. The next day, they met again and ran up the Confederate flag.[3]

Recent studies of the coming of the Civil War have emphasized that sectional rivalries had done much to create the party system, that the early system had kept sectional rancor in check, and that later partisan contests made sectional hostilities worse. According to Michael F. Holt, "the same reasons that explain why the political system could contain the smoldering sectional conflict for over thirty years before 1854 also explain why, after that date, the political system helped to fan that fire until it exploded into open warfare in

1. Fayetteville *Observer*, December 6, 1860.
2. *Ibid.*, April 18, 1861.
3. *Ibid.*

April 1861."[4] It was somewhat ironic that the citizens of Fayetteville began the Civil War with a disavowal of the parties which had guided them for a generation, but the gesture was appropriate. If the war was somehow the product of the second party system, it was also the system's death knell. The rhetoric and routines of partisanship had done much to drill the citizens in a knowledge of their rights, and this popular knowledge had given power to the politicians' demands for sectional vindication. As party competition had steadily escalated the intensity of sectional rivalries, the issues which the parties had been created specifically to address receded in importance and the agitation of slavery dominated public discourse.

Political participants in Cumberland County signaled their understanding of these changed conditions by numerous calls for an end to party spirit. "We think that partyism is pretty effectually worn out now in this State," declared the editor of the *North Carolinian* when Lincoln was elected. After the Farmer's Hall convention, the *Observer* opined that "the resolutions adopted embody the sentiments of the moderate men of both parties." "We desire to rise above party," vowed the inhabitants of Cedar Creek in January, 1861, "and survey the difficulties which beset us, as Patriots and Freemen." When elections were being held for a possible state convention in February, the *Observer* pronounced that "old party lines are forgotten as if they had never existed." A local convention of seventy-six delegates had nominated three unionist Democrats to represent Cumberland and Harnett counties at the proposed state gathering. According to the *Observer*, "not one of the 27 Whigs present, nor one of their Whig constituents at home, but heartily ignored all party ties in view of this great question, of Union or Disunion, of Peace or Civil War."[5]

Party spirit did not vanish overnight, and old alignments continued to affect North Carolina politics until 1864.[6] The citizens held on to a weakened party loyalty, but retained the political institutions and rhetoric of the second party system, even as the social and political framework of antebellum America disintegrated. The popular structures which had once been used to grapple with the Monster Bank and executive usurpation survived to be turned against Black Republicans and fire-eaters. Meeting in schoolhouses, churches, and stores in every captain's district, lawyers and farmers debated the Union's future in repeated neighborhood meetings, using the phrases and procedures of the old precinct conventions. As they dismantled the nation of Washington, Jefferson, and Lafayette, the citizens drew on the skills they had once learned

4. Holt, *The Political Crisis of the 1850s*, x.
5. Fayetteville *North Carolinian*, November 10, 1860; Fayetteville *Observer*, December 6, 1860, December 10, 1860, December 15, 1860, January 7, 1861, January 17, 1861, February 21, 1861.
6. Kruman, "Parties and Politics in North Carolina," 318–21.

in order to preserve the republic.[7] The legacy of the Age of Jackson was not easily put aside.

How the southern states came to choose secession is a well-known tale as well as a perennially perplexing one. Cumberland County's journey to the end of the Union was as complex a movement as the one already recounted here, and beyond the scope of this book to analyze in detail. The outlines of the story are clear, however. As political spokesmen indicated when they faced the crisis of 1860–1861, secession in the popular mind was a patriotic act that fulfilled the fundamental principles of the Jacksonian era. Whigs and Democrats had organized their parties to defend their rights and the government which embodied them. The succeeding generation of county leaders and voters left the Union for the same purpose. As the North Carolina electorate understood the matter, republicanism could not exist on the basis of coercion, where white men were forced to make war on their kindred, and where slavery faced unbending official hostility. The parties of the Jacksonian era had taught the citizens when and how to break the old republic just as they had also created the classic style, vocabulary, and institutions of American politics. Cumberland County's decision for secession was therefore the consummation of the second party system, the collapse of that system, and a sign of its continuing endurance.[8]

The political party structure which had laid so much of the basis for subsequent American history had originally served to express and to contain a specific set of community conflicts. The Cumberland County parties had grown out of a libertarian cultural heritage, a particular local history, and a pervasive social and economic challenge. The original settlers of colonial Cumberland had created a community which they hoped would be supportive of the families which composed it and would preserve maximum liberty for each individual householder. The American republic was the moral and political safeguard of their aspirations. By the second generation of independence, however, economic stagnation had undermined the blessings of liberty. Had not the Founding Fathers intended that the independent freeholder should enjoy the security of his property and the fruits of his labors? Diminished soil fertility made subsistence farming increasingly difficult, however, and the farmers of Cumberland County faced two ambiguous alternatives. Emigration to rich lands elsewhere was painful and dangerous. Production of exports for purchase by strangers—cotton for England's factories, flour and lumber for her sugar islands, or tar and pitch for her navy—invoked the twin pros-

7. Fayetteville *Observer*, December 3, 1860, December 10, 1860, December 15, 1860, January 7, 1861, January 17, 1861, February 18, 1861.
8. Kruman, "Parties and Politics in North Carolina," 198–245; Holt, *The Political Crisis of the 1850s*, 219–59; Thornton, *Politics and Power in a Slave Society*, 442–61.

pects of handsome profits on the one hand and slavery to banks, panics, and debt on the other.

Unique features of the southern economy made the second alternative especially distasteful to many farmers. In the agrarian slave South, the growth of a modern commercial infrastructure would not come about by the inadvertent operation of impersonal market forces. Even more than in other places, modernization there would be a political decision, undertaken deliberately by an ostensibly democratic state, and enforced by its powers of coercion. Cautious North Carolina farmers feared that state-sponsored modernization would inflate the legitimate powers of government and bankrupt the taxpayer. More fundamentally, banks and internal improvements would reshape rural society to conform more completely to the demands of the urban marketplace, a process which would undermine the moral and social order of the republic. Preservation of the republic and its moral and material blessings would require some painful choices for these citizens.

The existence of African slavery made Cumberland County's dilemma more complicated. If the fundamental question in Jacksonian-era politics was, as Rush Welter has argued, the proper means to preserve republicanism in a changing world, all white southerners firmly agreed that republicanism would not be safe unless slavery were safe as well. The glory of the republic was its ability to objectify the ideals of the white community and to protect the interests of all its members.[9] In a community based on slavery, how could it be republican to attack the interests of slaveholders? And how could there be any genuine American republic which was filled with free Negroes? To the racist mind, the very concept was a revolting contradiction in terms.[10] Every proffered formula for sectional improvement therefore included the implicit assurance that slavery would be strengthened by its enactment.

To strengthen slavery was not a simple business. The peculiar institution was a complex set of economic and political relationships as well as a labor system and a method of racial control. All of its aspects were closely interrelated, so the economic decline of the upper South was much more than a material inconvenience. Potentially, at least, it was a threat to the social position of all slaveholders and a danger to the safety of all whites. Without reaching any final conclusions, contemporaries and subsequent observers have all debated the question of whether the relative poverty which seemed to threaten slave society was in fact a product of the slave system itself. Few antebellum North Carolinians doubted that slavery and progress were compatible, but all

9. Welter, *The Mind of America*, 77–95.
10. George M. Fredrickson, *The Black Image in the White Mind: The Debate on Afro-American Character and Destiny, 1817–1914* (New York, 1971), 130–64.

admitted that some of the cures for the South's ills could be worse than the disease.

Some Old Republican orators had warned against the effects of a more dynamic commercial economy on the stability of the slave regime. More venturesome politicians held that North Carolina had more to fear from continued stagnation. Democrats tended to believe that a geographically expanding and agriculturally based society would best protect the interests of slaveholders and nonslaveholders alike, while modernizing Whigs expected that a developed and diversified regional economy would diminish southern dependence on the North and safeguard the future of southern institutions. Whatever their preferred solution, all realized on some level that the price of a mistake could be a future in which general emancipation would become inevitable. Every American community gambled on the direction of the future by the policies it took towards the Transportation Revolution and the expansion of the market, but for slaveholding localities like Cumberland County, the stakes were much higher than elsewhere.

The slavery issue shaped party formation by giving a special urgency to the economic questions debated by community leaders. During the 1830s in Cumberland County, the most sober political discussions and the most strident demagoguery all concerned themselves directly with the mechanics of political economy and indirectly with the preservation of liberty for whites, but usually not with slavery per se. By and large, the same issues of banks and internal improvements predominated in the election campaigns of the 1840s. The slavery question had intense emotional power, and speakers and audiences were ever sensitive to the institution's special needs, but the community's fundamental solidarity usually made overt discussion of the subject unnecessary. Proslavery bombast was mostly an adjunct to party formation in Cumberland County, not its fundamental cause. Eventually, the pressure of outside events forced some North Carolina politicians into the deadly game of racial one-upmanship which brought the citizens of Fayetteville to their resolutions of April, 1861. This denouement was still remote when the system began, but the slavery issue deeply affected the parties even then.[11]

Determination of Cumberland County's uncertain future was further hampered by the fact that prepartisan political culture prepared the citizens for competition over prestige among local gentry and for rhetorical defenses of republican values, but not for political action on social problems. Ethnic and geographical rivalries, and friction associated with social and economic in-

11. For a somewhat different interpretation of the role of slavery in party formation, see Cooper, *The South and the Politics of Slavery*, 43–97.

equality had affected the political climate since the eighteenth century, even though official values did not recognize the legitimacy of such concerns. A local elite which had not viewed universal suffrage with enthusiasm and which was itself internally divided faced a populace which had sometimes responded to dissident prophets of class-consciousness. It was a situation which would have challenged many American communities on the eve of the Transportation Revolution. If the national structure of presidential elections needed procedural adjustment, the apparatus of state and local government was equally due for an overhaul.[12] The prospect did not bode well for a fully harmonious resolution of a moral and material dilemma.

Political events of the 1820s established the framework within which officeholders would be forced to act. Solutions which mocked "the will of the people" could not hope for success, whereas faithful deference to the forms of popular sovereignty would be a prerequisite for all subsequent electoral victories. Political parties proved to be the means for dealing with the combined exigencies of choosing local officials, sharing in the choice of state and national leaders, and shaping a locality's future. As such, the party system took shape in a series of stages. The first was the clear emergence of county voting blocs based on divisive local issues involving ethnicity, economic development, urban-rural differences, and class tensions within Fayetteville itself. The second was an intellectual effort by party leaders to establish linkages between local and national issues and to create logical and consistent platforms which embodied these connections. This stage was completed when parties emerged in the Fayetteville town elections which sought office on the basis of interrelated local and national issues. The third stage was the extension of these party structures to the political environment of rural Cumberland and the firm establishment of an ongoing party routine. The process was complete by 1840.

As Richard P. McCormick pointed out, political activists took the initiative in party formation, perhaps with no higher goals than the achievement of their private ambitions.[13] But the organizers built parties with the social materials at hand and not from artificial enthusiasms. In some states, these social materials seem to have been ethnic and religious groups. In Cumberland County, party organizers faced a society divided into rival communities by the differential impact of regional decline and the market economy. Rival commercial and anticommercial groups among merchants and planters, small farmers and mechanics, fostered conflicting ideals for the future and for the republic. Appealing to the traditional fears of the abuse of power which were

12. McCormick, *The Second American Party System*, 330–33.
13. *Ibid.*, 351–52.

particular to these various segments of the population, the organizers translated national issues into the language of daily grievance and communal anxiety. In the process, an ancient rupture between Scottish and non-Scottish farmers healed over, and the breach between town and country deepened. The result was a party system which accurately reflected the tensions of local society at a particular historical moment. The Panic of 1837 strengthened the association of parties with the defense of private values and encouraged a new political culture in which party loyalty was no longer treason, nor even a necessary evil, but a positive benefit to the republic.

When seeking the citizens' allegiance, Whigs and Democrats both appealed to the quality of republicanism which diverse voters cherished for the nation and the community character they favored for their own neighborhoods. To this extent, moral and cultural sentiments underlay the second party system, and thus no rigid model of economic determinism can explain how any individual cast his vote. But republican culture for most Whigs depended on progress and banking and state-supported railroads, while a virtuous commonwealth for many Democrats rested on a dream of arcadian self-sufficiency. For both constituencies, desirable moral goals intertwined themselves with specific and mutually exclusive hopes for the future material basis of society. In Cumberland County, the positions of Whigs and Democrats at the beginning of the second party system resembled the shape of political alignments described in other settings by Charles Grier Sellers, Jr., Thomas B. Alexander, James R. Sharp, and J. Mills Thornton III.[14]

For many Democratic leaders, the modern commercial economy was never the unmitigated threat which it seemed to be for some of their followers. When several years had passed and the parties were well established, the hostility of Democratic voters to economic innovation softened. The menace of Fayetteville, banks, and internal improvements was obvious to them under certain conditions, but the blandishments of change were powerful under others. Paradoxically, the conflation of moral and material objectives eventually made it easier to accept the challenge of commercialized production while sustaining the values of an earlier age. The Democrats never discarded the eternal verities, but the party rather carefully enshrined them in its platforms, out of harm's way, while the forces of social change steamed along through daily life. As Marvin Meyers pointed out, when rural values were preserved in Democratic slogans and symbols, it became much easier to seek the rewards of material change with a clear conscience.[15] Likewise, the yeoman

14. Sellers, "Who Were the Southern Whigs?" 346; Alexander, *et al.*, "The Basis of Alabama's Ante-Bellum Two-Party System," 263–66; Sharp, *Jacksonians versus the Banks*, 215–84; Thornton, *Politics and Power in a Slave Society*, 45–57.
15. Meyers, *The Jacksonian Persuasion*, 121–41.

who settled for the symbols of self-sufficiency but not for its substance would be more likely to accept the penalties of a lost commercial gamble with confusion and self-accusation rather than protest. If Fayetteville's Whigs never gained the western railroad, they did obtain other material improvements without violating the expressed will of the people or attempting to impose alien values on an unwilling rural community. The county elite kept its position in a potentially rocky transition, moreover, without suffering the challenges which they had feared at an earlier period. Ingeniously, as it were, the second party system arose from a fundamental social conflict and then side-stepped it.

The example of Cumberland County suggests that the social and economic changes associated with the Transportation Revolution may have had more to do with American political development than historians have recently acknowledged. Though economic upheaval did not impinge directly on the county, it was nevertheless the experience of economic decline and the proposal to remedy it by political means that touched off the county's initial political explosion. When Cumberland voters turned from their neighborhood struggle and looked to Washington, moreover, they saw a repetition of their local drama. For all observers, the Bank War was a political battle to establish certain values by defending or attacking an agency of economic change. Reacting to local and national events, Cumberland County responded with massive political mobilization and the formation of the second American party system. For the most part, a variety of cultural lenses refracted perceptions of those events, but the dynamics of political transformation arose from the world of expanding commercial production.

The conceptions of social causation associated with ethnocultural and Progressive historians are both insufficient to explain the process of political development in Cumberland County. Economic pressures stimulated party development there without producing a system which gathered exploiters under one banner and their victims under another. Instead, rival communities struggled for predominance within the county. Roughly speaking, each arose from a different social framework, each had its own vision of the social future, and each followed its own privileged elite. Cultural conflict between these communities was indeed central to the process of political change, even though religious denominations and ethnic groups had little to do with the lines of battle. The outcome was a political system that preserved the values of one community without completely blocking the material goals of the other.

Cumberland County was not the United States, or even North Carolina, but its history suggests that the impact of a changing economy would have sparked analogous conflicts in a wide variety of contexts. Ethnocultural concerns may have shaped these tensions in some places and the points at issue may have been completely different in others, but not many counties could entirely escape the impact of nationwide social change. Repeated innumerable times, the basic process that evolved in Cumberland County would have furnished the powers of the Industrial Revolution the political assistance they required, and also kept the republic's values and institutions superficially intact. That development would carry the United States from the world of the Founding Fathers to the age of industrial supremacy.

When Cumberland County's parties were established, they normally operated in a framework that was truly a party system. Neither party could define itself in isolation from the other, nor could each act effectively without meaningful competition from the other. Even the humdrum business of nominating and electing local officeholders proceeded most efficiently when minority party opposition forced cooperation and mutual concessions on antagonistic personalities within the majority. The more complex activities of state and national elections and the ideological role of reconciling values and material conditions were even more difficult without credible local competition. Under normal conditions, the elements of the party system interacted smoothly to produce a viable government and an acquiescent climate of public opinion.

The contributions of the party system reached beyond the needs of local administration to the tasks of national integration. The necessity of winning elections against a well-organized foe forced state and national leaders to keep in close touch with the needs of Cumberland and her sister counties throughout the country. Bending repeatedly to disparate local wishes, national leaders created a flexible definition of what it meant to be American, and local communities grew accustomed to thinking of the nation as the hometown writ large. Fulsome generalities and partisan sleight of hand thus kept a diverse national family reasonably satisfied under one very broad but relatively insubstantial roof.

The desire of Martin Van Buren to create the Democratic party in order to unify "the Planters of the South and the plain Republicans of the North" is well-known.[16] Ever since Van Buren's day, numerous other commentators have pointed to the preservation of early national unity as the crowning achievement of the second party system, just as they have pointed to secession as the system's greatest failure. By concentrating on economic issues that divided every community and cut across sectional lines, these observers argue, the party system deflected the divisive issue of slavery from the arena of national politics. It does appear that the electoral mechanics of a two-party system kept regional spokesmen in a common national fold for many decades. The expansion of popular voting and other forms of political participa-

16. Martin Van Buren to Thomas Ritchie, January 13, 1827, quoted in Robert V. Remini, *Martin Van Buren and the Making of the Democratic Party* (New York, 1951), 132.

tion which the party system promoted was also a powerful agent to bring passive local inhabitants into active American citizenship. The expectation that the national government would exactly mirror local idiosyncracies gave the nation no more than a tenuous unity, however. By encouraging this expectation, the second party system actually drove the nation to the Civil War as much as it postponed the conflict.

As the war ultimately proved, the intersectional unity provided by the Jacksonian political system was actually its least enduring feature. The national consensus in favor of individual liberty and technological progress was a far more permanent legacy of the Whigs and the Democrats. When an expanding capitalist economy introduced the Industrial Revolution and the Transportation Revolution to towns and countrysides alike, the political parties gave government aid to the projects of the powerful, and at least the appearance of involvement and participation to those who doubted the benefits of progress. By diverting most challenges to economic development into noisy but harmless rituals, the Democratic party urged the farmers to defy and later to accept the onset of material revolution. In the process, it strengthened the national commitment to technological improvement and commercialized production, and hastened the end of a self-sufficient old order. Likewise, by forcing the modernizers to act within the limits set by the will of the people, the electoral needs of the Whig party made changes easier to swallow. A unique characteristic of United States history, variously known as the strength of the vital center and the riddle of American exceptionalism, grew out of this powerful political interaction. If Van Buren's instinct was correct and the Jacksonian party system postponed the Civil War, then the "bitter party combinations of the neighbourhood" did more than bind the Union. They knitted up the seams in a straining social fabric.

Appendix I. North Carolina Antebellum Tax Lists as Historical Sources

Tax lists in antebellum North Carolina were prepared every July by justices of the peace. Using information reported by the taxpayers themselves, the justices prepared an alphabetical list of all the property holders in each militia district in each county. These district lists were copied into a special ledger by the clerk of the county court, and kept as permanent county records.[1] If used with care, these tax lists are a valuable source of systematic information on antebellum society. In this research, the Cumberland County tax lists were the basis for comparison between Whigs and Democrats and for ecological data on electoral precincts.

Each entry in the tax list contains several kinds of information. Each taxpayer was listed by name. If the taxpayer was a minor, or a married woman, or incapacitated, then the name of his or her guardian, husband, or agent was listed also. Each property holder in the county was supposed to be listed only once, in the district where he resided. It was not necessary to search for every activist's name in every district of the county to determine his total taxable wealth in the county. By the same token, the aggregate figures for each district represented all the property owned by residents of that district, not just the property that actually lay within the district. However, property owned in other counties was not listed.

Separate columns on the list contained the number of white polls, free black polls, and slave polls for whom the taxpayer owed taxes. A free poll was a free male between twenty-one and forty-five years of age. A slave poll

---

1. The statutes governing tax collection were codified and published in 1821 and 1837. Potter, Taylor, and Yancey (comps.), *Laws of the State of North Carolina*, I, 425–26, 454–57, 549–51, II, 935–36; Nash, Iredell, and Battle (comps.), *The Revised Statutes of the State of North Carolina*, I, 123–27, II, 510–27. See also Herschal Luther Macon, "A Fiscal History of North Carolina, 1776–1860" (Ph.D. dissertation, University of North Carolina, 1932), 197–98.

was a slave of either sex between twelve and forty-five. A householder owed poll taxes for himself, his free servants, the adult sons in his household, his slaves, and any free black squatters on his land. Very few Cumberland County taxpayers paid tax on more than one free poll. Moreover, very few men who paid poll tax for themselves did not pay other property taxes. This was true even in Fayetteville, where there must have been a significant number of men who did not own real property. Many propertyless men apparently evaded the poll tax.

The most detailed information in the tax lists concerned landholdings. Each tract was listed separately under the owner's name. The list showed the number of acres in the tract, its general location, and its value in dollars. Before 1837, the value was declared under oath by the owner himself. In 1837, the land in each district was valued independently by a justice of the peace assisted by "two respectable freeholders." The legislature ordered general reassessments in 1846, 1855, and 1859.[2] Land valuations remained constant between these years, except for cases of individual adjustment. Town lots were listed in the same way as tracts of rural land, but their size was not specified.

A number of precautions must be taken in using these tax lists for historical research. It cannot be assumed that the taxable wealth declared by a property holder was the same as his actual net worth. Many forms of wealth were not taxable, and not all taxpayers declared all of their property.[3] Property held in another county did not appear in the tax list of a man's county of residence.

A single example illustrates the difficulty in using the tax lists to determine the net worth of an individual. In 1842, Louis D. Henry of Fayetteville was the Democratic candidate for governor of North Carolina. In the tax list of that year, Henry declared that he owned 8 slave polls, 5 town lots worth $3,300, and 530 acres of rural land, including a summer home worth $1,000. The greatest part of his holding in Fayetteville was accounted for by his residence, worth $2,500. During his campaign for governor, however, Henry was challenged to account for his property: "[Morehead] asked Mr. Henry, since he had answered this question how *he* had invested the wealth of which he was the reputed possessor. Mr. H. replied, that he had some real estate, some negroes, some 12 or $15,000 of Ohio State Stocks, some Louisiana Bank Stock, some Raleigh and Gaston Rail Road bonds, some Cape Fear and Bank of the State stock, but the chief part of his means was loaned out on bonds in the counties of Franklin, Warren, Cumberland, Sampson, &c."[4]

2. Nash, Iredell, and Battle (comps.), *The Revised Statutes of the State of North Carolina*, II, 519; Macon, "Fiscal History," 439.
3. In 1846, Governor William A. Graham complained that at least 7 percent of the state's land and 15 percent of its polls were unlisted and untaxed. Under the earlier self-assessment system, tax evasion was even more widespread. Macon, "Fiscal History," 442–43.
4. Fayetteville *Observer*, June 8, 1842.

In this candid reply, we see a very different man than the moderately well-off lawyer of the tax lists. Mr. Henry's intangible investments were not taxed by the state, so they were not listed. Henry implied, moreover, that the value of his stocks, bonds, slaves, and real estate was surpassed by his loans to individuals. If Henry had more than $20,000 earning interest in addition to his other property, then he was a very wealthy man. The size of his fortune, moreover, casts doubt on the value of his Fayetteville residence. Why should a man worth so much invest so little in his home? The answer is surely that the assessed value of his home was less than its actual market value. This is a common procedure in tax assessment today, but the student should be reminded that the practice occurred in the nineteenth century also. Instead of being worth a total of $4,300, Louis D. Henry was probably worth ten times that amount.

It would be fallacious to accept the information of the tax lists as an accurate account of the worth of individual taxpayers, even if one knew that the individual in question owned no intangible wealth. There has been no attempt here to determine the relationship between assessed land values and actual land values. Such an effort would be very difficult and probably unfruitful. The exact dollar value of an individual's wealth has not been important in this study. I have been more interested in the relative financial status of different groups than in the fortunes of individuals. For these purposes, the ratio between assessed value and real value has been irrelevant, as long as it is probable that assessment standards were applied equally among all groups in the county. Errors would be random in such a case and would therefore cancel each other out. This study is based on the assumption that assessment standards, however eccentric, were indeed applied impartially. I have found no widespread evidence that would contradict this assumption.

The fact that intangible assets were not taxed is potentially a graver threat to the usefulness of the tax lists. Other evidence about the Whigs suggests that they would have been more likely to own stocks and bonds and to be moneylenders than Democrats. If the two parties had shown equal holdings in real property, we might suspect that the superior wealth of the Whigs was disguised by these tax shelters. Tests show, however, that the Whigs were wealthier than the Democrats in taxable property alone. Information on intangible wealth would presumably only reinforce the conclusions of this study.

County tax lists can also be used to study neighborhoods as well as individuals. In Cumberland County, most tax districts also corresponded to election precincts. Data from the tax lists could therefore be used to examine the ecological correlates of voting behavior. This use of the tax lists is less reliable than the study of individuals. Modern survey research has shown that an individual's vote cannot be accurately predicted by facts about his social environment, or "ecological data." Thus, knowing that a voter's neighborhood is predominantly working-class does not guarantee that he or she will vote Democratic. Such a conclusion would be an example of the "ecological fallacy." Regardless of the behavior of specific individuals, it is still true that most working-class neighborhoods return Democratic majorities. Ecological data can at least explain something of the behavior of districts, if not of individuals. The Cumberland tax lists have been used with this caveat in mind.[5]

A second source of unreliability in the use of tax district data to study voting behavior is that voters were not required to vote in any particular precinct. Voter registration did not exist in antebellum North Carolina, nor did the various precincts have boundary lines. A citizen was free to vote wherever he chose in his county of residence. Poll lists were kept of the name of everyone casting a ballot at every polling place. Repeating voters could be detected from these lists, but only after the election. There were very few complaints of vote fraud in Cumberland County during the second party system. There is no assurance, however, that the voters in a precinct were drawn entirely from the taxpayers of that tax district. In the case of Fayetteville, it is certain that many rural residents voted there regularly. To use the tax lists for political analysis, one can only assume that, except for Fayetteville, most men voted in their own neighborhoods for the sake of convenience. This is a plausible assumption, but the surviving sources do not permit an easy test of it.

Cumberland County contained thirteen tax districts in 1836 and twelve polling places, or precincts. For the purpose of correlating socioeconomic data from the tax lists with information on voting behavior, it was necessary to establish an ordered one-to-one correspondence between the set of tax districts and the set of precincts. In most cases it was easy to match up tax districts and precincts because the same local place-name was used to refer to both units. In other cases, the precinct was called by the name of the person on whose property the election was held (*e.g.*, Murchison's Mills; Archibald Munroe's). These precincts were matched with tax districts in a variety of ways. In several cases the county court, when it established the precinct, mentioned the tax district in which it was located.[6] In other cases comparison of election returns over several years (or of the same set of returns between different sources) produced examples of the same precinct being called by different names, one of which would usually be the tax district name. Several precincts created problems, however. Captain John Munroe's did not corre-

---

5. Austin Ranney, "The Utility and Limitations of Aggregate Data in the Study of Electoral Behavior," in Ranney (ed.), *Essays on the Behavioral Study of Politics* (Urbana, 1962), 91–102.
6. See, for example, Minutes of the Cumberland County Court of Pleas and Quarter Sessions, March Term, 1827, in Cumberland County Records.

spond to any tax district since it was located on the border between two districts and drew voters from both. The votes from Captain Munroe's were prorated between its two neighboring precincts on the basis of the turnout at those two districts. Rockfish and Carver's Creek tax districts had no precinct at all; most of the inhabitants probably voted in Fayetteville if they voted at all, but rather than combine the fiscal data from these heavily agricultural districts with that of Fayetteville, they were simply omitted from the correlation. Thus by losing one precinct and two tax districts, we end up with a roughly matched set of eleven of each.

Naturally, when tax information is correlated with more tax information, the problem of matching does not arise, and table 21 therefore shows a value of N equal to all thirteen cases. One final complication of that table involves the constitutional referendum of 1835. No election was held on this occasion at Murchison's Mills (Upper Little River). In calculations involving the referendum, therefore, this case was treated as missing, and the value of N was reduced to ten.

Appendix II. Statistical Methods

Most of the statistical tests in this essay are tests of statistical significance. The following is a brief introduction to the concept of statistical significance that has been used here and a description of the tests themselves. These descriptions are not intended to be complete. Definitive explanations of these common methods should be sought in a standard text on statistics.[1]

We will begin with an example. In table 6, the seventy-five elite members for 1828 were divided into four groups by age and degree of activity. Thus, there were nineteen older passive men, thirty-eight younger passive men, five older active men, and thirteen younger active men. On their face, these figures seem to indicate that young men were slightly overrepresented among the active group. We might be tempted to conclude that youth gave an ambitious man an advantage in the world of Cumberland politics.

Without the use of a significance test, this conclusion would be too hasty. Table 6 divides the active members and passive members by age. We know, however, that the actives and the passives could be divided any number of ways, even randomly. If the seventy-five men were randomly divided over and over, most of the time the number of individuals falling into each cell of a two-by-two contingency table like table 6 would still be unequal. Before concluding that age gave an advantage to the ambitious amateur, we must be sure that the differences between young men and old men which appear in table 6 are greater than the differences that would commonly result by a random division of the group. Significance testing is a procedure for calculating the probability that observed differences between groups like the ones in table 6 could have resulted by chance alone.

1. A helpful introduction for this purpose is Hubert M. Blalock, *Social Statistics* (2nd ed.; New York, 1970).

An appropriate significance test for a contingency table like table 6 is called *chi-square*. This statistic is based on the difference between the actual number of cases falling into each cell of a contingency table and the number of cases that we would commonly expect to find in each cell if the distribution was strictly random. These differences are first computed for every cell, and then squared to eliminate differences in sign. The squares are then divided by the expected frequencies to standardize the value for each cell. The sum of all these quantities for every cell in the table is the chi-square statistic. The value of chi-square for table 6 is .02271.

A contingency table produced by a strictly random process would ordinarily show little difference between the observed and the expected frequencies in each cell. The value of chi-square for such a table would therefore be small. In the case of table 6, however, if youth did give an advantage, then chi-square should be relatively large. Even in a random process, high values of chi-square would occasionally occur. It is possible to calculate exactly how often any given value of chi-square would occur in a series of randomly produced contingency tables. Computer programs are available to perform these calculations, and one of them was used to prepare table 6. The computer reported that, in a table of the same size as table 6, we could expect a chi-square of .02271 or larger fully 88.0 percent of the time ($p = .8801$). Because the differences in table 6 could so easily have resulted from chance, it would be foolish to conclude that youth gave any advantage to the politically ambitious. The use of a significance test thus prevents the historian from reading imaginary relationships into his data.

When an observation could occur 88.0 percent of the time by chance alone, it is easy to say that the supposed relationship does not exist. How improbable should an observation be, however, before we conclude that a relationship between two variables does indeed exist? Social scientists commonly dismiss any observations which could occur randomly more often then 5 percent of the time. This criterion is known as the .05 level of significance. In their use of nonquantitative evidence, historians are frequently less rigid than this. No responsible historian would publish an explanation of an event if he felt that the chances of its being true were only 50 percent. Yet if the evidence on a particular problem is scanty, many sound historians are willing to publish explanations for which they have less than 95 percent certainty. These more tentative conclusions are announced to the reader by such phrases as "it is most likely that . . ." or "the bulk of the evidence suggests that such-and-such an explanation is correct." Parts of this essay are based on the belief that a similar informed permissiveness in the use of evidence should be available to the quantitative historian.

The use of significance tests enables the historian to replace vague qualifiers with exact statements like "the chances are better than 87.0 percent that town residents were more favorable to Adams than country residents." Such declarations fall considerably short of certainty. They are much too vulnerable to error for most social scientists to treat them as conclusive evidence. Among historians, however, they amount to a considerable advance in precision. Especially when the historian has not merely sampled a data source, but has used every possible case to make his analysis, such evidence should be accepted and used by historians in the same way that traditional evidence is used. For this reason, the .05 level of significance has guided my conclusions, but I have not adhered to it rigidly. Significance levels have not been used to accept or reject hypotheses. They have simply been used to assess the likelihood or the plausibility of the apparent relationships that occur in the quantitative evidence. Widespread use of significance tests for this purpose would improve the value of quantitative evidence in history.[2]

After chi-square, the *t-test* is the second common significance test in this essay. It is used to decide whether the mean value of some variable in one group is significantly different from the mean value of the same variable in the other group. The *t*-test is based on some of the same concepts as the chi-square test. If we divide the political activists by party and find the mean wealth of Whigs and Democrats, we will find that the means are different. We cannot automatically conclude, however, that there was a relationship between wealth and party. If we divided the activists randomly, we would still find that the mean wealth of the two groups was different. We must decide whether the observed difference of means between Whigs and Democrats is any larger than the differences we would commonly find in a series of random divisions. The *t*-statistic serves this purpose.

The derivation of *t* is complicated and will not be described here. Like chi-square, *t* reflects the difference between observed values (means, in this case) and the values that could be expected from chance. In addition, *t* takes into account the variance of the given variable in each group. "Variance" is a quantity in statistics that reflects the dispersal of a variable around its mean. If no party member were more than one hundred dollars richer or poorer than his copartisans, then the group's variance would be small and a difference of three hundred dollars between the mean wealth of the two parties would be very significant. If the range between the richest and the poorest members of both parties were several thousand dollars, then the variance would be large,

2. The concept of significance presented here is taken partly from Robert F. Winch and Donald T. Campbell, "Proof? No. Evidence? Yes. The Significance of Tests of Significance," in Denton E. Morrison and Ramon Henkel (eds.), *The Significance Tests Controversy—A Reader* (Chicago, 1970), 199–206.

and a three-hundred-dollar difference of means might not be significant at all.

The final result of the *t*-test is a significance level for *t*. This quantity is a percentage showing the probability of a real relationship between the interval-level variable and the dichotomous variable or in this case, between wealth and party. These significance levels have been used in the same way as those applying to chi-square tests.

Correlation coefficients (Pearson's *r*) have also been used in this study. Correlation coefficients are not significance tests, but significance tests can be applied to them. These coefficients are numbers that vary between +1.0 and −1.0 to express the degree of association between variables. A value of +1.0 expresses a perfect positive association, and a value of −1.0 expresses a perfect negative association. A value of zero expresses a perfect lack of any association. Any given correlation coefficient can be tested to determine if it is significantly different from zero or from another correlation coefficient. The significance levels that result are interpreted like other such figures.

Bibliography

PRIMARY SOURCES

Private Manuscripts

Duke University Library, Durham, N.C.
   Davis, Dolphin A., and John A. Mathews. Papers.
   McLaurin, Duncan. Papers.
   Robinson, Benjamin. Papers.
   Tillinghast Family. Papers.
   Van Noppen, Charles L. Papers.
Mr. and Mrs. Claude N. Kent, Columbus, Ga.
   Evans, James. Papers.
Library of Congress, Washington, D.C.
   Mallett, Edward J. Papers.
North Carolina State Archives, Raleigh, N.C.
   Account Book 341. Unidentified Merchant's Ledger, 1815–17.
   Account Book 345. Unidentified Merchant's Ledger, 1838–41.
   Deberry, Edmund. Papers. Microfilm copy.
   Hale, Edward J. Papers.
   Holeman Collection, Solomon Van Hook Correspondence. Microfilm copy.
   Skinner, McRae, Wooley, and Deberry Papers, 1808–1850. Microfilm copy.
   Wyatt, Arthur T. Papers.
Southern Historical Collection, University of North Carolina Library, Chapel Hill, N.C.
   Blake, William Kennedy. Reminiscences.
   Broadfoot, Charles W. Papers, 1806–1847.
   Caldwell, David Franklin. Papers, 1830–44.
   Cameron Family. Papers, 1808–1840.
   Cumberland Association. Papers.
   Davis, Orin Datus. Account Books, 1816–23.
   Deberry, Edmund. Papers.

Eccles Family. Papers, 1820–52.
Elliott, John. Papers.
Evans, Delancey. Papers.
Fuller, Bartholomew. Papers.
Fuller, Elijah. Papers.
Gaston, William. Papers, 1827–28.
Harnett County Papers.
Huske, Benjamin Robinson. Papers, 1799–1840, 1879.
Kenan, Thomas. Papers, 1838.
MacRae, Duncan G. Papers.
MacRae, John. Papers, 1820–50.
Newby, Larkin. Papers, 1800–1824.
Smith, Archibald A. T. Papers.
Strange, Robert, Jr. Papers.
Swain, David Lowry. Epistolatory Correspondence. Typed copies made from man-
    uscripts in bound volumes, Cobb Loan, North Carolina Collection, University of
    North Carolina Library.

Church Records

North Carolina Collection, University of North Carolina Library, Chapel Hill, N.C.
    Cape Fear Baptist Association. *Minutes*, 1806–1840. Microfilm copies.
North Carolina State Archives, Raleigh N.C.
    Cypress Presbyterian Church, Cumberland County, N.C. Session Minutes, 1833–
        54. Microfilm copy.
    First Baptist Church, Fayetteville, N.C. Church Minutes, 1837–50. Microfilm copy.
    First Presbyterian Church, Fayetteville, N.C. Session Minutes, 1832–58. Microfilm
        copy.
    Hay Street Methodist Church, Fayetteville, N.C. Quarterly Conference Record,
        1825–39. Microfilm copy.
    Mount Pisgah Presbyterian Church, Broadway, N.C. Session Minutes, 1835. Micro-
        film copy.
    Sardis Presbyterian Church, Linden, N.C. Session Minutes, *ca.* 1835. Microfilm
        copy.
    Saint John's Episcopal Church, Fayetteville, N.C. Parish Register, 1828–36. Micro-
        film copy.
Saint Patrick's Roman Catholic Church, Fayetteville, N.C. Parish Register, 1831–50.
    Manuscript copy in the church.

Unpublished Government Records

North Carolina Collection, University of North Carolina, Chapel Hill, N.C.
    United States Manuscript Census Returns. Cumberland County, North Carolina.
        Population Schedules, 1800–1850. Microfilm copy.
North Carolina State Archives, Raleigh, N.C.
    Miscellaneous Collections
        Compiled Election Returns, 1790–1860.
    Cumberland County Records
        Agricultural Society. Minutes.

Apprentice Bonds, 1820–50.
Court of Pleas and Quarter Sessions. Execution Docket, 1830–50.
————. Minute Docket, 1820–50.
Election Records, 1824–60.
Lists of Taxables, 1781, 1824–29, 1837–49.
Miscellaneous Papers, 1820–1917.
Officials' Bonds, 1790–1860.
Governors' Letter Books, 1803–1841.
Governors' Office Papers, 1839.
Governors' Papers, 1803–1841.
Legislative Papers, 1802–1840.
United States Manuscript Census Returns. Cumberland County, North Carolina. 1800–1850. Microfilm copies.

Published U.S. Census Reports

First Census. *Heads of Families at the First Census of the United States Taken in the Year 1790. North Carolina*. Washington, D.C.: Government Printing Office, 1908.
Second Census. *Return of the Whole Number of Persons Within the Several Districts of the United States*. N.p., n.d.
Third Census. *Aggregate Amount of Persons Within the United States in the Year 1810*. Washington, D.C.: n.p., 1811.
Fourth Census. *Census for 1820*. Washington: Gales and Seaton, 1821.
Fifth Census. *Fifth Census; or Enumeration of the Inhabitants of the United States: 1830*. Washington, D.C.: Duff Green, 1832.
Sixth Census. *Compendium of the Inhabitants and Statistics of the United States, As Obtained at the Department of State from the Returns of the Sixth Census*. Washington: Blair and Rives, 1841.
Seventh Census. *Statistical View of the United States . . . Being a Compendium of the Seventh Census*. Washington, D.C.: A. O. P. Nicholson, 1854.
Eighth Census. *Population of the United States in 1860, Compiled from the Original Returns of the Eighth Census, under the Direction of the Secretary of the Interior*. Washington, D.C.: U.S. Government Printing Office, 1864.
————. *Preliminary Report of the Eighth Census*. Washington, D.C.: U.S. Government Printing Office, 1861.
————. *Statistics of the United States (Including Mortality, Property, &c.) in 1860*. Washington, D.C.: U.S. Government Printing Office, 1866.

Other Government Publications

Biographical Directory of the American Congress, 1774–1971. Washington, D.C.: U.S. Government Printing Office, 1971.
Cheney, John L., Jr., ed. *North Carolina Government, 1585–1974: A Narrative and Statistical History*. Raleigh: N.C. Department of the Secretary of State, 1975.
Clark, Walter, ed. *The State Records of North Carolina*. Vol. XXII. Raleigh: State of North Carolina, 1905.
McIver, Colin, ed. *Laws of the Town of Fayetteville: Consisting of All the Acts and Parts of Acts Now in Force Passed in Relation to the Said Town . . . From A.D. 1762 to A.D. 1827*. Fayetteville, N.C.: Evangelical Printing Office, 1828.

"Memorial of the Convention upon the Subject of Internal Improvement; Held in Raleigh, November, 1833, to the General Assembly of North Carolina." *North Carolina Legislative Documents*, 1833, no. 4.

Nash, Frederick, James Iredell, and William H. Battle, comps. *The Revised Statutes of North Carolina*. 2 vols. Raleigh: Turner & Hughes, 1837.

North Carolina Board for Internal Improvements. *Reports*, 1823–33.

North Carolina General Assembly. House of Representatives. *Journal*, 1801–1860.

———. Senate. *Journal*, 1801–1860.

———. Session Laws, 1820–50.

Potter, Henry, J. L. Taylor, and Bartlett Yancey, comps. *Laws of the State of North Carolina*. 2 vols. Raleigh: J. Gales, 1821.

Proceedings and Debates of the Convention of North Carolina, Called to Amend the Constitution of the State, which Assembled at Raleigh, June 4, 1835. Raleigh: J. Gales & Son, 1836.

Richardson, James D., comp. *A Compilation of the Messages and Papers of the Presidents*. Vols. II and III. New York: Bureau of National Literature, Inc., 1927.

Saunders, William L., ed. *The Colonial Records of North Carolina*. Vol. IX. Raleigh: State of North Carolina, 1890.

U.S. Bureau of Soils. *North Carolina Soil Map*. Map Sheets for Cumberland, Harnett, and Hoke Counties. Washington, D.C.: n.p., 1916–22.

U.S. Congress. 25th Congress, 2nd Session. *Appendix to the Congressional Globe*.

———. 19th through 24th Congresses. *Register of Debates in Congress*.

———. House of Representatives. 8th Congress, 1st Session. "Contested Election of Samuel Purviance, A Representative from North Carolina," February 29, 1804. In *American State Papers*, vol. 037, no. 176, p. 389.

———. House of Representatives. 10th Congress, 1st Session. "Contested Election of John Culpepper, A Representative from North Carolina," December 17, 1807. In *American State Papers*, vol. 137, no. 234, pp. 652–54.

———. Senate. 23rd Congress, 1st Session. *Documents*, vols. I–IV.

Newspapers (Available on Microfilm at the North Carolina State Archives, Raleigh, N.C.)

Charlotte *Journal*, 1835–42.

Charlotte *Miners' and Farmers' Journal*, 1834.

Fayetteville *American*, 1813–18.

Fayetteville *Carolina Observer*, 1816–35.

Fayetteville *Gazette*, 1789, 1792–93, 1820–22.

Fayetteville *Intelligencer*, 1811.

Fayetteville *North Carolina Argus*, 1854–57.

Fayetteville *North Carolina Centinel*, 1795.

Fayetteville *North Carolina Chronicle*, 1790–91.

Fayetteville *North Carolina Intelligencer*, 1806–1808.

Fayetteville *North Carolina Journal*, 1826–38.

Fayetteville *North Carolina Minerva*, 1796–99.

Fayetteville *North Carolinian*, 1839–61.

Fayetteville *Observer*, 1835–61.

Fayetteville *People's Friend*, 1815.

Greensboro *Patriot*, 1836–42.

Halifax *North Carolina Journal*, 1792–1810.
Hillsborough *Recorder*, 1834.
New Bern *Spectator*, 1834–42.
Raleigh *Minerva*, 1799–1821.
Raleigh *North Carolina Standard*, 1834–42.
Raleigh *North Carolina Star*, 1830–42.
Raleigh *Register*, 1834–42.
Raleigh *Star and North Carolina State Gazette*, 1829.
Salisbury *Carolina Watchman*, 1832–42.
Salisbury *Western Carolinian*, 1833–42.
Tarboro *Free Press*, 1824–42.
Wilmington *Cape Fear Recorder*, 1831–32.
Wilmington *People's Press*, 1833–41.

Pamphlets, Addresses, and Broadsides

North Carolina Collection, University of North Carolina Library, Chapel Hill, N.C.
 *Address of the Administration Convention, Held in the Capitol at Raleigh, Dec.
  20th, 1827. To the Freemen of North Carolina.* Raleigh: J. Gales & Son, 1827.
 Address of the Central Jackson Committee to the Freemen of North Carolina.
  Raleigh: Lawrence & Lemay, 1828.
 *An Address to the Voters of the Electoral District Composed of the Counties of An-
  son, Richmond, Robeson, Cumberland and Moore.* Fayetteville, N.C.: North
  Carolina Journal Office, 1828.
 [Caldwell, Joseph.] *The Numbers of Carlton, Addressed to the People of North Car-
  olina, on a Central Rail-Road Through the State.* New York: G. Long, 1828.
 Dickins, Samuel. "To the Electors of the District Composed of the Counties of
  Wake, Orange and Person." Raleigh: n.p., July 6, 1816.
 A Few Citizens of Rowan, "To the Freemen of the Counties of Mecklenburg,
  Rowan, and Cabarrus." N.p., [1810?].
 Fisher, Charles. "To the Freemen of Rowan County." N.p., June 25, 1833.
 ———. "To the Freemen of Rowan County," N.p., August 6, 1833.
 Gaston, William. "To the Freemen of the Counties of Johnston, Wayne, Green,
  Lenoir, Jones, Carteret and Craven." New Bern: n.p., July 24. 1810.
 Hooper, William. *An Address Delivered Before the North Carolina Bible Society.*
  Fayetteville: n.p., 1819.
 *Journal of the Internal Improvements Convention Which Met at Raleigh on the 4th
  of July, 1833, Together with the Address of the Committee of that Body to the
  Citizens of North Carolina.* Raleigh: J. Gales & Son, 1833.
 McFarland, Duncan. "Communication." N.p., November 30, 1805.
 McPherson, Neill. "The Petition and Information of Thomas S. Ashe . . ." Fayette-
  ville: n.p., March 27, 1847.
 Presbyterian Church in the U.S.A. Synod of the Carolinas. *A Pastoral Letter, From
  the Synod of the Carolinas, to the Churches Under Their Care.* Fayetteville,
  N.C.: n.p. 1790.
 Purviance, Samuel D. "To the Freemen of the Fayetteville District." Fayetteville,
  N.C.: n.p. July 1, 1800.
 Williams, Lewis. "To the Freemen of the Counties of Wilkes, Surry, Iredell, and
  Ashe." N.p., [April, 1813].

North Carolina State Archives, Raleigh, N.C.
  McKay, Rev. Neill. *A Centenary Sermon, Delivered Before the Presbytery of Fay-
    etteville, at the Bluff Church, the 18th Day of October, 1858.* Fayetteville, N.C.:
    n.p., 1858. Microfilm copy.
Rare Book Room, Duke University Library, Durham, N.C.
  Huske, John, *et al.* "The Undersigned, Traders in the Town of Fayetteville." Fay-
    etteville, N.C.: n.p., October 24, 1833.
  McRae, D. G. "To My Fellow Citizens of the County of Cumberland." Fayette-
    ville, N.C.: n.p., July 23, 1836.

Books, Memoirs, and Published Collections

Bassett, John Spencer, ed. *Correspondence of Andrew Jackson.* Vol. III. Washington,
    D.C.: Carnegie Institution of Washington, 1928.
Battle, Kemp P., ed. *Letters of Nathaniel Macon, John Steele and William Barry
    Grove, with Sketches and Notes.* James Sprunt Historical Monographs, no. 3.
    Chapel Hill: The University Press, 1902.
Belden, Robert Cochran [Senex]. "Traditions of Cross Creek and Reminiscences of
    Fayetteville." Fayetteville *Observer*, September 28, 1893.
Brandon, Edgar Ewing, ed. *A Pilgrimage of Liberty: A Contemporary Account of the
    Triumphal Tour of General Lafayette Through the Southern and Western States in
    1825, As Reported in the Local Newspapers.* Athens, Ohio: The Lawhead Press,
    1944.
Coon, Charles L., ed. *The Beginnings of Public Education in North Carolina: A Doc-
    umentary History, 1790–1840.* Raleigh: North Carolina Historical Commission,
    1908.
Cooper, James Fenimore. *Home As Found.* New York: Hurd and Houghton, 1872.
Fries, Adelaide L., ed. and comp. *Records of the Moravians of North Carolina.* Vol.
    III. Raleigh: North Carolina Historical Commission, 1926.
Hall, Basil. *Travels in North America in the Years 1827 and 1828.* Vol. III. Edinburgh:
    Cadell and Marshall Co., 1829.
Hamilton, J. G. deRoulhac, ed. *The Papers of Thomas Ruffin.* Raleigh: North Carolina
    State Department of Archives and History, 1918–20.
Helper, Hinton R. *The Impending Crisis of the South: How to Meet It.* New York:
    Burdick Brothers, 1857.
Hoyt, William Henry, ed. *The Papers of Archibald D. Murphey.* Raleigh: North Car-
    olina Historical Commission, 1914.
Jefferson, Thomas. *Notes on the State of Virginia.* Edited by William Peden. Chapel
    Hill: University of North Carolina Press, 1954.
Levasseur, A. *Lafayette in America, in 1824 and 1825 or Journal of Travels in the
    United States.* Vol. II. New York: White, Gallaher & White, 1829.
[MacRae, Duncan G.] "Fayetteville!" Fayetteville *Observer*, June 27, 1889.
Newsome, A. R., ed. "Simeon Colton's Railroad Report, 1840." *North Carolina His-
    torical Review*, XI (July, 1934), 205–238.
Olmsted, Frederick Law. *A Journey in the Seaboard Slave States in the Years
    1853–1854, With Remarks on Their Economy.* Vol. I. New York: G. P. Putnam's
    Sons, 1904.
Pope-Hennessey, Una, ed. *The Aristocratic Journey: Being the Outspoken Letters Of
    Mrs. Basil Hall Written During a Fourteen Month Sojourn in America, 1827–28.*
    New York: G. P. Putnam's Sons, 1931.

Powell, William S., James K. Huhta, and Thomas J. Farnham, eds. *The Regulators of North Carolina: A Documentary History, 1759–1776*. Raleigh: North Carolina Department of Archives & History, 1971.

Royall, Anne. *Mrs. Royall's Southern Tour, or, Second Series of the Black Book*. Vol. I. Washington, D.C.: n.p., 1830.

Shanks, Henry Thomas, ed. *The Papers of Willie P. Mangum*. Raleigh: North Carolina Department of Archives and History, 1950–56.

Tolbert, Noble J., ed. *The Papers of John Willis Ellis*. Raleigh: North Carolina Department of Archives and History, 1964.

Wagstaff, H. M., ed. *The Papers of John Steele*. Raleigh: North Carolina Historical Commission, 1924.

Wheeler, John H. *Reminiscences and Memoirs of North Carolina and Eminent North Carolinians*. Columbus, Ohio: Columbus Printing Works, 1884.

SECONDARY SOURCES

Articles

Alexander, Thomas B., Kit C. Carter, Jack R. Lister, Jerry C. Oldshue, and Winfred G. Sandlin. "Who Were the Alabama Whigs?" *Alabama Review*, XIV (January, 1963), 5–19.

Alexander, Thomas B., Peggy Duckworth Elmore, Frank M. Lowery, Mary Jane Pickens Skinner. "The Basis of Alabama's Ante-Bellum Two-Party System." *Alabama Review*, XIX (October, 1966), 243–76.

Brewer, James Howard. "Legislation Designed to Control Slavery in Wilmington and Fayetteville." *North Carolina Historical Review*, XXX (April, 1953), 155–66.

Burnham, Walter Dean. "The Changing Shape of the American Political Universe." *American Political Science Review*, LIX (March, 1964), 7–28.

Counihan, Harold J. "The North Carolina Constitutional Convention of 1835: A Study in Jacksonian Democracy." *North Carolina Historical Review*, XLVI (October, 1969), 335–64.

Dorfman, Joseph. "The Jackson Wage-Earner Thesis." *American Historical Review*, LIV (January, 1949), 296–305.

Folsom, Burton J., II. "Party Formation and Development in Jacksonian America: The Old South." *Journal of American Studies*, VII (December, 1973), 217–29.

————. "The Politics of Elites: Prominence and Party in Davidson County, Tennessee, 1835–1861." *Journal of Southern History*, XXXIX (August, 1973), 359–78.

Formisano, Ronald P. "Analyzing American Voting, 1830–1860: Methods." *Historical Methods Newsletter*, II (March, 1969), 1–12.

————. "Deferential-Participant Politics: The Early Republic's Political Culture, 1789–1840." *American Political Science Review*, LXVIII (June, 1974), 473–87.

————. "Political Character, Antipartyism, and the Second Party System." *American Quarterly*, XXI (Winter, 1969), 683–709.

Gattell, Frank Otto. "Money and Party in Jacksonian America: A Quantitative Look at New York's Men of Quality." *Political Science Quarterly*, LXXXII (June, 1967), 235–52.

Goodman, Leo A. "Some Alternatives to Ecological Correlations." *American Journal of Sociology*, LXIV (May, 1959), 610–25.

Green, James. "Behavioralism and Class Analysis: A Methodological and Ideological Critique." *Labor History*, XIII (Winter, 1972), 89–106.

Hammond, Bray, "Jackson, Biddle, and the Bank of the United States." *Journal of Economic History*, VII (May, 1947), 1–23.

Hays, Samuel P. "History as Human Behavior." *Iowa Journal of History*, LVIII (July, 1960), 193–206.

————. "The Politics of Reform in Municipal Government in the Progressive Era." *Pacific Northwest Quarterly*, LV (October, 1964), 157–69.

————. "The Social Analysis of American Political History, 1880–1920." *Political Science Quarterly*, LXXX (September, 1965), 373–94.

Hoffman, William S. "The Downfall of the Democrats: The Reaction of North Carolinians to Jacksonian Land Policy." *North Carolina Historical Review*, XXXIII (April, 1956), 166–80.

————. "The Election of 1836 in North Carolina." *North Carolina Historical Review*, XXXII (January, 1955), 31–51.

————. "John Branch and the Origins of the Whig Party in North Carolina." *North Carolina Historical Review*, XXXV (July, 1958), 299–315.

Jeffrey, Thomas E. "Internal Improvements and Political Parties in Antebellum North Carolina, 1836–1860." *North Carolina Historical Review*, LV (April, 1978), 111–56.

Jensen, Richard. "The Religious and Occupational Roots of Party Identification: Illinois and Indiana in the 1870s." *Civil War History*, XVI (December, 1970), 325–43.

Johnson, Lucile. "Galatia Records Date Back to 1825." Fayetteville *Observer*, March 15, 1964, p. 10B.

Johnson, Lucile and Cathi Dixon. "The Men Who Wrote Their Names in Local History." Fayetteville *Observer*, June 22, 1975, sec. B, p. 1.

Kelley, Robert. "Ideology and Political Culture from Jefferson to Nixon." *American Historical Review*, LXXXII (June, 1977), 531–62.

Key, V. O., Jr. "Secular Realignment and the Party System." *Journal of Politics*, XXI (May, 1959), 198–210.

————. "A Theory of Critical Elections." *Journal of Politics*, XVII (February, 1955), 3–18.

McCormick, Richard L. "Ethno-Cultural Interpretations of Nineteenth-Century American Voting Behavior." *Political Science Quarterly*, LXXXIX (June, 1974), 351–77.

McCormick, Richard P. "New Perspectives on Jacksonian Politics." *American Historical Review*, LXV (January, 1960), 288–301.

————. "Suffrage Classes and Party Alignments: A Study in Voter Behavior." *Mississippi Valley Historical Review*, XLVI (December, 1959), 397–410.

McWhiney, Grady. "Were the Whigs a Class Party in Alabama?" *Journal of Southern History*, XXIII (November, 1957), 510–22.

Marshall, Lynn L. "The Genesis of Grass Roots Democracy in Kentucky." *Mid-America*, XLVII (October, 1965), 269–287.

————. "The Strange Stillbirth of the Whig Party." *American Historical Review*, LXXII (January, 1967), 445–68.

Montgomery, David. "The Shuttle and the Cross: Weavers and Artisans in the Kensington Riots of 1844." *Journal of Social History*, V (Summer, 1972), 411–46.

Morgan, J. Allen. "State Aid to Transportation in North Carolina: The Pre-Railroad Era (1776–1835)." *North Carolina Booklet*, X (January, 1911), 123–54.

Pessen, Edward. "Did Labor Support Jackson? The Boston Story." *Political Science Quarterly*, LXIV (June, 1949), 262–74.

———. "The Workingmen's Movement of the Jacksonian Era." *Mississippi Valley Historical Review*, XLIII (December, 1956), 428–43.

Phillips, Kim T. "The Pennsylvania Origins of the Jackson Movement." *Political Science Quarterly*, XCI (Fall, 1976), 489–508.

Pole, J. R. "Election Statistics in North Carolina to 1861." *Journal of Southern History*, XXIV (May, 1958), 225–28.

———. "Suffrage and Representation in Maryland from 1776 to 1810: A Statistical Note and Some Reflections." *Journal of Southern History*, XXIV (May, 1958), 218–25.

Pool, William C. "An Economic Interpretation of the Ratification of the Federal Constitution in North Carolina." *North Carolina Historical Review*, XXVII (April, July, October, 1950), 119–41, 289–313, 437–61.

Ratliffe, Donald J. "The Role of Voters and Issues in Party Formation: Ohio, 1824." *Journal of American History*, LIX (March, 1973), 847–870.

Richards, Leonard L. "John Adams and the Moderate Federalists: The Cape Fear Valley as a Test Case." *North Carolina Historical Review*, XLIII (January, 1966), 14–30.

Sellers, Charles Grier, Jr. "Who Were the Southern Whigs?" *American Historical Review*, LIX (January, 1954), 335–46.

Sitterson, J. Carlyle. "Economic Sectionalism in Ante-Bellum North Carolina." *North Carolina Historical Review* XVI (April, 1939), 134–46.

Smith, W. Wayne. "Jacksonian Democracy on the Chesapeake: Class, Kinship, and Politics." *Maryland Historical Magazine*, LXIII (March, 1968), 55–67.

Stalhope, Robert E. "Southern Federalists and the First Party Syndrome." *Reviews in American History*, VIII (March, 1980), 45–51.

Starling, Robert B. "The Plank Road Movement in North Carolina." *North Carolina Historical Review*, XVI (January, April, 1939), 1–22, 147–73.

Sullivan, William A. "Did Labor Support Andrew Jackson?" *Political Science Quarterly*, LXII (December, 1947), 569–80.

Vinson, John Chalmers. "Electioneering in North Carolina, 1800–1835." *North Carolina Historical Review*, XXIX (April, 1952), 171–88.

Wallace, Michael. "Changing Concepts of Party in the United States: New York, 1815–1825." *American Historical Review*, LXXIV (December, 1968), 453–91.

Ward, James A. "A New Look at Antebellum Southern Railroad Development." *Journal of Southern History*, XXXIX (August, 1973), 409–420.

Watson, Harry L. "Squire Oldway and His Friends: Opposition to Internal Improvements in Antebellum North Carolina." *North Carolina Historical Review*, LIV (April, 1977), 105–119.

Wilson, Major L. "The Concept of Time and the Political Dialogue in the United States, 1828–1848." *American Quarterly*, XIX (Winter, 1967), 619–44.

Books

Apter, David E., ed. *Ideology and Discontent*. New York: Free Press, 1964.

Aronson, Sidney H. *Status and Kinship in the Higher Civil Service: Standards of Selection in the Administrations of John Adams, Thomas Jefferson, and Andrew Jackson*. Cambridge, Mass.: Harvard University Press, 1964.

Ashe, Samuel A., *et al.*, eds. *Biographical History of North Carolina From Colonial Times to the Present.* Greensboro, N.C.: Charles L. Van Noppen, 1905–1917.

Bailey, Hugh C. *Hinton Rowan Helper: Abolitionist-Racist.* University, Ala.: University of Alabama Press, 1965.

Bailyn, Bernard. *The Ideological Origins of the American Revolution.* Cambridge, Mass.: Harvard University Press, 1967.

Bemis, Samuel Flagg. *John Quincy Adams and the Union.* New York: Alfred A. Knopf & Co., 1956.

Benson, Lee. *The Concept of Jacksonian Democracy: New York as a Test Case.* Princeton, N.J.: Princeton University Press, 1961.

———. *Toward the Scientific Study of History: Selected Essays.* Philadelphia: J. B. Lippincott Co., 1972.

Biographical Sketches of Distinguished American Lawyers. New York: n.p., 1852.

Black, George F. *The Surnames of Scotland: Their Origin, Meaning, and History.* New York: New York Public Library, 1962.

Blalock, Hubert M. *Social Statistics.* 2nd ed. New York: McGraw-Hill Book Co., 1970.

Bogue, Allan G., ed. *Emerging Theoretical Models in Social and Political History.* Sage Contemporary Social Science Issues, Vol. IX. Beverly Hills, Calif.: Sage Publications, 1973.

Boyd, William K. *The History of North Carolina.* Vol. II. *The Federal Period, 1783–1860.* Chicago: Lewis Publishing Co., 1919.

Broadfoot, C. W. *The Address of Col. C. W. Broadfoot at the Centennial Celebration of St. John's Church, Fayetteville, N.C..* Fayetteville, N.C.: n.p., 1917.

Campbell, Angus, Phillip E. Converse, Warren E. Miller, and Donald E. Stokes. *The American Voter.* New York: John Wiley & Sons, Inc. 1960.

———. *Elections and the Political Order.* New York: John Wiley & Sons, 1966.

Campbell, Randolph, and Richard Lowe. *Wealthholding and Power in Antebellum Texas.* College Station, Tex.: Texas A & M University Press, 1977.

Cash, W. J. *The Mind of the South.* New York: Alfred A. Knopf, Inc., 1941.

Catterall, Ralph C. H. *The Second Bank of the United States.* Chicago: University of Chicago Press, 1903.

Cave, Alfred A. *Jacksonian Democracy and the Historians.* University of Florida Monographs: Social Sciences, No. 22. Gainesville, Fla.: University of Florida Press, 1964.

Chambers, William Nisbet. *Political Parties in a New Nation: The American Experience, 1776–1809.* New York: Oxford University Press, 1963.

Chambers, William Nisbet, and Walter Dean Burnham, eds. *The American Party Systems: Stages of Political Development.* New York: Oxford University Press, 1967.

Cole, Arthur Charles. *The Whig Party in the South.* Washington, D.C.: American Historical Association, 1913.

Connor, R. D. W. *North Carolina: Rebuilding an Ancient Commonwealth, 1584–1925.* Chicago: Lewis Publishing Co., 1929.

———. *Race Elements in the White Population of North Carolina.* North Carolina State Normal and Industrial College Historical Publications, No. 1. Raleigh: North Carolina Normal and Industrial College, 1920.

Cooper, William J. *The South and the Politics of Slavery, 1828–1856.* Baton Rouge: Louisiana State University Press, 1978.

Corbitt, David Leroy. *The Formation of the North Carolina Counties, 1663–1943*. Raleigh: State Department of Archives and History, 1950.

Crotty, William J., ed. *The Study of Party Organization*. Boston: Allyn and Bacon, Inc., 1968.

Crucial American Elections. Memoirs of the American Philosophical Society, Vol. XCIX. Philadelphia: American Philosophical Society, 1973.

Dawley, Alan. *Class and Community: The Industrial Revolution in Lynn*. Cambridge, Mass.: Harvard University Press, 1976.

DeMond, Robert O. *The Loyalists of North Carolina During the Revolution*. Durham, N.C.: Duke University Press, 1940.

Dorfman, Joseph. *The Economic Mind in American Civilization*. Vol. II. New York: Viking Press, 1946.

Edelman, Murray. *The Symbolic Uses of Politics*. Urbana, Ill.: University of Illinois Press, 1964.

Fisher, David Hackett. *The Revolution of American Conservativism: The Federalist Party in the Era of Jeffersonian Democracy*. New York: Harper & Row, 1965.

Fogel, Robert William, and Stanley L. Engerman. *Time on the Cross: The Economics of American Negro Slavery*. Boston: Little, Brown and Co., 1974.

Foner, Eric. *Free Soil, Free Labor, Free Men: The Ideology of the Republican Party Before the Civil War*. New York: Oxford University Press, 1970.

Foote, William Henry. *Sketches of North Carolina, Historical and Biographical, Illustrative of the Principles of a Portion of Her Early Settlers*. New York: Robert Carter, 1846.

Formisano, Ronald P. *The Birth of Mass Political Parties: Michigan, 1827–1861*. Princeton, N.J.: Princeton University Press, 1971.

Frederickson, George M. *The Black Image in the White Mind: The Debate on Afro-American Character and Destiny, 1817–1914*. New York: Harper & Row, 1971.

Freehling, William W. *Prelude to Civil War: The Nullification Controversy in South Carolina, 1816–1836*. New York: Harper & Row, 1965.

Geertz, Clifford. *The Interpretation of Cultures: Selected Essays*. New York: Free Press, 1973.

Genovese, Eugene D. *The Political Economy of Slavery: Studies in the Economy and Society of the Slave South*. New York: Pantheon Books, 1965.

Gilpatrick, Delbert Harold. *Jeffersonian Democracy in North Carolina, 1789–1816*. New York: Columbia University Press, 1931.

Graham, Ian Charles Carghill. *Colonists From Scotland: Emigration to North America, 1707–1783*. Ithaca, N.Y.: Cornell University Press, 1956.

Grodzins, Morton. *The Loyal and the Disloyal: Social Boundaries of Patriotism and Treason*. Chicago: University of Chicago Press, 1956.

Gunderson, Robert Gray. *The Log Cabin Campaign*. Lexington, Ky.: University of Kentucky Press, 1957.

Hamilton, J. G. deRoulhac. *Party Politics in North Carolina, 1835–1860*. James Sprunt Historical Publications, Vol. 15, Nos. 1 and 2. Chapel Hill: University of North Carolina, 1916.

Hammond, Bray. *Banks and Politics from the Revolution to the Civil War*. Princeton: N.J.: Princeton University Press, 1957.

Hartz, Louis. *The Liberal Tradition in America: An Interpretation of American Political Thought Since the Revolution*. New York: Harcourt, Brace and Co., 1955.

Hobbs, S. H., Jr. *North Carolina: Economic and Social*. Chapel Hill: University of North Carolina Press, 1930.

Hoffman, William S. *Andrew Jackson and North Carolina Politics*. James Sprunt Studies in History and Political Science, Vol. 40. Chapel Hill: University of North Carolina, 1958.

Hofstadter, Richard. *The American Political Tradition: And the Men Who Made It*. New York: Alfred A. Knopf, Inc., 1948.

————. *The Idea of a Party System: The Rise of Legitimate Opposition in the United States, 1780–1840*. Berkeley: University of California Press, 1972.

Holt, Michael F. *Forging a Majority: The Formation of the Republican Party in Pittsburgh*. New Haven, Conn.: Yale University Press, 1969.

————. *The Political Crisis of the 1850s*. New York: John Wiley & Sons, 1978.

Hugins, Walter. *Jacksonian Democracy and the Working Class: A Study of the New York Workingmen's Movement, 1829–1837*. Stanford: Stanford University Press, 1960.

James, Marquis. *The Life of Andrew Jackson*. Indianapolis: Bobbs-Merrill, Inc., 1938.

Johnson, Guion Griffis. *Ante-Bellum North Carolina: A Social History*. Chapel Hill: University of North Carolina Press, 1937.

Johnson, Paul E. *A Shopkeeper's Millennium: Society and Revivals in Rochester, New York, 1815–1837*. New York: Hill and Wang, 1978.

Kelley, Robert. *The Cultural Pattern of American Politics: The First Century*. New York: Alfred A. Knopf, Inc., 1979.

Kleppner, Paul. *The Cross of Culture: A Social Analysis of Midwestern Politics, 1850–1900*. New York: Free Press, 1970.

Lamb, Elizabeth. *Historical Sketch of Hay Street Methodist Episcopal Church, South, Fayetteville, North Carolina*. Fayetteville, N.C.: n.p., 1934.

Lefler, Hugh Talmadge, and Albert Ray Newsome. *North Carolina: The History of a Southern State*, 3rd. rev. ed. Chapel Hill: University of North Carolina Press, 1973.

Lipset, Seymour Martin. *Political Man: The Social Bases of Politics*. Garden City, N.Y.: Doubleday & Co., Inc., 1960.

McCormick, Richard P. *The Second American Party System: Party Formation in the Jacksonian Era*. Chapel Hill: University of North Carolina Press, 1966.

Mathews, Donald G. *Religion in the Old South*. Chicago: University of Chicago Press, 1977.

Merrens, Harry Roy. *Colonial North Carolina in the Eighteenth Century: A Study in Historical Geography*. Chapel Hill: University of North Carolina Press, 1964.

Meyer, Duane. *The Highland Scots of North Carolina, 1732–1776*. Chapel Hill: University of North Carolina Press, 1961.

Meyers, Marvin. *The Jacksonian Persuasion: Politics and Belief*. Stanford: Stanford University Press, 1957.

Morrison, Denton E., and Ramon Henkel, eds. *The Significance Test Controversy: A Reader*. Chicago: Aldine Publishing Co., 1970.

Nelson, William H. *The American Tory*. London: Clarendon Press, 1961.

Newsome, Albert Ray. *The Presidential Election of 1824 in North Carolina*. James Sprunt Studies in History and Political Science, Vol. 23, No. 1. Chapel Hill: University of North Carolina Press, 1939.

Norton, Clarence Clifford. *The Democratic Party in Ante-Bellum North Carolina, 1835–1861*. James Sprunt Historical Studies, Vol. 21, Nos. 1 and 2. Chapel Hill: University of North Carolina Press, 1930.

Oates, John A. *The Story of Fayetteville and the Upper Cape Fear*. 2nd ed. Fayetteville, N.C.: The Fayetteville Women's Club, 1972.

Parton, James. *Life of Andrew Jackson*. New York: Mason Brothers, 1861.

Pegg, Herbert Dale. *The Whig Party in North Carolina*. Chapel Hill: Colonial Press, Inc., n.d.

Pessen, Edward. *Jacksonian America: Society, Personality, and Politics*. 2nd rev. ed. Homewood, Ill.: Dorsey Press, 1978.

————. *Riches, Class, and Power Before the Civil War*. Lexington, Mass.: D. C. Heath and Co., 1973.

Potter, Jack M., May N. Diaz, and George M. Foster, eds. *Peasant Society: A Reader*. Boston: Little, Brown and Co., 1967.

Rankin, Harriet Sutton, comp. *History of the First Presbyterian Church, Fayetteville, North Carolina*. Fayetteville, N.C.: n.p., 1928.

Ranney, Austin, ed., *Essays on the Behavioral Study of Politics*. Urbana, Ill.: University of Illinois Press, 1962.

Remini, Robert V. *Martin Van Buren and the Making of the Democratic Party*. New York: Columbia University Press, 1951.

Ridgway, Whitman. *Community Leadership in Maryland, 1790–1840: A Comparative Analysis of Power in Society*. Chapel Hill: University of North Carolina Press, 1979.

Rose, Lisle A. *Prologue to Democracy: The Federalists of the South, 1789–1800*. Lexington, Ky.: University of Kentucky Press, 1968.

Rosenbaum, Walter A. *Political Culture*. New York: Praeger Publishers, 1975.

Schauinger, Joseph H. *William Gaston, Carolinian*. Milwaukee: Bruce Publishing Co., 1949.

Schlesinger, Arthur M., Jr. *The Age of Jackson*. Boston: Little, Brown and Co., 1946.

Sellers, Charles. *James K. Polk: Continentalist, 1843–1846*. Princeton, N.J.: Princeton University Press, 1966.

Shade, William Gerald. *Banks or No Banks: The Money Issue in Western Politics, 1832–1865*. Detroit: Wayne State University Press, 1972.

Sharp, James R. *Jacksonians versus the Banks: Politics in the States After the Panic of 1837*. New York: Columbia University Press, 1970.

Silbey, Joel, and Samuel T. McSeveney, eds. *Voters, Parties, and Elections: Quantitative Essays in the History of American Popular Voting Behavior*. Lexington, Mass.: Xerox College Publishing, 1972.

Sitterson, J. Carlyle, ed. *Studies in Southern History in Memory of Albert Ray Newsome, 1891–1951*. James Sprunt Studies in History and Political Science, Vol. 39. Chapel Hill: University of North Carolina Press, 1957.

Somkin, Fred. *Unquiet Eagle: Memory and Desire in the Idea of American Freedom*. Ithaca, N.Y.: Cornell University Press, 1967.

Stone, Robert Hamlin. *A History of Orange Presbytery, 1770–1970*. Greensboro, N.C.: n.p., 1970.

Temin, Peter. *The Jacksonian Economy*. New York: W. W. Norton & Co., 1969.

Thompson, Ernest Trice. *Presbyterians in the South*. Vol. I. Richmond: John Knox Press, 1963.

Thornton, J. Mills III. *Politics and Power in a Slave Society: Alabama, 1800–1860*. Baton Rouge: Louisiana State University Press, 1978.

Trenholme, Louise Irby. *The Ratification of the Federal Constitution in North Carolina*. New York: Columbia University Press, 1932.

Troxler, Carole Watterson. *The Loyalist Experience in North Carolina*. Raleigh: North

Carolina Department of Cultural Resources, Division of Archives and History, 1976.

Wagstaff, Henry McGilbert. *States Rights and Political Parties in North Carolina, 1776–1861*. Johns Hopkins University Studies in Historical and Political Science, Series 24, Nos. 7–8. Baltimore: Johns Hopkins University Press, 1906.

Ward, John William. *Andrew Jackson: Symbol for an Age*. New York: Oxford University Press, 1955.

Weaver, Charles Clinton. *Internal Improvements in North Carolina Previous to 1860*. Johns Hopkins University Studies in History and Political Science, Series 21, Nos. 3–4. Baltimore: Johns Hopkins University Press, 1903.

Welter, Rush. *The Mind of America, 1830–1860*. New York: Columbia University Press, 1975.

Wheeler, John H. *Historical Sketches of North Carolina From 1584 to 1851*. Philadelphia: Lippicott, Grambo and Co., 1851.

Wiebe, Robert H. *The Search for Order, 1877–1920*. New York: Hill & Wang, 1967.

Wilburn, Jean Alexander. *Biddle's Bank: The Crucial Years*. New York: Columbia University Press, 1967.

Williamson, Chilton. *American Suffrage from Property to Democracy, 1760–1860*. Princeton, N.J.: Princeton University Press, 1960.

Wilson, Edwin Mood. *The Congressional Career of Nathaniel Macon*. James Sprunt Historical Monographs, No. 2. Chapel Hill: The University Press, 1900.

Wilson, Major L. *Space, Time, and Freedom: The Quest for Nationality and the Irrepressible Conflict, 1815–1861*. Westport, Conn.: Greenwood Press, 1974.

Wooster, Ralph. *Politicians, Planters, and Plain Folk: Courthouse and Statehouse in the Upper South, 1850–1860*. Knoxville: University of Tennessee Press, 1975.

Wright, Gavin. *The Political Economy of the Cotton South: Households, Markets, and Wealth in the Nineteenth Century*. New York: W. W. Norton & Co., 1978.

Young, James Sterling. *The Washington Community, 1800–1828*. New York: Columbia University Press, 1966.

Theses, Dissertations, and Other Unpublished Works

Byrd, Luther Nicholson. "The Life and Public Services of Edward Bishop Dudley, 1789–1855." M.A. thesis, University of North Carolina, 1949.

Counihan, Harold J. "North Carolina, 1815–1836: State and Local Perspectives on the Age of Jackson." Ph.D. dissertation, University of North Carolina, 1971.

Jeffrey, Thomas Edward. "The Second Party System in North Carolina, 1836–1860." Ph.D. dissertation, Catholic University of America, 1979.

Kruman, Marc Wayne. "Parties and Politics in North Carolina, 1846–1865." Ph.D. dissertation, Yale University, 1978.

McFarland, Daniel M. "Duncan McFarland." Manuscript in North Carolina Collection, University of North Carolina, Chapel Hill.

———. "Rip Van Winkle: Political Evolution in North Carolina, 1815–1835." Ph.D. dissertation, University of Pennsylvania, 1954.

Macon, Herschal Luther. "A Fiscal History of North Carolina, 1776–1860." Ph.D. dissertation, University of North Carolina, 1932.

Matthews, Catherine Barden. "John Culpepper: A Biographical Sketch." Manuscript in North Carolina Collection, University of North Carolina, Chapel Hill.

Index

Abolitionism, 204–207, 275–77, 290, 292, 293, 295. *See also* Slavery

Adams, John, 87, 88, 176

Adams, John Quincey: as president, 20–21, 21*n*11, 68, 69, 73–76, 109, 117, 176; 1824 election, 99–102; support for, 110, 112–13, 119–26, 128–29, 138–39, 147–49, 180–81, 209, 219, 230; opposition to, 114–18, 176, 179, 292

Age of party leaders, 130, 138–39, 221, 223–24, 228–29, 242

Agriculture. *See* Cotton; Farmers

Alabama, 8, 12, 70, 311

Alexander, Thomas B., 321

Alston, Willis, 57, 59

Anderson, David, 94, 95

American Revolution, 17, 19, 20, 29–30, 48, 70, 83–85, 87, 88, 101, 126, 148

Armstrong, John, 200

Army, 275

Atkins, Benjamin F., 301*n*46

Badger, George E., 295

Bank of the United States, 36, 42, 67, 126, 150, 152, 159–62, 165–68, 172, 175, 176, 184–85, 188–90, 194, 195, 199, 205, 244, 246, 250, 256, 260–66, 289–91, 294, 296, 298, 322

Banks and banking, 8, 14, 15, 36, 42, 78, 159–69, 187, 190, 194, 246–47, 249–60, 262–70, 275–80, 289–90, 293, 299, 318–21. *See also* Economic policies

Baptists, 39–41, 41*n*58, 57–58, 98, 99, 240–42, 284

Barbour, Phillip, 154, 177–80, 178*n*73, 184, 204

Barclay, John, 170–71

Bayne, William H., 292, 293, 299, 301

Beard, Charles, 3

Belden, Robert Cochran, 22, 192

Belden, Simeon, 93–97

Benson, Lee, 4–6, 61*n*1

Benton, Thomas Hart, 265, 276

Bethune, Lauchlin, 161, 164–67, 169, 180, 201, 202, 205–206, 264–67, 301

Biddle, Nicholas, 36, 159–60, 173, 289

Blacks, free, 24, 39, 43–45, 61, 95, 191–93, 195, 200, 201, 240. *See also* Slavery

Blake, Isham, 19

Blake, William Kennedy, 19, 42

Bloodworth, Timothy, 87, 95

Branch, John, 111*n*9

Branson, Henry, 92–97, 127*n*49

Breckinridge, John C., 305*n*53

Britain. *See* Great Britain

Brown, Bedford, 185, 187, 195

Bryan, John H., 121–22

Burnham, Walter Dean, 312

Business and businessmen, 34–37, 41–42, 48–49, 54–59, 172–73, 205–207, 234–35, 243, 245, 252–54, 266–69, 298–99, 302, 320

Caldwell, Joseph, 154–55

Calhoun, John C., 67, 111, 153, 154, 176–77, 181, 268

Cameron, Duncan, 68, 158

Cameron, John A.: support for Jackson, 1–2, 72–73, 76, 114–17, 122, 127–28, 127*n*49, 140–41, 152; on political activities, 65, 75–76, 122; biographical information, 67–69, 77–80, 101, 129, 157, 158, 167,

169, 200, 300; opponent of J. Q. Adams, 74, 117, 123; as political candidate, 72, 92–97, 111, 123, 132, 172
Cameron, Thomas N., 157, 169, 197, 300, 303
Cameron, William, 101, 102
Canals, 50, 51, 53, 56, 87, 154. *See also* Internal improvements
Carolina Observer, 66–67, 98
Carter, A. G., 78
Carver, David, 257
Cash, W. J., 53
Catholics, 39–40, 41*n*58, 238, 267
Churches, 5–7, 38–41, 41*n*58, 57–58, 117–18, 238–43. *See also* names of specific churches
Civil War, 16, 50, 67, 315–16, 324
Class differences, 91, 102, 108, 116, 172–75, 191–92, 195, 205–207, 270–71, 320
Clay, Henry, 21*n*11, 22, 74, 109, 115, 160, 173, 177–84 *passim*, 285, 286, 290, 297, 310
Colton, Simeon, 247–48
Congressional elections, 63–65, 98, 164–65
Constitutions. *See* State constitution; United States Constitution
Converse, Philip E., 6
Cooper, William J., 8, 276
Corporations. *See* Business and businessmen
Corruption in government, 63, 114, 117, 179, 180, 211, 291–92
Cotton, 31, 33–36, 41, 46, 250, 251, 253, 253–54*n*22
Cotton mills, 42–44, 145, 248, 249, 285–87
Counihan, Harold J., 62
Country-town differences. *See* Urban versus rural residence
Crawford, William H., 21*n*11, 67, 99–102, 110, 114, 177, 209, 263
Culpepper, John, 88, 96, 98
Cumberland County, 24, 24*n*19, 27, 31, 32, 45–46, 128–29, 215, 283
Cushing, Isaac, 94, 95

Davie, William R., 86
Deberry, Edmund, 78–80, 99, 172, 183, 241–42, 295
Democratic party: election returns, 65, 66, 111*n*9, 147, 193–97, 208–13, 272, 274, 305–10; characteristics, 2–4, 13–15, 187–88, 198, 205–207, 243, 245, 279–81, 290–91, 321–24; beginning, 149, 152; economic views, 173, 184–89, 194, 205, 260, 262–70, 298–99; party loyalty, 190, 193,

195, 202–204, 304, 304*n*51, 307–10; leaders, 103, 210–12, 220, 222, 227–35, 243–45, 266–69, 279–80, 300–303
Democratic-Republicans. *See* Republican party
Depression. *See* Panic of 1837
Dickins, Samuel, 71
Dobbin, James C., 42, 246, 263, 268–69, 300, 301
Donaldson, Henry A., 145
Douglas, Stephen A., 305*n*53
Dudley, Edward B., 51, 111, 195, 201, 203, 204, 208, 209, 249, 251, 309

Eccles, John D., 95, 101, 193, 197
Economic policies, 8, 53–59, 260, 262–66, 269–70, 276, 289–90, 298–99. *See also* Bank of the United States; Banks and banking
Elections. *See* Congressional elections; Gubernatorial elections; Presidential elections; Town elections; Voting records
Elliott, Alexander, 28, 161
Elliott, Henry, 28, 146
Ellis, John W., 52*n*89
Emigration, 46–50, 55, 108, 175
England. *See* Great Britain
Episcopalians, 38–39, 41*n*58, 239
Erambert, Henry, 238
Ethnic groups. *See* Scots
Evangelicalism, 40–41, 117, 118, 238, 240–41
Evans, Henry, 28, 39
Evans, James, 54, 257
Evans, John, 54
Evans, Jonathan, 27, 146
Evans, Jonathan, Jr., 28
Evans, Josiah, 28, 54, 146

Factories. *See* Cotton mills
Farmers, 27–35, 49, 50, 53–59, 107, 164, 172–74, 203, 206–207, 211, 253, 261, 263, 269–71, 274, 282–85, 287, 301, 302, 371–81, 320, 324
Fayetteville, N.C., 31–32, 35–37, 41–46, 52–56, 107, 283
Fayetteville *Observer*, 203, 274
Federalist party, 2, 18, 63, 67, 68, 75, 76, 86–92, 95–99, 101, 110, 112, 116, 122, 126–27, 127*n*49, 147, 148, 157, 161, 169, 190, 191, 195, 206, 267
Fillmore, Millard, 295
Financial policies. *See* Bank of the United States; Banks and banking; Economic policies

Fisher, Charles, 78, 79
Fisher, David Hackett, 91
Folsom, Burton W., II, 7–8
Foner, Eric, 70
Formisano, Ronald P., 3, 6, 7, 75
Free Blacks. *See* Blacks, free
Freehling, William W., 153
Fuller, Bartholomew, 48
Fuller, Elijah, 34, 48–49, 54, 250–52, 252n19
Fuller, Jones, 48–49, 250, 252, 252n19
Fuller, Thomas, 48–49
Fuller, Willie J., 48–49

Gales, Joseph, 67
Gallagher, P., 261–63, 264
Gardner, Charles T., 43
Gaston, William, 75, 77, 112, 121–22, 126, 127, 140, 141, 157, 194, 200
Gee, David, 43
Gee, James, 43
Gee, James R., 43
Georgia, 73, 76, 114, 176
Giddings, Joshua, 292
Gilmore, John T., 290
Graham, William A., 326n3
Great Britain, 83–86, 88, 89, 256, 265, 317
Grodzins, Morton, 311
Grove, William Barry, 63, 87–91, 93, 95, 98, 121
Gubernatorial elections: of 1836, pp. 15, 201, 203–13, 277, 308, 309, 310, 312; of 1838, pp. 111n9, 259, 265, 308, 312; of 1840, pp. 271, 277, 308–10, 312; of 1842, pp. 155, 277, 288, 289, 308, 312; of 1844, pp. 277, 288, 290, 308; of 1846, pp. 111n9, 297, 308; of 1860, p. 309

Hale, Edward Jones: biographical information, 67, 176–77, 192, 245, 300, 315; anti-party feelings, 71, 76, 193, 203, 204, 315; and J. Q. Adams, 73, 112, 114, 176; and Van Buren, 74, 179–80, 258–60, 275; and Jackson, 73–74, 110, 152, 160, 176–77, 178n73; party bickering, 77–78, 123, 152, 168, 192, 196, 298, 298n41; and party issues, 105, 153, 158, 168, 170, 183, 200, 247, 266, 286; as Whig, 176–77, 183, 184, 193, 200, 203, 258–60, 270, 274, 291–95; party loyalty, 183, 193, 256
Hall, Basil, 30, 37
Hamilton, Alexander, 86, 97
Harrison, William Henry, 206, 259, 261, 269, 270, 276, 284, 297

Hart, James, 48, 54, 251, 252n19
Hartz, Louis, 4, 5
Hays, Samuel P., 5, 10
Haywood, William H., Jr., 185, 247
Helper, Hinton Rowan, 287–88, 288n13
Henry, Louis D., 113, 153, 155, 157, 169–71, 186, 192, 266–67, 288, 289, 326–27
Hofstadter, Richard, 4, 5
Holmes, Hardy L., 256–57, 262, 268–69, 274, 298n41
Holt, Michael F., 315
Hooper, William, 83, 84, 86
Huske, John Winslow, 42, 178n73, 276
Hussey, Miles, 96–97, 116
Hybart, Thomas L., 22, 43, 167–75, 180, 187–93, 196, 245, 261, 266

Internal improvements, 15, 50–57, 81, 87, 98, 108, 152–59, 163–65, 169–71, 175–76, 185–90, 194–95, 199–201, 206, 247–48, 282–83, 290–91, 303, 318–21. *See also* Canals; Railroads; Roads
Iredell, James, 86

Jackson, Andrew: support for, 2, 14, 73–74, 76, 110, 112–21, 123–29, 138–50, 139–40n54, 168–69, 176–78, 178n73, 190, 204, 220, 228, 230; 1824 election, 21–22, 21n11, 22n14, 67, 99–102, 110; as president, 68, 69, 126, 152, 153, 159–60, 168–69, 175, 177, 181–82, 190, 256, 262, 263; opposition to, 74–75, 119–24, 126, 178–79, 181–82, 184, 186, 190, 206, 211, 258
Jacksonian democracy, 3–4, 23–24, 126, 148–49. *See also* Democratic party
Jefferson, Thomas, 76, 86, 89, 106, 148, 264
Jeffersonian Republicans. *See* Republican party
Johnson, Guion G., 239–40
Johnson, Neill, 171
Johnson, Paul E., 7
Johnson, Richard M., 202, 205, 212, 228, 276
Johnston, Samuel, 86
Jones, Jacup, 283–85
Jordan, Dillon, Jr., 127n49, 188–90, 245
Jordan, Dillon, Sr., 39, 95, 238

Kelley, Robert, 4
Kelly, John, 145, 238, 266–67
Key, V. O., 111
King, Rufus, 204
Kruman, Marc W., 309–10

Laborers. *See* Workers
Lafayette, Marquis de, 17–23, 49, 52, 59,
    60, 313
Landowners. *See* Property owners
Latta, John C., 288
Leaders of political parties. *See* Political
    parties
Leake, Walter F., 111*n*9
Lefler, Hugh Talmage, 46
Lilly, E. J., 22
Lincoln, Abraham, 314–16
Lord, William, 27, 145
Loyalists, 29–30, 84–85, 88, 101

McBryde, Archibald, 88, 98
McCormick, Richard P., 2, 4–5, 7, 243*n*60,
    320
McDiarmid, Angus, 38, 103
McDiarmid, Archibald, 43*n*64, 103–107,
    149, 151, 175–76, 178*n*73, 236*n*41, 301,
    304, 304*n*51
McDiarmid, Daniel, 103
McDonald, Alexander, 94, 95
McFarland, Duncan, 89–91, 96
McKay, John, 301*n*46
McKay, William McL., 276
McKethan, Alfred A., 43
Maclaine, Archibald, 86
McLane, Louis, 121
McLean, Archibald, 315
McLean, John, 193, 269–70
McLerran, John, 95
McMillan, Alexander, 98
McMillan, John, 94, 95
McNeill, Alexander, 171, 178*n*73
McNeill, Archibald, 88, 98
McNeill, David, 171
Macon, Nathaniel, 51, 263
MacRae, Duncan, 19, 95
MacRae, John, 113–14
McSeveney, Samuel T., 6
Madison, James, 86
Mallett, Charles Beatty, 42, 285
Mallett, Charles P., 42, 249
Mallett, Peter, 42
Mangum, Willie P., 74, 184–85, 187
Manly, M. E., 194
Martin, John B., 102
Martin, Josiah, 82–85
Martin, William, 88
Mathews, Donald G., 118, 240
Matthews, John, 93, 95, 101, 127*n*49
Merchants. *See* Business and businessmen
Methodists, 39, 40, 41*n*58, 242

Mexican War, 294, 296
Meyers, Marvin, 267, 321
Money. *See* Bank of the United States; Banks
    and banking; Economic policies
Monroe, James, 1, 97
Montague, Charles, 39
Montgomery, David, 7
Morality in government, 71–75, 117–18, 180
Morehead, John Motley, 249, 276, 288, 289,
    310, 326
Morris, William, 99, 241
Munroe, John, 328–29
Murchison, Angus, 93
Murchison, William, 161
Murphy, Archibald D., 49–52, 58–59,
    97–98

Negroes. *See* Blacks, free; Slaves
Newby, Larkin, 94, 95
Newsome, Albert Ray, 46
Newspapers. *See* Fayetteville *Observer*;
    North Carolina Journal; *North Carolinian*;
    Political parties
Nixon, Lewis A., 191
North Carolina, 46–49, 154, 170
North Carolina Journal, 66–69, 167, 261
North Carolinian, 256, 262, 265, 274,
    298*n*41
Nullification, 73, 153, 154, 173, 177, 206

Olmsted, Frederick Law, 29, 285, 287

Panic of 1837, pp. 245–47, 252–58, 262–
    66, 268, 280, 321
Parties, political. *See* Democratic party; Fed-
    eralist party; Political parties; Republican
    party; Whig party
Party leaders. *See* Political parties
Party press. *See* Fayetteville *Observer*; *North
    Carolina Journal*; *North Carolinian*; Politi-
    cal parties
Pemberton, James D., 260
Person, Samuel J., 295
Pessen, Edward, 4
Pierce, Franklin, 269
Planters, 27–28, 31, 31*n*32, 42, 52, 53, 62,
    102, 245, 254, 268, 278–79, 287, 301,
    302, 320
Platforms. *See* Political parties
Pole, J. R., 63
Political parties: resistance to partisanship, 2,
    21, 70–71, 75–77, 98, 108, 189–91,
    202–204, 297, 315–16; role of, 2–5,
    323–24; in the South, 7–9; organization

of, 9–16, 111–13, 152, 244–45, 271–72, 274, 303–304; stages in formation, 14–15, 81, 108, 152–53, 162–63, 184, 256, 320; party press, 66–68, 171, 190, 203, 244, 256, 261–62, 271–74, 298, 298*n*41; leaders in 1828, pp. 128–35, 138–50, 139–40*n*54, 214–20, 223, 227, 230; linking of local and national issues, 151–52, 163, 164, 167, 184, 189–90, 193–96, 243–44, 296–97, 320; platforms, 153, 163, 186–88, 199, 244, 303, 320; party loyalty, 183, 190–91, 195, 202–204, 294, 297, 304, 304*n*51, 307–12; leaders in 1836, pp. 213–35, 242–45; definition, 213*n*36; leaders in the 1840s, 300–303; and Civil War, 315–16. *See also* Democratic party; Federalist party; Republican party; Whig party

Polk, James K., 310

Poll taxes, 62*n*4, 127, 200, 201, 210, 211, 325–26

Poor, 29, 43–44, 172–75, 279

Potter, Henry, 178*n*73

Potts, Jesse, 88–89, 91, 95

Power: disapproval of, 73–76, 108, 109, 114, 291; use of, in government, 109, 114, 117–18

Presbyterians, 24, 30, 38, 40, 41*n*58, 57, 98, 103, 148, 211, 239

Presidential elections: of 1824, pp. 2, 21–22, 21*n*11, 22*n*14, 99–102, 109, 110, 114, 115, 147, 149, 209; of 1828, pp. 22, 23, 110–26, 146–49; of 1832, pp. 147, 173, 178, 180; of 1836, pp. 15, 147, 201–208, 305–306; of 1840, pp. 2, 254, 256, 258, 271, 277–80, 297, 305–307; of 1844, pp. 285, 292–94, 305–307, 310; of 1848, pp. 292–94, 305–307; of 1852, pp. 305–306; of 1856, pp. 305–306; of 1860, pp. 305–306

Property owners, 28–32, 128, 134–35, 138–45, 215–20, 224–28, 230–35, 325–27

Protestant churches. *See* names of specific churches

Purviance, Samuel, 88, 89

Railroads, 50–52, 56, 78, 103, 107, 154–58, 163, 169–72, 175–76, 185–89, 194–95, 199, 201, 235–36, 236*n*41, 243, 245, 247–48, 267, 283, 303, 321, 322

Randolph, John, 109, 263

Religious groups. *See* Churches; names of specific churches

Republican party, 2, 63, 71, 76, 86–89, 92, 96–98, 101, 110, 127*n*49, 147, 169, 180–84, 186, 190, 203, 263, 269, 288*n*13, 290, 314

Republicanism, 57, 59, 66, 69–70, 81, 98, 114, 180, 181, 206, 313, 318

Revivalist movement, 40–41, 103, 240

Revolutionary War. *See* American Revolution

Ridgely, Henry Moore, 121

Ridgway, Whitman H., 311

Roads, 50, 52–53, 56, 104–107, 126, 244, 282–84, 297. *See also* Internal improvements

Robeson, Thomas J., 127*n*49

Robinson, Benjamin, 42*n*59, 113, 181–82, 300

Roman Catholics. *See* Catholics

Rowan, Robert, 87

Rowland, Alexander, 95

Royall, Anne, 30, 37*n*46, 69

Rural-urban differences. *See* Urban versus rural residence

Saunders, Romulus, 276

Schlesinger, Arthur M., 3–4

Scots, 24, 29–32, 38, 84–85, 89–90, 98, 100–103, 108, 110, 123, 131–33, 139–40, 139–40*n*54, 146–48, 210–13, 215, 221, 228–29, 238–42, 279, 285, 321

Seawell, James, 22, 47, 103–107, 149, 151, 156, 157, 169, 175–76, 184, 186–93, 195, 245

Secession, 51–52, 74, 314–15, 317, 323

Sellers, Charles Grier, Jr., 321

Shade, William G., 6

Sharp, James R., 321

Shaw, John, 95

Shepard, Charles, 194, 196, 297

Shepard, James B., 111*n*9

Sherwood, Daniel, 195

Silbey, Joel H., 6

Slave owners, 27–28, 31, 31*n*32, 42, 94–95, 97, 128, 134–35, 141–46, 195, 210–12, 215, 217–20, 223–27, 230–33, 242–45, 325–26

Slavery, 8, 24, 32, 36, 43–46, 51, 53, 54, 70, 73, 86, 99, 102, 113–18, 200, 204–207, 275–77, 287, 292–96, 314–19, 323. *See also* Abolitionism

Smith, Archibald A. T., 300

Social classes. *See* Class differences

Somkin, Fred, 20

South Carolina, 74, 153, 154

Spaight, Richard Dobbs, 201, 208–13

Spoils system, 74, 207, 258, 260, 291

Stanly, Edward, 51
State aid, 56, 81, 108, 152–59, 163–65,
    169–71, 175–76, 185–90, 194–95, 247–
    50, 283, 290–91, 295, 303
State constitution, 194, 196–201, 210, 211
States' rights, 114, 116, 153–54, 176, 178,
    268, 275
Stedman, Elisha, 42n59
Strange, Robert, 157, 158, 202, 263–64
Strange, William F., 167–75, 180, 261
Suffrage. See Voting requirements
Swain, David Lowry, 156–58, 169

Tariffs, 50, 153, 154, 164, 173–74, 176, 179,
    274, 285, 290–96 passim
Taylor, Zachary, 291
Taxes. See Poll taxes; Tariffs
Temin, Peter, 256
Textile industry. See Cotton; Cotton mills
Thomas, Aaron, 34
Thornton, J. Mills, III, 8, 12, 70, 115, 311,
    321
Tocqueville, Alexis de, 58
Toomer, John B., 18, 21, 49, 52, 54, 59, 196
Town-country differences. See Urban versus
    rural residence
Town elections: of 1810, pp. 92–97, 127n49;
    of 1834, pp. 15, 22–23, 163, 184–93, 196
Transportation. See Canals; Internal improve-
    ments; Railroads; Roads
Trueman, Timothy, 284
Turner, Frederick Jackson, 3
Turner, Nat, 153

United States Constitution, 78, 85–88, 110
Urban versus rural residence: and party is-
    sues, 8, 35, 164–65, 171–72, 175, 182,
    206–207, 211, 278–80, 298–99, 312–13,
    318, 320–22; description, 31, 41–44; con-
    flicts, 102–108, 149, 167; and party leader-
    ship, 130–34, 139, 143–47, 215, 216,
    221–34 passim, 242–44, 301

Van Buren, Martin: opposition to, 74, 177–
    82, 191, 200, 203–204, 207, 212, 228,
    257–59, 270, 275; as president, 111n9,
    185, 246, 255, 261, 275, 276; as vice-pres-
    ident, 154, 169, 180; support for, 169,
    201–202, 205–208, 279, 290, 323, 324
Van Hook, Solomon, 268–69

Vesey, Denmark, 113
Voting records, 2–3, 6–7, 11–12, 62–66,
    108, 146, 152, 213–14, 242, 277. See also
    Congressional elections; Gubernatorial
    elections; Presidential elections; Town
    elections
Voting requirements, 61–62, 82–84, 116,
    193, 197, 200

Waddil, William, Jr., 155
War of 1812, pp. 67, 79, 86–88, 127n49
Washington, George, 17, 86, 88, 125
Wealth: in Cumberland County, 31, 32; and
    party preference, 100, 205–207, 210–12,
    269–70, 279–80, 327; and party leaders,
    128–29, 134–35, 138, 140–45, 215–20,
    224–28, 230–35, 242–45. See also Busi-
    ness and businessmen; Property owners;
    Slave owners
Wellborne, James, 107
Welter, Rush, 69, 318
Whig party: characteristics, 3, 13–15, 117,
    186–87, 198, 202–205, 208–13, 243, 245,
    279–80, 291–92, 321–22; antiparty feel-
    ings, 75, 180, 182–83, 189–91, 202–204,
    297; party leaders, 103, 217, 219, 222,
    227–35, 242–45, 272, 274, 300–303;
    election returns, 111, 111n9, 196–97, 306,
    307, 309, 312–13; beginning, 149, 152,
    174, 176, 186n92, 309; and National Re-
    publicans, 180–84; economic views,
    184–87, 190, 194, 270, 275, 289–91,
    298–99
White, Hugh Lawson, 201–202, 204, 206,
    207
Wiebe, Robert H., 23
Wilkings, Edward R., 157
Williams, Lewis, 75
Wilmot Proviso, 294–95
Winslow, Edward Lee, 22, 41, 129, 145, 156,
    158, 184, 247, 250–52
Winslow, John, Jr., 41, 88, 95, 263, 270
Winslow, John, Sr., 41–42
Winslow, Warren, 41, 156, 178n73, 250,
    252n19
Wooster, Ralph A., 62
Workers, 43–44, 172–75, 191–92, 195,
    206–207, 236–37, 243, 274, 285–87, 320
Wright, Gavin, 53
Wright, William B., 178n73